To Alison -
Happy Birthday 1996!
Enjoy.
Joan

NOTEWORTHY *two*

A NEW RECIPE COLLECTION FROM THE RAVINIA FESTIVAL

Additional copies of NOTEWORTHY TWO may be
obtained by writing or faxing:

NOTEWORTHY TWO
Ravinia Festival
P.O. Box 1603
Highland Park, Illinois 60035

Telephone 708/266-5043
Fax 708/433-7983

All proceeds from the sale of NOTEWORTHY TWO
will support the Steans Institute for Young Artists
at the Ravinia Festival.

First Edition, First Printing: February, 1995

Printed in the United States of America
The Lakeside Press
RR Donnelley & Sons Company

NOTEWORTHY TWO is dedicated to the Ravinia Festival's
loyal audiences whose devotion does not waiver through rain or shine.

Editor:
Joan Freehling

Co-Editor:
Jan Weil

Production:
Dorothy Haber

Testing:
Susan Spears

Collection:
Jean McClung

Index:
Parsla Mason

Consultant:
Lois Steans

Marketing:
Mary Kay Eyerman
Courtney MacDonald

Retail:
Nancy Woulfe
Patricia Schnadig

Wholesale:
Barbara Daniels

Treasurers:
Lou Guthrie
Ann McDermott

Design:
Diane Kavelaras
Teubner Kavelaras Associates, Inc.

Photography:
Tim Turner

Food Stylist:
Bonnie Rabert

Prop Stylist:
Renée Miller

Editing Consultant:
Margot Goldsmith

Office Liaison:
Sharon Sklansky

Ravinia Liaison:
Charlis McMillan

Typesetting:
CarElz Graphics

CONTENTS

RAVINIA—the Past Decade

Ravinia. To some the word conjures up a verdant lawn and a sunset filtering through the stately trees, providing a flawless backdrop for a picnic. To others, Ravinia is embodied by the tuxedo-clad, world-renowned Chicago Symphony Orchestra who claim the dignified Pavilion as their summer home. The reality is that the Ravinia Festival fuses each element; the wonder of a summer evening under the stars, the pleasure of an alfresco supper, and the excitement of the first downbeat summoning the magic of music.

Harza Building–home of the Steans Institute for Young Artists.

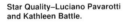

Star Quality–Luciano Pavarotti and Kathleen Battle.

The Ravinia Festival celebrated its first half-century in 1985. It was a memorable season honoring the Festival's proud past, glorious present, and exciting future. Two gentlemen, Edward Gordon, Executive Director, and James Levine, Music Director, earned high praise from both audiences and music critics for shaping a world-class festival.

Nineteen eighty-eight marked the inaugural season of the Steans Institute for Young Artists. Located in the Harza Building, the Institute's mission is to bring young, outstanding musicians to study with a distinguished faculty in a unique summer program.

A new Executive Director, Zarin Mehta, was appointed in 1990. The same year the "Rising Stars" series was introduced. This continues to be a showcase for young musicians performing in Bennett Hall during the fall, winter, and spring seasons. In 1991 another new series, Jazz In June, opened the season early, presenting a selection of great jazz artists including the Oscar Peterson Quartet, Gerry

Orchestra and chorus performing Prokofiev's original score for the classic film, Alexander Nevsky.

Tony Bennett–the singer's singer and a perennial favorite.

A summer evening at Ravinia.

Mulligan, and Ella Fitzgerald. Starring in a concert version of The Elixir of Love were Luciano Pavarotti and Kathleen Battle. The same year the classic film, Alexander Nevsky, was shown with the Ravinia Festival Orchestra playing

The one, the only ELLA!

Prokofiev's original sound track. In 1992 Placido Domingo made his Ravinia debut in a concert version of Samson and Delilah. Alfred Brendel played Beethoven's piano sonatas in the newly remodeled theater at Ravinia. Charlie Chaplin's inimitable silent film, "City Lights", was shown accompanied live by Chaplin's original score. After 20 years' service as Music Director, James Levine conducted his farewell concert in 1993. The same year the Israel Philharmonic returned for three concerts under the direction of Zubin Mehta. Ravinia's "Musica Viva" series presented the latest in world music, new music, and off-beat eclecticism. In 1994 Plácido Domingo returned to conduct the Chicago Symphony and, in a second performance, sang for a Gala Benefit Evening. The season brought innovative and diversified programming with performances by Alicia de Larrocha, Tony Bennett, and Marilyn Horne.

Nineteen ninety-five marks Ravinia's 60th season and the appointment of the new Musical Director, Christophe Eschenbach. In celebration and to expand and further enhance Ravinia, there will be major renovation and modernization of the grounds and facilities. The Women's Board has chosen this special anniversary to introduce its new cookbook, NOTEWORTHY TWO.

APPETIZERS & MORE

SALMON TORTILLA BITES

SERVES 4

8	ounces cream cheese
½	cup mayonnaise
1	tablespoon chopped parsley
2	teaspoons dill weed
2	teaspoons chopped fresh chives
½	teaspoon seasoned salt
2	teaspoons fresh lemon juice
	freshly ground pepper to taste
2	9- or 10-inch flour tortillas, room temperature
4	ounces smoked salmon, thinly sliced
1-2	ripe tomatoes, in 6 to 8 thin slices

In food processor or blender combine cream cheese, mayonnaise, parsley, dill weed, chives, seasoned salt, lemon juice, and pepper. Blend well. Spread each tortilla thinly with mixture.

Arrange salmon slices on half of each tortilla. Arrange 3 to 4 tomato slices in center of each tortilla. Roll tortillas tightly. Wrap in plastic wrap. Refrigerate 1 to 2 hours. Serve sliced diagonally.

SPINACH TORTILLAS

YIELD: FOUR 8- OR 9-INCH TORTILLAS

10	ounces frozen spinach, thawed, drained, finely chopped
2	green onions, finely chopped
.02	ounces ranch salad dressing mix
2	thick slices bacon, crisply cooked, drained, crumbled
2¼	ounces canned sliced black olives
3	tablespoons mayonnaise
3	tablespoons plain yogurt or sour cream
4	8- or 9-inch flour tortillas

In large bowl combine spinach, green onions, salad dressing mix, bacon, olives, mayonnaise, and yogurt. Mix well. Spread mixture on tortillas. Roll up tightly. Wrap in plastic wrap. Refrigerate 2 hours. Slice to serve.

PIZZA PARTY

**YIELD: TWO
6-INCH PIZZAS**

QUICK CRUST:

2   6-inch flour tortillas or 1 pita bread split horizontally

TOPPINGS:

Choose one of the following toppings. Spread on crusts.

Bake on ungreased baking sheet in preheated 425-degree oven 7 to 9 minutes or until crusts are brown.

JALAPEÑO PEPPER AND CHEESE:

2   tablespoons pizza sauce
3   tablespoons chopped jalapeño slices, mild, medium, or hot
2   slices bacon, crisply cooked, drained, crumbled
2   tablespoons grated Cheddar cheese
2   tablespoons grated mozzarella cheese

Spread each crust with pizza sauce. Sprinkle with remaining ingredients.

GOAT CHEESE AND SAGE:

1/4 cup ricotta cheese
2   tablespoons goat cheese
1   teaspoon chopped fresh sage or 1/4 teaspoon dried sage, crumbled
2   tablespoons chopped Canadian bacon or prosciutto
1   plum tomato, thinly sliced, seeded
2   teaspoons toasted pine nuts
2   teaspoons grated Parmesan cheese

In small bowl, combine ricotta, goat cheese, and sage. Mix well. Spread on crusts. Sprinkle with remaining ingredients.

PESTO AND TOMATO:

3   tablespoons pesto sauce
1   tablespoon toasted pine nuts
2   teaspoons chopped sun-dried tomatoes (in oil), drained
2   tablespoons grated mozzarella cheese
2   tablespoons grated Asiago cheese

Spread each crust with pesto sauce. Sprinkle with remaining ingredients.

continued

MEDITERRANEAN CHEESE AND WALNUT:
1 **tablespoon roasted garlic, mashed**
2 **tablespoons toasted walnuts, broken**
2 **slices small red onion, divided into rings**
1 **teaspoon chopped parsley**
2 **tablespoons goat cheese, crumbled**
3 **tablespoons shredded four cheese mixture or mozzarella cheese**

Spread each crust with mashed garlic. Sprinkle with remaining ingredients. See photo page 83.

TURKEY TORTILLA BITES

YIELD: 24

8 **ounces cream cheese, softened**
4 **ounces canned chopped green chilies**
4 **ounces canned chopped black olives**
½ **medium tomato, seeded, juice removed, finely chopped**
6 **medium flour tortillas**
8 **ounces finely sliced turkey breast**
1 **head Bibb lettuce**

In medium bowl stir cream cheese until smooth. Add chilies, olives, and tomato. Mix well. Spread mixture equally on tortillas. Cover with turkey slices. Top with lettuce. Roll each tortilla jelly-roll fashion. Wrap each roll in paper towel. Place rolls in plastic bag and refrigerate 6 hours or overnight. Serve in ½-inch slices.

THIN CRUSTED PIZZA

SERVES 6

6 **6-inch flour tortillas**
12 **tablespoons tomato base pasta sauce**
1½ **teaspoons oregano, thyme, or basil**
12 **tablespoons grated pizza cheese**
6 **tablespoons grated Chihuahua cheese**
3 **ounces sliced pepperoni**

Spread each tortilla with 2 tablespoons sauce, ¼ teaspoon oregano, 2 tablespoons pizza cheese, 1 tablespoon Chihuahua cheese, and 8 pepperoni slices. Arrange tortillas on baking sheet. Bake in preheated 450-degree oven 10 to 12 minutes or until bottoms are crisp.

SMOKED SALMON PIZZA

SERVES 8 TO 10

2 **8- to 10-inch flour tortillas**
8 **ounces cream cheese**
1/2 **cup mayonnaise**
1 **tablespoon chopped parsley**
2 **teaspoons dill weed**
2 **teaspoons chopped fresh chives**
1/2 **teaspoon seasoned salt**
2 **teaspoons fresh lemon juice**
1/4 **teaspoon freshly ground pepper**
4-6 **ounces smoked salmon, thinly sliced**
2-3 **teaspoons black caviar**

Bake tortillas on baking sheet in preheated 425-degree oven until lightly browned. If tortillas puff while baking, pierce with sharp knife. Cool.

In food processor or blender combine cream cheese, mayonnaise, parsley, dill weed, chives, seasoned salt, lemon juice, and pepper. Blend well.

No longer than 1 hour before serving, gently spread cream cheese mixture over cooled tortillas, leaving 1-inch border uncovered. (Tortillas break easily.) Arrange salmon over cream cheese mixture. Spoon caviar in center and slice in wedges.

SPINACH, MUSTARD SEED, AND GOAT CHEESE PIZZA

**YIELD: ONE
12-INCH PIZZA**

*1 **12-inch pizza crust**
2 **tablespoons olive oil**
1 **cup grated mozzarella cheese**
3 1/2 **ounces goat cheese, crumbled**
2 **tablespoons butter**
1 **tablespoon mustard seed**
18 **fresh small spinach leaves or strips of larger leaves**

Brush pizza crust with olive oil. Cover with mozzarella cheese. Sprinkle goat cheese over top.

In small skillet melt butter. Sauté mustard seed in butter until it pops. Sprinkle over cheeses. Arrange spinach leaves over all. Bake in preheated 500-degree oven 10 to 12 minutes.

*See Pizza Dough page 11.

ROASTED RED PEPPER WITH CAPERS PIZZA

YIELD: ONE
12-INCH PIZZA

*1 12-inch pizza crust, partially baked
4 teaspoons olive oil
1/2 cup shredded mozzarella cheese
1/2 cup shredded Fontina cheese
2 to 3 red peppers, roasted**, cut up
1 tablespoon capers

Brush pizza crust with olive oil. Cover with cheeses. Arrange peppers over cheese. Sprinkle with capers. Bake in preheated 425-degree oven 10 minutes or until cheese is melted.

*See Pizza Dough below.

**For roasting instructions, see page 162.

PIZZA DOUGH

YIELD: ONE
12-INCH PIZZA
CRUST

1 teaspoon active dry yeast
1 teaspoon sugar
3/4 cup warm water (105 degrees to 115 degrees), divided
2 3/4 cups flour
1 teaspoon salt
1 tablespoon olive oil

In small bowl combine yeast, sugar, and 1/4 cup warm water. Let stand a few minutes until frothy.

In medium bowl sift together flour and salt. Add yeast mixture, remaining 1/2 cup water, and olive oil. Mix well.

On floured surface knead dough until smooth and elastic. Place in greased bowl. Cover with plastic wrap. Let rise in warm place 45 minutes or until double in size. Punch down dough and knead briefly.

Transfer to oiled 12-inch pizza pan. Press dough to edges, pinching up edge to create rim. Fill and bake according to directions.*

*May be used with Spinach, Mustard Seed, and Goat Cheese Pizza, page 10, or Roasted Red Pepper with Capers Pizza, above.

SONATINA SPIRAL SANDWICH

SERVES 8 TO 10

1   15-inch round lahvosh (Armenian sesame seed cracker bread)
8   ounces Neufchâtel cheese, softened
1   tablespoon tarragon
1   tablespoon chopped fresh chives, optional
2   teaspoons dill weed
1/2 teaspoon garlic salt
4   ounces very thinly sliced ham or smoked turkey
2   large firm tomatoes, very thinly sliced
8   ounces thinly sliced Swiss cheese
1/2 cup alfalfa sprouts
1   large romaine lettuce leaf, rib removed, halved lengthwise

Submerge lahvosh briefly in bowl of cold water. Place inverted lahvosh on damp dish towel. Cover with another damp dish towel. Let stand 1 hour or until soft and pliable.

In small bowl combine Neufchâtel cheese, tarragon, chives, if desired, dill weed, and garlic salt. Mix well. Spread mixture over entire surface of softened lahvosh. Arrange ham or turkey over cheese mixture, leaving 1-inch margin. Top with sliced tomatoes. Cover with Swiss cheese followed by alfalfa sprouts and romaine. Starting with edge closest to you gently roll up lahvosh.

Transfer seam side down to platter or cutting board. Cover with foil. Refrigerate until served. Slice into 1-inch pieces with sharp knife.

RED ONION TART WITH STILTON AND ROSEMARY

SERVES 6 TO 8

1   cup plus 2 tablespoons flour
2   pinches salt, divided
4   tablespoons butter, in chunks
4   ounces cream cheese, in chunks
1   egg
1   tablespoon ice water
2   tablespoons olive oil
3   large red onions, thinly sliced
    freshly ground pepper to taste
1   teaspoon chopped fresh rosemary or
        1/2 teaspoon dried rosemary
1/4 pound Stilton cheese (without rind), crumbled

In food processor combine flour and pinch salt. Add butter and cream cheese. Process with quick on and off turns until mixture resembles coarse meal. Beat egg lightly with ice water. Add to flour mixture. Process with on and off turns until dough forms large lumps, not single ball. Turn dough onto lightly floured surface. Knead gently 6 times. Shape into smooth, flat cake. Wrap in foil. Refrigerate at least 15 minutes.

In large skillet heat olive oil. Add onions, pinch salt, and pepper. Gently cook covered 15 minutes until onions are soft but not brown, stirring occasionally. Increase heat. Remove cover and cook 5 minutes or until liquid in skillet has evaporated, stirring frequently. Remove onions from skillet with slotted spoon. Cool.

Roll out dough to conform to size of large, rimless baking sheet. Transfer to lightly greased baking sheet. Spread onions over pastry to within 1 inch of border. Sprinkle with pepper, rosemary, and Stilton cheese. Roll up edges of pastry until they reach onion mixture.

Bake in preheated 400-degree oven 30 minutes or until pastry edges are golden brown. Cool on rack 5 minutes. Slice into serving pieces.

MONTRACHET TORTE

YIELD: 16 TO 20 SQUARES

7	**sheets 14- by 18-inch filo dough**
5	**tablespoons butter, melted**
8	**tablespoons freshly grated Parmesan cheese, divided**
1	**cup coarsely grated mozzarella cheese**
4	**ounces Montrachet cheese, crumbled**
1	**cup very thinly sliced onions**
2	**pounds Italian plum tomatoes, in 1/4- inch slices**
1/2	**cup chopped fresh basil**
1/2	**teaspoon dried oregano**
1/4	**teaspoon dried thyme**
	salt to taste and pepper to taste

Lay sheet of filo on lightly buttered baking sheet. Brush lightly with butter. Sprinkle with 1 tablespoon Parmesan cheese. Repeat procedure with remaining sheets of filo, stacking 1 on another.

Sprinkle top sheet with all mozzarella and Montrachet. Spread all onion slices over top followed by all tomato slices. Sprinkle remaining Parmesan, basil, oregano, thyme, salt, and pepper over all. Bake in preheated 375-degree oven 30 to 35 minutes. Slice into squares. Serve warm.

QUESADILLA PIE

SERVES 6 TO 8

8   ounces canned green chilies, chopped, drained
4   cups grated sharp Cheddar cheese (may use lowfat)
2   cups milk
1   cup buttermilk baking mix
4   eggs
    sour cream, guacamole, and salsa are each optional

In greased 10-inch pie pan sprinkle chilies and cheese. In medium bowl combine milk, baking mix, and eggs. Beat until smooth. Pour into pie pan.

Bake in preheated 425-degree oven 25 to 30 minutes or until knife inserted between center and edge comes out clean. Let stand 10 minutes before slicing. Serve with sour cream, guacamole, and/or salsa, if desired.

SCALLOP PUFFS

YIELD: 48

3   tablespoons unsalted butter
1   pound bay scallops or quartered sea scallops
2   teaspoons finely grated lemon zest
3   cloves garlic, minced
3   tablespoons chopped fresh dill plus sprigs dill, divided
2½ cups grated Swiss or Gruyère cheese
1   cup mayonnaise
    freshly ground pepper to taste
4   dozen melba or bread rounds
    sweet Hungarian paprika
    lemon wedges

In medium skillet melt butter over medium-high heat. Add scallops, lemon zest, and garlic. Cook 1 to 2 minutes or until opaque,* stirring constantly. Add chopped dill. Cook 30 seconds. Remove from heat. Add cheese, mayonnaise, and pepper. Mix well. Transfer scallop mixture to bowl. Cover. Refrigerate until ready to use.

Top each melba round with heaping teaspoon of scallop mixture. Sprinkle lightly with paprika. Arrange rounds ½ inch apart on baking sheets.

Broil rounds in preheated broiler 5 inches from heat 1 to 2 minutes until lightly browned. Transfer to platter. Garnish with dill sprigs and lemon wedges. Serve immediately.

*CAUTION:
Scallops toughen if overcooked.

COCONUT SHRIMP WITH
ORANGE HORSERADISH SAUCE

SERVES 6

1	tablespoon cayenne pepper
2¼	teaspoons salt
1½	teaspoons paprika
1½	teaspoons freshly ground pepper
1½	teaspoons garlic powder
¾	teaspoon onion powder
¾	teaspoon chopped fresh thyme
¾	teaspoon chopped fresh oregano
1¾	cups flour, divided
2	large eggs, separated
¾	cup beer (not dark)
24	large shrimp, uncooked, shelled, deveined, tails and last joint intact
3	cups sweetened flaked coconut
	vegetable oil

In small bowl combine cayenne, salt, paprika, pepper, garlic powder, onion powder, thyme, and oregano. Mix well. In second bowl blend 1¼ cups flour, 2 teaspoons cayenne mixture, 2 egg yolks, and beer. In third bowl beat 2 egg whites until peaks form. Fold whites gently into beer mixture. Chill batter at least 30 minutes.

In another small bowl combine remaining ½ cup flour with ½ teaspoon cayenne mixture. Pour remaining cayenne mixture into plastic bag. Add shrimp. Shake, coating shrimp, then dredge shrimp in flour-cayenne mixture until well covered. Shake off excess. Dip shrimp into beer batter and coat with coconut.

Pour at least 2 inches oil into deep fryer heated to 325 degrees. Fry shrimp 2 minutes on each side or until golden brown. With slotted spoon remove shrimp to paper towel to cool. Serve with sauce.

ORANGE HORSERADISH SAUCE:

¾	cup orange marmalade
2½	tablespoons Dijon mustard
	prepared horseradish to taste

In small saucepan combine marmalade and mustard. Heat until warm. Stir in horseradish.

See photo page 77.

BROILED OR GRILLED JUMBO SCAMPI

SERVES 12

MARINADE:
1 cup olive oil
1/2 cup white wine
3 tablespoons chopped fresh basil
juice of 1/2 lemon
1 teaspoon salt
1/4 teaspoon pepper
1 clove garlic, minced

24 jumbo scampi, uncooked, shelled, deveined, tails intact
*1 cup clarified butter
3 tablespoons chopped parsley
1 tablespoon lemon juice
1/2 teaspoon salt
1 clove garlic, minced

In large bowl combine all marinade ingredients. Mix well. Marinate scampi in mixture overnight in refrigerator. Broil or grill scampi just until flesh turns from opaque to white.

In small saucepan combine clarified butter, parsley, lemon juice, salt, and garlic. Mix well. Heat mixture. Serve with warm scampi.

*Melt unsalted butter. Discard white foam on top and white liquid on bottom, keeping only golden liquid.

GRAVLAX ROLLS

YIELD: 20 TO 30

1 1/2 pounds salmon fillet
2 tablespoons coarse salt
2 tablespoons sugar
1 tablespoon peppercorns
large bunch fresh dill, divided
5 ounces smoked salmon
3 ounces cream cheese
1/4 cup whipping cream, more if necessary
salt and pepper to taste
2 ounces caviar, optional
2 small cucumbers, sliced, optional

To make gravlax,* season both sides of salmon fillet with coarse salt, sugar, and peppercorns. Set salmon skin side down on large sheet of plastic wrap. Top with dill. Wrap fish tightly in plastic wrap. Set in shallow dish with heavy plate on top.

Refrigerate 2 days, turning every 8 hours. Wipe gravlax with paper towel to remove dill and seasoning.

In food processor or blender puree smoked salmon and cream cheese. With motor running pour in enough whipping cream to bring mixture to spreading consistency. Season to taste. Refrigerate.

Cut gravlax (or smoked salmon) in thinnest possible diagonal slices, discarding skin. Spread spoonful of smoked salmon mixture on each slice of gravlax. Roll up gravlax. Trim ends of rolls. If rolls are very long, cut in half. Dip 1 end of roll in caviar to coat lightly, if desired. Before serving, insert toothpick in each roll or place on cucumber slice and garnish with dill sprig. Serve at room temperature.

Smoked salmon mixture may be made 2 days ahead and refrigerated.

Gravlax rolls may be made 1 day ahead and refrigerated before proceeding with serving directions. See photo page 77.

*May substitute smoked salmon for gravlax, eliminating procedure for gravlax in first paragraph.

FRESH BASIL-TOMATO TOAST

SERVES 12

1   cup coarsely chopped ripe, firm tomatoes
1/2   cup chopped fresh basil
3   tablespoons chopped Belgian endive
2   tablespoons extra virgin olive oil
1/4   teaspoon salt
1/8   teaspoon pepper
1   teaspoon butter, softened
12   slices baguette, 1 1/2 inches in diameter, 1/2 inch thick
1   clove garlic, halved, optional
2   tablespoons grated Parmesan cheese

In small bowl combine tomatoes, basil, endive, olive oil, salt, and pepper. Mix well.

Lightly butter bread. Lightly toast bread in preheated 400-degree oven 5 minutes or until center is firm. Rub cut ends of garlic on toasted bread, if desired. Sprinkle with Parmesan cheese.

Shortly before serving spread toast with tomato mixture. Toast will become soggy if assembled too early.

SUN-DRIED TOMATO PASTRY

YIELD: 25 TO 30 TRIANGLES

1/2   **pound feta cheese**
1   **pound nonfat cottage cheese**
1   **egg, lightly beaten, plus 1 egg white, lightly beaten, divided**
2   **tablespoons chopped sun-dried tomatoes**
1   **package frozen puff pastry, thawed**

In medium bowl combine cheeses, 1 beaten egg, and tomatoes. Mix well. Roll out 1 sheet puff pastry onto greased baking sheet. Spread cheese mixture over pastry. Cover with second sheet of pastry. Brush with egg white.

Bake in preheated 375-degree oven 30 to 35 minutes or until brown. Slice into triangles. Serve warm.

MUSHROOM PALMIERS

YIELD: 36 SLICES

5   **tablespoons butter**
1   **pound fresh mushrooms, chopped**
1-2   **medium onions, finely chopped**
3/4   **teaspoon lemon juice**
2   **tablespoons flour**
2   **teaspoons dried thyme**
     dash Worcestershire sauce
     salt to taste
     pepper to taste
2   **sheets frozen puff pastry, thawed**
1   **egg, beaten with 2 teaspoons water**

In large skillet melt butter. Cook mushrooms and onions over medium heat until soft and all juices have evaporated, stirring occasionally. Blend in lemon juice, flour, thyme, and Worcestershire sauce. Cook 2 minutes, stirring constantly. Season to taste. Cool.

Spread half of mushroom mixture over each puff pastry sheet. Starting from short sides of pastry sheets, roll each short side toward center. Press together. Transfer to ungreased baking sheet. Cover. Refrigerate at least 1 hour until firm. (May be frozen at this point.)

Slice pastry into 1/4-inch slices. Arrange on ungreased baking sheet. Brush with egg wash. Bake in preheated 350-degree oven 20 minutes or until golden brown. Serve warm.

TOASTED CHÈVRE BAGUETTES

SERVES 6

6 ¼- to ½-inch slices Montrachet cheese
   virgin olive oil
2 cloves garlic, slivered
¼ teaspoon chopped fresh thyme
¼ teaspoon chopped fresh basil
¼ teaspoon chopped parsley
⅛ teaspoon chopped fresh oregano
   butter or margarine
6 thin slices baguette, lightly toasted
2 tablespoons olivada San Remo (olive spread)

In shallow bowl combine cheese with enough olive oil to cover. Add garlic, thyme, basil, parsley and oregano. Marinate 1 to 4 days.

Lightly butter toasted baguette slices. Spread olivada sparingly on baguette slices. Top with cheese slice. Broil 3 to 4 minutes or until cheese begins to melt and brown.

GOAT CHEESE APPETIZER

SERVES 12

½ pound Montrachet cheese
½ pound cream cheese or lowfat cream cheese
1 clove garlic, minced
½ tablespoon chopped fresh basil plus ½ basil branch
3 tablespoons extra virgin olive oil, divided
   salt to taste
½ small onion, finely chopped
8 ounces canned stewed tomatoes
1 cup peeled, chopped fresh tomatoes
   freshly ground pepper to taste

In large bowl combine Montrachet, cream cheese, garlic, chopped basil, 2 tablespoons olive oil, and pinch salt. Blend until smooth. Cover and refrigerate.

In medium skillet sauté onion in remaining 1 tablespoon olive oil until soft. Add tomatoes and ½ basil branch. Simmer 1 hour. Remove basil branch. Season to taste. Transfer cheese mixture to center of ovenproof baking dish. Surround with tomato mixture.

Bake in preheated 350-degree oven until warm or top is browned. Serve with small rounds of toasted bread lightly seasoned with garlic or herb butter.

See photo page 77.

BAKED BOURSIN AND TOMATO APPETIZER

SERVES 6

2/3 **pint cherry tomatoes, quartered**
3 **tablespoons minced fresh basil leaves, divided**
5 **ounces Boursin pepper cheese**
5 **ounces Boursin herb cheese**
6-8 **tablespoons milk**

Spread tomatoes in single layer over bottom of shallow 2- to 2½-quart baking dish. Sprinkle 1½ tablespoons basil leaves over tomatoes.

In small bowl combine cheeses. Add enough milk to form thick, lumpy sauce. Pour mixture over tomatoes and basil, covering completely. Sprinkle with remaining 1½ tablespoons basil. Bake in preheated 350-degree oven 15 to 18 minutes. Serve hot with crackers.

May be assembled 1 day ahead, refrigerated, and brought to room temperature before baking.

PEPPERED CHEESE CRISPS

YIELD: 50 TO 60

1/2 **pound extra sharp Cheddar cheese, grated**
1/4 **pound margarine**
1 **teaspoon Tabasco**
1/8 **teaspoon cayenne pepper**
1 **cup flour**
1½ **cups Rice Krispies**
1/2-1 **cup chutney, chopped, optional**
1/2-1 **cup grated Parmesan cheese, optional**

In food processor or blender combine Cheddar cheese, margarine, Tabasco, and cayenne. Blend well. Add flour. Process until blended. Fold in Rice Krispies.

Roll dough into balls. Arrange balls 2 inches apart on ungreased baking sheet. Flatten each ball with bottom of glass to half-dollar size. Brush with thin layer of chopped chutney or sprinkle with grated Parmesan cheese, if desired. Bake in preheated 350-degree oven 15 minutes.

Dough freezes well.

TINY CORN FRITTERS

SERVES 6

16 ounces canned corn, drained
2 eggs
6 tablespoons flour
1/2 teaspoon baking powder
1/4 teaspoon salt
1/8 teaspoon nutmeg
3 tablespoons butter

In food processor puree corn. In small bowl beat eggs until light. In medium bowl combine corn, eggs, flour, baking powder, salt, and nutmeg. Drop batter by heaping tablespoonfuls onto hot buttered griddle. Brown on both sides.

Batter may be prepared early in day and refrigerated before frying.

PEPPER STRIPS WITH ANCHOVIES

SERVES 8 TO 10

1 large red pepper, in 1/2-inch strips
1 large yellow pepper, in 1/2-inch strips
2/3 cup vegetable oil
1/3 cup lemon juice
1/2 teaspoon paprika
1/2 teaspoon dry mustard
1/2 teaspoon salt
1/8 teaspoon freshly ground pepper
2 teaspoons confectioners sugar
2 ounces canned flat anchovies

In large saucepan combine pepper strips with water to cover. Parboil until tender-crisp. Drain.

In jar with tight-fitting lid combine oil, lemon juice, paprika, mustard, salt, ground pepper, and sugar. Cover and shake well.

In large bowl marinate pepper strips in dressing mixture overnight. Drain strips on paper towel. Blot well. Top each strip with anchovy.

POT STICKERS WITH DIPPING SAUCE

SERVES 8 TO 10

1 head napa (Chinese cabbage), leaves separated
1 pound lean ground pork
10 green onions, chopped
9 cloves garlic, minced
1 teaspoon salt
1 tablespoon soy sauce
1 tablespoon cornstarch
60 wonton wrappers
1 tablespoon vegetable oil
1/2 cup water

DIPPING SAUCE:
1 tablespoon rice vinegar
1 teaspoon soy sauce
3 drops sesame oil
1 drop hot chili oil, optional

In large pot of boiling water cook cabbage leaves 3 minutes. Drain. Blot dry with paper towel. Chop finely.

In large bowl combine cabbage, pork, green onions, garlic, salt, soy sauce, and cornstarch. Mix well. Moisten all edges of wonton wrapper. Place teaspoon of pork mixture in center. Fold into triangle and crimp shut.

In large heavy skillet heat vegetable oil over medium heat. Add dumplings. Cook covered 8 minutes or until bottoms brown. (May do in batches.) Return all browned dumplings to skillet. Add water. Cover and cook 10 minutes. Remove from skillet by inverting onto plate.

DIPPING SAUCE:
In small bowl combine all ingredients. Mix well. Serve pot stickers with dipping sauce or sweet and sour sauce.

CRISPY WONTONS

1   tablespoon olive oil, heated
1   clove garlic, crushed
12 wonton wrappers, 3½ by 3½ inches each
    cooking spray
    salt to taste, optional
3   tablespoons freshly grated Parmesan cheese
1½-2 tablespoons finely chopped fresh herbs (chives, basil, parsley)

In small bowl combine olive oil and garlic. Mix well. Cut wontons diagonally, creating triangles. Arrange on baking sheet sprayed with cooking spray.

Brush wontons with olive oil mixture. Salt to taste, if desired. Sprinkle with cheese and herbs. Bake in preheated 450-degree oven 3 to 4 minutes, watching carefully as wontons brown rapidly.

Best used same day.

MARINATED CHICKEN WINGS

SERVES 12

1   cup orange juice
2   tablespoons soy sauce
2   tablespoons honey
1   tablespoon minced fresh ginger root
3   cloves garlic, minced
½   cup vegetable oil
24 chicken wings, separated at joints, tips discarded

In large bowl combine all ingredients except chicken. Mix well. Marinate chicken in mixture at least 3 hours or overnight. Remove from marinade. Bake on rack in pan in preheated 400-degree oven until browned.

HUNAN HACKED CHICKEN

SERVES 8 TO 10

8-10	romaine lettuce leaves, shredded
3	whole chicken breasts, cooked, boned, skinned, in thin slices
3	tablespoons rice vinegar
2	tablespoons soy sauce
6	tablespoons smooth peanut butter
2	teaspoons sugar
3	tablespoons cream sherry
3	tablespoons sesame oil
1-2	teaspoons chili paste with garlic, or to taste
6	tablespoons water
4-5	green onions, minced
3	cloves garlic, minced
3	teaspoons peeled, minced fresh ginger root

On serving platter arrange lettuce. Layer chicken over top. In food processor slowly add vinegar and soy sauce to peanut butter. Add sugar, sherry, sesame oil, chili paste, and water. Process with quick on and off turns until smooth.

In jar with tight-fitting lid combine peanut butter mixture, green onions, garlic, and ginger root. Shake well. Pour desired amount over chicken. Serve remaining sauce on side.

ISLAND CHICKEN BITS

YIELD: 40 PIECES

3½	cups sweetened grated coconut
2	teaspoons ground cumin
¾	teaspoon ground coriander
½	teaspoon cayenne pepper
	salt to taste
	freshly ground pepper to taste
2	pounds boned, skinned chicken breasts, in 1-inch pieces
2	eggs, beaten
4	tablespoons butter

Spread coconut on large ungreased baking sheet. Bake in preheated 325-degree oven 15 minutes or until golden brown, stirring frequently. Cool. Transfer in batches to food processor. Process until coarsely ground.

In large bowl combine cumin, coriander, cayenne, salt, and pepper. Mix well. Add chicken pieces, turning to coat. Add eggs. Toss well. Dredge chicken pieces in coconut, coating completely. Spread chicken pieces on 2 large buttered baking sheets. Cover. Refrigerate 1 hour.

Bake chicken in preheated 400-degree oven 12 minutes or until crisp and golden brown, turning pieces once. Serve warm or at room temperature with Orange Horseradish Sauce, page 15.

May be prepared 1 day ahead, refrigerated, and baked before serving.

ANTIPASTO CHEESE LOAF

SERVES 8 TO 10

16 ounces cream cheese, softened, divided
¼ pound calamata olives, pitted, chopped
2 tablespoons sliced green onion tops
2 tablespoons chopped roasted red pepper, well drained
1 tablespoon vegetable oil
8 ounces Gruyère or Swiss cheese, in ⅛-inch slices
2 tablespoons poppy seed
2 tablespoons chopped parsley

In medium bowl beat cream cheese until light and fluffy. Combine half of cream cheese with olives. Combine a fourth of cream cheese with green onion tops. Combine a fourth of cream cheese with red pepper.

Brush 7½- by 4- by 2¼-inch loaf pan with vegetable oil. Line loaf pan with plastic wrap, leaving 1-inch overhang on long sides.

Trim 1 or 2 slices Gruyère cheese to fit bottom of pan in single layer. Spread with a third of olive-cheese mixture. Place in pan spread side down. Trim Gruyère for next layer. Spread with green onion-cheese mixture. Place in pan spread side down. Repeat layers with a third of olive-cheese spread on Gruyère followed by red pepper-cheese spread on Gruyère, ending with remaining olive-cheese spread on Gruyère. Bring plastic wrap over top. Chill several hours or overnight.

Remove from pan. Peel off plastic wrap. Press poppy seed and parsley on top and sides of loaf. Chill. To serve, slice with sharp or electric knife.

See photo page 77.

MIXED SATAYS

YIELD: 30

3/4 **pound beef, in 1/2- by 2-inch strips**
3/4 **pound chicken, in 1/2- by 2-inch strips**
3/4 **pound pork, in 1/2- by 2-inch strips**
30 **bamboo skewers, presoaked in water**

MARINADE:
2 **tablespoons sugar**
1 **tablespoon turmeric**
1 **teaspoon coriander**
1 **teaspoon cumin**
   pinch salt
1/2 **cup vegetable oil**
2 **tablespoons fish sauce**
4 **cloves garlic, minced**

Thread 3 to 4 pieces mixed meat on each skewer. Place skewers in shallow dish. In food processor or blender combine all marinade ingredients. Process until smooth. Pour over skewers. Marinate 1 hour, rotating skewers occasionally.

Grill meat on skewers over high heat 3 minutes on each side. Serve with Satay Sauce and Sweet and Sour Cucumber Relish.

SATAY SAUCE

2 **cups unsweetened coconut milk**
2 **teaspoons red curry paste**
2 **teaspoons paprika**
8 **tablespoons peanut butter, more if desired**
3 **tablespoons sugar**
2 **teaspoons garlic salt**

While meat marinates bring coconut milk to boil in small saucepan. Add red curry paste, paprika, peanut butter, sugar, and garlic salt.

continued

SWEET AND SOUR CUCUMBER RELISH

1/2   **cup vinegar**
1   **cup sugar**
1   **teaspoon salt**
3   **tablespoons water**
1   **small onion, finely chopped**
1   **small carrot, finely chopped**
1   **medium cucumber, finely chopped**
  fresh coriander leaves, chopped

In small saucepan combine vinegar, sugar, salt, and water. Boil 1 minute. In serving bowl combine onion, carrot, and cucumber. Pour syrup over vegetables until just covered. Garnish with chopped coriander leaves. See photo page 77.

MUSHROOM PECAN PÂTÉ

YIELD: 2 CUPS

3   **tablespoons butter or margarine**
1   **pound fresh mushrooms, finely chopped**
2   **green onions, finely chopped**
1   **tablespoon plus 1 teaspoon sherry, sweet vermouth, or Marsala**
1/2   **cup fresh whole wheat bread crumbs**
1/2   **cup finely chopped pecans**
1/8   **teaspoon Tabasco**
1/4   **cup finely chopped parsley**
2   **tablespoons sour cream or lite sour cream**
1/2   **teaspoon dill weed**
1/4   **teaspoon garlic powder**
  pinch nutmeg
1 1/2   **teaspoons Dijon mustard**
  salt to taste
  freshly ground pepper to taste

In large skillet melt butter. Add mushrooms and green onions. Cook over medium heat 8 to 10 minutes or until mushrooms begin to brown and liquid has evaporated. Stir in sherry, bread crumbs, pecans, and Tabasco. Remove from heat.

Add parsley, sour cream, dill weed, garlic powder, nutmeg, mustard, salt, and pepper. Mix well. Chill. Taste to adjust seasoning. Serve with crackers.

TURKEY TERRINE

SERVES 16

1½   **pounds ground turkey, white or dark meat**
1   **medium-large onion, finely chopped**
2   **large cloves garlic, minced**
1   **egg, beaten**
¼   **cup milk**
2   **teaspoons white wine Worcestershire sauce**
¼   **teaspoon savory**
1½   **teaspoons salt**
½   **teaspoon pepper**
10   **ounces frozen chopped spinach, thawed, drained**
½   **cup pesto sauce**
5   **ounces pimiento, rinsed, drained**
    chopped parsley
    red or green leaf lettuce
    cornichons
    Dijon mustard

In large bowl combine turkey, onion, garlic, egg, milk, Worcestershire sauce, savory, salt, and pepper. Mix well. In medium bowl combine spinach and pesto. Mix well.

Spread a third of turkey mixture firmly and evenly over bottom of lightly greased 9- by 5-inch loaf pan. Arrange pimiento pieces evenly over turkey. Follow with another third of turkey mixture. Top with layer of all spinach mixture, pressing down with spoon. Cover spinach layer with remaining turkey mixture. Wrap pan tightly in foil. Place in large baking pan. Pour hot water into outer pan, halfway up sides of loaf pan.

Bake in preheated 350-degree oven 1½ to 1¾ hours or until center of terrine is firm to touch. Remove loaf pan from water and unwrap. Cool 20 minutes. Drain any fat. Cover loosely with foil. Place second empty 9- by 5-inch loaf pan bottom side down on top of terrine. Place several heavy cans in empty pan for weight. Refrigerate overnight or several days.

To unmold, run knife carefully around sides of pan. Invert onto serving platter. Garnish with parsley and lettuce. Serve in ½-inch slices, accompanied by cornichons and Dijon mustard.

CHICKEN PÂTÉ

SERVES 10

1   whole chicken breast, boned, skinned,
      poached in 2 cups water or chicken broth
1   cup finely chopped walnuts
1/4   cup minced green onions
3   tablespoons minced, crystallized ginger
1 1/2   tablespoons soy sauce
1   tablespoon wine vinegar
1/8   teaspoon garlic powder
1/3   cup mayonnaise
    salt to taste
    chopped chives or parsley

In food processor puree chicken breast. Add remaining ingredients except chives. Blend with quick on and off turns. Pack in crock or oiled mold. Cover with plastic wrap. Chill at least 24 hours. Unmold or serve directly from crock. Garnish with chives or parsley. May be served with sour cream and melba toast or bread rounds.

WHITEFISH SALAD APPETIZER

YIELD: 1 CUP

    juice of 1/2 lemon
1/4   cup mayonnaise or lite mayonnaise
1/4   cup chopped red onion
1   cup flaked smoked whitefish, mashed

In medium bowl combine lemon juice, mayonnaise, and onion. Mix well. Add whitefish. Blend well. Serve with crackers.

VARIATION:
To use as a salad, serve on bed of lettuce.

GLAZED WHITEFISH MOUSSE PÂTÉ

SERVES 8

MOUSSE:
1 pound fresh whitefish, boned
1½ cups whipping cream
2 teaspoons chopped onions
2 teaspoons dried chives
2 teaspoons dill weed
1 teaspoon lemon juice
1 teaspoon salt
¼ teaspoon cayenne pepper

GLAZE:
1 pint sour cream
¼ cup mayonnaise
2 teaspoons Dijon mustard
1 teaspoon lemon juice
½ teaspoon white pepper
½ teaspoon salt
1 envelope unflavored gelatin
¼ cup dry vermouth

fresh dill or parsley, optional

In food processor grind fish 2 to 3 seconds. Add remaining mousse ingredients. Process 6 to 8 seconds until just smooth. Do not overprocess or fish will be tough and dry.

Pour mixture into buttered loaf pan or 2½-cup fish mold. Place filled pan in larger pan. Pour hot water into outer pan, halfway up sides of filled pan. Bake in preheated 350-degree oven 45 minutes. May be served hot without glaze or cold with glaze.

For glaze, combine sour cream, mayonnaise, mustard, lemon juice, white pepper, and salt in medium bowl. In small bowl soak gelatin in vermouth. Dissolve mixture over hot water. Rapidly whip gelatin-vermouth into sour cream mixture.

Unmold cooled mousse. Frost with glaze. Refrigerate 2 hours. Garnish with fresh dill or parsley, if desired. Serve with crackers or toast points.

TUNA MOUSSE RING
WRAPPED IN SMOKED SALMON

SERVES 8 TO 10

10	tablespoons unsalted butter
14	ounces canned white tuna in water, drained
2	tablespoons lemon juice
	pinch white pepper
2	tablespoons chopped fresh dill
1	cup mayonnaise
3	teaspoons capers
8-9	ounces smoked salmon, in long strips

In food processor cream butter. Add tuna. Blend. Add lemon juice, white pepper, and dill. Process until smooth. Stir in mayonnaise and capers.

Line 6-cup ring mold with plastic wrap, leaving at least 3-inch overhang. Line mold with salmon strips. Spoon tuna mixture into mold. Fold salmon strips over top of tuna. Bring plastic wrap over top to cover. Refrigerate overnight. To serve, unwrap plastic wrap, invert onto serving platter, and unmold, peeling off plastic.

Attractive centered with cherry tomatoes and surrounded by lettuce.

SALMON AND CARROT SPREAD

SERVES 8

8	ounces fresh salmon, cooked, cooled
8	ounces lite cream cheese
2	teaspoons lemon juice
2	teaspoons prepared horseradish
1/3	cup chopped cooked carrot
2	tablespoons minced parsley
2	tablespoons chopped green onion
1/4	teaspoon dill weed
1/8	teaspoon white pepper
	salt to taste, optional
1	small, round loaf of dark rye or pumpernickel bread, unsliced

In large bowl combine all ingredients except bread. Mix well. Hollow out bread. Spoon mixture into remaining loaf. Cut cubes from cutout bread. Serve with spread.

SAVORY CHEESE LOG

YIELD: 6-INCH LOG

3   **ounces cream cheese**
4   **ounces extra sharp or aged Cheddar cheese, grated**
1   **large clove garlic, minced**
1/4   **cup finely chopped onion**
1/3   **cup plus 2 tablespoons finely chopped walnuts, divided**
*1/8   **teaspoon chili paste**
2   **tablespoons minced parsley**
1½   **teaspoons paprika**
1½   **teaspoons chili powder**
1½   **teaspoons curry powder**
1   **teaspoon dill weed**

In food processor or blender combine cheeses, garlic, onion, 1/3 cup walnuts, and chili paste. Blend well. Chill mixture 1 hour or until firm. Transfer mixture to sheet of wax paper. Shape into log about 6 by 1½ inches. Wrap in wax paper. Refrigerate.

In small bowl combine remaining 2 tablespoons walnuts, parsley, paprika, chili powder, curry powder, and dill weed. Mix well. Roll log in mixture, coating well on all sides. Roll log in wax paper. Press mixture firmly to adhere. Transfer to foil or plastic wrap. Chill several hours or overnight. Serve with crackers.

*Available in Oriental sections of some supermarkets and Oriental markets.

LAYERED PESTO CHEESE SPREAD

SERVES 10 TO 12

11   **ounces cream cheese, softened**
6   **tablespoons unsalted butter**
2/3   **cup grated Parmesan cheese**
1²/3   **cups lightly packed fresh basil or parsley leaves, divided**
3   **tablespoons olive oil**
3   **tablespoons pine nuts, divided**

Blend cream cheese and butter until well mixed. In food processor or blender combine remaining ingredients, reserving 6 basil leaves and 6 to 8 pine nuts. Process until paste forms.

Line small bowl with plastic wrap. Spread a third of cream cheese mixture over bottom. Top with half of basil mixture. Repeat layers. Cover with remaining cheese mixture. Cover and chill 2 hours.

To serve, invert bowl onto serving plate and peel off plastic wrap. Garnish with reserved basil leaves and pine nuts. Serve with bread rounds or crackers.

May be made 2 days ahead.

SALSA CHEESECAKE

SERVES 16 TO 18

1/2 **pound cream cheese, room temperature**
1/2 **pound lite cream cheese, room temperature**
1/2 **cup grated Romano cheese**
1 1/2 **cups grated Monterey Jack cheese**
2 **cups lite sour cream, divided**
1 **tablespoon flour**
3 **eggs or equivalent egg substitute**
1 1/2 **tablespoons minced green onion**
8 **ounces medium or hot salsa**
4 **ounces canned green chilies, diced, drained**
1 **teaspoon chopped fresh cilantro or parsley, optional**
6 **ounces guacamole, optional**
1/3 **cup chopped red pepper, optional**
sprigs fresh cilantro or parsley
tortilla chips or crackers

In large bowl combine cream cheese, lite cream cheese, Romano, and Monterey Jack. Beat until light and fluffy. Add 1 cup lite sour cream and flour. Add eggs all at once. Mix well. Stir in green onion, salsa, chilies, and cilantro, if desired.

Pour into ungreased 9-inch springform pan. Place pan on baking sheet in center of preheated 350-degree oven. Bake 40 to 45 minutes. Center will be nearly set. Remove from oven. Spread remaining 1 cup lite sour cream over top of hot cheesecake. Cool on rack. Refrigerate covered at least 4 hours.

To serve, remove sides of pan. If desired, swirl guacamole around outer edge of cheesecake. Sprinkle guacamole with red pepper, if desired. Garnish top with sprigs cilantro. Serve with tortilla chips.

ROQUEFORT WHIPPED WITH BRIE

7   ounces Brie cheese, rind removed
2   ounces Roquefort cheese
3   tablespoons unsalted butter, room temperature
1/4 cup whipping cream
    freshly ground pepper to taste

In food processor combine cheeses and butter. Mix with 6 on and off turns. Add cream and pepper. Blend until smooth, stopping to scrape sides of bowl. Cover.

Let stand at room temperature 1 hour before serving. Serve with Walnut Wheatberry Bread, page 343.

SPICY EGGPLANT SPREAD

SERVES 6

1   large eggplant (about 2 pounds)
6   tablespoons olive oil, divided
1/2 pound tomatoes, seeded, chopped
1   medium onion, chopped
1   cup pitted, chopped black olives
1   cup dried currants
2   tablespoons curry powder
1   tablespoon chopped fresh thyme or 1 1/2 teaspoons dried thyme
1   teaspoon celery salt
    salt to taste
    pepper to taste
    lemon wedges
    pita bread, in wedges

Cut eggplant in half lengthwise. Remove flesh and reserve, leaving 1/4-inch shell. Pour 2 tablespoons olive oil into 9- by 13-inch baking pan. Place shells skin side down in pan. Chop reserved eggplant.

In large skillet heat remaining 4 tablespoons olive oil. Add eggplant, tomatoes, onion, olives, currants, curry powder, thyme, and celery salt. Mix well. Cook over medium heat 15 minutes or until eggplant and onion are soft. Season to taste. Spoon mixture into eggplant shells. Bake uncovered in preheated 300-degree oven 1 hour. Cover with foil. Bake additional hour. Remove from oven and cool.

Transfer to serving platter. Garnish with lemon wedges. Serve at room temperature with pita bread.

May be made 1 to 2 days ahead, covered, and refrigerated.

SUN-DRIED TOMATO SPREAD

YIELD: 1½ CUPS

8	ounces cream cheese
1	clove garlic, minced
1	ounce Gruyère cheese, grated
1	ounce white Cheddar cheese, grated
2	large sun-dried tomatoes (in oil)
4-5	fresh basil leaves, finely chopped
1-2	tablespoons half and half
	salt to taste

In food processor combine all ingredients. Process with several quick on and off turns until tomatoes are in small pieces. Serve on melba toast or with fresh vegetables.

RED PEPPER RELISH

YIELD: APPROXIMATELY 5 CUPS

6	red peppers, seeded, in chunks
2	medium onions, quartered
½	tablespoon mustard seed
½	tablespoon salt
¾	cup white vinegar
¾	cup sugar

In food processor or blender combine all ingredients. Process until chopped and well blended. Transfer to bowl. Refrigerate covered.

An excellent topping for crackers spread with cream cheese.

HOT MEXICAN DIP

YIELD: 4 CUPS

8	ounces cream cheese, softened
10¾	ounces canned chili beef soup
1½	cups salsa (hot or mild)
2	cups shredded Monterey Jack, Cheddar, or taco cheese
	tortilla chips

Spread cream cheese over bottom of shallow 9- by 9-inch ovenproof dish. Layer chili beef soup over cream cheese. Spread salsa over soup. Sprinkle shredded cheese over top. Bake in preheated 350-degree oven 30 minutes. Serve with tortilla chips.

HOT BLUE CHEESE DIP

SERVES 8

16 ounces cream cheese
1 cup milk
1 teaspoon Worcestershire sauce
pinch garlic powder
pinch salt
1/2 pound blue cheese

In double boiler over simmering water combine cream cheese, milk, Worcestershire sauce, garlic powder, and salt. Stir until creamy. Add blue cheese. Stir until melted. Serve hot or warm. Use as dip for fresh vegetables or chunks of French bread.

SANTA FE SPINACH DIP

YIELD: 4 CUPS

2 tablespoons vegetable oil
1 medium onion, chopped
1/2 red pepper, chopped
3 tablespoons chopped chilies, mild or hot
8 ounces cream cheese
1/2 cup half and half
10 ounces frozen chopped spinach, thawed, well drained
2 cups grated Monterey Jack or Colby cheese
2 1/4 ounces sliced black olives
1 tablespoon red wine vinegar
salt to taste
pepper to taste
tortilla chips

In medium skillet heat oil over medium heat. Add onion. Sauté until soft but not brown. Add red pepper and chilies. Sauté 2 to 3 minutes.

In large bowl beat cream cheese and half and half until smooth. Add sautéed vegetables and remaining ingredients except tortilla chips. Mix well. Transfer to lightly greased casserole. Bake in preheated 400-degree oven 25 to 35 minutes or until brown and bubbly. Serve with tortilla chips.

CURRY VEGETABLE DIP

YIELD: 1½ CUPS

1½ cups mayonnaise or lite mayonnaise
1 teaspoon curry powder
1 teaspoon garlic salt
1 teaspoon onion powder
1 teaspoon dry mustard
1 teaspoon prepared yellow mustard
1 teaspoon prepared horseradish
1 teaspoon cider vinegar

In small bowl combine all ingredients. Mix well. Serve mixture as dip for vegetables.

DIP FOR ARTICHOKES

YIELD: APPROXIMATELY 1 CUP

2 tablespoons white wine vinegar
1 teaspoon Dijon mustard
1 clove garlic, crushed
¼ teaspoon dried thyme
¼ teaspoon salt
1 teaspoon chopped parsley
1 tablespoon toasted, ground sesame seed
¼-½ cup olive oil
2 tablespoons plain yogurt
1 tablespoon mayonnaise
2-3 artichokes, cooked, chilled

In small bowl combine all ingredients except artichokes. Mix well. Serve mixture as dip for artichokes.

SAVORY PECANS

3 tablespoons margarine or butter
1 pound pecan halves
1½ tablespoons curry powder
1 tablespoon cumin
1½ teaspoons salt
½ teaspoon sugar

In large skillet melt margarine over medium heat. Add pecans. Cook several minutes until pecans sizzle. Sprinkle with curry powder, cumin, salt, and sugar. Continue cooking 2 minutes, stirring constantly. Cool. Store in airtight container.

SPICED ALMONDS

2 cups whole natural almonds
1 egg white, lightly beaten
¾ cup superfine sugar
1-1¼ teaspoons cumin
½ teaspoon cayenne pepper
   salt to taste
4 tablespoons butter, melted

In large baking pan arrange almonds in single layer. Toast in preheated 325-degree oven 5 minutes. Cool. Mix almonds with egg white until well coated.

In small bowl combine sugar, cumin, cayenne, and salt. Mix well. Add a third of sugar mixture to coated almonds. Mix well. Spread melted butter in large baking pan. Arrange almonds in single layer. Bake in preheated 325-degree oven 20 to 30 minutes, stirring and turning every 7 minutes. Remove almonds to rack covered with wax paper. Cool 4 to 5 minutes.

With fine sieve sprinkle almonds with remaining sugar mixture. Stir to coat both sides of almonds. Cool completely before storing in airtight container.

HAM AND CHEESE MINI BUNS

YIELD: 24 TO 36

1/2 **pound butter or margarine, softened**
3/4 **cup chopped green onions with tops**
3 **tablespoons Dijon mustard**
1 **tablespoon poppy seed**
3 **dozen cocktail size hamburger buns, 2 inches in diameter,**
    or 2 dozen dinner rolls, 3 inches in diameter
1 1/4 **pounds sliced ham**
12 **ounces sliced Swiss cheese**

In small bowl combine butter, green onions, mustard, and poppy seed. Split buns. Spread each side with butter mixture, using 1 teaspoonful per side. Place ham on bun bottoms and cover with Swiss cheese. Close sandwiches and wrap individually in foil. Freeze in plastic bags, if desired.

When ready to serve, remove sandwiches from plastic bags, keeping foil wrapping, and place on baking sheet. Bake in preheated 350-degree oven 15 to 20 minutes. Remove from foil.

DAGWOOD LOAF

SERVES 6 TO 8

1 **loaf Rhodes bread dough, thawed**
1/2 **green pepper, julienned**
1/2 **red pepper, julienned**
2 **tablespoons vegetable oil**
1/4 **teaspoon garlic salt**
1/8 **pound ham, sliced**
1/8 **pound provolone cheese, sliced**
1/8 **pound pepperoni, sliced**
1/8 **pound American cheese, sliced**
1 **egg white, lightly beaten**

Knead dough 15 times. Place in greased bowl and cover. Let rise in warm place 2 hours. Punch down dough. On floured surface roll out to length of baking sheet and half of width.

In small skillet sauté peppers in oil. Drain on paper towel. Sprinkle peppers and garlic salt over center of dough. Top with ham, followed by provolone cheese, pepperoni, and American cheese. Fold up ends and sides of dough to seal. Brush with egg white. Bake in preheated 425-degree oven 30 minutes.

SUPER BOWL BITES

YIELD: 40

1   **pound ground chuck**
8   **ounces grated Cheddar cheese**
1   **tablespoon mayonnaise**
1   **package dry onion soup mix**
2   **packages baked miniature dinner rolls in foil pans**

In medium bowl combine ground chuck, cheese, mayonnaise, and onion soup mix. Mix well. Slice unseparated rolls in half horizontally. Spread meat mixture over bottoms of rolls. Top with remaining halves. Wrap filled rolls in foil. Bake in preheated 350-degree oven 30 to 35 minutes.

May be prepared, wrapped, frozen, and baked frozen 45 minutes.

FRESH VEGETABLE TORTE

SERVES 6 TO 8

1   **large round country bread (about 2 pounds)**
5   **medium cloves garlic**
2   **shallots**
1/4   **pound plus 4 tablespoons butter or margarine**
1   **cup chopped parsley**
12   **ounces fresh spinach, stems removed**
2   **tomatoes, thinly sliced**
8   **ounces fresh mushrooms, thinly sliced**
2 1/4   **ounces canned chopped black olives**
2   **cups grated mozzarella cheese**

Cut circular top from bread. Remove top. Scoop out inside to create basket.*

In food processor combine garlic and shallots. Chop finely. Add butter and parsley. Process until well blended.

Spread thin layer of garlic butter on inside of bread. Add thin layer of spinach leaves followed by thin layer of tomato slices, garlic butter, mushrooms, olives, and mozzarella cheese. Repeat layering until filling is higher than bread (it will fall as it cooks), mounding cheese on top.

Bake on baking sheet in preheated 350-degree oven 35 to 45 minutes. Serve warm or at room temperature. Slices beautifully.

*Save top and inside of bread for another use.

SOUPS

SUMMER TOMATO AND ORANGE SOUP

YIELD: 6 CUPS

1½ tablespoons butter
¾ cup thinly sliced onion
½ cup thinly sliced fennel
1¼ pounds plum tomatoes, quartered
3 large oranges, peeled
⅓ cup dry white wine
1 tablespoon grated orange rind
1 bay leaf
½ teaspoon salt, or to taste
¼ teaspoon white pepper, or to taste
2 large cloves garlic, minced
2 teaspoons basil
1 teaspoon allspice

In large saucepan melt butter. Add onion and fennel. Sauté 10 minutes until soft. Add tomatoes.

Working over bowl to catch juice, cut between orange membranes to remove segments. Add segments and juice to tomato mixture. Simmer 15 minutes, stirring occasionally. Add wine, orange rind, bay leaf, salt, and white pepper. Bring to boil. Reduce heat. Cover. Simmer over medium heat 10 minutes, stirring occasionally. Remove bay leaf.

In food processor or blender puree soup in batches. Stir in garlic, basil, and allspice. Refrigerate. Serve cold.

CLAMATO SOUP

SERVES 12

3 medium tomatoes, seeded, finely chopped
2 medium zucchini, seeded, finely chopped
4-6 green onions with tops, minced
½ green pepper, seeded, finely chopped
6 ounces canned minced clams
2 avocados, finely chopped
2-3 ribs celery, finely chopped
¼ cup Worcestershire sauce
3 tablespoons fresh lemon juice
1 tablespoon prepared horseradish
64 ounces Clamato juice

In large bowl combine all ingredients. Mix well. Cover and refrigerate. Serve cold. See photo page 78.

CHICKEN SOUP BOMBAY

SERVES 8

2   leeks, split, rinsed, chopped, including 3 inches of green tops
2   medium onions, chopped
5   ribs celery, chopped
1/4 pound butter
1   tablespoon curry powder
3   tablespoons flour
2   quarts chicken broth
2   medium potatoes, peeled
1   cup plain yogurt, milk, or whipping cream, optional
    salt to taste
    pepper to taste
2   chicken breasts, cooked, boned, skinned, slivered

In medium pot brown leeks, onions, and celery in butter about 15 minutes. Stir in curry powder and flour. Mix well. Add chicken broth. Simmer 30 minutes.

Strain vegetables from pot, reserving broth. In food processor or blender puree vegetables with 1 cup of reserved broth. Return pureed vegetables to liquid in pot.

In small pot boil potatoes until soft. Strain. In food processor or blender puree potatoes with 1 cup soup. Add to soup. Add yogurt, if desired. Season to taste. Mix well. Chill. Fill bowls and top with slivered chicken.

CURRIED EGGPLANT SOUP WITH JICAMA

SERVES 4

1   medium onion, chopped
2   shallots, chopped
4   tablespoons margarine
1¼   pounds eggplant, peeled, in 1-inch cubes
1   quart chicken broth
1½   teaspoons curry powder
1/2 cup non-dairy creamer or half and half
     salt to taste
     pepper to taste
1/2 cup julienned jicama

continued

In medium pot sauté onion and shallots in margarine just until soft. Do not brown. Add eggplant, chicken broth, and curry powder. Bring to boil. Reduce heat. Simmer 40 minutes or until eggplant is tender.

In food processor or blender puree soup in batches. Strain back into pot. Heat mixture over medium heat. Stir in creamer, salt, and pepper. Blend well. Remove from heat. Cool. Refrigerate. Serve chilled garnished with jicama.

CREAM OF BROCCOFLOWER SOUP

SERVES 8

4 **cups broccoflower flowerets (may substitute broccoli or cauliflower)**
5 **cups chicken broth, divided**
4 **tablespoons unsalted butter**
1/4 **cup flour**
2 **cups hot milk**
1 **teaspoon salt**
1/4 **teaspoon white pepper**
1/4 **teaspoon dry mustard**
  pinch cayenne pepper
1/2 **cup whipping cream**
  minced fresh coriander or parsley

In medium pot combine broccoflower flowerets and 3 cups chicken broth. Cook over medium heat about 20 minutes until flowerets are tender. In food processor or blender puree mixture. Strain and reserve.

In large pot melt butter over medium heat. Blend in flour. Cook several minutes until bubbly but not brown, stirring constantly. Remove from heat.

Blend in hot milk with wire whisk until smooth. Bring to boil, stirring constantly. Add remaining 2 cups chicken broth, salt, white pepper, mustard, and cayenne. Return to boil. Add pureed broccoflower. Simmer 5 minutes. Stir in cream.

Serve garnished with coriander. May be served hot or cold.

RASPBERRY BEET SOUP

SERVES 8

2 **pounds fresh beets, tops removed**
3 **tablespoons chopped shallots**
2 **cups raspberries**
2 **cups skim milk**
5 **tablespoons red wine vinegar**
4 **tablespoons fresh lemon juice**
2 **tablespoons sugar**
salt to taste
pepper to taste

In large pot cover beets with cold water. Bring to boil. Reduce heat. Simmer covered 30 to 40 minutes or until tender. Remove from heat and cool.

Drain beets, reserving 3 cups cooking liquid. Peel beets. Julienne 2 beets and set aside. Cut remaining beets into pieces.

In food processor or blender combine beet pieces, shallots, and raspberries. Puree, adding reserved cooking liquid as needed for smooth consistency. Strain pureed mixture to remove seeds.

In large bowl combine strained mixture, milk, vinegar, lemon juice, and sugar. Mix well. Season to taste. Refrigerate covered until chilled. Garnish each portion with julienned beets.

CHILLED BLUEBERRY SOUP

SERVES 6

4½ **cups fresh blueberries, divided**
1¾ **cups cold water**
¾ **cup red Burgundy wine**
⅓ **cup sugar**
2 **teaspoons grated orange rind**
¼-⅓ **cup fresh orange juice**

Reserving ½ cup blueberries, combine remaining ingredients in medium saucepan. Stir well. Bring to boil. Reduce heat and simmer 7 to 8 minutes. Remove from heat.

Puree in food processor or strain through fine strainer. Chill thoroughly.

Top each serving with dollop of Lemon Sauce page 413 and several fresh blueberries.

LEEK AND PEAR BISQUE

YIELD:
12 TO 14 CUPS

5   large leeks, split, rinsed, thinly sliced crosswise
4   tablespoons butter or margarine
3   medium potatoes, peeled, in 1-inch cubes
2   pounds canned pear halves (may use lite), liquid reserved
46 ounces chicken broth
1   cup half and half
1/4 pound blue cheese, crumbled, optional
    chopped chives, optional

In large pot sauté leeks in butter 5 minutes. Add potatoes. Sauté 5 minutes. Add liquid from pears and chicken broth. Bring to boil. Reduce heat and simmer covered 15 minutes or until potatoes are soft.

In food processor or blender puree mixture from pot in batches. Return puree to pot. In food processor or blender puree pears. Add to pot with half and half. Blend well. Reheat over medium heat, stirring constantly. Do not boil. Serve sprinkled with cheese and chives, if desired.

ASPARAGUS SOUP

SERVES 4

    cooking spray
1   cup chopped leek
1   pound asparagus, in 1-inch pieces
10 ounces chicken broth
1/4 cup flour
1/2 cup water
1/2 teaspoon tarragon
12 ounces evaporated skim milk
1/4 cup plain lowfat yogurt

Coat 2-quart microwavable casserole liberally with cooking spray. Add leek to casserole. Microwave uncovered on high 2 minutes. Stir in asparagus and chicken broth. Microwave covered on high 10 minutes or until asparagus is tender.

In small bowl combine flour and water. Mix well. Stir into asparagus mixture.

In food processor or blender puree asparagus mixture until smooth. Return mixture to casserole. Blend in tarragon and milk. Microwave uncovered on high 7 minutes. Serve warm or chilled with dollop of yogurt.

PEPPER SOUP WITH
PARMESAN BUTTER CROUTONS

8   **tablespoons unsalted butter, room temperature, divided**
4   **large red or yellow peppers, seeded, quartered**
2   **large leeks, split, rinsed, sliced (white part only)**
3   **cloves garlic, divided**
3   **cups chicken broth**
    salt to taste
    pepper to taste
3/4   **cup whipping cream**
2   **tablespoons dry sherry**
1   **ounce Parmesan cheese**
6   **fresh basil leaves**
1   **tablespoon fresh parsley leaves**
6   **slices French bread, 3/8 inch thick**
2   **tablespoons olive oil**

In large pot melt 4 tablespoons butter. Add peppers and leeks. Mince and add 2 cloves garlic. Cover. Cook 5 minutes. Add chicken broth, salt, and pepper. Cover. Simmer 30 minutes. Strain, returning liquid to pot.

In food processor or blender puree vegetables until smooth. With motor running add 1/4 cup liquid from pot. Process until mixed.

Transfer puree to pot. Mix with liquid. Stir in cream and sherry. Add salt and pepper, if desired. Warm on low heat until heated through, stirring occasionally.

In food processor finely chop Parmesan cheese. Add basil and parsley. Process briefly. Add remaining 4 tablespoons butter. Process until smooth. Set aside.

In medium skillet sauté bread slices in olive oil until golden brown. Drain on paper towel. Rub both sides of toast with halved clove garlic.

Garnish each serving of soup with bread topped with dollop of Parmesan butter.

ROASTED PEPPER SOUP

SERVES 4

1	**teaspoon olive oil**
2	**cloves garlic, minced**
1	**onion, minced**
1	**large carrot, minced**
4	**ribs celery, minced**
1	**quart chicken or vegetable broth**
1	**teaspoon dried thyme**
6	**red peppers, roasted*, seeded, peeled, quartered**
1	**cup skim buttermilk**
1/2	**teaspoon salt, or to taste**
	pepper to taste
1/2	**cup minced fresh basil leaves**
2	**green onions, minced**

In large pot heat olive oil. Add garlic and onion. Cook over medium heat about 5 minutes until soft. Add carrot, celery, broth, and thyme. Simmer 25 minutes. Add peppers. Simmer 5 minutes.

In food processor or blender puree mixture in batches until smooth. Return mixture to pot.

Warm over medium-low heat. Stir in buttermilk. Season to taste. Heat well. Serve in individual bowls garnished with basil and green onions.

*For roasting instructions, see page 162.

ZUCCHINI BISQUE WITH SHERRY

SERVES 8

1	medium onion, chopped
1	medium clove garlic, minced
2	tablespoons margarine or butter
2	medium potatoes, peeled, grated
1	pound grated zucchini, divided
14	ounces chicken broth
22	ounces water
1	medium carrot, grated
3	tablespoons sherry
1	tablespoon chopped fresh dill
1/8	teaspoon nutmeg
1	cup whipping cream
	salt to taste
	pepper to taste

In large pot sauté onion and garlic in margarine. Add potatoes. Cover. Cook 3 minutes. Add ½ pound grated zucchini. Cook 3 minutes or until vegetables are tender.

In food processor or blender puree vegetable mixture. Return puree to pot.

Add chicken broth and water to puree in pot. Add carrot, sherry, dill, and nutmeg. Cook covered 5 to 10 minutes or until boiling. Add remaining ½ pound zucchini. Cook 4 minutes or until vegetables are tender. Stir in cream, salt, and pepper. Serve hot.

CAULIFLOWER AND WATERCRESS SOUP

SERVES 6

1½	cups cauliflower flowerets
	lowfat milk
3/4	cup finely chopped green onions
6	tablespoons unsalted butter
3/4	teaspoon salt
1½	cups peeled, finely diced potatoes
1½	cups chicken broth
8	ounces watercress, stems removed, divided
1/4	teaspoon white pepper
3/4	cup crème fraîche

continued

In small pan combine cauliflower with enough milk to cover. Simmer about 10 minutes until fork tender. Set aside.

In large pot sauté green onions in butter over medium-low heat until soft. Add salt, potatoes, and chicken broth. Simmer covered 10 minutes. Add watercress, reserving 12 leaves. Simmer covered 10 minutes until potatoes are fork tender, shaking pot occasionally. Add white pepper.

Reserving milk, drain cauliflower. Transfer vegetables from pot and cauliflower to food processor or blender. Puree until smooth. Return to pot. Add reserved cauliflower milk and additional plain milk, if necessary. Mix well. Heat until warm but not hot. Serve garnished with crème fraîche and reserved watercress leaves.

SPICY TOMATO DILL SOUP

SERVES 8 TO 10

7½	**tablespoons butter, divided**
1	**onion, chopped**
1	**clove garlic, minced**
4	**cups chicken broth**
½	**cup flour**
29	**ounces tomato puree**
16	**ounces whole peeled tomatoes with juice, chopped**
3	**tablespoons honey**
1	**tablespoon dill weed**
1	**teaspoon basil**
½	**teaspoon pepper**
½	**teaspoon chili powder**

In large pot melt 3 tablespoons butter. Add onion. Cook until soft. Add garlic. Cook 2 minutes. Add chicken broth. Bring to boil. Reduce to simmer.

In small saucepan melt remaining 4½ tablespoons butter. Stir in flour until blended. Cook over low heat 2 minutes, stirring constantly. Add flour mixture to large pot. Stir until completely blended and soup is thickened.

Add remaining ingredients. Simmer 30 minutes, stirring bottom frequently to prevent scorching. Serve hot. If thinner consistency is desired, add more chicken broth.

HERB GARDEN TOMATO SOUP

SERVES 10

3 medium yellow onions, thinly sliced
2 tablespoons unsalted butter
2 tablespoons olive oil
8 large or 10 medium tomatoes, peeled, coarsely chopped
6 ounces tomato paste
6 cups chicken broth
1 tablespoon chopped fresh basil
1 tablespoon chopped fresh thyme
1 teaspoon salt
1/2 teaspoon pepper
   chives, chopped

In large pot sauté onions in butter and olive oil until soft and golden. Add remaining ingredients except chives. Bring to boil over medium-high heat. Reduce heat to low. Cover. Simmer 30 minutes.

In food processor or blender puree soup in batches. Pour through strainer into pot. Simmer 30 to 40 minutes until mixture is reduced to desired thickness.

Serve hot or cold garnished with chives.

TOMATO BLUE CHEESE SOUP

YIELD: 12 CUPS

2 1/2 medium onions, chopped
5 tablespoons finely chopped garlic
3 ribs celery, chopped
6-7 green onions, sliced
2-3 tablespoons butter
30 ounces tomato juice
44 ounces low sodium chicken broth
28 ounces tomato puree
*1/2-1 pound blue cheese, crumbled
1 tablespoon chopped fresh basil
1/2 teaspoon Tabasco
   salt to taste
   pepper to taste

continued

In large pot sauté onions, garlic, celery, and green onions in butter. Add tomato juice, chicken broth, and tomato puree. Simmer until vegetables are very soft. Add cheese to taste.

In food processor or blender puree soup in batches. Return to pot. Add basil and Tabasco. Season to taste.

*1 pound cheese is very strong flavoring.

APPLE GINGER SQUASH SOUP

SERVES 6

3-4	**tablespoons butter or margarine**
1½	**pounds yellow crookneck or butternut squash, peeled, seeded, in chunks**
1	**medium onion, sliced**
1	**large Granny Smith apple, peeled, cored, chopped**
1	**slice white bread, cubed**
2	**cups chicken broth**
1	**sprig thyme or ½ teaspoon dried thyme**
2	**tablespoons chopped crystallized ginger**
	salt to taste
	pepper to taste
1	**cup whipping cream**
	chopped fresh chives

In large heavy pot melt butter. Add squash, onion, apple, and bread. Sauté 5 minutes. Add chicken broth and thyme. Bring to boil. Cover. Reduce heat. Simmer about 40 minutes or until squash is tender. Remove thyme sprig. Cool.

In food processor or blender puree soup in batches, adding some ginger with each batch. Blend well, thoroughly processing ginger into mixture. Season to taste. Cool. Cover and refrigerate up to 2 days ahead.

Before serving stir in cream and heat to simmer. Ladle into bowls and sprinkle with chives.

BUTTERNUT SQUASH PEAR SOUP

SERVES 6 TO 8

1½   **quarts chicken broth**
2½   **pounds butternut squash, peeled, seeded, in 2-inch pieces**
3   **Bosc pears, peeled, cored, quartered**
1   **large onion, chopped**
2   **medium shallots, peeled, chopped**
¼-½   **teaspoon nutmeg**
½   **cup half and half**
  salt to taste
  pepper to taste
6-8   **tablespoons sour half and half, optional**
1-2   **teaspoons cinnamon, optional**

In large pot heat chicken broth. Add squash, pears, onion, shallots, and nutmeg. Bring to boil. Reduce heat. Simmer 30 minutes or until tender.

In food processor or blender puree mixture in small batches. Strain back into pot. Stir in half and half, salt, and pepper. Cook over low heat just until hot.

Serve with dollop of sour half and half, sprinkle of cinnamon, or Cinnamon Croutons, if desired.

CINNAMON CROUTONS

SERVES 6 TO 8

6   **slices 2½- by 3½-inch French bread, in ½-inch cubes**
4   **tablespoons margarine or butter**
3   **teaspoons sugar**
¾   **teaspoon cinnamon**

Place bread cubes on ungreased jelly-roll pan. In small saucepan melt margarine. Add sugar and cinnamon. Mix well. Pour over bread cubes. Toss to coat evenly. Arrange cubes in single layer.

Bake in preheated 350°-degree oven 12 minutes, tossing every 3 to 4 minutes. Cool on pan. Store in plastic bag.

AUTUMN BISQUE

1/4 **pound unsalted butter**
1 **cup diced Spanish onion**
1/2 **cup diced carrots**
1/2 **cup diced celery**
1 **pound butternut squash, peeled, seeded, diced**
2 **teaspoons sage**
1 **tablespoon thyme**
1/2 **cup flour**
1 **quart chicken broth**
1 **cup whipping cream**
   pinch nutmeg
   salt to taste
   white pepper to taste
1/2 **cup cooked wild rice**
1/2 **cup blanched morels, chanterelles, or button mushrooms, sliced**
1/2 **cup julienned smoked chicken breast, optional**

In large pot melt butter. Sauté onion, carrots, celery, and squash until golden brown. Reduce heat. Add sage and thyme. Cook 5 minutes. Gradually add flour, blending well. Add chicken broth. Simmer 1 hour.

In food processor or blender puree mixture until smooth. Return to pot. Add cream, nutmeg, salt, and white pepper. Reheat.

To serve, divide rice, mushrooms, and chicken, if desired, among 8 soup bowls. Fill with hot soup.

See photo page 78.

MARKET BASKET SOUP

SERVES 4

1 small onion, chopped
1 rib celery, chopped
3 tablespoons margarine
2 tablespoons minced garlic
3 pounds tomatoes, peeled, seeded, chopped
1 quart chicken broth
1 cup diced squash (hubbard, banana, acorn)
1 cup diced rutabaga
1 cup diced sweet potato or yam
1 cup diced parsnips or carrots
1/4 pound prosciutto, julienned
1/4 cup chopped Italian parsley
  salt to taste
  pepper to taste

In large pot sauté onion and celery in margarine until soft. Add garlic. Cook 2 minutes. Add tomatoes. Cook 2 minutes. Add chicken broth, squash, rutabaga, sweet potato, and parsnips. Simmer gently until vegetables are fork tender. Add prosciutto and parsley. Cook 1 minute. Season to taste.

WILD RICE SOUP

SERVES 8 TO 10

8-10 acorn squash
1/2 cup sliced fresh mushrooms
1 cup chopped onion
3/4 cup chopped celery
1/2 cup chopped green pepper
2 teaspoons butter
1/2 cup wild rice, cooked
1 pound Canadian bacon, diced
32 1/4 ounces canned cream of mushroom soup
28 ounces chicken broth

continued

Trim just enough from bottom of each squash so it will "sit up." Cut off top. Save for lid. Scoop out seeds. Bake squash on greased baking sheet in preheated 375° degree oven 30 minutes.

In medium skillet sauté mushrooms, onion, celery, and green pepper in butter. In large pot combine sauteed vegetables and remaining ingredients. Simmer until vegetables are tender, stirring occasionally. Ladle into squash "tureens." Cover. Serve immediately.

May also be served from a large pumpkin "tureen."

See photo page 82.

MUSHROOM PARSNIP SOUP

SERVES 6

2 tablespoons butter or margarine
8 ounces fresh mushrooms, coarsely chopped
1 pound parsnips, peeled, sliced
1 small onion, sliced
1 quart beef broth
 salt to taste
 pepper to taste
8 ounces sour half and half

In medium pot melt butter over medium heat. Add mushrooms, parsnips, and onion. Sauté 10 minutes. Add beef broth. Increase heat to high. Bring soup to boil. Reduce heat. Simmer soup about 30 minutes until vegetables are tender. Remove from heat.

Strain soup into large bowl. In food processor or blender puree vegetables until very smooth. Return vegetables and soup stock to pot. Season to taste. Bring to boil.

Top each serving with dollop of sour half and half.

POTATO MUSHROOM SOUP

SERVES 4

3 medium onions, sliced
1 clove garlic
3 tablespoons butter
8 ounces fresh mushrooms, sliced
  salt and pepper to taste
  oregano to taste
13¾ ounces beef broth
¾ pound new potatoes, in small cubes
13¾ ounces chicken broth
2 tablespoons finely chopped parsley

In large pot sauté onions and garlic in butter until light golden. Add mushrooms. Cook over low heat 10 minutes. Remove garlic. Add salt, pepper, oregano, and beef broth. Simmer covered 10 minutes.

In medium pot boil potatoes in chicken broth until just tender. Add chicken broth and potatoes to onion mixture. Mix well. Serve garnished with parsley.

SWEET POTATO PANCETTA SOUP

SERVES 6 TO 8

½ pound sliced pancetta (Italian bacon) or bacon, divided
¼ pound butter
9 medium leeks, split, rinsed, thinly sliced (white part only)
3 medium sweet potatoes, peeled, thinly sliced
2 quarts chicken broth
4 ounces sour half and half, optional
¼ cup chopped fresh chives

In large pot cook pancetta until crisp. Drain well on paper towel. Crumble. Reserve 2 to 3 tablespoons drippings. Discard remaining fat.

Return reserved drippings to pot. Add butter. Melt butter over low heat. Add leeks. Cook over low heat 20 to 25 minutes until leeks are soft, stirring frequently. Add sweet potatoes and chicken broth. Cover. Bring to boil. Reduce heat. Simmer 30 minutes or until potatoes are soft. Add half of crumbled pancetta. Cool soup slightly.

In food processor or blender puree soup in batches until very smooth. Return to pot. Reheat.

Ladle soup into serving bowls. Stir 1 teaspoon to 1 tablespoon sour half and half into each bowl, if desired. Top with remaining pancetta and chives.

CREAMED WINTER VEGETABLE SOUP

SERVES 8

7   **cups chicken broth**
4   **cups peeled, diced new potatoes**
4   **cups peeled, diced turnips**
2   **cups diced celery**
1   **cup diced carrots**
1/2 **cup sliced green onions with tops**
1   **parsnip, peeled, diced**
3   **tablespoons butter or margarine**
2   **tablespoons flour**
1   **cup whipping cream or half and half, optional**
2   **teaspoons salt, or to taste**
   white pepper to taste
1/2 **cup chopped parsley**

In large pot bring chicken broth to boil. Add vegetables. Return to boil. Reduce heat. Simmer covered 15 to 20 minutes until vegetables are tender. Remove 2 cups vegetables. Reserve.

In food processor or blender puree remaining vegetables. Stir pureed vegetables into broth. In small skillet melt butter over low heat. Stir in flour. Cook 2 minutes, stirring constantly. Combine flour mixture with broth. Bring to boil. Stir in cream, if desired. Reduce heat. Simmer uncovered 10 minutes. Stir in reserved vegetables. Season to taste. Serve garnished with chopped parsley.

SPRING VEGETABLE SOUP

SERVES 4

3   **medium onions, chopped**
2   **tablespoons butter**
1 1/2 **cups chopped carrots**
1/2 **cup fresh parsley**
1/4 **cup celery leaves**
10 **ounces beef broth**
20 **ounces V8 juice**
1   **cup uncooked angel hair pasta, optional**

In large skillet sauté onions in butter until soft. Transfer to food processor. Add carrots, parsley, celery leaves, and beef broth. Process finely.

In large pot heat V8 juice. Add chopped mixture. Heat thoroughly. If thicker soup is desired, add pasta. Cook over medium heat several minutes until pasta softens.

TEN VEGETABLE BEEF SOUP

SERVES 10

3	pounds beef stew meat, in bite-size pieces
2	pounds beef bones
2¼	quarts water
1	large clove garlic, minced
4	teaspoons salt
¼	teaspoon freshly ground pepper
1	bay leaf
⅓	cup barley
½	cup chopped celery leaves
2	cups chopped onions
28	ounces canned tomatoes with juice, coarsely chopped
1½	cups thinly sliced celery
1	cup diced carrots
1	cup fresh green beans, in 1-inch pieces
1	cup peeled, diced potatoes
1	cup coarsely grated cabbage
¼	pound unsalted margarine
10	ounces frozen baby peas
5	ounces fresh or frozen leaf spinach

In large pot combine beef and bones with water. Cook over medium heat 30 minutes. Skim. Add garlic, salt, pepper, bay leaf, barley, celery leaves, and onions. Simmer partially covered 3 hours. Cover.

Refrigerate several hours or overnight. Skim fat. Remove meat and bones, reserving meat. Add tomatoes to soup.

In large skillet sauté celery, carrots, green beans, potatoes, and cabbage in margarine 7 minutes. Add to soup. Simmer 20 minutes. Add peas, spinach, and reserved meat. Simmer 10 minutes. Add more salt and pepper, if desired.

HEARTY VEGETABLE SOUP

SERVES 12

2	**pounds veal bones**
2	**pounds beef bones**
2	**pounds beef brisket, in 2-inch chunks**
2	**medium onions, chopped**
1/4	**cup barley**
2	**small turnips, peeled, sliced**
4	**large carrots, sliced**
2-3	**large ribs celery with leaves, sliced**
1	**large parsnip, peeled, sliced**
1/2	**pound green beans, sliced**
14 1/2	**ounces canned tomatoes**
	salt to taste
	pepper to taste
4	**quarts water**
3	**sprigs parsley**

In large pot combine all ingredients except parsley. Bring to boil over high heat. Reduce heat. Cover. Simmer 4 hours. Remove and discard bones. Reserve 3 cups vegetables.

In food processor or food mill puree remainder of soup. Combine whole vegetables with puree and refrigerate. Skim fat. Reheat soup. Serve hot, garnished with parsley.

SWEET AND SOUR CABBAGE SOUP

SERVES 8

1 1/2	**pounds beef short ribs**
3	**quarts water**
2	**pound head cabbage, in 1-inch pieces**
1	**onion, chopped**
2	**cups canned chopped tomatoes with juice**
1	**cup ketchup**
1/2	**cup sugar**
1/3	**cup fresh lemon juice**
2	**teaspoons salt, or to taste**

In large pot combine short ribs with water. Bring to boil. Reduce heat. Simmer 1 hour.

With slotted spoon transfer ribs to cutting board. Slice beef into 1-inch cubes, discarding fat and bones. Skim fat from broth. Add beef and remaining ingredients to broth. Simmer 30 minutes.

ITALIAN VEGETABLE CHOWDER
IN SOURDOUGH BOWLS

SERVES 6

6	**½-pound round sourdough loaves**
½	**pound zucchini, halved lengthwise, thinly sliced**
2	**onions, halved, thinly sliced**
4	**medium tomatoes, peeled, seeded, chopped**
8	**ounces garbanzo beans**
1	**small red pepper, seeded, julienned**
8	**ounces fresh mushrooms, thinly sliced**
2	**cups dry white wine**
2	**teaspoons minced garlic**
5	**tablespoons minced parsley**
1	**teaspoon basil**
1	**bay leaf**
2	**teaspoons salt**
¼	**teaspoon pepper**
6	**ounces Monterey Jack cheese, grated**
1	**cup freshly grated Romano cheese**
1	**cup half and half**
1½	**cups milk**
¾	**pound cooked crab meat**

Slice lid-shaped piece from top of each bread loaf. Hollow out loaves, leaving ½-inch shell. Set aside.

In heavy 4- to 5-quart casserole combine zucchini, onions, tomatoes, beans, red pepper, mushrooms, wine, garlic, parsley, basil, bay leaf, salt, and pepper. Mix well. Bake covered in preheated 400°-degree oven 30 minutes. Stir thoroughly. Bake additional 30 minutes. Remove from oven.*

Stir in cheeses, half and half, and milk. Bake covered in 350°-degree oven 15 minutes. Stir in crab meat. Bake covered 5 minutes. Remove from oven. Cheese will not be completely melted. Blend well. Ladle into prepared bread bowls. Serve immediately.

*May be prepared ahead to this point and refrigerated. To proceed, heat on stove top until very hot, stirring constantly. Continue with remainder of recipe.

CHEDDAR VEGETABLE BISQUE

SERVES 6 TO 8

1	medium clove garlic, minced
1	cup finely chopped onion
2	tablespoons butter or margarine
1	cup thinly sliced fresh mushrooms (if mushrooms are large, halve before slicing)
1	red pepper, seeded, diced
1/2	cup diced celery
1 1/4	pounds extra sharp Cheddar cheese, grated
2	tablespoons cornstarch
2	cups chicken broth
1/2	pound bacon, cooked, drained, crumbled
1	teaspoon Worcestershire sauce
2	cups half and half or whole or skim milk
3/4	cup diced, cooked carrots
1/2	cup finely chopped, cooked broccoli
	salt to taste
	pepper to taste

In medium skillet sauté garlic and onion in butter until soft but not brown. Add mushrooms, red pepper, and celery. Cook 3 to 4 minutes, stirring constantly. Set aside.

In small bowl combine cheese and cornstarch. In large pot bring chicken broth to boil. Reduce heat. Add cheese mixture a fourth at a time, stirring until smooth. Reserving a few spoonfuls of bacon, add remaining ingredients and onion mixture. Heat well. Serve garnished with reserved bacon.

MISO SOUP

SERVES 4 TO 6

5	cups water
*5	rounded teaspoons miso (soy bean paste)
2	cups cooked millet or cooked rice
3	green onions, sliced horizontally in 1/4-inch slices
1/2	cup sliced shiitake mushrooms
2	tablespoons chopped fresh cilantro

In large pot heat water. In small bowl dissolve miso in 1/2 cup of the heated water. Add to water in pot. Add remaining ingredients over medium heat. Heat only until greens are bright in color and crunchy. Serve hot.

*Available in ethnic groceries or health food stores.

MINESTRONE

1 **pound dried white beans, rinsed**
6 **quarts plus 1/4 cup water, divided**
2 **packages George Washington seasoning**
1/4 **cup vegetable oil**
2 **small cloves garlic, minced**
2 **small onions, chopped**
4 **ribs celery, chopped**
1 **teaspoon rosemary**
2 **tablespoons tomato paste**
1/3 **small cabbage, chopped**
2 **zucchini, diced**
2 **teaspoons chopped parsley**
2 **teaspoons salt, or to taste**
  freshly ground pepper to taste
1 **teaspoon basil**
4 **carrots, diced**
2-3 **red or Idaho potatoes, diced**
10 **ounces frozen peas**
14 1/2 **ounces canned tomatoes**
6 **tablespoons butter**
6 **tablespoons margarine**
13 3/4 **ounces chicken broth, optional**
  freshly grated Romano or Parmesan cheese

Soak beans in 6 quarts water overnight. Transfer beans and water to large pot. Add George Washington seasoning. Bring to boil and simmer until beans are tender.

In another large pot heat oil. Brown garlic, onions, celery, and rosemary. Add tomato paste mixed with remaining 1/4 cup water. Cook 5 minutes. Add cabbage, zucchini, parsley, salt, pepper, and 2 cups liquid from pot with beans. Cook 15 minutes.

Pour mixture into pot with beans. Add basil, carrots, potatoes, peas, tomatoes, butter, and margarine. Simmer 1 to 2 hours. Add chicken broth, if desired. Serve hot with grated cheese.

ST. JOSEPH'S SOUP

SERVES 14

1 pound dried navy beans, rinsed
$1/2$ pound dried kidney beans, rinsed
$1/2$ pound dried lentils, rinsed
$1/2$ pound dried split peas, rinsed
96 ounces chicken broth plus 8 cups water
4 sun-dried tomatoes, chopped
1 tablespoon fennel seed, optional
3 onions, chopped
7 ribs celery, chopped
1 small cabbage, sliced
1 small bulb fennel, including greens
1 pound fresh spinach, shredded
16 ounces canned garbanzo beans
    salt to taste
    pepper to taste
    chopped parsley, optional
    slices of Italian bread, toasted, buttered, optional

Soak navy and kidney beans in water to cover overnight. In morning add lentils and split peas to beans. Soak for 2 hours. Drain.

In large pot combine beans, lentils, peas, chicken broth, and water. Bring to boil. Reduce heat. Simmer $1^1/2$ hours. Add tomatoes, fennel seed, if desired, and onions. Simmer $1^1/2$ hours. Add celery, cabbage, fennel, spinach, and garbanzo beans. Cook 10 minutes. Season to taste.

Serve sprinkled with parsley or topped with Italian bread slice, if desired.

See photo page 78.

BEAN AND BARLEY SOUP

SERVES 6

3	quarts water
3	pound stewing hen
3	carrots, thinly sliced
3	medium onions, thinly sliced
1/2	cup dried lima beans, rinsed
1/2	cup barley
1/2	cup dried navy beans, rinsed
1	medium sweet potato, peeled
1	medium parsnip, peeled
1	pound fresh mushrooms, quartered
	medium bunch fresh dill or 2 tablespoons dill weed
2	tablespoons salt
1/2	teaspoon black pepper

In large pot bring water to boil. Add stewing hen. Reduce heat. Simmer 30 minutes. Skim top of water. Add remaining ingredients. Bring to boil. Reduce to strong simmer. Cover. Cook 2 1/2 hours, stirring frequently.

Remove chicken. Bone chicken, cut into pieces, and set aside. Remove sweet potato and parsnip. Mash or puree. Return vegetables and chicken to soup.

Soup is more flavorful if made 1 day ahead.

CAJUN PINTO BEAN SOUP

SERVES 12

2	cups dried pinto beans, rinsed
1	ham bone
1	pound ham, cubed
1	quart water
1	quart chicken broth
3	cups tomato juice
1	medium onion, chopped
2	medium cloves garlic, minced
3	tablespoons chopped parsley
1/4	cup chopped green pepper
1/4	cup brown sugar
	salt to taste
1	teaspoon crumbled bay leaves
1/2	teaspoon celery seed
4	whole cloves
1 1/2	teaspoons fines herbes, optional
	Tabasco to taste
1/4	cup dry sherry or dry vermouth, optional

CAJUN PINTO BEAN SOUP, *continued*

Soak pinto beans in water to cover overnight. Drain. Rinse.

In 5-quart or larger pot combine beans with remaining ingredients except sherry. Bring to boil. Reduce heat and simmer covered 2 hours or until beans are tender. Add sherry, if desired.

Freezes well.

SOUTH CAROLINA LOW COUNTRY BEAN SOUP

SERVES 6 TO 8

*1	**pound bean mix**
1	**cup chopped onion**
1	**cup chopped celery**
1/2	**cup chopped green pepper**
2	**carrots, chopped**
16	**ounces canned stewed tomatoes**
	juice of 1 large lemon
1/4	**cup Worcestershire sauce**
2	**tablespoons dried basil, or to taste**
2	**tablespoons dried parsley**
2	**cloves garlic, minced**
2	**teaspoons salt, or to taste**
1/2	**teaspoon Tabasco**
1/2	**teaspoon black pepper**
1/2	**teaspoon cayenne pepper, or to taste**
1/2	**pound smoked ham or sausage, in small cubes**
	freshly grated Parmesan cheese

Rinse beans in strainer. Place in large pot. Soak in water to cover 3 to 4 hours or overnight. Drain.

Return to pot. Add 3 quarts fresh water. Simmer gently 1 hour. Add remaining ingredients except meat and cheese. Simmer 1 hour. Add meat. Simmer 1 hour. Serve hot sprinkled with cheese.

If thicker consistency is desired, puree some beans from soup in food processor or blender and return to soup.

*Available in 15 bean combination packages or use any dried bean combination of your choice.

SHERMAN OAKS PIQUANT LENTIL SOUP

SERVES 6

1½   **cups dried lentils, preferably red, rinsed**
2   **quarts water**
¾   **cup chopped onion**
½   **cup olive oil**
5   **cloves garlic, slivered**
½   **cup fresh lemon juice**
1½   **teaspoons salt**
2   **bunches spinach or chard**
1   **bunch cilantro, reserving 6 small sprigs**
6   **ounces jumbo, pitted black olives, thickly sliced**
8   **ounces sour cream**

In large pot cook lentils in water until tender. In small skillet sauté onion in olive oil until soft. Add garlic. Sauté briefly until soft. Add onion and garlic to lentils. Stir in lemon juice and salt. Add enough water to create soup consistency. Simmer 10 minutes. Add spinach and cilantro. Simmer 10 minutes. Add olives. Simmer 5 minutes. Add more water if necessary.

Serve in soup bowls with large dollop of sour cream and sprig of cilantro.

SOUTH OF THE BORDER CHILI-BEAN SOUP

SERVES 8 TO 10

1   **cup dried navy beans, rinsed**
1   **tablespoon vegetable oil**
1   **cup chopped onion**
2   **teaspoons minced garlic**
1   **bay leaf**
1   **teaspoon oregano**
6   **cups chicken or vegetable broth**
1   **small banana pepper, seeded, chopped**
1   **small jalapeño pepper, seeded, chopped**
16   **ounces canned chopped tomatoes with juice**
16   **ounces canned dark red kidney beans, undrained**
4   **ounces canned mild green chilies, chopped**
1   **teaspoon cumin**
¼   **teaspoon cayenne pepper**
16   **ounces canned refried beans**
2   **tablespoons chopped cilantro**
2   **tablespoons chopped parsley**
  salt and freshly ground pepper to taste
  tortilla chips

Soak navy beans in water to cover 4 hours. Drain and rinse.

In large heavy pot heat oil. Add onion. Cook until tender. Add garlic. Cook 1 minute. Add bay leaf, oregano, broth, and navy beans. Bring to simmer. Cook about 1 hour until beans are tender and beginning to split. Add banana and jalapeño peppers, tomatoes with juice, kidney beans, chilies, cumin, and cayenne. Add refried beans, stirring until no lumps remain. Simmer 20 minutes. Add cilantro, parsley, salt, and pepper. Serve with tortilla chips.

Flavor improves if made 1 day ahead.

SPICY CHICKEN TORTILLA SOUP

SERVES 8

A fiery meal in a bowl.

2	tablespoons vegetable oil
1	small onion, chopped
4½	ounces canned green chilies, chopped
2	teaspoons minced garlic
15	ounces canned stewed tomatoes
13¾	ounces beef broth
10¾	ounces canned cream of chicken soup
1½	cups chicken broth
1	teaspoon salt
1	teaspoon sugar
½	teaspoon lemon pepper
2	teaspoons Worcestershire sauce
1	teaspoon chili powder
1	teaspoon cumin
1	teaspoon Tabasco
2	cups diced, cooked chicken
4-8	corn tortillas, in strips
2	avocados, in chunks
2	cups grated Monterey Jack cheese

In large pot heat oil. Sauté onion, chilies, and garlic. Add tomatoes, beef broth, cream of chicken soup, chicken broth, salt, sugar, lemon pepper, Worcestershire sauce, chili powder, cumin, and Tabasco. Simmer 1 hour.

To serve, combine ¼ cup chicken, tortilla strips as desired, and several avocado chunks in each of 8 soup bowls. Pour soup into bowls. Top generously with grated cheese. Serve immediately.

LENTIL AND BROWN RICE SOUP

SERVES 8 TO 10

10-12	**cups beef or chicken broth**
1½	**cups dried lentils, rinsed**
1	**cup brown rice**
28	**ounces canned tomatoes, chopped**
2	**cups sliced carrots**
1½	**cups chopped onion**
1	**cup chopped celery**
3	**cloves garlic, minced**
½	**teaspoon basil**
½	**teaspoon oregano**
¼	**teaspoon thyme**
1	**bay leaf**
½	**cup minced parsley**
1	**tablespoon cider vinegar**
	salt and pepper to taste

In large pot combine all ingredients except parsley, vinegar, salt, and pepper. Bring to boil. Reduce heat. Simmer 1 hour. Stir in remaining ingredients. Add additional broth if too thick.

SAUSAGE SOUP

SERVES 10 TO 12

1	**pound mild or spicy Italian sausage, casing removed**
1	**large onion, chopped**
1	**quart water**
32	**ounces canned navy or butter beans**
29	**ounces canned tomatoes with juice**
1	**bay leaf**
1	**clove garlic, minced**
½	**teaspoon thyme**
½	**teaspoon cumin seed**
1½	**teaspoons salt**
½	**teaspoon pepper**
1	**green pepper, seeded, chopped**
1	**large potato, peeled, diced**

In large pot brown sausage. Add onion. Sauté until soft. Drain fat. Add water, beans, tomatoes with juice, bay leaf, garlic, thyme, cumin seed, salt, and pepper. Cover and simmer 1 hour. Add green pepper and potato. Cook 15 minutes or until potato is tender.

SALADS

CHICKEN TORTILLA SALAD

SERVES 9

MARINADE:

1	cup red wine
3	tablespoons chopped shallots
2²/₃	cups balsamic vinegar
¹/₃	cup honey
¹/₄	cup chopped fresh basil
1¹/₂	teaspoons salt
	freshly ground pepper to taste
2¹/₃	cups canola oil
¹/₃	cup olive oil
2	jicama, peeled, julienned
3	chicken breasts, boned, skinned, halved
1	quart canola oil
9	12-inch flour tortillas
1-2	heads red or green leaf lettuce, in pieces or shredded
2¹/₄	cups guacamole
8	ounces sour cream, optional
3	tomatoes, chopped
4	ounces sliced, pitted, drained black olives
1	cup grated Monterey Jack cheese

For marinade, combine wine and shallots in large saucepan. Simmer until mixture is reduced to ¹/₂ cup. Add vinegar, honey, basil, salt, and pepper. Slowly blend in oils.

In medium bowls marinate jicama and chicken breasts separately in refrigerator 4 to 5 hours, using a third of marinade for each. Turn several times. Reserve remaining third of marinade for dressing.

In large deep skillet heat 1¹/₂ to 2 inches canola oil over high heat. Fry tortillas singly, slightly indenting center with large spoon to form shallow bowl shape. Cook until golden. Remove with tongs. Drain on paper towel. Place 1 tortilla on each individual serving plate.

Grill marinated chicken breasts. Cool. Slice into strips.

Spread layer of lettuce over each tortilla shell. Arrange 5 to 6 chicken strips and 5 to 6 marinated jicama strips over lettuce. Spoon ¹/₄ cup guacamole on side. Top guacamole with dollop of sour cream, if desired. Sprinkle tomatoes over all, followed by olives. Top with cheese and reserved marinade.

ORANGE CHICKEN SALAD

SERVES 6

- 3 large chicken breasts, poached, boned, skinned
- 4 navel oranges
- 1/2 pound bacon, crisply cooked, drained, crumbled
- 8 green onions with tops, thinly sliced
- 2/3 cup coarsely chopped pecans
- 2 jalapeño peppers, seeded, finely julienned

ORANGE DRESSING:
- 1/2 cup orange juice
- 2 tablespoons lemon juice
- 2/3 cup olive oil
- 1 teaspoon sugar
- 1 teaspoon salt, or to taste
- 1/2 teaspoon white pepper, or to taste
- 1/2 teaspoon cumin
- 4 teaspoons Dijon mustard

  leaf lettuce
- 3 kiwis, peeled, sliced, optional

Slice chicken into medium julienne strips. Using fine grater or zester remove 4 tablespoons of zest from oranges. Set aside. Peel oranges, removing all membrane. Section oranges. In large bowl combine chicken, orange sections, bacon, green onions, pecans, and peppers.

In jar with tight-fitting lid combine all dressing ingredients. Shake well.

Before serving pour dressing over salad and toss. Serve on leaf lettuce. Garnish top with reserved orange zest and kiwis, if desired.

NAPA CHICKEN SALAD

SERVES 6

- 4-5 chicken breast halves, boned, skinned
- 1/4-1/2 cup soy sauce
- 1 tablespoon sesame seed
- 1 head napa (Chinese cabbage)
- 6 cups mixed greens (Boston, red leaf, and green leaf lettuce)
- 1 cup blanched green beans, in 1-inch pieces
- 4 1/2 ounces Sesame Stix
- 8 ounces canned sliced water chestnuts, drained
- 1 cup chopped celery

DRESSING:

1	**tablespoon Dijon mustard**
1/2	**cup finely chopped parsley**
2	**tablespoons finely chopped onion**
1	**clove garlic, minced**
2/3	**cup red wine vinegar or rice vinegar**
1 1/2	**tablespoons soy sauce**
3/4	**cup peanut oil**
1/2	**cup olive oil**
2	**tablespoons sesame oil**
1/4	**cup honey**
1	**egg, optional**

In large saucepan simmer chicken breasts in water 15 to 20 minutes. Remove chicken from liquid. Cool. Cut into strips. In large bowl combine soy sauce and sesame seed. Marinate chicken strips in soy sauce mixture in refrigerator 4 to 5 hours.

When ready to serve, assemble chicken and remaining salad ingredients in large salad bowl. In jar or blender combine all dressing ingredients. Mix well. Pour over salad and toss.

CURRIED CHICKEN SALAD WITH MANGO

SERVES 4 TO 6

4	**cups bite-size pieces cooked chicken breast (about 3 pounds)**
2	**tablespoons fresh lime juice**
2	**mangoes, peeled, pitted, in 1-inch pieces**
1	**cup chopped celery**
4	**green onions with tops, thinly sliced**
1/4	**cup plain yogurt**
1/4	**cup lite mayonnaise**
1 1/2	**teaspoons curry powder**
1/2	**teaspoon cumin**
	salt and pepper to taste
1	**cup chopped cashews**

In large bowl combine chicken, lime juice, mangoes, celery, and green onions. Mix well. In small bowl combine yogurt, mayonnaise, curry powder, and cumin. Blend well. Add to chicken mixture, mixing thoroughly. Season to taste. Sprinkle cashews over top.

CHICKEN SALAD WITH VEGETABLES

SERVES 4 TO 6

1   cup mayonnaise
2   teaspoons Dijon mustard
2   tablespoons lemon juice
    salt to taste
    pepper to taste
*5-6 pound capon, roasted, boned, skinned, in large
     bite-size pieces

VINAIGRETTE DRESSING:
1/4 cup red wine vinegar
2   teaspoons Dijon mustard
1/2 cup olive oil
    salt to taste
    pepper to taste

1   large head red or green leaf lettuce, in bite-size pieces
1   celery root, peeled, julienned
4   medium fresh beets, cooked, sliced
4   carrots, cooked, sliced
10 spears fresh asparagus, cooked "al dente" (slightly
     underdone), in 1-inch pieces
1   Belgian endive, in 1-inch pieces
1/2 cup coarsely chopped walnuts
1/2 cup Roquefort cheese, crumbled

In large bowl combine mayonnaise, mustard, lemon juice, salt, and pepper. Mix well. Add capon. Toss well.

For vinaigrette dressing, combine vinegar and mustard in medium bowl. Mix well. Slowly add olive oil, whisking well with each addition. Season to taste.

Line serving platter with lettuce. Drizzle part of vinaigrette dressing over lettuce. In small bowl marinate celery root in small amount of vinaigrette dressing. Set aside.

Arrange chicken over lettuce on platter. Garnish with beets, carrots, asparagus, and endive. Add spoonful of celery root at intervals along side of platter. Spoon remaining vinaigrette over salad. Sprinkle with walnuts and top with cheese.

*May substitute 4 whole chicken breasts, cooked, boned, skinned, in bite-size pieces.

CLOCKWISE FROM UPPER LEFT: GRAVLAX ROLLS, MIXED SATAYS, COCONUT SHRIMP WITH ORANGE HORSERADISH SAUCE, GOAT CHEESE APPETIZER, AND ANTIPASTO CHEESE LOAF

TOP TO BOTTOM:
JALAPEÑO PEPPER
AND CHEESE PIZZA,
GOAT CHEESE AND
SAGE PIZZA, MEDITER-
RANEAN CHEESE AND
WALNUT PIZZA, AND
PESTO AND TOMATO
PIZZA

WILD RICE SOUP

CURRIED CHICKEN SALAD IN SWEET POTATO BASKETS

SERVES 4 TO 6

2   **chicken breasts, boned, skinned, halved**
1/2   **cup sliced celery**
1   **green onion with top, thinly sliced**
1/4   **cup golden raisins**
3   **tablespoons slivered almonds, toasted**
1   **tablespoon currants**
1   **teaspoon crystallized ginger, in small pieces**

DRESSING:
1/2   **cup mayonnaise**
1 1/2   **tablespoons chopped chutney**
2   **teaspoons lemon juice**
3/4   **teaspoon curry powder**
    salt to taste
    pepper to taste

In medium saucepan poach chicken gently in water or chicken broth. Drain and cool. Slice into bite-size pieces. In large bowl combine chicken and remaining salad ingredients.

In small bowl combine all dressing ingredients. Mix well. Stir into chicken mixture. Chill.

Just before serving spoon chicken salad into Sweet Potato Baskets.

SWEET POTATO BASKETS

2   **medium sweet potatoes, peeled**
1 1/2   **quarts vegetable oil**
    salt to taste

Shred sweet potatoes with carrot peeler. Dry between 2 sheets of paper towel. In large deep saucepan heat oil to 350 to 360 degrees, measured on deep-frying thermometer. With long-handled basket utensil (1 small basket within larger basket) fill larger basket with 1/3 cup shredded sweet potatoes. Secure smaller basket over larger and dip into hot oil. Cook until potatoes turn golden brown, taking care not to burn. Remove from oil. Release smaller basket and remove sweet potato nest, using small knife if necessary. Drain on paper towel. Salt to taste. Repeat procedure with remaining shredded sweet potatoes.

TUSCAN
BREAD SALAD

GINGER CHICKEN SALAD WITH SPINACH

SERVES 4 TO 6

2   **pounds chicken breasts, boned, skinned**
3   **tablespoons soy sauce, divided**
10   **tablespoons extra virgin olive oil, divided**
1   **clove garlic, minced**
2   **teaspoons peeled, grated fresh ginger root, divided**
2   **teaspoons grated lemon rind, divided**
2   **tablespoons lemon juice**
1   **pound fresh spinach, stems removed**
11   **ounces canned mandarin oranges, chilled, drained**
1   **cup toasted, chopped walnuts**

Slice chicken into long strips. Slice strips into bite-size pieces. In large bowl combine 1 tablespoon soy sauce, 2 tablespoons olive oil, garlic, 1 teaspoon ginger root, and 1 teaspoon lemon rind. Mix well. Toss chicken with mixture. Cover. Chill 2 to 3 hours.

In large skillet heat 2 tablespoons olive oil. Add chicken. Sauté over medium heat 3 to 4 minutes. In food processor or blender combine remaining 6 tablespoons olive oil, 2 tablespoons soy sauce, 1 teaspoon ginger root, 1 teaspoon lemon rind, and lemon juice. Blend until well combined. Mix well with cooked chicken. Refrigerate at least 1 hour.

Working in small batches shred spinach into thin strips. Arrange on large serving dish. Spoon chicken and dressing over spinach. Top with oranges. Sprinkle walnuts over all.

SPINACH CHICKEN SALAD

SERVES 6 TO 8

3   **whole chicken breasts**
2   **quarts chicken broth**
2   **oranges, peeled, sectioned**
1   **cup bean sprouts**
2   **avocados, cubed**
1/4   **cup orange juice**
3   **ribs celery, sliced horizontally**
10   **ounces fresh spinach, stems removed**

Poach chicken in chicken broth. Drain and cool. Discard skin and bones. Cut chicken into chunks. In large salad bowl combine chicken, orange sections, bean sprouts, avocados mixed with orange juice to retain color, celery, and spinach.

continued

DRESSING:

¼   **cup sugar**
¾   **cup vinegar**
½   **cup vegetable oil**
¼   **cup olive oil**
2   **tablespoons ketchup**
2   **tablespoons tomato sauce**
2   **teaspoons dry mustard**
1   **teaspoon celery salt**
    freshly ground pepper and paprika to taste

In jar with tight-fitting lid combine all dressing ingredients. Shake well. Just before serving add dressing to salad and toss.

GRILLED CHICKEN CAESAR SALAD

SERVES 6

DRESSING:

2   **large cloves garlic**
2   **ounces canned flat anchovies, drained**
1½ **cups canola or safflower oil**
    juice of 1 lemon
3   **tablespoons red wine vinegar**
2   **tablespoons Worcestershire sauce**
1   **teaspoon Dijon mustard**

3   **chicken breasts, boned, skinned**
1   **large head romaine lettuce, in bite-size pieces**
1   **cup croutons**
1   **cup grated Parmesan cheese**
    freshly ground pepper to taste
*1 **egg, coddled, reserving yolk only, optional**

For dressing, mince garlic in food processor or blender. Add anchovies and puree. Add canola oil, lemon juice, vinegar, Worcestershire sauce, and mustard. Blend well.

Arrange chicken in shallow dish. Pour ½ cup dressing over chicken. Cover and refrigerate 2 to 3 hours. Drain. Discard dressing in dish.

Grill or broil chicken. Cool slightly. Slice into long strips. Just before serving combine lettuce, croutons, cheese, pepper, egg yolk, if desired, and chicken strips in large salad bowl. Toss with remaining dressing.

*To coddle egg boil water, remove from heat, and submerge egg for 1 minute.

TURKEY SALAD WITH CHUTNEY DRESSING

SERVES 4 TO 6

*2   **pounds cooked turkey breast, skinned, in bite-size chunks**
1   **cup thinly sliced celery**
2/3   **cup green onions with tops, chopped, divided**

YIELD: 2 CUPS

CHUTNEY DRESSING:
3/4   **cup vegetable or peanut oil**
1/2   **cup plus 1 tablespoon mango chutney**
1/4   **cup plus 2 tablespoons white wine vinegar**
1/4   **cup fresh lemon juice**
1   **tablespoon Dijon mustard**
1   **tablespoon soy sauce**
1   **tablespoon sesame oil**
3/4   **teaspoon dried crushed red pepper**
2   **large cloves garlic, minced**
   salt to taste
   pepper to taste

1/2   **cup salted cashews**
2   **cups small cantaloupe balls**

In large bowl combine turkey, celery, and 1/2 cup green onions. Cover. Refrigerate.

In food processor or blender combine all dressing ingredients. Process until smooth.

Just before serving add cashews and cantaloupe balls to salad. Toss with enough dressing to moisten. Garnish with remaining green onions. Pass remaining dressing.

*May substitute cooked chicken or duck.

SERVES 6 TO 8

*3/4 **cup quinoa, rinsed**
3 **cups 1/2-inch cubes smoked turkey
2 **cups cooked or canned black beans**
1 **cup cooked fresh or frozen corn**
1/2 **cup chopped red pepper**
1/2 **cup chopped green pepper**
1/2 **cup chopped red onions**
1/4 **cup thinly sliced green onions with some tops**

VINAIGRETTE DRESSING:
1/3 **cup olive oil**
3 **tablespoons sherry or red wine vinegar**
1 **tablespoon Dijon mustard**
1/2 **teaspoon salt**
1/2 **teaspoon freshly ground pepper**
pinch sugar

2-4 **tablespoons minced cilantro**
6-8 **cherry tomatoes, halved, optional**
6-8 **radishes, optional**
6-8 **lettuce leaves, optional**

Place quinoa in fine mesh strainer, discarding any impurities. Place strainer in bowl. Fill with cold water. Rub quinoa with fingers until water becomes sudsy and cloudy. Lift strainer from bowl. Discard water. Repeat process until water stays clear, about 3 rinsings.

In large saucepan filled with 6 cups boiling salted water cook quinoa 12 minutes or until grains are transparent. Drain. Transfer to large bowl. Add turkey, beans, corn, peppers, and onions.

In jar with tight-fitting lid combine all vinaigrette dressing ingredients. Shake until mixed.

Toss salad with vinaigrette. Cover and refrigerate. Just before serving toss salad with cilantro. Transfer to serving bowl and decorate with tomatoes, radishes, and/or lettuce, if desired.

See photo page 81.

*Available in health food stores or health food section of supermarket.

**May substitute cooked chicken.

SMOKED TURKEY SALAD

SERVES 4

DRESSING:

1	green onion
2	cloves garlic
3	tablespoons tarragon white wine vinegar
1	tablespoon lemon juice
1/4	cup olive oil
1/4	cup vegetable oil
1/8	teaspoon salt
1/8	teaspoon freshly ground pepper
3/4	pound smoked turkey, in 1/3-inch strips
1	cup julienned jicama
1/2	cup julienned green pepper
1/4	cup julienned yellow pepper
6	dried pear halves, in strips
1/2	pound fresh spinach leaves, in pieces
8	romaine lettuce leaves, in strips
8	red or green leaf lettuce leaves, in pieces
2	Belgian endives, optional

In food processor or blender blend all dressing ingredients. In medium bowl mix turkey, jicama, peppers, and pears with half of dressing. In large bowl mix spinach, romaine, and leaf lettuce with remaining dressing.

On 4 salad plates arrange greens. Arrange several endive leaves decoratively with other greens, if desired. Top with turkey mixture.

STEAK AND ARTICHOKE SALAD

SERVES 6 TO 8

2   **pounds top sirloin, London broil, or butt steak**
14   **ounces canned artichoke hearts, drained, in bite-size pieces**
1/3   **cup coarsely chopped red pepper**
1/3   **cup coarsely chopped green pepper**
1/4   **pound mozzarella cheese, in 1-inch cubes**

DRESSING:
1/4   **cup dry white wine**
3   **tablespoons white wine vinegar**
1/3   **cup finely chopped red onion**
1   **large clove garlic, crushed**
1/2   **cup olive oil**
1   **tablespoon Dijon mustard**
1/4   **cup chopped parsley**
1/4   **teaspoon oregano**
1/4   **teaspoon basil**
1/4   **teaspoon sugar**

8-10   **romaine lettuce leaves, shredded in 1-inch strips**
1   **red onion, in thinly sliced rings, optional**
2   **tomatoes, sliced, optional**
3   **eggs, hard-boiled, quartered, optional**

Broil steaks to desired doneness, preferably medium-rare. Cool. Cut into thick julienne slices. In large bowl combine meat with artichoke hearts, peppers, and cheese.

In jar with tight-fitting lid combine all dressing ingredients. Shake well to blend. On serving platter arrange lettuce. Mix dressing with meat and vegetables. Mound mixture on lettuce. Garnish with onion, tomatoes, and/or eggs, if desired.

SPICY STRIP STEAK SALAD

SERVES 4

- ¾ cup soy sauce, divided
- 1 tablespoon peeled, finely grated fresh ginger root
- 6 tablespoons sugar
- 1 tablespoon minced garlic
- 1 12-ounce top loin New York steak, 1 inch thick
- 8 cups bite-size pieces mixed greens (escarole, radicchio, Boston lettuce, and red leaf lettuce)
- ¼ cucumber, julienned
- 1⅓ cups thinly sliced red onion
- 2 tablespoons fresh lemon juice
- ¾ teaspoon hot green chili, minced (jalapeño or Thai)
- 2 tablespoons peanut oil
- 2 tablespoons olive oil
- 1 teaspoon black sesame seed
- 12 sprigs cilantro

In large shallow dish combine ½ cup soy sauce, ginger root, sugar, and garlic. Mix well. Add steak, turning to coat. Cover and refrigerate 2 hours, turning occasionally.

In large bowl combine greens, cucumber, and onion. In small bowl combine remaining ¼ cup soy sauce, lemon juice, and chili. Gradually whisk in peanut and olive oils.

Grill steak to desired doneness, about 3 minutes per side for rare. Toss salad with dressing and divide salad among 4 plates. Slice steak thinly across grain. Arrange over salad. Sprinkle with sesame seed. Garnish with cilantro.

See photo page 80.

REGAL LOBSTER SALAD

SERVES 6

- 1 teaspoon salt
- *6 medium lobster tails
- 4 tablespoons butter
- 6 tablespoons garlic-flavored olive oil
- 5 large cloves garlic, minced
- ¼ cup chopped chives
- 5 tablespoons Dijon mustard
  juice of ½ lemon
  grape leaves
- 3 tomatoes, in wedges

Fill large kettle with water. Add salt. Bring to boil. Submerge lobster tails in water. Cook 10 minutes or until shell is red. Remove lobster from kettle. Drain in colander. Cool. Keeping shells intact, remove lobster meat. Cut into 1-inch chunks. Set aside.

**In large skillet melt butter. Add olive oil and garlic. Cook over medium heat until garlic browns lightly. Stir in lobster chunks, chives, mustard, and lemon juice. Cook 1 minute. Remove and cool.

Line 6 serving plates with grape leaves. Place 1 lobster shell in center of each plate. Spoon equal amount of cooked mixture into each shell, spilling over side. Garnish with tomato wedge on each side.

*May substitute 1½ pounds cooked, shelled, deveined large shrimp, halved lengthwise, and start from **.

HONEY-MUSTARD SHRIMP SALAD

SERVES 4

1   **pound cooked, shelled, deveined shrimp**
2   **large oranges (navel or Valencia), peeled, in**
      horizontal slices
1   **ripe avocado, scooped into small balls**
1   **medium red onion, thinly sliced**

HONEY-MUSTARD VINAIGRETTE DRESSING:
⅓   **cup cider vinegar**
3   **tablespoons honey**
1   **tablespoon dry mustard**
      juice and zest of ½ lemon
½   **teaspoon salt**
¼   **teaspoon freshly ground pepper**
1   **cup olive oil**

1   **head romaine or red leaf lettuce, in bite-size pieces**

In large bowl combine shrimp, oranges, avocado, and onion. In food processor or blender combine all dressing ingredients. Blend 1 minute.

Dress shrimp mixture with vinaigrette as desired. Arrange lettuce on individual serving plates. Drizzle remaining vinaigrette over lettuce as desired. Top with shrimp mixture.

SHRIMP AND SCALLOP SALAD WITH CITRUS DRESSING

SERVES 4

6   **jumbo sea scallops**
12   **medium shrimp in shells**
1-2   **tablespoons virgin olive oil**
    salt to taste
    pepper to taste

MARINADE:
½   **cup virgin olive oil**
1   **teaspoon lime juice**
2   **teaspoons chopped cilantro**
½   **teaspoon chopped serrano chili**
¼   **teaspoon dried crushed red pepper**

TOMATO HERB COULIS:
¼   **cup virgin olive oil**
2   **tomatoes, peeled, seeded, chopped**
2   **teaspoons chopped shallots**
½   **clove garlic, minced**
2   **teaspoons rice vinegar**
2   **teaspoons chopped chives**
2   **teaspoons chopped fresh basil**
2   **teaspoons chopped parsley**
¼   **teaspoon tarragon**

CITRUS DRESSING:
4   **tablespoons orange juice**
1   **tablespoon lemon juice**
4   **teaspoons lime juice**
2   **teaspoons chopped shallots**
2   **tablespoons mayonnaise**
½   **cup whipping cream, whipped**

SALAD:
6   **cups torn radicchio, romaine, and spinach leaves, combined**
1   **artichoke bottom or 4 canned marinated artichoke hearts, drained, sliced**
1   **avocado, sliced**
1   **orange, sliced**

Lightly brush scallops and shrimp with olive oil. Grill on both sides to medium rare. Cool. Shell shrimp. Season to taste.

MARINADE:
In large bowl combine all marinade ingredients. Mix well. Add scallops and shrimp. Refrigerate at least 3 hours or overnight.

TOMATO HERB COULIS:

In medium skillet heat olive oil over medium-high heat. Add tomatoes, shallots, and garlic. Cook briefly until heated. Stir in vinegar. Remove from heat. Add chives, basil, parsley, and tarragon. Blend well. Cool. Refrigerate.

CITRUS DRESSING:

Just before serving mix juices and shallots in large bowl. Blend in mayonnaise. Combine with whipped cream.

SALAD:

In large bowl toss radicchio, romaine, and spinach with dressing. Divide among 4 serving plates. Remove scallops and shrimp from marinade. Dry with paper towel. Slice scallops in half horizontally. Arrange 3 scallop halves grilled side up and 3 shrimp on each salad. Garnish with slices of artichoke, avocado, and orange. Spoon tomato herb coulis liberally over salads.

SHRIMP LUTÈCE

SERVES 6

DRESSING:

- ¾ **teaspoon salt**
- **pinch pepper**
- ½ **teaspoon prepared mustard**
- ½ **clove garlic, minced**
- ¼ **cup tarragon vinegar, divided**
- 1 **small egg yolk**
- 1 **cup vegetable oil**
- ¼ **teaspoon sugar**
- 1 **tablespoon Worcestershire sauce**
- ¼ **cup chili sauce**

- 14 **ounces canned artichoke hearts, drained, quartered**
- 2 **large avocados, sliced**
- 2½ **pounds cooked, shelled, deveined medium shrimp**
- 4 **eggs, hard-boiled, quartered**
- 6 **small heads Bibb lettuce**

For dressing, make paste of salt, pepper, mustard, garlic, and 2 teaspoons vinegar in food processor or blender. Blend in egg yolk until smooth. With motor running add part of oil in slow steady stream until mixture has consistency of mayonnaise. Add remaining oil alternately with remaining vinegar. Blend in sugar and Worcestershire sauce. Fold in chili sauce. Chill.

Just before serving combine dressing with artichoke hearts, avocado slices, shrimp, and hard-boiled eggs. Serve on 6 plates lined with lettuce.

SHRIMP AND ORZO SALAD

SERVES 4

¾	cup orzo, cooked, drained
1	teaspoon vegetable oil
1	pound cooked, shelled, deveined large shrimp
3½	ounces feta cheese, crumbled
1	large tomato, seeded, diced
12	black olives, pitted, chopped
2	green onions, sliced

DRESSING:

⅛-¼	cup chopped fresh dill, or to taste
1½	cloves garlic
3	tablespoons olive oil
3	tablespoons fresh lemon juice
1½	tablespoons red wine vinegar
½	teaspoon salt
¼	teaspoon freshly ground pepper
	lettuce leaves
	sprigs dill

Toss orzo with vegetable oil. Transfer to salad bowl. Add shrimp, feta cheese, tomato, olives, and green onions.

For dressing, place dill in food processor. With motor running add garlic. Mince. Add olive oil, lemon juice, vinegar, and salt. Scrape sides. Add pepper. Blend 5 seconds.

Pour dressing over salad. Toss well. Serve at room temperature on lettuce leaves. Garnish with sprigs dill.

May be assembled 3 hours ahead and refrigerated.

RICE SALAD WITH CUCUMBERS AND SHRIMP

SERVES 4 TO 6

3	small cucumbers, seeded, thinly sliced
2	teaspoons salt plus salt to taste, divided
2½	quarts water
2	cups rice
1	clove garlic
½	cup virgin olive oil
¼	cup white wine vinegar
½	cup chopped walnuts
½	cup finely chopped fresh mint

½   **cup sliced, pitted, small green olives**
   pepper to taste
2   **teaspoons lemon juice**
2   **pounds cooked, shelled, deveined shrimp**
¼   **cup chopped chives**
6   **green onions, chopped**

Sprinkle cucumbers with ½ teaspoon salt. Let stand at least 30 minutes. In large saucepan combine water and 1 teaspoon salt. Bring to boil. Add rice. Cook 14 minutes. Drain well. Transfer to large bowl.

In small bowl mash garlic with ½ teaspoon salt. Add olive oil and vinegar. Mix well. Pour over rice. Toss well. Cool. Add walnuts, mint, olives, well-drained cucumbers, salt, pepper, and lemon juice. Mix well. Stir in shrimp. Top with chives and green onions. Serve cold. See photo page 278.

SMOKED TURKEY PASTA SALAD

SERVES 4 TO 6

8   **ounces fettucine**
½   **pound smoked turkey, julienned in ¼- by 2-inch strips**
⅓   **pound mozzarella cheese, julienned in ¼- by 2-inch strips**
1-2 **large sun-dried tomatoes, in strips**
1   **teaspoon fresh thyme**
1   **teaspoon finely chopped parsley**
   freshly ground pepper to taste
¼   **cup coarsely chopped walnuts, optional**

DRESSING:
1   **large shallot, diced**
1   **small or medium clove garlic, minced**
1   **teaspoon Dijon mustard**
3   **tablespoons lemon juice**
1   **tablespoon balsamic vinegar**
1   **tablespoon red wine vinegar**
   salt and pepper to taste
⅓   **cup virgin olive oil**

Cook fettucine until "al dente" (slightly underdone). Drain well. Cool. In large serving bowl combine fettucine and remaining salad ingredients.

In small bowl combine all dressing ingredients, adding olive oil last. Mix well. Stir dressing into salad. Mix well.

CHICKEN LINGUINE ORIENTAL

1   **pound linguine**
3   **large cloves garlic, minced**
1   **tablespoon red wine vinegar**
1   **tablespoon brown sugar**
6   **tablespoons chunky peanut butter**
1/4   **cup soy sauce**
6   **tablespoons sesame oil**
1½   **tablespoons hot chili oil**
4   **chicken breasts, boned, skinned, halved, poached**
5   **tablespoons sesame seed, toasted, divided**
1   **pound thin asparagus**
3   **green onions, white part plus 3 inches green,**
      slivered finely lengthwise
1   **small cucumber, seeded, in 1/4-inch pieces**

In large kettle of boiling water cook linguine until just tender. Drain. Rinse. Drain again. Transfer to large bowl.

In food processor combine garlic, vinegar, brown sugar, peanut butter, and soy sauce. Process until blended. Slowly add sesame and chili oils through feed tube, continuing to process until well blended.

Slice chicken into strips. Combine with linguine. Add peanut butter sauce and 4 tablespoons sesame seed. Mix well.

Slice asparagus diagonally into 1-inch pieces. Blanch 1 minute. Drain. Rinse in cold water. Dry well.

Transfer linguine to large, flat serving plate. Arrange asparagus over top. Sprinkle with green onions, cucumber, and remaining 1 tablespoon sesame seed. Serve at room temperature.

ORIENTAL PASTA SALAD

SERVES 8 TO 10

Robust flavor. With addition of chicken could be served as entree.

1	**pound udon noodles* or egg noodles**
2	**tablespoons dark sesame oil**
6	**tablespoons peanut butter**
6	**tablespoons tahini (sesame paste)**
6	**tablespoons dark soy sauce**
3	**tablespoons light soy sauce**
2	**tablespoons sherry**
4	**teaspoons rice wine vinegar**
1/4	**cup honey**
4	**medium cloves garlic, minced**
2	**teaspoons minced fresh ginger root**
1-2	**tablespoons hot chili oil**
1/4	**cup cold water**
1/2	**cup hot water**
3	**tablespoons chopped green onions**

In large saucepan of unsalted boiling water cook noodles until "al dente" (slightly underdone). Drain immediately. Rinse with cold water. Drain. Transfer to large bowl. Toss with dark sesame oil.

In food processor or blender combine remaining ingredients except hot water and green onions. Blend well. Add hot water. Just before serving toss mixture with noodles. Garnish with green onions.

Dressing may be made 1 week ahead.

*Eggless Oriental noodles.

COLD CHINESE SESAME VERMICELLI

SERVES 4

Delicately flavored. Excellent accompaniment for fish or poultry.

9	**ounces vermicelli or pasta of choice**
3	**tablespoons soy sauce**
2	**tablespoons sesame seed**
2	**tablespoons sesame oil**
1/2	**teaspoon hot chili oil**
1	**green onion, thinly sliced**

Cook pasta according to package directions. Drain. In large bowl combine pasta and remaining ingredients. Mix well. Serve cold or at room temperature.

BROWN RICE SALAD

3 tablespoons red wine vinegar
6 tablespoons vegetable oil, divided
5 cups cooked brown rice
*1 teaspoon ginger juice
2 tablespoons lime juice
2 teaspoons sugar
1 canned jalapeño pepper, chopped
1 clove garlic, crushed
1 tablespoon anchovy paste, optional
2 cups snow peas, blanched, trimmed, cut in thirds
1 whole chicken breast, cooked, boned, skinned, cubed
  salt to taste
  pepper to taste
1/2 cup chopped Italian parsley

In large bowl combine vinegar and 4 tablespoons oil. Mix well. Add rice. Blend well. Marinate in refrigerator at least overnight.

In small bowl combine ginger juice, lime juice, sugar, jalapeño pepper, garlic, remaining 2 tablespoons oil, and anchovy paste, if desired. Mix well. Add to rice with peas, chicken, salt, and pepper. Toss. Garnish with parsley.

*Squeeze peeled, freshly grated ginger root.

FRIJOLES NEGROS SALAD

1 1/2 cups canned small black beans, drained, rinsed
1 1/2 cups cooked corn, drained
1/4 cup chopped red onion
1 small clove garlic, minced
4 plum tomatoes, diced
2 jalapeño peppers, seeded, finely chopped
  salt to taste
  pepper to taste
1 1/2 tablespoons finely chopped cilantro

DRESSING:
2 tablespoons dry white wine
1 1/2 tablespoons lime juice
2 tablespoons olive oil
1 tablespoon Dijon mustard

In large bowl combine all salad ingredients. Mix well.

In small bowl combine all dressing ingredients. Mix well. Pour dressing over salad. Toss thoroughly.

May be made 1 day ahead.

LENTIL SALAD WITH GOAT CHEESE

SERVES 8 TO 10

2	**cups dried lentils, rinsed**
1	**teaspoon salt**
10-12	**sprigs Italian parsley, divided**
12-15	**sprigs basil, divided**
6-8	**cloves garlic, minced, divided**
1	**carrot, chopped**
1	**red onion, chopped**
1	**rib celery, chopped**
1	**cup olive oil, divided**
1/3	**cup red wine vinegar**
8	**ounces goat cheese, crumbled**
1/2	**cup minced chives**
	salt to taste
	freshly ground pepper to taste
1-2	**tomatoes, in wedges**
8-10	**basil leaves, in strips**

In medium saucepan combine lentils with water barely to cover. Add salt. Make bouquet garni bag by tying half of parsley, basil, and garlic in cheesecloth. Add to lentils. Simmer 10 minutes. Add carrot, onion, and celery. Simmer 10 to 15 minutes until lentils are tender but "al dente" (slightly underdone). Add more hot water if necessary to prevent lentils from sticking. There should be very little liquid left when lentils are done.

Discard bouquet garni. Toss lentils and vegetables with 1/2 cup olive oil. Spread on baking sheet to cool. Finely chop remaining parsley, basil, and garlic. When lentils are cool, combine with parsley, basil, garlic, remaining 1/2 cup olive oil, vinegar, cheese, and chives. Season to taste. Refrigerate at least 2 hours. Serve garnished with tomato wedges and basil strips.

See photo page 81.

BEAN SALAD

*1   cup dried navy beans, rinsed
1   cup dried light red kidney beans, rinsed
1   cup dried cranberry beans, rinsed

DRESSING:
1/2   cup ketchup
1/4   cup barbecue sauce
3/4   cup chopped green onions
3   tablespoons balsamic vinegar
3   tablespoons white wine vinegar
3/4   cup vegetable oil
7   tablespoons sugar
1 1/2   teaspoons paprika
1/2   teaspoon salt

OPTIONAL:
1 1/2   cups diced cooked ham
1   large green pepper, seeded, thinly sliced, each slice halved
1   cup diced celery

In large kettle combine beans with water to cover by 3 inches. Bring to boil. Cook 2 to 3 minutes. Reduce heat. Simmer 20 minutes. Beans will be slightly softened. Remove from heat. Cover and let stand 1 hour.

In large bowl combine all dressing ingredients. Mix well. Drain beans. Rinse under cold water. Drain well. Add beans to dressing. Toss to combine well. Refrigerate covered 6 hours or overnight. Before serving mix in any or all of optional ingredients, if desired.

*May use combination of beans or single variety to total 3 cups.

WARM BAVARIAN POTATO SALAD

SERVES 6

5	large red potatoes, unpeeled
5	slices bacon
1/2	cup chopped onion
2	tablespoons sugar
1	tablespoon flour
1 1/2	teaspoons salt
1-2	teaspoons Tabasco, or to taste
1/2	cup water
1/4	cup vinegar
1/2	cup sliced red radishes

Cook potatoes in boiling water about 20 minutes or until tender. Peel and slice.

In large skillet fry bacon until crisp. Reserving drippings, drain bacon and crumble. Set aside. Sauté onion in bacon drippings 5 minutes until partially tender.

In small bowl combine sugar, flour, salt, Tabasco, water, and vinegar. Mix well. Add to onion. Cook about 5 minutes until mixture thickens and bubbles, stirring constantly. Remove from heat. Add potatoes to onion mixture. Heat 5 minutes. Add radishes and toss. Top with reserved bacon. Serve warm or at room temperature.

ARTICHOKE POTATO SALAD

SERVES 6

1 1/2-2	pounds red potatoes, peeled, in bite-size pieces
14	ounces canned quartered artichoke hearts, drained, halved
10	large sun-dried tomatoes (in oil), drained, in strips
12	large calamata olives, drained, pitted, sliced
1 1/2	tablespoons drained capers

DRESSING:

1	large clove garlic, minced
3	tablespoons white wine vinegar
1	tablespoon Dijon mustard
1/2	cup olive oil

Steam potatoes until tender. Cool 15 minutes. In large bowl combine potatoes, artichoke hearts, tomatoes, olives, and capers.

In jar with tight-fitting lid combine all dressing ingredients. Shake well. Pour 1/3 cup dressing over salad. Mix well. Toss with enough additional dressing to moisten. Serve at room temperature.

May be made 1 day ahead.

SWEET POTATO SALAD

SERVES 4

1½   **pounds sweet potatoes, peeled, in ½-inch pieces**
2   **tablespoons white wine vinegar**
3   **tablespoons Dijon mustard**
½   **cup safflower oil**
2   **cups thinly sliced celery**
½   **cup sliced red pepper**
½   **cup thinly sliced green onions**
  salt to taste
  pepper to taste
⅔   **cup chopped walnuts**
  lettuce leaves

Steam potatoes 10 minutes or until tender. Transfer to medium bowl and cool.

In small bowl combine vinegar, mustard, and safflower oil. Mix well. Pour over potatoes. Add celery, red pepper, green onions, salt, pepper, and walnuts. Mix well. Divide among 4 plates lined with lettuce.

ROASTED EGGPLANT SALAD

SERVES 6

1   **large eggplant (1¼ to 1½ pounds)**
1   **teaspoon vegetable oil**
½   **cup diced ripe tomato**
*½   **cup diced roasted red pepper**
¼   **cup chopped parsley**
2   **tablespoons sliced green onions**
2   **teaspoons fresh lemon juice**
¾   **teaspoon salt**
½   **teaspoon freshly ground pepper**

Rub eggplant with oil. Grill until very soft or bake in preheated 400-degree oven 45 to 55 minutes. Cool. Slit skin and remove. Cut flesh into chunks.

In medium serving bowl combine eggplant chunks and remaining ingredients. Mix well. Serve at room temperature.

*For roasting instructions, see page 162.

CHILLED ASPARAGUS ORIENTAL

SERVES 6

For a different twist, try it with tender-crisp broccoli flowerets and red onion rings.

1½   **pounds asparagus, trimmed**
1½   **tablespoons sesame oil**
¼   **cup cider vinegar**
¼   **cup soy sauce**
1   **tablespoon sugar, or to taste**
  red leaf lettuce
1   **cup chopped walnuts**
  freshly ground pepper to taste

Steam asparagus until tender-crisp. Rinse under cold water. Drain. Chill. In small bowl combine sesame oil, vinegar, soy sauce, and sugar. Mix well. Line 6 plates with lettuce leaves. Arrange asparagus on plates. Pour dressing over asparagus. Sprinkle with walnuts and pepper.

See photo page 279.

BROCCOLI NUT SALAD

SERVES 6 TO 8

2   **large bunches broccoli**
10   **slices bacon, crisply cooked, drained, crumbled**
⅔   **cup golden raisins**
1   **medium red onion, in thinly sliced rings**
1   **cup mayonnaise**
2   **tablespoons white wine vinegar**
¼   **cup sugar**
½   **cup finely chopped pecans**

Break broccoli flowerets into small pieces. Slice tender stems. In large bowl combine flowerets and stem pieces with bacon, raisins, and onion. Mix well.

In small bowl combine mayonnaise, vinegar, and sugar. Mix well. Pour over broccoli mixture. Cover and refrigerate 4 to 5 hours or overnight, stirring occasionally.

Just before serving add pecans to salad. Toss to combine.

MUSHROOM CHEESE SALAD

SERVES 8

1   **pound fresh mushrooms, sliced**
1   **bunch green onions with tops, sliced**
1   **small bunch parsley, chopped**
1/2 **pound Swiss cheese, finely grated**
3   **teaspoons Cavender's Greek seasoning**
1/4 **cup white wine vinegar**
1   **tablespoon sugar**
1/2 **cup safflower oil**

In medium salad bowl combine mushrooms, green onions, parsley, and cheese. In small bowl combine remaining ingredients. Mix well. Just before serving toss dressing with salad.

ROASTED PEPPER AND SNOW PEA SALAD

SERVES 4

2   **red peppers**
3/4 **pound snow peas**
    salt to taste
1   **small red onion**

DRESSING:
1   **tablespoon Dijon mustard**
2   **tablespoons red wine vinegar**
1/2 **teaspoon cumin**
    freshly ground pepper to taste
1/4 **cup olive oil**
1/2 **cup finely chopped parsley**

Place peppers under broiler or on grill. Cook on all sides until well charred. Split peppers in half. Remove skin and seeds. Cut lengthwise into thin strips.

In medium saucepan bring to boil enough water to cover snow peas. Add snow peas and salt. Boil 2 minutes. Drain. Rinse peas in cold water. Drain.

Cut onion in half. Cut each half crosswise into thin slices. In medium salad bowl combine pepper strips, snow peas, and onion. For dressing, combine mustard, vinegar, cumin, and salt and pepper to taste in small bowl. Beat well with whisk, gradually adding olive oil. Stir in parsley. Pour dressing over vegetables and toss.

BEAN SPROUT SALAD

SERVES 4 TO 6

2	**tablespoons vegetable oil**
1	**slice peeled fresh ginger root, any size**
1	**clove garlic, minced**
1	**green onion, sliced**
¾	**pound fresh bean sprouts**
1	**green pepper, thinly sliced**
4	**ounces canned sliced water chestnuts, drained**
*½-1	**teaspoon salt**
½	**teaspoon sesame oil, optional**

In wok or skillet heat vegetable oil. Cook ginger root, garlic, and green onion until dark brown. Remove from oil with slotted spoon. Discard.

Add bean sprouts and green pepper to hot oil. Stir fry 1 minute or until pepper turns bright green and sprouts become opaque, turning quickly. Remove from heat. Add water chestnuts, salt, and sesame oil, if desired. May be served hot or cold.

*Soy sauce may be substituted for some of the salt.

GARDEN SPINACH SALAD

SERVES 6

10	**ounces fresh spinach, stems removed, in bite-size pieces**
6	**slices bacon, crisply cooked, drained, crumbled**
3	**tablespoons diced green pepper**
3	**tablespoons diced red pepper**
1	**cup broccoli flowerets**
1	**avocado, in ½-inch pieces**
5	**radishes, thinly sliced**
6-8	**cherry tomatoes, halved**
4-6	**fresh mushrooms, sliced**

DRESSING:

⅔	**cup sugar**
	pinch salt
1	**small onion, chopped**
½	**cup cider vinegar**
⅓	**cup ketchup**
1	**tablespoon Worcestershire sauce**
1	**cup vegetable oil**

In large serving bowl combine all salad ingredients. Mix well. In medium bowl whisk together all dressing ingredients. Pour over salad. Toss well.

SPINACH SALAD

SERVES 4

10 ounces fresh spinach, stems removed
*2 tablespoons pine nuts, toasted
*1/2 cup toasted croutons
sections of 1 pear, 4 clementine oranges, or 1 avocado, or
    combination of all

ANCHOVY DRESSING:

5 flat anchovies, crushed
2 cloves garlic, minced
1 tablespoon fresh lemon juice
2 tablespoons balsamic vinegar
6 tablespoons olive oil
salt to taste
pepper to taste

ALTERNATE DRESSING:

grated rind of 1 clementine orange
1 tablespoon clementine orange juice
4-5 shallots, minced
1/4 cup olive oil

In large bowl assemble spinach, pine nuts, croutons, and fruit sections. In jar with tight-fitting lid combine all dressing ingredients. Shake well. Just before serving toss dressing with salad.

*May use either or both.

TRICOLOR COLE SLAW

SERVES 8

4 cups grated red cabbage
4 cups grated green cabbage
2 large carrots, finely grated
5 tablespoons white wine vinegar
2 tablespoons soy sauce
1/2 tablespoon peeled, coarsely grated fresh ginger root
6 tablespoons vegetable oil
2 tablespoons sesame oil
Tabasco to taste
1/2 cup chopped dry roasted peanuts

continued

In large bowl combine cabbage and carrots. Refrigerate.

In jar with tight-fitting lid combine remaining ingredients except peanuts. Shake vigorously until well mixed. Just before serving toss dressing with slaw mixture. Sprinkle peanuts over cole slaw.

CREATIVE COLE SLAW

SERVES 10 TO 12

3   **pounds green cabbage, coarsely chopped**
1   **green pepper, chopped**
2   **white onions, chopped**
1½ **cups sugar**
1   **cup vegetable oil**
1   **cup cider vinegar**
2   **tablespoons celery seed**
1   **tablespoon salt**

OPTIONAL:
1   **red pepper, coarsely chopped**
1   **small red cabbage, chopped or grated**
4   **green onions with tops, finely sliced**
5   **carrots, grated**
½   **cup chopped walnuts**
3   **McIntosh or Rome Beauty apples, unpeeled, cored, coarsely chopped**

In large bowl combine cabbage, green pepper, onions, and sugar. Mix well. In small saucepan combine oil, vinegar, celery seed, and salt. Bring to boil. Pour over cabbage mixture. Blend well.

Refrigerate in airtight container at least 3 days, stirring several times daily. Will keep up to 2 weeks. Flavor improves with age. Any or all of the optional ingredients may be added on day of serving, if desired.

LEMON COLE SLAW

SERVES 6 TO 8

1½ pounds green cabbage, shredded
½ red pepper, julienned
½ green pepper, julienned
½ red onion, finely chopped
1 large carrot, grated
2 tablespoons chopped parsley
2 teaspoons grated lemon rind

DRESSING:
½ cup mayonnaise or lite mayonnaise
½ cup sour half and half
¼ cup fresh lemon juice
2 tablespoons Dijon mustard
2 tablespoons olive oil
2 tablespoons sugar
1 tablespoon white wine vinegar
1 tablespoon prepared horseradish
1 teaspoon salt
½ teaspoon celery seed
½ teaspoon pepper

In large bowl combine cabbage, peppers, onion, carrot, parsley, and lemon rind.

In small bowl combine all dressing ingredients. Mix well. Pour over cabbage mixture. Blend well.

HOT GOAT CHEESE SALAD

SERVES 4

1½ cups chopped ripe tomatoes
3 tablespoons capers
1 tablespoon white wine vinegar
2 tablespoons light olive oil
salt to taste
freshly ground pepper to taste
1 egg white
1 tablespoon water
7 ounces round goat cheese, cut into 12 slices
1 cup plain bread crumbs
2 tablespoons butter
red leaf and Boston lettuce and Belgian endive
12 calamata olives

In large glass or ceramic bowl combine tomatoes, capers, vinegar, olive oil, salt, and pepper. Let stand 1 hour. In small bowl combine egg white and water. Coat each cheese slice with egg-water mixture and then with bread crumbs. In medium skillet brown cheese slices lightly in butter on each side, 1 to 2 minutes.

Arrange mixed greens on 4 plates. Top each with 3 slices cheese and tomato mixture. Garnish each plate with 3 olives. Serve warm.

TUSCAN BREAD SALAD

SERVES 4

- 1²/₃ cups cold water
- ¹/₂ cup red wine vinegar
- 10 ounces stale premium Italian bread, crusts removed, in 1-inch chunks
- 3 large ripe tomatoes, seeded, diced
- 1 red or Vidalia onion, coarsely chopped
- 2 ribs celery, in ¹/₂-inch slices
- ¹/₂ medium cucumber, seeded, coarsely chopped
- 2 tablespoons drained capers
- 1 clove garlic, minced
- 4 ounces mozzarella cheese, cubed, optional
- 12 calamata olives, optional
- 12 large green olives, optional
- ¹/₃ cup olive oil
- ³/₄ teaspoon anchovy paste
- ¹/₄ teaspoon dried crushed red pepper
- salt to taste
- pepper to taste
- ²/₃ cup slivered fresh basil leaves

In large bowl pour water and vinegar over bread chunks. Toss lightly until bread is soaked. Let stand 10 minutes. Gently squeeze bread to remove most of moisture. Return bread to dry bowl. Add tomatoes, onion, celery, cucumber, capers, and garlic. Add cheese and olives, if desired.

In small bowl combine olive oil, anchovy paste, red pepper, salt, and pepper. Pour over bread mixture. Toss well. Stir in basil.

See photo page 84.

TOFU TOMATO SALAD WITH PEANUT DRESSING

SERVES 14

For those who enjoy spicy food.

*8	ounces extra firm tofu, cubed
7-8	large tomatoes, in wedges
3	large cucumbers, peeled, sliced
1	cup broccoli flowerets
2	red peppers, in strips
4	onions, in finely sliced rings
12	green onion tops, curled
7	eggs, hard-boiled, quartered
2	large heads romaine lettuce

PEANUT DRESSING:

3/4	pound unsalted peanuts
1 1/2	cups fresh lemon juice
6	tablespoons vinegar
10	cloves garlic
1/2	cup chopped cilantro
7	tablespoons sugar
1	tablespoon salt, or to taste
4	tablespoons fish sauce
1	whole fresh chili, optional
3	tablespoons water
2	eggs, hard-boiled, sliced
	cilantro leaves, optional

Arrange salad ingredients on bed of lettuce.

In food processor or blender combine all dressing ingredients. Blend well. Pour dressing over salad.

Garnish with sliced eggs and cilantro leaves, if desired.

*May be brushed with oil and lightly browned.

EGGLESS CAESAR SALAD

SERVES 6 TO 8

1-2   **cloves garlic, minced**
1   **teaspoon salt**
1/4   **teaspoon celery salt**
1   **teaspoon dry mustard**
1   **teaspoon Worcestershire sauce**
1/4   **teaspoon freshly ground pepper**
2   **ounces canned flat anchovies, drained, divided**
1/4   **cup lemon juice**
1/4   **cup olive oil**
2   **heads romaine lettuce, in 1-inch pieces**
1-2   **cups croutons**
    grated Parmesan cheese

Place garlic in wooden salad bowl. Sprinkle with salt. Mash well. Add celery salt, mustard, Worcestershire sauce, and pepper. Mix well.

Reserving 4 anchovy fillets, mash remainder into mixture. Blend in lemon juice. Add olive oil slowly, whisking 1 minute. Add lettuce. Toss with croutons. Sprinkle liberally with Parmesan cheese. Garnish with reserved anchovies.

If desired, coddled egg may be mixed with dressing.

TOSSED SALAD WITH
BLUE CHEESE DRESSING

SERVES 4

1   head Boston lettuce, in bite-size pieces
1   head red leaf lettuce, in bite-size pieces
1   tomato, peeled, in wedges
1   avocado, sliced
6   ounces marinated artichoke hearts, drained
1   cup croutons

DRESSING:
1/2   cup crumbled blue cheese
3   tablespoons half and half
1/2   teaspoon Dijon mustard
1/8   teaspoon Worcestershire sauce
    pinch salt
    freshly ground pepper to taste
2   tablespoons balsamic vinegar
6   tablespoons olive oil

In large salad bowl combine all salad ingredients.

In food processor or blender combine all dressing ingredients. Blend well.
Drizzle dressing over top of salad. Toss well.

WINTER SALAD VINAIGRETTE

1   **large head leaf lettuce, in bite-size pieces**
1   **large head radicchio, in bite-size pieces**
1   **large bunch watercress, stems removed**
2   **medium Belgian endives, in 1-inch horizontal pieces**

RED WINE VINAIGRETTE:
2   **medium flat anchovies, rinsed**
1   **medium clove garlic**
1/4   **teaspoon salt**
1/2   **teaspoon freshly ground pepper**
1/4   **cup red wine vinegar**
1   **tablespoon balsamic vinegar**
2   **sun-dried tomatoes (in oil), drained, minced**
1   **tablespoon finely chopped parsley**
2   **teaspoons coarse-grained mustard**
2/3   **cup extra virgin olive oil**

12   **1-inch rounds goat cheese**

In large bowl combine leaf lettuce, radicchio, watercress, and endives. Toss. Place greens on individual plates.

For red wine vinaigrette, combine anchovies, garlic, and salt in medium bowl. Mash to form coarse paste. Blend in pepper. Add vinegars, tomatoes, parsley, and mustard. Mix well. Whisk in olive oil in steady stream until well blended. Add 2 tablespoons dressing to each individual salad plate.

Place cheese rounds on baking sheet. Bake in preheated 300-degree oven until just brown. Place warm cheese on cold salad.

Dressing may be made ahead and refrigerated. Bring to room temperature before serving.

LUNCHEON SALAD WITH
MUSTARD TARRAGON CROUTONS

SERVES 4 TO 5

1   **head romaine lettuce, in bite-size pieces**
1   **head Boston lettuce, in bite-size pieces**
1   **Belgian endive, in 1-inch pieces**
12   **cherry tomatoes, halved**
2   **tablespoons toasted pine nuts or sunflower seeds**
1   **tablespoon minced red onion**
1/2 **cup crumbled blue or feta cheese**
1   **ripe avocado, coarsely chopped**

DRESSING:
2-3 **tablespoons mayonnaise**
1   **tablespoon prepared horseradish**
1   **tablespoon Dijon mustard**
1/4 **cup balsamic vinegar**
1/4 **cup olive oil**

In large salad bowl combine all salad ingredients. Toss well. In jar with tight-fitting lid combine all dressing ingredients. Shake well. Just before serving add dressing to salad. Toss. Sprinkle with Mustard Tarragon Croutons.

MUSTARD TARRAGON CROUTONS

1/4 **cup olive oil**
1 1/2 **tablespoons Dijon mustard**
1 1/2 **teaspoons tarragon**
1 1/2 **cups cubed sourdough, French, or pumpernickel bread**

In medium bowl combine olive oil, mustard, and tarragon. Mix well. Toss with bread cubes. Bake in preheated 350-degree oven 12 minutes until toasted, turning frequently.

WATERCRESS, PEAR, AND
BLUE CHEESE SALAD

2   **large bunches watercress, tough stems removed**
1   **small head Boston lettuce, leaves separated**
2   **ripe pears, Bosc or Comice, peeled, sliced**
1/2 **cup crumbled blue cheese**
1/2 **cup walnut halves, lightly toasted**

DRESSING:
2   **tablespoons white vinegar**
2   **tablespoons fresh lemon juice**
1   **large shallot, minced**
1   **teaspoon salt**
1   **teaspoon freshly ground pepper**
1/2 **cup walnut oil**

In large salad bowl combine watercress, lettuce, pears, cheese, and walnuts.

In small bowl whisk all dressing ingredients. Fifteen minutes before serving toss salad with dressing. Let marinate briefly before serving.

See photo page 80.

ENDIVE AND APPLE SALAD

SERVES 6

2   **tablespoons Dijon mustard**
2   **tablespoons red wine or balsamic vinegar**
1/4 **teaspoon salt**
1/4 **teaspoon sugar**
     freshly ground pepper to taste
1/2 **cup vegetable oil**
5   **Belgian endives (about 1 pound)**
*1 **large sweet apple, peeled, cored, diced**
1   **tablespoon chopped green onion tops**

In small bowl combine mustard and vinegar. Mix well. Stir in salt, sugar, and pepper. Slowly beat in oil.

Remove and discard stem ends from endives. Cut 2 endives in half, reserving top portions. Slice bottom halves and remaining endives crosswise in 1/4-inch rounds. Transfer to salad bowl. Add apple and green onion tops. Just before serving toss salad with dressing. Arrange reserved endive tops upright around salad.

*Do not chop early. Apple will discolor.

JICAMA CITRUS SALAD

1½-2   **pounds jicama, peeled, in 1½- to 2-inch julienne strips**
1   **small red onion, very thinly sliced**
2   **small red peppers, thinly sliced, each slice halved**
3   **pears, in thin wedges**
3   **large navel oranges, peeled, membranes removed from each section**
⅔   **cup vegetable oil**
¼   **cup fresh lime juice**
3   **tablespoons fresh lemon juice**
1   **tablespoon finely grated lime rind**
1   **tablespoon superfine sugar**
1½   **teaspoons dried crushed red pepper**
1   **teaspoon coriander**
   Bibb lettuce and watercress to cover bottoms of 10 salad plates
3-4   **Belgian endives, ends trimmed, separated into leaves**

In large glass or ceramic bowl combine jicama, onion, peppers, pears, and oranges. Sprinkle with oil, juices, rind, sugar, red pepper, and coriander. Toss to coat well. Cover with plastic wrap. Refrigerate 1 to 4 hours.

Cover salad plates with Bibb lettuce and watercress. Arrange endive leaves in spoke fashion. Toss jicama mixture. Using slotted spoon arrange mixture on prepared plates. Sprinkle with remaining marinade or pass marinade with salad.

MELON AND JICAMA SALAD

2   **cups bite-size melon (honeydew or cantaloupe)**
2   **cups peeled, bite-size jicama**
½   **cup minced red onion**
   grated zest of 1 orange
   juice of 1 orange
   juice of 1 lime
1   **canned jalapeño pepper, seeded, minced**
1   **teaspoon Dijon mustard**
½   **cup olive oil**
¼   **teaspoon salt**
⅛   **teaspoon freshly ground pepper**
   greens of choice

continued

In large bowl combine melon, jicama, and onion. Mix well. In small bowl or blender combine remaining ingredients except greens. Mix well.

Toss dressing with melon mixture. Let stand 1 hour. Serve at room temperature on bed of greens.

MOLDED FRUIT SALAD

SERVES 12 TO 14

An attractive addition to a summer luncheon.

1¼   **pounds frozen rhubarb, sliced**
¾   **cup cold water, divided**
6   **ounces lemon gelatin**
2   **cups boiling water**
½   **cup sugar**
1   **pound frozen sliced strawberries, thawed**
2   **pink grapefruit, peeled, sectioned**
1   **cup fresh strawberries, thickly sliced**
    lettuce leaves

SWEET FRENCH DRESSING:
¼   **cup sugar**
1   **teaspoon salt**
1   **teaspoon celery seed**
1   **teaspoon dry mustard**
1   **teaspoon paprika**
1   **medium shallot, finely chopped**
¼   **cup vinegar**
1   **cup vegetable oil**

In large saucepan combine rhubarb and ¼ cup cold water. Cook over low heat 5 minutes or until rhubarb softens. Set aside.

In large bowl combine remaining ½ cup cold water and gelatin. Mix well. Add boiling water. Stir until gelatin dissolves. Add sugar, reserved rhubarb, and thawed strawberries. Mix well. Refrigerate until mixture thickens but is not jelled. Stir in grapefruit sections and fresh strawberries.

Pour into greased 12-cup mold. Refrigerate 3 hours or until well set. Unmold onto serving plate lined with lettuce leaves. Serve with dressing on side.

For sweet French dressing, combine sugar, salt, celery seed, mustard, paprika, shallot, and vinegar in small bowl. Mix well. Slowly add oil, mixing constantly.

SUN-DRIED TOMATO VINAIGRETTE

YIELD:
APPROXIMATELY
1 CUP

*1/2 **red pepper, roasted, peeled, finely chopped**
4 **ounces sun-dried tomatoes (in oil), drained, chopped**
1/3 **cup chopped, pitted calamata olives**
2 **cloves garlic, minced**
1/2 **teaspoon salt**
1/4 **cup red wine vinegar**
3 **tablespoons balsamic vinegar**
3/4 **cup olive oil**

In medium bowl combine all ingredients. Mix well. Cover and refrigerate until used.

*To roast, hold pepper with long fork over flame or place under broiler, turning until blackened. Place in paper bag. Close. Let steam 5 minutes. Skin will peel easily.

TANGERINE VINAIGRETTE

YIELD: 2 CUPS

3/4 **cup plus 2 tablespoons balsamic vinegar**
1 **cup plus 2 tablespoons vegetable oil**
2 **medium cloves garlic, quartered**
1/4 **cup sugar**
1/2 **teaspoon chili powder**
1/2 **teaspoon paprika**
1/2 **teaspoon salt**
1/2 **teaspoon pepper**
1/2 **teaspoon dry mustard**
1/4 **cup tangerine juice**
1 1/2 **teaspoons grated tangerine zest**

In food processor or blender combine all ingredients. Process until well blended. Store covered in refrigerator.

WALNUT VINAIGRETTE

YIELD: 2 CUPS

4	tablespoons coarse-grained mustard
1	tablespoon plus 1 teaspoon Dijon mustard
1½	teaspoons balsamic vinegar
¼	cup rice vinegar
¼	cup vegetable oil
¼	cup olive oil
2	tablespoons water
¼	cup honey
2	tablespoons coarsely chopped walnuts

In food processor or blender combine all ingredients except walnuts. Blend well. Stir in walnuts. Refrigerate in jar with tight-fitting lid.

Excellent with fresh spinach, greens, or fresh fruit.

FRENCH DRESSING

YIELD: 2 CUPS

1	large clove garlic
½	teaspoon salt
½	teaspoon freshly ground black pepper
½	teaspoon dry mustard
½	teaspoon paprika
1	teaspoon Worcestershire sauce
3	tablespoons fresh lemon juice
½	cup cider vinegar
½	cup chili sauce
¾	cup vegetable oil
¼	cup olive oil

In large wooden bowl mash garlic and salt together. Add pepper, mustard, and paprika. Blend well. Stir in Worcestershire sauce, lemon juice, vinegar, and chili sauce. Mix well. Slowly add combined vegetable and olive oils, whisking constantly. Refrigerate in jar with tight-fitting lid.

MUSTARD GARLIC SALAD DRESSING

YIELD: 2¹/₂ CUPS

3	cloves garlic
1¹/₂	teaspoons salt
1¹/₂	teaspoons freshly ground pepper
2	tablespoons Worcestershire sauce
3	heaping tablespoons Dijon mustard
4	heaping tablespoons mayonnaise
¹/₂	cup cider vinegar
1¹/₂	cups vegetable oil

In large wooden bowl finely mash garlic and salt together. Add pepper, Worcestershire sauce, mustard, and mayonnaise. Blend well. Whisk in vinegar. Slowly add oil until well blended, stirring constantly. Refrigerate in jar with tight-fitting lid.

SESAME DRESSING

YIELD: 1 CUP

1	tablespoon sesame seed
¹/₂	teaspoon salt
¹/₂	teaspoon dry mustard
1	teaspoon Dijon mustard
1-2	cloves garlic, minced
¹/₄	teaspoon thyme
¹/₄	teaspoon rosemary
¹/₄	teaspoon basil
1	teaspoon chopped parsley
2	tablespoons white wine vinegar
1	teaspoon lemon juice
³/₄	cup vegetable oil
2	tablespoons olive oil

In dry small skillet toast sesame seed over medium heat until light brown and popped, stirring constantly. Remove from skillet. Cool.

In food processor or blender process sesame seed to coarse powder. Add salt, mustards, garlic, thyme, rosemary, basil, parsley, vinegar, and lemon juice. With motor running add oils in slow steady stream until blended.

May be used for dip with equal amounts of dressing, mayonnaise, and lowfat yogurt. Refrigerate in jar with tight-fitting lid.

SESAME ORANGE DRESSING

YIELD: 2 CUPS

4   ounces frozen orange juice
4   tablespoons Dijon mustard
2/3   cup red currant jelly
1/4-1/2   teaspoon cayenne pepper
3   tablespoons red wine vinegar
3   tablespoons vegetable oil
3   tablespoons sesame seed, toasted

In small saucepan bring orange juice, mustard, and jelly to boil. Remove from heat. Add remaining ingredients. Blend well. Refrigerate in jar with tight-fitting lid.

SESAME MAYONNAISE

YIELD: 3 1/2 CUPS

1   egg plus 2 egg yolks
2 1/2   tablespoons rice vinegar
2 1/2   tablespoons soy sauce
3   tablespoons Dijon mustard
1/4   cup sesame oil
2 1/2   cups corn oil
  *drops of hot chili oil, optional

In food processor or blender combine egg, egg yolks, vinegar, soy sauce, and mustard. Process 1 minute. With motor running add sesame and corn oils in slow steady stream. Add hot chili oil, if desired. Mix well.

Serve on asparagus, broccoli, sandwiches, or as dip or salad dressing.

Keeps well in refrigerator for weeks.

*Found in Oriental section of supermarket.

CELERY DRESSING

YIELD: 2 CUPS

1 small onion, quartered
2 large ribs celery, in 1-inch pieces
1 tablespoon dry mustard
1 teaspoon salt
1/2 teaspoon white pepper
1 cup vegetable oil
1/3 cup white wine vinegar
3/4 cup sugar

In food processor or blender combine all ingredients. Blend until well combined. Chill.

Especially good drizzled on fruit.

SWEET AND SOUR FRUIT SALAD DRESSING

YIELD: 2 CUPS

2 eggs, beaten
1 cup sugar
1 tablespoon cornstarch
1/4 teaspoon salt
1/4 teaspoon dry mustard
1/4 teaspoon celery seed
3/4 cup white vinegar
1/4 cup water

In medium bowl combine all ingredients except vinegar and water. Beat well. In medium saucepan heat vinegar and water. Add egg mixture. Mix well. Cook about 10 minutes until thick and glossy, stirring constantly. Remove from heat. Cool and refrigerate.

EGGS & CHEESE

POLENTA-CHEESE SOUFFLÉ WITH FRESH TOMATO SAUCE

SERVES 6 TO 8

2¹/₂   **cups water**
1¹/₂   **tablespoons olive oil**
  6   **tablespoons yellow cornmeal**
  5   **teaspoons butter, divided**
  8   **eggs, separated**
  2   **cups freshly grated Parmesan cheese, divided**
     salt to taste
     pepper to taste

FRESH TOMATO SAUCE:

  3   **tablespoons olive oil**
4-5   **green onions, including 1 inch of green tops, finely chopped**
  3   **tablespoons finely chopped parsley**
  2   **teaspoons basil**
¹/₂   **teaspoon dried thyme**
4¹/₂   **cups coarsely pureed plum tomatoes**

In medium saucepan bring water to boil. Stir in olive oil. Slowly add cornmeal, stirring constantly. Cook over medium heat 10 minutes, stirring constantly. Remove from heat. Stir in 3 teaspoons butter. Beat in egg yolks with spoon. Reserving 2 tablespoons, stir in cheese. Season to taste. Refrigerate. May be prepared ahead to this point.

In medium bowl beat egg whites and pinch salt until stiff peaks form. Stir a fourth of whites into cheese mixture. Fold in remaining whites.

Grease 8-cup soufflé dish with remaining 2 teaspoons butter. Dust with 1 tablespoon reserved Parmesan cheese to coat inside of dish. Spoon cheese mixture into prepared dish. Smooth top. Sprinkle with remaining 1 tablespoon Parmesan cheese.

Bake in preheated 350-degree oven 30 to 35 minutes or until browned, puffed, and firm.

FRESH TOMATO SAUCE:

While soufflé bakes heat olive oil in large heavy pot. Add green onions. Sauté until onions are soft but not browned. Add remaining sauce ingredients. Stir, reduce heat, and simmer 15 minutes. Serve baked soufflé immediately. Top with warm sauce.

LUNCHEON TORTE

SERVES 10 TO 12

*CRUST:

1/4   **pound unsalted butter, in pieces**
1   **egg**
1 1/3   **cups flour**
1 1/4   **teaspoons baking powder**
1/8   **teaspoon salt**

FILLING:

1/2   **pound baked ham, in small pieces**
1/4   **pound Fontina cheese, in pieces**
1 1/2   **pounds ricotta cheese, drained dry**
12   **ounces cream cheese**
1/4   **cup whipping cream**
4   **eggs**
1/2   **teaspoon salt**
1/4   **teaspoon pepper**
   dash Tabasco
2-4   **tablespoons Dijon mustard**
1   **cup pesto sauce**

For crust, blend butter in food processor with 2 quick on and off turns. Add egg. Turn on and off twice. Add flour, baking powder, and salt. Process until lumps form. Transfer mixture to plastic bag. Refrigerate 45 minutes.

On lightly floured surface roll out pastry. Cut out circle to line bottom of springform pan. Cut long rectangle to line side of springform. Moisten seam edges and pinch together. (Crust may be frozen for 1 week.)

For filling, puree ham in food processor. Set aside. In food processor puree Fontina cheese. Set aside. In food processor combine ricotta cheese, cream cheese, cream, eggs, salt, pepper, and Tabasco. Process until smooth.

Brush mustard over crust. Cover with 1 1/2 cups ricotta cheese mixture. Spread with half of ham. Cover with half of Fontina cheese. Top with half of pesto sauce. Repeat layers, ending with remaining ricotta mixture. Bake in preheated 325-degree oven 1 to 1 1/4 hours or until golden brown. Serve at room temperature.

May be assembled 1 day ahead, refrigerated, and baked.

*May substitute prepared deep dish crust.

SAVORY PICNIC PIE

SERVES 10

pastry for 10-inch double crust pie
2 **tablespoons olive oil**
1 **tablespoon unsalted butter**
3 **medium onions, chopped**
12 **ounces frozen spinach soufflé, thawed, in small pieces**
12 **ounces cooked ham, chopped**
1½ **cups grated Parmesan cheese**
1 **cup ricotta cheese**
5 **large eggs, beaten, divided**
¼ **teaspoon freshly ground pepper**
pinch nutmeg
8 **ounces Monterey Jack cheese, grated**

Roll out half of pastry to fit 10-inch pie pan. Fit into pie pan, leaving 1-inch overhang.

In large skillet heat olive oil and butter. Add onions. Cook until onions are transparent. Remove skillet from heat. Stir in soufflé pieces, ham, Parmesan and ricotta cheeses, 4 beaten eggs, pepper, and nutmeg. Mix well. Pour into pie shell. Sprinkle Monterey Jack cheese over top.

Roll out remaining pastry to fit top of pie pan. Place over filling, turning edges from bottom over top crust. Pinch or flute edges. Brush top with remaining beaten egg. Cut vent in crust.

Bake in center of preheated 425-degree oven 25 minutes. Check pastry edges. If browning quickly, cover edges with foil. Bake 25 to 35 minutes longer or until crust is golden brown. Let stand 20 minutes before serving.

ONION AND TWO-CHEESE TART

SERVES 4 TO 6

1   9-inch unbaked deep dish pie shell
      (may use frozen)
1   large onion, thinly sliced
1   tablespoon butter or margarine, optional
3   ounces blue cheese, crumbled
1   cup milk or half and half
3   large eggs, lightly beaten
1   cup grated, firmly packed aged Cheddar cheese
1/4 teaspoon salt
1/4 teaspoon white pepper

If using frozen pie shell, thaw 10 minutes. Pierce shell thoroughly with fork. Bake in preheated 400-degree oven 10 minutes. Remove from oven. Microwave onion on high 3 to 4 minutes or sauté in butter until soft. Spread onion over bottom of pie shell.

In medium bowl mash blue cheese with milk. Stir in eggs, Cheddar cheese, salt, and white pepper. Pour mixture over onion.

Bake in preheated 350-degree oven 40 to 45 minutes or until filling is firm in center. If crust browns too quickly during baking, cover with strips of foil.

May be made several days ahead, refrigerated, and reheated.

SWEET ONION PIE

SERVES 6 TO 8

1   pound sweet onions, thinly sliced
1/2 green pepper, chopped
8   medium fresh mushrooms, sliced
1/4 pound butter or margarine
3   eggs, well beaten
8   ounces sour cream
4   ounces grated Jarlsberg cheese
1/4 teaspoon salt
1/2 teaspoon white pepper
1/4 teaspoon Tabasco
1   unbaked pie shell (deep dish, if frozen)
      grated Parmesan cheese

continued

In large skillet sauté onions, green pepper, and mushrooms in butter. Drain excess liquid. In large bowl combine eggs, sour cream, Jarlsberg cheese, salt, white pepper, and Tabasco. Mix well. Stir in onion mixture. Pour into pie shell. Sprinkle with Parmesan cheese.

Bake in preheated 450-degree oven 10 minutes. Reduce heat to 325 degrees. Bake 20 minutes or until pie is set.

GOAT CHEESE WEDGES

SERVES 4

8	**ounces refrigerated crescent rolls**
8	**1/8-inch slices large red onion, halved, separated**
1/3	**cup chopped green onions, including some of green tops**
1	**teaspoon sugar**
7	**tablespoons butter or margarine, room temperature, divided**
8	**ounces Montrachet or other goat cheese**
2	**eggs**
1/2	**cup whipping cream**
	salt to taste
	pepper to taste
2	**tablespoons chopped fresh basil**
2	**medium plum tomatoes, seeded, in thin julienne strips**

Pinch seams of crescent roll dough together. Form into square. Flatten slightly with rolling pin. Drape over 9-inch removable bottom tart pan, fitting into bottom and up sides. Trim upper edge. Pierce bottom and sides several times with fork. Bake in preheated 375-degree oven 5 to 6 minutes or until golden brown. Cool on rack.

In medium skillet sauté red and green onions with sugar in 3 tablespoons butter 3 to 4 minutes. Remove from heat.

In food processor or blender combine cheese, eggs, cream, salt, pepper, and remaining 4 tablespoons butter. Process until well blended. Stir in basil. Spread onions over baked crust. Pour cheese mixture over onions. Decorate with tomatoes.

Place tart pan on baking sheet. Bake in preheated 375-degree oven 30 to 35 minutes. Tart will rise as it bakes and settle when removed from oven. Cool before removing pan sides. Serve in wedges warm or at room temperature.

SUMMER TOMATO AND BASIL SLICES

SERVES 12 TO 15

CRUST:

2 **cups flour**
¼ **pound cold, unsalted butter, in small pieces**
2 **tablespoons cold shortening**
8 **slices bacon, crisply cooked, drained, crumbled**
3-4 **tablespoons ice water**
   dried navy beans

FILLING:

6 **large tomatoes, in ¼-inch horizontal slices**
3 **teaspoons salt, divided**
2 **cups firmly packed fresh basil leaves**
1 **pound whole milk ricotta cheese**
4 **large eggs, slightly beaten**
½ **pound whole milk mozzarella cheese, coarsely grated**
1 **cup freshly grated Parmesan cheese**
   freshly ground pepper to taste
   olive oil

For crust, combine flour, butter, shortening, and bacon in food processor. Process with on and off turns until well mixed. Through feed tube, with motor running, add ice water. Process until dough forms ball. Transfer dough to sheet of wax paper. Flatten dough. Cover with another sheet of wax paper. Refrigerate 1 hour.

Press dough into bottom and sides of 10- by 15-inch ungreased jelly-roll pan. Pierce dough several times with fork. Refrigerate 30 minutes. Cover dough with foil. Fill foil with navy beans. Bake in lower third of preheated 425-degree oven 15 minutes. Carefully remove beans and foil. Bake crust 3 to 5 minutes or until pale golden. Cool on rack.

For filling, sprinkle tomato slices with 1 teaspoon salt. Drain slices on paper towels. In food processor combine basil (reserving several sprigs), ricotta, and eggs. Blend well. Add remaining 2 teaspoons salt, mozzarella, Parmesan, and pepper. Puree.

Pat tomato slices dry with paper towel. Line bottom of crust with tomato end slices, reserving 20 good slices. Spread cheese mixture smoothly over tomato slices in pan. Arrange reserved tomato slices over top. Brush slices with olive oil. Bake in preheated 350-degree oven 40 to 50 minutes or until cheese mixture is set. Cool on rack 10 minutes. Garnish with reserved basil sprigs. Serve hot or at room temperature.

FRESH GARDEN QUICHE

pastry for 9-inch pie or quiche pan

2   tablespoons butter or margarine, divided

2   tablespoons finely chopped green pepper plus
       3 green pepper rings, divided

2   tablespoons finely chopped onion

1/2   cup (more if desired) halved cherry or 1/4-inch slices plum
       tomatoes, plus 3 cherry tomatoes, halved

1/2   cup flour

1   teaspoon finely chopped fresh thyme

1   teaspoon finely chopped fresh oregano

1   cup freshly grated Swiss cheese

3   eggs, beaten

1 1/3   cups half and half

1   teaspoon seasoned salt
       pinch cayenne pepper

2   tablespoons sliced black olives
       freshly ground pepper to taste

Fit pastry into bottom and up sides of 9-inch pie or quiche pan, leaving high edge. Pierce bottom with fork. Bake in preheated 400-degree oven 8 minutes.

In large skillet heat 1 tablespoon butter. Add chopped green pepper and onion. Sauté until golden. Remove vegetables from skillet. Set aside.

Add remaining 1 tablespoon butter to skillet. Dredge 1/2 cup tomatoes in flour. Sauté quickly. Drain on paper towel. Arrange on bottom of cooled baked pastry shell. Sprinkle with thyme and oregano. Cover with cooked green pepper and onion. Sprinkle with Swiss cheese.

In medium bowl combine eggs, half and half, seasoned salt, and cayenne. Mix well. Pour over filling. Garnish with green pepper rings, 3 halved cherry tomatoes, and olives. Bake in preheated 375-degree oven 40 minutes or until inserted knife comes out clean. Remove from oven. Season with freshly ground pepper. Let stand 10 minutes before serving.

ASPARAGUS QUICHE

SERVES 4 TO 6

1   9-inch unbaked pie shell
8   slices bacon, crisply cooked, drained, crumbled
2   cups cooked asparagus, in 1-inch pieces
1   cup shredded Gruyère cheese
1   cup half and half
3   eggs, slightly beaten
1   teaspoon tarragon
¼   teaspoon nutmeg
½   teaspoon salt
    pepper to taste

Pierce pie shell with fork. Bake in preheated 450-degree oven 7 minutes. Cool. Sprinkle bacon over shell. Add asparagus, then cheese.

In medium bowl combine half and half, eggs, tarragon, nutmeg, salt, and pepper. Mix well. Pour gently over cheese. Bake in preheated 350-degree oven 30 minutes or until set.

MOCK CHEESE SOUFFLÉ

SERVES 6 TO 8

8   ounces sharp Cheddar cheese, grated
10   slices white or whole wheat bread
1½   tablespoons butter
4   eggs plus 2 egg whites
2   cups milk
1   teaspoon salt
1   teaspoon dry mustard

In food processor or blender combine all ingredients. Process until well mixed. Pour into greased 1½-quart casserole. Bake in preheated 350-degree oven 1 hour. Serve immediately.

VARIATIONS:
Add 1 or more of the following: cubed ham; sausage pieces, crumbled; crisply cooked bacon; chopped red or green peppers, sautéed; sliced mushrooms; chopped green onions; chopped chives.

RICOTTA DILL SOUFFLÉ

SERVES 8

$^1/_2$ **cup ricotta cheese**
$1^1/_2$ **teaspoons coarse-grained mustard**
$1^1/_2$ **teaspoons dill weed**
$1^1/_8$ **cups freshly grated Parmesan cheese**
$^1/_4$ **cup skim milk**
1   **egg yolk**
2   **teaspoons safflower oil**
   pinch cayenne pepper
8   **egg whites, stiffly beaten**

In large bowl combine all ingredients except egg whites. Mix well. Gently fold in egg whites. Divide mixture among eight 4-ounce custard cups or ramekins. Place cups in baking pan with sides. Add hot water to reach $^1/_2$ inch up sides of cups. Bake in preheated 400-degree oven 20 minutes. Serve immediately.

May be held a short while by leaving in oven, with heat off and door open.

CORN CUSTARD WITH SMOKED SALMON AND CURRY SAUCE

SERVES 6 AS
FIRST COURSE

1¾ cups whipping cream, divided
1 cup cooked corn
¼ cup milk
4½ tablespoons flour
1 large egg plus 3 egg yolks
1 tablespoon butter
4 ounces smoked salmon, coarsely chopped, plus 2 ounces smoked salmon slices, divided
1¼ cups fish stock or clam juice
1 tablespoon curry powder
¼ red pepper, finely chopped
1½ teaspoons finely chopped parsley

In food processor puree 1¼ cups cream, corn, milk, flour, egg, and yolks. Butter six ¾-cup custard cups or ramekins. Line bottoms with parchment paper. Butter parchment. Divide chopped salmon among prepared cups. Pour pureed mixture over. Arrange cups in large baking pan. Add enough hot water to come halfway up sides of cups. Bake in preheated 325-degree oven 45 minutes or until custard is set.

While custards bake boil fish stock and curry powder in small saucepan about 8 minutes until reduced to ½ cup. Add remaining ½ cup cream. Simmer about 5 minutes.

Remove cooked custards from water. Cool slightly. Run sharp knife around sides of cups to loosen custards. Invert 1 onto each plate. Top with salmon slices. Sprinkle with red pepper and parsley. Spoon sauce around custard.

STACKED SAUSAGE TORTE

SERVES 6

2   tablespoons butter, divided
4   eggs plus 1 egg, separated
17   ounce package frozen puff pastry, thawed, divided
1   pound fresh spinach or 10 ounces frozen spinach, cooked,
    squeezed very dry
8   ounces grated mozzarella or Swiss cheese, divided
5½   ounces cooked ham, cubed
1   red pepper, in strips
8   ounces brown and serve sausage links
1   cup cubed salami
1   teaspoon water

In 8-inch omelet pan heat 1 tablespoon butter. In medium bowl beat 4 eggs and 1 egg white together, reserving yolk. Pour half of beaten eggs into pan. Cook until set, turning if needed to cook top. Remove from pan but do not fold. Repeat with remaining 1 tablespoon butter and beaten eggs.

Roll 1 sheet puff pastry into 12-inch square. Carefully place into 8-inch spring-form pan fitting excess pastry up sides of pan. Place 1 omelet in bottom of springform pan. Spread spinach over omelet. Sprinkle half of cheese over spinach. Top with ham and red pepper. Add second omelet. Layer sausage links over omelet. Top with salami. Sprinkle with remaining cheese.

Trim second pastry sheet into 8-inch circle, reserving excess scraps. Place pastry circle over top of cheese. Pinch edges of pastry top with top edges of bottom pastry. In small bowl beat reserved egg yolk and water. Brush pastry with yolk. Cut decorative shapes from reserved scraps of pastry and arrange over top. Brush with yolk.

Bake in preheated 375-degree oven 70 to 75 minutes. Cover. Cool 10 minutes before slicing. Serve warm or cold.

GOAT CHEESE CHILES RELLENOS

SERVES 6

12	Anaheim or poblano peppers
1	clove garlic, minced
1/2	pound goat cheese, crumbled
1/2	pound Monterey Jack cheese, grated
2	tablespoons chopped green onions
1	tablespoon sun-dried tomatoes (in oil), chopped
1/2	cup chopped fresh cilantro
1/2	cup chopped fresh basil
2	tablespoons chopped fresh marjoram
2	sprigs thyme or 1/2 teaspoon dried thyme
1/2	cup finely chopped pecans
	salt and pepper to taste
1	quart vegetable oil
1	egg, beaten
1	cup yellow cornmeal
	salsa or picante sauce
2	avocados, sliced

Arrange peppers on broiling pan. In preheated broiler broil 4 to 5 inches from heat until blistered. Carefully turn and broil on other side. Remove from broiler and wrap in towel 10 minutes. Remove from towel and cut small slit in side of each pepper. Under running water remove all seeds. (Peppers will be unbearably hot to eat if any seeds remain.) Carefully peel blistered outer skin, leaving stem. Set aside.

In medium bowl combine garlic, cheeses, green onions, tomatoes, cilantro, basil, marjoram, thyme, pecans, salt, and pepper. Mix well. Shape mixture into 12 rolls similar in size to peppers. Gently work mixture into each pepper. Do not overfill. Close each pepper with toothpick. Refrigerate until 15 minutes before serving.

In large deep skillet heat oil to 375 degrees. Dip each pepper into egg and then roll in cornmeal. Fry peppers a few at a time (do not crowd) several minutes until lightly browned, turning frequently. Drain on paper towel. Serve with salsa or picante sauce and avocado slices.

PANCAKE POPOVERS

SERVES 3 TO 4

4	eggs
1	cup milk
1	cup flour
	pinch salt
6	tablespoons butter or margarine
	maple syrup

In medium bowl combine eggs, milk, flour, and salt. Beat well.

Place two 9-inch pie pans, each with 3 tablespoons butter, in preheated 450-degree oven. Heat until butter melts. Remove from oven. Pour half of batter into each heated pie pan. Bake 20 minutes. Serve immediately with maple syrup.

VARIATION:
Strawberries and whipped cream may be substituted for maple syrup.

See photo page 186.

FLUFFY ORANGE PANCAKES

YIELD: 20

1½ **cups flour**
3 **tablespoons sugar**
2 **teaspoons baking powder**
½ **teaspoon salt**
2 **eggs, separated**
1 **cup milk**
½ **cup orange juice**
3 **tablespoons butter, melted, or vegetable oil**
1 **teaspoon grated orange rind**
6 **tablespoons margarine or vegetable oil, divided**

TOPPING:
¼ **pound butter, softened**
1 **cup confectioners sugar**
2 **teaspoons grated orange rind**

sliced strawberries or peaches

In large bowl sift together flour, sugar, baking powder, and salt. In small bowl beat egg yolks lightly. Add milk, orange juice, melted butter, and orange rind. Mix well. Add to dry ingredients, blending well. In another small bowl beat egg whites until soft peaks form. Fold into batter.

Heat griddle over medium heat. Add 2 teaspoons margarine. Pour batter by ¼ cupfuls onto griddle. Cook 1 to 1½ minutes until bubbles appear. Turn pancakes. Cook 1 to 1½ minutes on second side until light golden brown. Transfer to heated ovenproof platter. Repeat until all batter is used, regreasing griddle as necessary. Keep warm in 250-degree oven.

In medium bowl combine all topping ingredients. Serve with warm pancakes. Pass strawberries or peaches to spoon over top.

OATMEAL PANCAKES

SERVES 4

1½   **cups quick-cooking oats**
½   **cup flour**
1   **tablespoon brown sugar**
1   **teaspoon baking soda**
¼   **teaspoon salt**
2   **cups buttermilk**
3   **tablespoons vegetable oil**
2   **eggs, beaten**
1   **teaspoon vanilla**
½   **teaspoon maple flavoring, optional**

In large bowl combine oats, flour, brown sugar, baking soda, and salt. Mix well. Add remaining ingredients. Blend well. Let stand at room temperature 15 minutes.

Spoon onto hot, lightly greased griddle. Cook until golden brown on both sides.

PUFFY APPLE PANCAKE

SERVES 4 TO 6

6   **eggs**
1½   **cups milk**
1   **cup flour**
3   **tablespoons sugar**
1   **teaspoon vanilla**
½   **teaspoon salt**
¼   **teaspoon cinnamon**
¼   **pound butter**
2   **apples, peeled, thinly sliced (McIntosh, Granny Smith, Rome Beauty)**
3   **tablespoons brown sugar**

In large bowl combine eggs, milk, flour, sugar, vanilla, salt, and cinnamon. Mix well.

In 12-inch fluted or 9- by 13-inch baking dish melt butter in preheated 425-degree oven. Spread apples in dish. Return dish to oven until butter sizzles. Do not brown butter. Remove dish from oven. Immediately pour batter over apples. Sprinkle with brown sugar.

Bake in preheated 425-degree oven 25 to 30 minutes or until puffed and golden brown. Serve immediately. Pancake will collapse soon after removal from oven.

FISH & SEAFOOD

SHRIMP RATATOUILLE

SERVES 4

2	**teaspoons salt, divided**
2	**medium zucchini, cut lengthwise and then into ¹/₄-inch slices**
1	**medium eggplant, peeled, in ¹/₄-inch slices**
7-8	**tablespoons olive oil, divided**
2	**large cloves garlic, minced**
1	**medium onion, chopped**
1	**medium to large green pepper, seeded, chopped**
6	**pinches cayenne pepper, divided**
28	**ounces canned Italian plum tomatoes, cut in pieces, juice reserved**
¹/₄	**pound feta cheese, crumbled into pea-size pieces**
1¹/₂	**pounds cooked, shelled, deveined shrimp**

In colander liberally salt zucchini and eggplant. Let stand 30 minutes, turning several times.

In medium skillet heat 3 tablespoons olive oil over low heat. Add garlic. Sauté 2 minutes, stirring occasionally. Add onion, green pepper, ¹/₂ teaspoon salt, and 3 pinches cayenne. Cover and cook gently 15 minutes or until onion and pepper are soft, stirring occasionally and adding more olive oil if necessary. Transfer to large pot.

Rinse zucchini and eggplant. Dry with paper towel. In large skillet heat 3 table-spoons olive oil. Brown eggplant slices on each side. Cut eggplant into 1-inch cubes and add to large pot.

Add 1 tablespoon olive oil to skillet. Brown zucchini. Add to large pot with 3 pinches cayenne, ¹/₂ teaspoon salt, tomatoes, tomato juice, and cheese. Simmer over low heat 20 minutes, stirring occasionally. Increase heat to evaporate juice if mixture appears soupy. Remove from heat. Add shrimp.

May be made ahead, adding shrimp when ready to serve.

SHRIMP FLORENTINE

SERVES 6

1½ pounds shelled, deveined shrimp
4 tablespoons chopped garlic
6 tablespoons butter
19 ounces frozen creamed spinach
½ teaspoon garlic powder
2 tablespoons lemon juice
3 ounces bacon bits
4 ounces grated Swiss cheese

In large skillet sauté shrimp and garlic in butter 3 minutes. Remove from heat. Transfer shrimp to 9- by 13-inch baking dish, arranging in tight rows. Pour remaining butter sauce from skillet over shrimp.

Prepare spinach according to package directions. Stir in garlic powder and lemon juice. Spoon spinach mixture over shrimp. Top with bacon bits and cheese. Bake uncovered in preheated 400-degree oven 20 minutes.

STIR-FRIED SWEET AND SOUR PRAWNS

SERVES 2 TO 3

12 prawns, shelled, deveined
2½ teaspoons salt, divided
1 tablespoon Chinese yellow wine or sweet sherry
1 egg white
4 tablespoons vegetable oil, divided
2 slices unpeeled fresh ginger root
1 clove garlic, minced
1 green onion
1 green pepper, in bite-size pieces
⅓ cup sliced bamboo shoots
1 cup canned, drained pineapple chunks
½ teaspoon sugar
3 tablespoons ketchup
  cooked rice

continued

In large bowl combine prawns and 2 teaspoons salt. Blend well with fingers. Rinse prawns. Dry with paper towel. In shallow dish combine wine and egg white. Mix well. Marinate prawns in mixture 30 minutes.

In hot wok or large heavy skillet heat 3 tablespoons oil. Cook ginger root, garlic, and green onion until dark brown. Remove and discard.

Add prawns to hot oil. Stir fry until prawns become white. Transfer to warm serving platter. Add remaining 1 tablespoon oil to wok. Stir fry green pepper until bright green and crispy. Add bamboo shoots and pineapple chunks. Heat through. Return prawns to mixture. Stir in remaining $1/2$ teaspoon salt, sugar, and ketchup. Serve over rice.

THAI SHRIMP AND PINEAPPLE WITH RICE

SERVES 4 TO 6

$2^{1/2}$	**tablespoons soy sauce**
$1^{1/2}$	**teaspoons sugar**
$1/2$	**teaspoon turmeric**
1	**tablespoon water**
2	**tablespoons vegetable oil, divided**
1	**pound medium or large shrimp, shelled, deveined**
2	**large cloves garlic, minced**
4	**cups cooked rice**
1	**teaspoon ground coriander seed**
2	**cups inch-long julienned slices fresh pineapple**
$3/4$	**cup coarsely chopped red pepper**
2	**teaspoons minced jalapeño pepper with seeds, or to taste**
3	**green onions with tops, finely sliced**

In small bowl combine soy sauce, sugar, turmeric, and water. Mix well. Set aside.

In large heavy skillet or wok heat 1 tablespoon oil until hot but not smoking. Stir fry shrimp about 2 minutes only until shrimp are pink and lose transparency. Remove from skillet.

In skillet heat remaining 1 tablespoon oil. Add garlic. Stir until golden. Add rice. Stir fry about 1 minute until hot. Add reserved soy sauce mixture. Blend well. Add shrimp, coriander seed, pineapple, peppers, and green onions. Stir until very hot.

SHRIMP PIRI PIRI

Not for the timid palate.

2	teaspoons cider vinegar
1	teaspoon cumin
1	teaspoon curry powder
1/2	teaspoon cayenne pepper
1/2	teaspoon salt
1/4	teaspoon turmeric
2	large cloves garlic, minced
1	pound jumbo shrimp, shelled, deveined, tails intact, if desired
2	tablespoons vegetable oil
2 1/2	teaspoons Oriental sesame oil, divided
1	large onion, thinly sliced
10	tablespoons fresh orange juice, divided
12	ounces fresh spinach, stems removed
12-16	orange, peach, or nectarine slices
	fresh currants, optional

In large bowl combine vinegar, cumin, curry powder, cayenne, salt, turmeric, and garlic. Mix well. Blend to smooth paste. Add shrimp, tossing to coat.

In large skillet heat vegetable oil and 1 teaspoon sesame oil over medium heat. Add onion. Sauté until lightly browned, stirring occasionally. Increase heat to high. Add shrimp with paste mixture and 5 tablespoons orange juice. Cook about 3 minutes or until shrimp are just pink, turning occasionally. Remove from heat.

In large saucepan of boiling water cook spinach 1 minute. Drain well. Toss spinach with remaining 5 tablespoons orange juice and 1 1/2 teaspoons sesame oil. Divide spinach among individual plates. Top with shrimp mixture. Garnish with orange, peach, or nectarine slices. Sprinkle with currants, if desired.

See photo page 185.

HOT SPICED CURRIED SHRIMP

SERVES 4

RAITA:

1	teaspoon cumin seed
1	cup plain yogurt
1	cucumber, peeled, seeded, finely chopped
1/2	teaspoon salt, optional

1/2-1	teaspoon ground chilies or cayenne pepper
2	tablespoons dry sherry or white wine
1/2	teaspoon black pepper
3	tablespoons soy sauce
2	cups chicken broth
2	teaspoons cornstarch
1	tablespoon water
4	tablespoons vegetable oil, divided
1 1/2-2	pounds shrimp, shelled, deveined
1	tablespoon minced fresh ginger root
4-6	cloves garlic, minced, or to taste
1 1/2	teaspoons tandoori powder
1 1/2	teaspoons curry powder
2	teaspoons sugar
	cooked rice

For raita, cook cumin seed in small dry skillet over high heat until they begin to pop and become fragrant. Cool seed. In small bowl combine cumin seed, yogurt, cucumber, and salt, if desired. Mix well. Chill.

In small bowl combine chilies, sherry, pepper, soy sauce, and chicken broth. Mix well. In another small bowl mix cornstarch and water. Set aside.

Heat dry wok or large skillet 1 to 2 minutes. Add 3 tablespoons oil. Heat until smoking. Add shrimp. Stir fry until shrimp start to curl and become opaque. Do not overcook. Remove shrimp with slotted spoon. Add remaining 1 tablespoon oil and ginger root. Stir fry 15 seconds. Do not burn. Add garlic. Stir fry 10 seconds. Add tandoori and curry powders. Cook 30 seconds, stirring constantly. Color will darken. Add sugar and cook about 5 seconds until dissolved. Stir in broth mixture. Cook until reduced to 3/4 cup.

Add shrimp and cornstarch mixture to wok. Cook until shrimp are heated. Do not overcook. Serve over rice with raita accompaniment. May also be served cold as appetizer.

SCALLOPS WITH SAFFRON LEEK SAUCE

1/2 teaspoon firmly packed saffron threads
1/4 cup hot water
2 tablespoons unsalted butter
2 large leeks, halved lengthwise, thinly sliced across
2/3 cup dry vermouth
3 teaspoons tomato paste
1 cup whipping cream
1/2 teaspoon grated fresh ginger root
1 teaspoon salt, divided
   freshly ground black pepper to taste
1 cup 2% milk
1/4 teaspoon white pepper
1 pound sea scallops, halved
4 sprigs parsley

In small bowl combine saffron and hot water. Set aside.

In medium saucepan melt butter. Add leeks. Reduce heat to low, cover, and cook 20 minutes until leeks are soft, stirring occasionally. Add vermouth. Increase heat to medium. Cook 6 minutes or until vermouth is almost evaporated. Stir in tomato paste, cream, ginger root, and reserved saffron liquid. Simmer until mixture is thick and creamy. Season with 1/2 teaspoon salt and black pepper.

While sauce cooks bring milk to boil in large saucepan. Season with remaining 1/2 teaspoon salt and white pepper. Remove from heat. Add scallops. If liquid does not cover scallops add boiling water to cover. Cover. Let scallops poach in milk 5 minutes or until opaque through center. Drain liquid.

Ladle leek sauce on 4 individual serving plates. Place scallops on sauce. Spoon additional sauce as desired over top. Garnish with parsley.

See photo page 184.

SEA SCALLOPS WITH ENDIVE AND CHERRY TOMATOES

SERVES 4

6	**Belgian endives, cored, thinly sliced lengthwise**
2	**teaspoons minced garlic**
13	**tablespoons butter, divided**
16-20	**sea scallops**
2	**tablespoons dry white wine or vermouth**
2	**tablespoons white wine vinegar**
1	**tablespoon lemon juice**
1	**tablespoon minced shallots**
1/4	**teaspoon salt**
	pinch white pepper
2-4	**tablespoons whipping cream**
1	**teaspoon tomato paste**
12	**cherry tomatoes**

In large skillet sauté endives and garlic in 3 tablespoons butter over medium heat 6 to 8 minutes. Remove from heat. Arrange scallops 1 inch apart on greased baking sheet. Bake in preheated 500-degree oven 15 minutes.

While scallops bake gently boil wine, vinegar, lemon juice, shallots, salt, and white pepper in small saucepan until mixture reduces to ¾ tablespoon. Beat in remaining 10 tablespoons butter over low heat. Add cream and tomato paste. Mix well. Keep sauce over very low heat.

Add cherry tomatoes to endives. Reheat endives over medium heat 3 minutes. Divide scallops browned side up among serving plates. Surround scallops with endives and tomatoes. Drizzle tomato sauce over all.

BAKED SCALLOPS WITH MUSHROOMS

SERVES 3

2   **tablespoons margarine, divided**
1½ **tablespoons flour**
¼   **cup white wine**
¼   **cup chicken broth**
3   **tablespoons whipping cream**
    salt to taste
    pepper to taste
1-2 **tablespoons lemon juice**
¾   **pound fresh mushrooms, finely chopped**
1   **pound sea scallops, quartered**
    paprika to taste
    chopped parsley

In medium saucepan melt 1 tablespoon margarine. Add flour. Blend well over low heat. Gradually stir in wine and chicken broth, continuing to stir until thickened. Slowly stir in cream. Blend in salt, pepper, and lemon juice. Remove from heat.

In medium skillet sauté mushrooms in remaining 1 tablespoon margarine. Cook 5 to 10 minutes until all liquid has evaporated.

Divide scallops among 3 individual baking shells. Spoon sauce over each. Top with mushrooms, paprika, and parsley. Bake in preheated 450-degree oven 10 to 12 minutes.

CRAB CAKES

YIELD:
EIGHT 2-INCH OR
SIX 3-INCH

2   tablespoons minced onion
3   tablespoons butter, divided
2   eggs, beaten
1/4 cup half and half
1/2 cup soft bread crumbs
2   cups fresh crab meat
1/2 cup minced celery
2   tablespoons chopped parsley
2   tablespoons mustard
1/2 teaspoon Worcestershire sauce, or to taste
    Tabasco to taste
    salt to taste
    dried crushed red pepper to taste
2   tablespoons flour

In small skillet sauté onion in 2 tablespoons butter 3 minutes. In medium bowl combine sautéed onions with remaining ingredients except flour and remaining butter. Mix well. Cover and refrigerate 2 hours.

Shape crab meat mixture into eight 2-inch or six 3-inch disks. Dust "cakes" lightly with flour. In large skillet melt remaining 1 tablespoon butter. Sauté cakes 3 minutes on each side or until browned. Serve immediately with tartar sauce, if desired.

TARTAR SAUCE

YIELD: 1 1/2 CUPS

1   cup mayonnaise
2   tablespoons fresh lemon juice
1   teaspoon Worcestershire sauce
3   drops Tabasco
1/3 cup chopped sweet and sour pickles
2   tablespoons finely chopped shallots
2   tablespoons capers
1/3 cup chopped parsley
1/4 teaspoon curry powder
    salt to taste
    pepper to taste

In small bowl combine and mix all ingredients. Mix well. Refrigerate covered until served.

WOVEN SALMON WITH TOMATO AND SPINACH SAUCES

SERVES 4

4   **large ripe tomatoes, peeled, seeded, chopped, divided**
²⁄₃   **cup whipping cream, divided**
¹⁄₂   **teaspoon sugar**
    salt to taste
    pepper to taste
1   **pound fresh spinach, stems removed**
*24   **ounces salmon fillets, skinned, in 24 4- by ¹⁄₂-inch strips**
2   **tablespoons butter, melted**

In medium saucepan combine 3 chopped tomatoes, ¹⁄₃ cup cream, sugar, salt, and pepper. Simmer about 30 minutes until thick, stirring occasionally. Remove from heat.

Reserving 4 spinach leaves, combine remaining spinach, remaining ¹⁄₃ cup cream, salt, and pepper in another medium saucepan. Simmer until spinach wilts. Remove from heat. In food processor puree tomato and spinach mixtures separately. Return to original saucepans. Keep warm.

Sprinkle salmon strips with salt and pepper. Line broiler pan with foil. Grease foil. Weave 3 salmon strips in each direction into square shape. Repeat procedure with remaining strips to create 3 additional squares. Brush salmon with melted butter. Broil 6 to 8 minutes without turning.

To serve, spoon small amount of each sauce onto individual serving plates. With wide spatula, carefully lift woven salmon square, blot on paper towel, and place on sauces. Garnish with reserved spinach leaves and remaining chopped tomato.

*May be prepared without braiding using four 6-ounce salmon fillets, skinned, broiled.

See photo page 183.

GRILLED SALMON STEAKS

SERVES 4

4 8-ounce salmon steaks, 1¼ inches thick
⅓ cup fresh lime juice
2-3 tablespoons red wine vinegar
2 teaspoons chopped fresh mint
1 shallot, minced
1 large egg yolk
¾ teaspoon cornstarch
⅓ cup plain yogurt
1 teaspoon Dijon mustard
2 teaspoons unsalted butter
1 tablespoon vegetable oil
   pinch paprika

In large shallow dish arrange salmon steaks in single layer. Pour lime juice over salmon. Marinate at least 30 minutes, turning occasionally.

In double boiler combine vinegar, mint, and shallot. Cook over medium heat until vinegar is almost evaporated. Remove from heat. Whisk in egg yolk and cornstarch. Return mixture to double boiler.

Cook over simmering water about 1 minute until slightly thickened, stirring constantly. Remove from heat. Whisk in yogurt and mustard. Cook over simmering water 1 minute, stirring constantly. Remove from heat. Whisk in butter. Keep sauce warm over warm water, whisking occasionally.

Brush salmon steaks with oil. Sprinkle with paprika. Broil or grill salmon 3 to 4 minutes on each side or until fish flakes easily. Serve with warm sauce.

Sauce may be kept over warm water for up to 1 hour.

DIJON BROILED SALMON

SERVES 4

4 ½-pound salmon steaks, 1 inch thick
1½-2 teaspoons Dijon mustard
⅛-¼ teaspoon freshly ground black pepper
1 teaspoon dill weed

Arrange salmon on foil-covered broiler pan. Spread thick layer of mustard over each steak. Grind several turns pepper over mustard. Sprinkle ¼ teaspoon dill weed over each steak. Broil 4 inches from heat 15 to 20 minutes or until done.

SMOKED SALMON

Delicious recipe requiring a smoker.

1/3   cup sugar
2   cups light soy sauce
1/2   teaspoon onion powder
1/2   teaspoon garlic powder
1/2   teaspoon pepper
1/2   teaspoon Tabasco
1   cup dry white wine
5   pound whole king salmon, filleted, skin on
2-3   panfuls alder or apple wood chips

In large shallow dish combine sugar, soy sauce, onion and garlic powders, pepper, Tabasco, and wine. Mix well. Submerge fish in mixture. Marinate covered in dish 8 hours or overnight in refrigerator.

Arrange salmon on smoker racks with thickest fillets on bottom racks. Light wood chips under racks. When chips have burned, continue smoking using only heating element for total smoking time of 8 to 12 hours, depending on thickness of salmon fillets. Fish should be moist. Let salmon cool in smoker. Keeps 2 to 3 weeks in refrigerator.

TUNA CAPRI

SERVES 3

1   cup olive oil
3   tablespoons white wine vinegar
5   cloves garlic, minced
1/4   cup chopped parsley
1/4   cup chopped fresh mint
      salt to taste
      pepper to taste
1 1/2 pounds tuna steaks (swordfish or other firm fish may be used)

In large bowl combine all ingredients except fish. Mix well. Add fish to mixture. Pierce fish with fork in several places. Cover and refrigerate at least 2 hours. Broil or grill fish to desired doneness.

SWORDFISH WITH GRAPEFRUIT AND ROSEMARY SAUCE

SERVES 2

2 **6-ounce swordfish steaks, 1 to 1¼ inches thick**
   salt to taste
   pepper to taste
3 **tablespoons butter, divided**
2 **shallots, minced**
1 **teaspoon dried rosemary, crumbled**
¾ **cup grapefruit juice**
   sprigs parsley

Season fish to taste. In heavy skillet melt 1 tablespoon butter over medium heat. Add fish. Cook about 9 minutes per inch of thickness until just opaque, turning once. Transfer fish to warm platter. Tent with aluminum foil to retain heat.

To same skillet add shallots and rosemary. Stir over medium heat about 2 minutes until shallots soften. Add grapefruit juice. Increase heat. Bring to boil, scraping sides of skillet. Add juices from fish platter. Boil about 5 minutes or until sauce becomes syrupy. Remove from heat.

Stir in remaining 2 tablespoons butter. Season sauce to taste. Spoon sauce over fish. Garnish with sprigs parsley.

GRILLED SWORDFISH WITH TOMATO COULIS

SERVES 4

TOMATO COULIS:

3   pounds ripe tomatoes, peeled
2   tablespoons butter
2   tablespoons olive oil
3   medium onions, chopped
2   cloves garlic, finely minced
1½ teaspoons salt
     pepper to taste
½   teaspoon sugar
2   tablespoons chopped parsley
1   tablespoon chopped fresh basil
*3 sun-dried tomatoes, optional
2   teaspoons Dijon mustard
2   tablespoons crème fraîche

4   6-ounce swordfish steaks, ¾ to 1 inch thick
1-2 tablespoons olive oil
     pepper to taste

For tomato coulis, halve tomatoes horizontally. Remove seeds and juice. Chop pulp and set aside. In large saucepan heat butter and olive oil. Sauté onions 5 minutes. Add garlic. Sauté 2 minutes. Add tomatoes, salt, pepper, sugar, parsley, basil, sun-dried tomatoes, if desired, and mustard. Simmer uncovered until very thick. Add crème fraîche. Set aside.

Brush swordfish steaks with olive oil. Season with pepper. Grill over hot coals about 5 minutes on each side, turning once. Serve topped with warm tomato coulis.

*Sun-dried tomatoes add to flavor but should be removed when sauce is cool.

STUFFED SOLE FILLETS

SERVES 4
AS MAIN COURSE;
8 AS APPETIZER

4   slices white bread, crusts removed
1   cup milk
2   shallots, finely chopped
*1/2   pound butter, clarified, divided
1   pound cooked, shelled crevettes (tiny pink shrimp),
       finely chopped
    salt to taste
    pepper to taste
2   Dover sole, skinned, in 4 fillets
1   cup crème fraîche
1   tablespoon lemon juice
1/4   cup light cream (option for clarified butter)
2   tablespoons finely chopped parsley

In medium shallow bowl soak bread in milk. Squeeze out all liquid. In small skillet sauté shallots in 1 tablespoon clarified butter. Combine bread, shallots, and crevettes. Mix well. Season to taste. Divide mixture into 4 balls. Wrap sole fillet around each ball, securing with string or toothpick.

In medium skillet sauté stuffed fillets in clarified butter as needed 5 to 10 minutes until fish is cooked and stuffing heated.

In small saucepan warm crème fraîche. Add lemon juice and 1/4 cup clarified butter or light cream. Mix well and heat briefly. Serve fillets with sauce over top and sprinkle with parsley.

*CLARIFIED BUTTER DIRECTIONS:

In small saucepan melt butter. Remove from heat. Let stand 10 minutes. Skim white foam from top. Carefully pour golden liquid into small bowl, discarding white foam and liquid on bottom of saucepan. Golden liquid can be used for sautéing at higher temperature than regular butter without burning.

CATFISH TRICOLORE IN PARCHMENT

SERVES 6

6   medium catfish fillets
    salt to taste
    pepper to taste
    pinch thyme
1   red pepper, seeded, in strips
1   medium carrot, julienned
6   green onions, in strips
1   tablespoon extra virgin olive oil

Place each fillet on individual rectangle of parchment or aluminum foil. Season to taste. Sprinkle with thyme. Add several strips of red pepper, carrot, and green onions. Drizzle olive oil over top. Fold opposite corners of parchment or foil together. Bunch together remaining 2 corners. Place on baking sheet.

Bake in preheated 375-degree oven 20 to 25 minutes or until fish interior is white. Place each serving on individual plate. Open slightly.

See photo page 184.

GRILLED BLACK SEA BASS

SERVES 4

1   tablespoon lime juice
1   tablespoon soy sauce
2   cloves garlic, crushed
1/3   cup olive oil
1 1/2-2 pound black sea bass (or shrimp, tuna,
        mahi mahi, or other similar fish)

In large shallow dish combine lime juice, soy sauce, garlic, and olive oil. Mix well. Marinate fish in mixture 2 hours in refrigerator. Grill fish over white hot coals or broil 7 to 10 minutes on each side.

TILAPIA WITH GINGER SAUCE

SERVES 6

1/3   **cup soy sauce**
1/3   **cup chicken broth**
1/2   **teaspoon sugar**
1/3   **cup plus 1 tablespoon water, divided**
1   **teaspoon cornstarch**
3   **tablespoons corn oil, divided**
2   **green onions**
2   **tablespoons finely grated fresh ginger root**
3   **pounds tilapia**
   juice of 1 lemon
   salt to taste
   pepper to taste

In small bowl combine soy sauce, chicken broth, sugar, and 1/3 cup water. Mix well. Mix cornstarch with remaining 1 tablespoon water. Add to soy sauce mixture.

In small saucepan heat 2 tablespoons corn oil. Chop white part of green onions, reserving green tops. Add chopped green onions and ginger root to saucepan. Cook until light brown. Add soy sauce mixture. Bring to boil. Reduce heat. Keep sauce warm.

Place fish in large baking dish. Season with lemon juice, salt, and pepper. Rub fish with remaining 1 tablespoon corn oil. Bake fish in preheated 350-degree oven 15 to 20 minutes. Transfer fish to platter and pour ginger sauce over top. Garnish with reserved green onion tops, sliced into julienne strips.

Sauce may be used for other fish.

RED SNAPPER IN WALNUT BUTTER
AND ARUGULA

SERVES 2

1-2	tablespoons walnut oil
2	red snapper fillets
	salt to taste
	cayenne pepper to taste
½	cup chopped walnuts
1	teaspoon finely minced shallots
2	tablespoons dry white wine
½	cup fish stock or clam juice
2	tablespoons margarine
1	teaspoon lemon juice
10	fresh arugula leaves, julienned

In large skillet heat walnut oil over high heat. Make 3 diagonal slits on skin side of each fillet. Season fillets with salt and cayenne. Place fillets skin side down in hot oil. Cook 2 minutes. Turn and cook 1 minute. Transfer fillets skin side up to ovenproof dish. Set aside.

Add walnuts to skillet. Toss in hot oil until golden. Remove with slotted spoon. Set aside. Add shallots, wine, and stock to skillet. Cook until liquid is reduced by two-thirds. Remove from heat. Stir in reserved walnuts, margarine, and lemon juice.

Bake fish in preheated 350-degree oven 10 minutes. Divide sauce between 2 serving plates. Place 1 fillet skin side up in center of each plate. Surround with arugula.

BAKED RED SNAPPER WITH PEPERONATA SAUCE

SERVES 4

SAUCE:

2	**tablespoons olive oil**
2	**large cloves garlic, minced**
1	**teaspoon basil**
1	**teaspoon oregano**
1/2	**teaspoon dried crushed red pepper**
1	**teaspoon salt, or to taste**
1/2	**teaspoon pepper**
1	**green pepper, seeded, in 1/3-inch strips**
1	**red pepper, seeded, in 1/3-inch strips**
1	**orange pepper, seeded, in 1/3-inch strips**
1/2	**pound onions, in 1/4-inch crosswise slices**
1	**pound plum tomatoes, seeded, coarsely chopped**
1	**tablespoon red wine vinegar**
1 1/2	**pounds skinned red snapper, orange roughy, or sole fillets**
2	**tablespoons olive oil**
	salt to taste
	pepper to taste

For sauce, heat olive oil in large skillet. Add garlic, basil, oregano, crushed red pepper, salt, and pepper. Cook over medium-high heat 1 minute, stirring constantly. Add green, red, and orange pepper strips and onions. Cook 6 to 7 minutes or until tender-crisp, stirring frequently. Stir in tomatoes and vinegar.

Place fillets in shallow baking pan. Brush with olive oil. Season to taste. Bake in preheated 450-degree oven 10 minutes or just until fish flakes easily. Serve sauce over fillets.

HALIBUT STEAKS WITH RED PEPPER SAUCE

SERVES 2

RED PEPPER SAUCE:
2 large red peppers
1/2 teaspoon salt
1/4 teaspoon freshly ground pepper
1 tablespoon lowfat plain yogurt
3 tablespoons lite ricotta cheese

2 7- to 8-ounce halibut steaks (may substitute grouper, cod,
   red snapper, or turbot)
2 tablespoons olive oil

For red pepper sauce, cook peppers over open flame or under broiler until skin blisters and turns black on all sides. Transfer peppers to paper bag. Close bag and set aside for 15 to 20 minutes. Remove peppers from bag. Split each pepper. Remove skin and seeds. Do not rinse.

In food processor combine peppers, salt, pepper, yogurt, and ricotta. Process until smooth. Transfer to small saucepan. Warm sauce over low heat.

Brush halibut with olive oil. Grill over hot coals 4 to 5 minutes on each side or until just cooked through. Spoon red pepper sauce onto individual serving plates and top with fish.

Sauce may also be served with grilled chicken.

GROUPER IN ROSEMARY VINAIGRETTE

SERVES 4

1   **teaspoon Dijon mustard**
2   **tablespoons red wine vinegar**
2   **teaspoons chopped fresh rosemary or ¹/₂ teaspoon**
       dried rosemary
1   **clove garlic, minced**
¹/₄ **teaspoon salt**
     freshly ground pepper to taste
2   **teaspoons olive oil**
4   **6- to 8-ounce grouper steaks**

In large bowl combine mustard, vinegar, rosemary, garlic, salt, and pepper. Mix well. Whisk in olive oil. Marinate fish in mixture 20 minutes, turning once.

Transfer fish to broiling pan. Spoon marinade over fish. Broil 4 to 5 minutes on each side. Serve sprinkled with pepper.

CRISPY FISH STICKS

SERVES 3

1   **egg, lightly beaten**
1   **cup vegetable oil plus oil as needed for frying, divided**
1   **cup milk plus 1 or 2 tablespoons as needed, divided**
1   **cup flour**
     pinch salt
1   **pound halibut, cod, or sea bass fillets, in 1-inch strips**

In large bowl combine egg, 1 cup oil, and 1 cup milk. Mix well. Add flour and salt. Beat well. Place fish strips in batter.

Fill large skillet with 2 inches oil and place over high heat. When oil reaches 350 degrees remove fish strips from batter 1 at a time with tongs. Drop strips into oil. Cook no longer than 3 minutes or until firm. Remove and drain on paper towel. If thinner crispy coating is desired after first strip is cooked, dilute batter with 1 or 2 tablespoons milk.

FISH STEW

2 teaspoons minced garlic
1/2 cup finely chopped onion
3 tablespoons olive oil
1 cup dry white wine or chicken broth
1 pound fresh tomatoes (preferably plum) or canned
      tomatoes, drained, in 1/2-inch cubes
1 bay leaf
1/2 teaspoon dried crushed red pepper
     salt to taste
     pepper to taste
1/4 pound sea scallops, in 1-inch cubes
3/4 pound red snapper or other non-oily fish, in 1-inch cubes
2 tablespoons chopped parsley

In large skillet sauté garlic and onion in olive oil until onion is soft. Add wine. Simmer 3 minutes. Add tomatoes, bay leaf, red pepper, salt, and pepper. Bring to boil. Reduce heat and simmer covered 5 minutes. Stir in scallops and fish. Simmer covered 5 minutes. Remove bay leaf. Pour into individual serving bowls. Sprinkle with parsley.

MEAT

KENTUCKY BOURBON BARBECUED RIBS

SERVES 8 TO 10

SAUCE:

- 1½ **cups ketchup**
- 6 **tablespoons white vinegar**
- ¼ **cup water**
- ¼ **cup light brown sugar**
- 1 **tablespoon Worcestershire sauce**
- 1 **tablespoon molasses**
- 1 **tablespoon soy sauce**
  juice of 1 lemon
- 2 **teaspoons Pickapeppa sauce**
- 2 **teaspoons dry mustard**
- 1 **large clove garlic, minced**
- 1-2 **teaspoons coarsely ground pepper**
- 1-2 **tablespoons bourbon**

- 6 **slabs baby back ribs**
  salt to taste
  pepper to taste
- 1 **teaspoon paprika**

In medium saucepan combine all sauce ingredients except bourbon. Bring to boil. Reduce heat. Simmer gently about 10 minutes until lightly thickened. Add bourbon just before using.

Season ribs with salt, pepper, and paprika. Place ribs in shallow roasting pan. Cover tightly with foil. Bake in preheated 350-degree oven 1 hour, basting with sauce twice during last 30 minutes of cooking.

Brush cooked ribs on both sides with sauce. Grill over hot coals 20 minutes, turning and basting occasionally with sauce.

Ribs may also be left in oven and baked at 350 degrees 20 to 30 minutes, basting occasionally.

Sauce may also be used on chicken.

SERVES 4

3-5 tablespoons canola or safflower oil, divided
1 large clove garlic, minced
3-4 green onions, in ¼-inch slices, including some green
2 8-ounce pork tenderloins, trimmed, in 3-inch strips,
    ½ inch wide
2 cups broccoli flowerets
*2 cups sliced portobello mushrooms, in 3-inch strips,
    ½ inch thick
2 teaspoons grated fresh ginger root
1 red pepper, seeded, in strips
1 yellow pepper, seeded, in strips
1 green pepper, seeded, in strips
1 tablespoon soy sauce
3 tablespoons dry sherry
    freshly ground pepper to taste, optional
    cooked rice or couscous

In wok or large heavy skillet heat 2 tablespoons canola oil until very hot. Add garlic and green onions. Stir fry 1 to 2 minutes. Add meat. Cook until brown on all sides, stirring constantly. Remove from wok with slotted spoon. Set aside.

Add 1 tablespoon canola oil and broccoli to wok. Cook 2 minutes, stirring constantly. Remove with slotted spoon. Set aside. Add mushrooms and ginger root. Cook 1 to 2 minutes, stirring constantly. Remove with slotted spoon. Set aside. Add more canola oil if necessary. Stir in peppers and cook 2 to 3 minutes. Blend in soy sauce, sherry, and pepper, if desired.

Return meat and green onions, broccoli, and mushrooms to wok. Mix well. Heat through. Serve with rice or couscous.

*May substitute other mushrooms if portobellos are not available.

PORK MEDALLIONS WITH ORANGE ROSEMARY GLAZE

SERVES 4

1/2   **cup white vinegar**
1/4   **cup sugar**
1   **cup fresh orange juice**
1   **tablespoon fresh lime juice**
1/2   **teaspoon dried rosemary, crumbled**
    salt to taste
    pepper to taste
1 1/2-2   **pound pork tenderloin, fat trimmed, in 1-inch slices**

In small saucepan combine vinegar and sugar. Simmer until sugar is dissolved and liquid is reduced by half, stirring occasionally. Add orange juice. Simmer 20 to 25 minutes or until syrup is thick enough to coat wooden spoon. Remove from heat. Add lime juice, rosemary, salt, and pepper. Set aside.

Season pork to taste. Grill or broil on lightly oiled rack 2 to 3 minutes per side or to desired doneness. Brush pork with reserved glaze during last minute of cooking. Serve with remaining warm glaze.

See photo page 188.

PORK CHOPS IN ORANGE SAUCE

SERVES 4

4   **pork loin chops**
5   **tablespoons butter, divided**
3   **tablespoons flour**
1   **teaspoon ginger**
1   **cup orange juice**
1/2   **cup water**
1/2   **cup Sauterne**
1/2   **cup brown sugar**
2   **tablespoons grated orange rind**
1/2   **teaspoon salt**

In large skillet brown chops in 2 tablespoons butter. Remove chops from skillet. Add remaining 3 tablespoons butter and melt. Blend in flour and ginger to make smooth paste. Add orange juice, water, and Sauterne. Cook until mixture comes to boil stirring constantly. Blend in brown sugar, orange rind, and salt. Return meat to skillet. Cover and simmer 45 minutes, turning and basting chops occasionally.

SESAME PORK KABOBS

SERVES 6

MARINADE:

1/2   **cup unsweetened pineapple juice**
1/4   **cup soy sauce**
1/4   **cup finely sliced green onions**
4   **teaspoons sesame seed**
1   **tablespoon brown sugar**
1   **clove garlic, peeled**
1/8   **teaspoon pepper**

2   **whole 1¾- to 2-pound pork tenderloins,
      in 1½- to 2-inch pieces**
1/2   **teaspoon cornstarch**
2   **tablespoons water**
2   **large onions, sliced**
1   **pound fresh mushrooms**
2   **red peppers, seeded, in chunks**
2   **green peppers, seeded, in chunks**

In large bowl combine all marinade ingredients. Mix well. Add pork to marinade. Cover. Refrigerate overnight.

Drain pork, reserving marinade. In small bowl blend cornstarch and water. Stir into marinade. In small saucepan cook marinade over medium heat until thickened. Thread pork on skewers, alternating with onions, mushrooms, and peppers. Brush with marinade. Grill over hot coals 12 minutes or to desired doneness, turning frequently and brushing with marinade.

SMOTHERED PORK CHOPS

SERVES 4

4   **pork chops, 1½ inches thick**
3   **tablespoons butter**
3   **cups very thinly sliced potatoes, divided**
1   **teaspoon salt, divided**
½   **teaspoon freshly ground pepper, divided**
1   **large onion, thinly sliced**
2   **tablespoons flour**
14½   **ounces canned plum tomatoes with juice, cut in pieces**
½   **teaspoon marjoram**

In large skillet brown chops in butter on both sides. In medium casserole layer 1½ cups potatoes. Sprinkle with a fourth of salt and pepper. Place onion over potatoes. Season with a fourth of salt and pepper. Cover with remaining 1½ cups potatoes. Season with a fourth of salt and pepper. Place chops over potatoes.

Add flour to drippings in skillet. Mix until smooth. Slowly add tomatoes and juice over low heat. Season with remaining salt and pepper and marjoram. Pour sauce over chops. Cover. Bake in preheated 350-degree oven 45 minutes.

MEDALLIONS OF PORK TENDERLOIN

SERVES 3 TO 4

1½   **pound pork tenderloin, sliced into 1½-inch pieces**
4   **teaspoons lemon pepper**
4   **tablespoons butter**
4   **tablespoons lemon juice**
2   **tablespoons Worcestershire sauce**
2   **teaspoons Dijon mustard**
2   **tablespoons minced parsley and/or chives**

Place each piece of tenderloin between 2 sheets of plastic wrap. Flatten slightly with heel of hand. Sprinkle meat with lemon pepper. In medium heavy skillet heat butter. Cook pork slices 3 to 4 minutes on each side or until desired doneness. Remove meat to serving platter. Keep warm.

Add lemon juice, Worcestershire sauce, and mustard to skillet. Cook, stirring with pan juices until heated. Pour sauce over meat. Sprinkle with parsley and/or chives.

SERVES 4

2	**pounds boneless pork loin, in 1½-inch slices**
1	**cup fresh orange juice**
⅓	**cup fresh lemon juice**
1⅓	**teaspoons oregano**
1⅓	**teaspoons cumin**
1⅓	**teaspoons white pepper**
10	**cloves garlic, peeled, quartered**
1	**bay leaf**
1¼	**cups chopped Spanish onions**
5-6	**tablespoons orange marmalade**
2	**oranges, peeled, sectioned**

Place pork in shallow ovenproof casserole. In medium bowl combine orange juice, lemon juice, oregano, cumin, white pepper, garlic, bay leaf, and onions. Mix well. Pour over pork slices. Turn meat to coat well. Cover casserole with plastic wrap. Refrigerate 3 hours or overnight, turning meat occasionally. Remove plastic wrap. Cover casserole with lid or foil.

Bake in preheated 325-degree oven 3 hours or until done. Remove pork slices to serving dish. Keep warm. Pour remaining marinade and pan drippings into small saucepan. Stir marmalade into saucepan over medium heat until melted. Add orange sections. Heat. Pour over meat.

CHILE VERDE

SERVES 10   *Hot and delicious !*

1/3 **cup bacon drippings**
4   **pounds pork shoulder, in 1- to 1½-inch cubes**
1   **large yellow onion, diced**
5   **cloves garlic, minced**
1   **large tomato, seeded, chopped**
7   **ounces canned green chilies, diced**
     vegetable oil as needed
1   **tablespoon freshly ground pepper**
1   **tablespoon Cajun spice**
1/2 **teaspoon cumin**
16   **ounces prepared green chili salsa, hot, medium, or mild**
2½   **cups water**
     salt to taste

In large pot heat bacon drippings to very hot. Brown pork cubes, 1 cup at a time. Remove pork and all but ⅓ cup drippings.

Sauté onion, garlic, tomato, and green chilies in drippings, adding vegetable oil if drippings are insufficient. Add pepper, Cajun spice, and cumin. Mix well. Add pork, salsa, water, and salt. Simmer covered 1½ hours. Uncover and cook 30 minutes.

GRILLED VEAL CHOPS

SERVES 2

1   **shallot, minced**
3   **tablespoons margarine or butter, melted**
1/2 **cup fresh lemon juice**
1   **tablespoon coarsely chopped fresh basil**
     freshly ground pepper to taste
2   **veal chops, 1 to 1½ inches thick**

In medium bowl combine shallot, margarine, lemon juice, basil, and pepper. Mix well. Marinate chops in mixture at room temperature 1 hour. Remove chops to hot grill. Baste with marinade. Cover grill. Grill 12 to 15 minutes or to desired doneness, turning 2 or 3 times and basting well with marinade each time.

RACK OF VEAL WITH GARLIC AND ROSEMARY

SERVES 6

6 tablespoons unsalted butter, room temperature
6 large cloves garlic
1/3 cup fresh rosemary leaves or 5 teaspoons dried
      rosemary, crumbled
2 tablespoons minced parsley
1 teaspoon salt
1 teaspoon freshly ground pepper
2 lemons, thinly sliced
4 pound rack of veal (6 ribs)
1 cup chicken broth or veal stock
   sprigs rosemary
   lemon slices

In food processor combine butter, garlic, rosemary, parsley, salt, and pepper. Process until smooth. Arrange lemon slices in roasting pan. Rub butter mixture over veal. Place veal over lemon slices. Bake in lower third of preheated 350-degree oven 1¼ to 1½ hours or until meat thermometer registers 130 degrees. Let veal stand 15 minutes. Transfer to platter.

Add chicken broth to roasting pan and heat on top of stove until boiling. Stir vigorously to scrape up brown bits. Strain into gravy boat. Slice veal. Garnish with sprigs rosemary and lemon slices. Pass sauce.

SICILIAN VEAL CHOP

SERVES 4

3/4 cup toasted bread crumbs
3/4 cup freshly grated Parmesan cheese
3/4 teaspoon salt
2 large cloves garlic, minced
4 veal chops with rib bone, 1 inch thick
2 eggs, beaten
1/4 pound butter or margarine

In medium shallow bowl combine bread crumbs, cheese, salt, and garlic. Mix well. Dip each chop in egg and then in bread crumb mixture.

In medium skillet sauté coated chops in butter until well browned on both sides. Arrange chops in foil-lined baking pan. Bake in preheated 450-degree oven 10 minutes.

VEAL BRISKET

SERVES 6

3-4 **pound veal brisket**

2 **tablespoons vegetable oil**

1/2 **teaspoon salt, plus salt to taste, divided**

freshly ground pepper to taste

1 **large onion, chopped**

1 **clove garlic, sliced or minced**

1 **tablespoon tomato paste**

1/4 **cup white wine**

1 **tablespoon chopped parsley**

1/4-1/2 **teaspoon dried thyme**

1/8 **teaspoon celery salt**

2 **carrots, sliced**

sprigs dill or 1/2 teaspoon dill weed

1/2 **pound fresh mushrooms, sliced**

1 **tablespoon margarine**

In large roasting pan place large sheet heavy-duty foil. Lay brisket on foil. Drizzle oil over brisket. Add 1/2 teaspoon salt, pepper, onion, and garlic. Fold foil tightly around brisket. Bake in preheated 350-degree oven 1 hour.

Uncover meat but do not remove from pan or foil. Remove all juices to medium saucepan. Add tomato paste, wine, parsley, thyme, and celery salt to juices. Bring to boil. Reduce heat. Simmer 3 minutes. Pour over brisket in foil. Add carrots and dill. Partially close foil. Bake in 350-degree oven 1 hour or until tender, basting frequently. Add boiling water as needed if gravy evaporates.

In small skillet sauté mushrooms in margarine. Set aside. Remove brisket to serving platter. Pour juice from foil into saucepan. Add water if needed and season to taste. Heat. Cover meat with carrots, onion, and mushrooms. Pour gravy over vegetables and meat.

VEAL GOULASH

3   **onions, chopped**
6   **tablespoons butter, divided**
3   **pounds veal, in 1-inch cubes**
1/2 **cup chicken broth**
1   **cup dry white wine**
1   **tablespoon paprika**
2 1/2 **teaspoons salt, or to taste**
1/4 **teaspoon pepper**
1   **teaspoon lemon juice**
2   **tablespoons flour**
8   **ounces sour cream or lite sour cream**
1/2 **pound sliced fresh mushrooms**
1/4 **cup chopped parsley**
6   **cups hot cooked noodles**

In Dutch oven sauté onions in 4 tablespoons butter about 10 minutes until tender. Add veal. Cook 5 minutes, stirring frequently. Blend in chicken broth, wine, paprika, salt, and pepper. Bring to boil. Reduce heat. Simmer covered 1 to 1 1/2 hours until meat is tender. With slotted spoon remove veal. Set aside. Strain sauce, reserving strained onion mixture. Return liquid to Dutch oven.

In food processor or blender process strained onion mixture until smooth. Add to Dutch oven. Stir in lemon juice.

In small bowl combine flour and sour cream. Mix well. Stir into sauce. Add veal.

In small skillet sauté mushrooms in remaining 2 tablespoons butter. Stir into goulash. Simmer uncovered 10 minutes. Serve sprinkled with parsley over noodles.

NOODLE PANCAKE WITH BEEF
AND GREEN ONIONS

SERVES 6

1½   teaspoons cornstarch
2½   teaspoons oyster sauce
6   tablespoons soy sauce, divided
2¼   teaspoons sesame oil, divided
4   teaspoons sherry, divided
2   pounds flank steak, cut in thirds lengthwise, then
      cut thinly against grain
10   ounces uncooked Chinese noodles
9   tablespoons vegetable oil, divided
16   large green onions with tops
2   large cloves garlic, minced
2½   teaspoons hoisin sauce
1⅓   tablespoons brown sugar

In small bowl combine cornstarch, oyster sauce, 4 tablespoons soy sauce, 1½ teaspoons sesame oil, and 2⅔ teaspoons sherry. Mix well. Place sliced beef in large plastic bag. Pour cornstarch mixture over beef. Seal bag. Marinate beef at room temperature 2 hours. In medium saucepan cook noodles in boiling water 5 minutes. Drain.

In large skillet heat 3 tablespoons vegetable oil over high heat. Spread noodles evenly over bottom of skillet and press down to form pancake. Cook 10 minutes or until crisp and golden brown. Turn carefully, adding additional 3 tablespoons oil if needed. Cook until crisp and golden brown. Transfer to large ovenproof serving platter. Place in preheated 250-degree oven.

Cut green onions to fit horizontally in feed tube of food processor. Slice lengthwise in processor.

Add remaining 3 tablespoons vegetable oil to skillet over medium heat. Add beef. Cook 3 minutes or until beef is no longer pink. Add garlic and green onions. Cook 30 seconds or until just wilted.

In small bowl combine hoisin sauce, brown sugar, remaining 1⅓ teaspoons sherry, 2 tablespoons soy sauce, and ¾ teaspoon sesame oil. Add to beef mixture. Cook 1 to 2 minutes until heated, stirring constantly. Pour beef mixture over pancake.

May substitute thinly sliced, boned, skinned chicken breast or shrimp for flank steak.

SHORT RIBS BISTRO STYLE

SERVES 4

1/4 cup flour
   salt to taste
   freshly ground pepper to taste
4 pounds beef short ribs, in 3- to 4-inch pieces
4 tablespoons olive oil, divided
4 cloves garlic, finely chopped
1 1/2 cups coarsely chopped onions
1 1/2 cups dry red wine
4 tablespoons tomato paste
3 cups beef broth
2 bay leaves
1 1/2 teaspoons marjoram
2 large potatoes, cubed
4 large carrots, in 2-inch pieces
2 medium turnips, peeled, in 2-inch cubes
6 sprigs parsley, chopped

In small bowl combine flour, salt, and pepper. Mix well. Sprinkle ribs with mixture, coating well.

In large heavy pot heat 2 tablespoons olive oil. Brown ribs on all sides about 10 minutes. Remove ribs to plate. Pour off and discard fat from pot. Add remaining 2 tablespoons olive oil. Sauté garlic and onions over medium heat about 10 minutes. Add wine. Boil about 7 minutes until thick. Stir in tomato paste, beef broth, bay leaves, and marjoram. Return ribs to pot. Bring to boil. Reduce heat and simmer covered 1 1/2 hours.

Add potatoes, carrots, turnips, and parsley to pot. Simmer covered 50 minutes or until meat and vegetables are tender and sauce thickens.

Transfer ribs to serving platter. Skim surface fat from sauce. Season to taste. Pour sauce over ribs.

BRAISED POT ROAST

SERVES 6 TO 8

4	**pound lean pot roast**
2	**tablespoons vegetable oil**
2	**onions, thinly sliced**
1	**green pepper, seeded, in small pieces**
1	**cup ketchup**
2	**tablespoons prepared horseradish**
1½	**cups water**
½	**teaspoon garlic powder**
	pinch basil
	salt and freshly ground pepper to taste

In Dutch oven brown pot roast in oil. Pour off oil. In medium saucepan combine remaining ingredients. Simmer 10 minutes. Pour mixture over meat. Bake tightly covered in preheated 300-degree oven 3 hours.

VARIATION:
Substitute 4 pounds lean short ribs for pot roast.

CHARCOAL GRILLED FLANK STEAK

SERVES 4 TO 6

¾	**cup vegetable oil**
¼	**cup soy sauce**
3	**tablespoons honey**
2	**tablespoons red wine vinegar**
1	**clove garlic, crushed**
1	**green onion, chopped**
2	**pound flank steak**

In small bowl combine all ingredients except flank steak. Place steak in large plastic bag. Add marinade. Seal bag. Refrigerate overnight, turning occasionally. Drain steak and grill over very hot coals 4 to 5 minutes on each side. To serve, slice in thin diagonal slices across grain.

MUSHROOM STUFFED GRILLED FLANK STEAK

SERVES 4

1/2	**cup soy sauce (may use lite)**
2	**tablespoons dry sherry**
1/2	**teaspoon ginger or 1 tablespoon chopped fresh ginger root**
3/4	**teaspoon pepper, divided**
1 1/2	**pound flank steak**
2	**ounces shallots, peeled, chopped**
2	**tablespoons butter or margarine**
3	**ounces shiitake mushrooms, thinly sliced**
3	**ounces oyster mushrooms, thinly sliced**
4	**ounces white mushrooms, thinly sliced**
1/4	**teaspoon salt**

In large shallow dish combine soy sauce, sherry, ginger, and 1/2 teaspoon pepper. Mix well. Marinate flank steak in mixture 1 hour. Drain meat, reserving marinade.

In medium skillet sauté shallots in butter until opaque. Add mushrooms, salt, and remaining 1/4 teaspoon pepper. Sauté until tender. Cool. Spread mushroom mixture over steak. Roll steak from long side. Tie with string in 4 or 5 places. Secure ends with toothpicks. Grill 5 minutes or to desired doneness on each of 4 sides, basting with marinade.

ON PLATTER UPPER LEFT: LEMON BLUEBERRY CORNMEAL MUFFINS, MORNING GLORY MUFFINS, CHEATER SCHNECKEN, AND SWIRLED APRICOT CREAM CHEESE BREAD. AT RIGHT: VEGETABE TORTE.

CLOCKWISE
FROM UPPER LEFT:
ROCK CORNISH
HENS WITH GINGER

CLEMENTINE SAUCE
AND PAN-FRIED
GARLIC POTATOES

WOVEN SALMON
WITH TOMATO AND
SPINACH SAUCES

LEFT TO RIGHT:
SCALLOPS WITH SAF-
FRON LEEK SAUCE,
CATFISH TRICOLORE
IN PARCHMENT, AND
SHRIMP PIRI PIRI

CLOCKWISE
FROM UPPER LEFT:
BEST EVER CORN
BREAD, TURKEY LOAF
WITH HERBS, MASHED
POTATOES WITH
HORSERADISH, AND
TEQUILA CHICKEN
WITH CITRUS SALSA

PEPPER STEAK

SERVES 4 TO 5

2	**pounds beef tenderloin tips, in 1/2-inch slices or strips**
1/4	**pound butter or margarine**
	salt to taste
	pepper to taste
1/2	**teaspoon basil, divided**
1/2	**teaspoon rosemary, divided**
1	**medium onion, chopped**
1	**green pepper, julienned**
1/2	**pound fresh mushrooms, sliced**
1	**cup white wine, preferably Chablis**
28	**ounces canned crushed tomatoes**
1/4-1/2	**cup minced parsley**
12	**ounces canned Chinese chow mein or rice noodles, optional**

In large skillet cook meat in butter over high heat until rare. Season with salt, pepper, 1/4 teaspoon basil, and 1/4 teaspoon rosemary. With slotted spoon remove meat from skillet. Set aside.

In same skillet combine onion, green pepper, mushrooms, remaining 1/4 teaspoon basil, and remaining 1/4 teaspoon rosemary. Cook 2 to 3 minutes. Add wine. Bring to boil. Reduce heat and simmer 1 minute. Add tomatoes. Simmer uncovered 4 minutes. Add reserved meat and parsley. Cook several minutes until liquid is reduced. Serve over Chinese noodles, if desired.

TOP TO BOTTOM:
PORK MEDALLIONS
WITH ORANGE ROSE-
MARY GLAZE, RACK
OF LAMB WITH ROSE-
MARY SAUCE, AND
PISTACHIO CRUSTED
SWEET POTATOES.

2-HOUR MARINATED BEEF TENDERLOIN

SERVES 8 TO 10

2/3 **cup wine vinegar**
1/2 **cup ketchup**
4 **tablespoons vegetable oil**
4 **tablespoons soy sauce**
2 **tablespoons Worcestershire sauce**
1 **teaspoon dry mustard**
1 **teaspoon salt**
1/2 **teaspoon pepper**
1/2 **teaspoon garlic salt**
4-5 **pound beef tenderloin**

In medium bowl combine all ingredients except meat. Mix well. Place meat in large plastic bag. Pour marinade in bag. Seal bag. Place bag in deep bowl. Marinade meat at room temperature 2 hours.

Remove meat from marinade. Transfer to rack in shallow roasting pan. Bake uncovered in preheated 475-degree oven 35 to 45 minutes for rare (140 degrees on meat thermometer), or 60 minutes for medium (160 degrees on meat thermometer). Remove from oven and let stand 15 minutes before slicing.

Marinade is also excellent with pork, lamb, flank steak, and meat kabobs.

OVERNIGHT MARINATED BEEF TENDERLOIN

SERVES 8 TO 10

1½   cups beer
½   cup vegetable oil
3   cloves garlic, divided
2   tablespoons lemon juice
1   tablespoon sugar
1   teaspoon salt
2   tablespoons dried marjoram, crushed
4-5 pound beef tenderloin

In medium bowl combine beer, oil, 1 minced clove garlic, lemon juice, sugar, salt, and marjoram. Mix well. Slice remaining 2 cloves garlic into 3 to 4 pieces each. Insert garlic evenly throughout tenderloin with small cuts in meat. Place tenderloin in large glass or enamel dish. Pour marinade over meat. Refrigerate covered overnight.

Before baking let meat return to room temperature. Remove tenderloin from marinade and transfer to rack in shallow roasting pan. Bake uncovered in pre-heated 475-degree oven 35 to 45 minutes for rare (140 degrees on meat thermometer), or 60 minutes for medium (160 degrees on meat thermometer). Remove from oven and let stand 15 minutes before slicing.

ROUND-UP STEAK

SERVES 4

3   teaspoons vegetable oil, divided
1   Spanish onion, thinly sliced
1   red pepper, in thin strips
2   tablespoons coarse-grained mustard
¼   cup water
     salt to taste
     freshly ground pepper to taste
4   4-ounce beef tenderloin steaks, 1 inch thick, fat trimmed

In large skillet heat 2 teaspoons oil over medium heat. Add onion and cook 5 minutes, stirring constantly. Add red pepper. Cook about 5 minutes.

In small bowl combine mustard and water. Mix well. Add to onion mixture. Cook 2 minutes or until most of liquid has evaporated. Season to taste. Keep warm.

Brush steaks with remaining 1 teaspoon oil. Season with salt and liberally with pepper. Grill steaks to desired doneness. Serve with onion-pepper mixture.

STIR-FRIED BEEF AND BROCCOLI

SERVES 3 TO 4

4   **teaspoons plus 1 tablespoon soy sauce, divided**
1/4   **teaspoon sugar**
3/4   **pound 1/2-inch-thick sirloin or tenderloin steak, in 3-inch julienne strips**
1   **tablespoon cornstarch**
1   **tablespoon sherry**
1/2   **teaspoon beef concentrate**
1/4   **cup plus 1/3 cup water, divided**
2   **teaspoons sesame oil**
1   **pound fresh broccoli**
3   **tablespoons vegetable oil, divided**
1   **tablespoon minced fresh ginger root**
2   **large cloves garlic, minced**
1/2   **teaspoon dried crushed red pepper, or to taste**
  Chinese rice noodles or rice, cooked

In medium bowl combine 4 teaspoons soy sauce and sugar. Mix well. Add meat. Blend well. Set aside. In small bowl mix cornstarch and 1 tablespoon soy sauce. Add sherry. In another small bowl mix beef concentrate and 1/4 cup water. Add to cornstarch mixture with sesame oil. Set aside.

Separate broccoli into flowerets and cut stems into 1/2 inch pieces. In wok or large heavy skillet heat 2 tablespoons vegetable oil until hot. Add beef. Stir briefly until meat loses red color. Transfer to bowl.

Add remaining 1 tablespoon vegetable oil to wok. Stir in ginger root, garlic, and red pepper. Add broccoli. Stir fry 1 minute. Add 1/3 cup water. Cover and steam 1 minute or until tender-crisp. Stir in cornstarch mixture and beef and its juices. Stir mixture over medium heat until sauce is thickened and hot. Serve with Chinese rice noodles or over rice.

OVEN BARBECUED BRISKET

SERVES 8 TO 10

2	tablespoons brown sugar
1	teaspoon celery seed
1/4	teaspoon garlic powder
1/4	teaspoon paprika
1/4	teaspoon onion powder
1/2	teaspoon salt
1/2	teaspoon freshly ground pepper
1	teaspoon Liquid Smoke
3 1/2-4	pound beef brisket, fat trimmed
1 1/4	cups barbecue sauce

In small bowl combine brown sugar, celery seed, garlic powder, paprika, onion powder, salt, pepper, and Liquid Smoke. Mix well. Score brisket. Coat both sides of meat with seasoning paste. Wrap meat tightly in plastic wrap. Place in plastic bag. Refrigerate at least 12 hours. Unwrap brisket. Transfer to roasting pan.

Bake brisket in preheated 300-degree oven 45 minutes per pound or until tender. Cool. Refrigerate at least 1 hour. Reserving juices, remove fat particles. Slice beef across grain into thin slices.

In small bowl mix 1 cup pan juices and barbecue sauce. Return sliced meat to pan. Pour barbecue sauce mixture over meat. Cover pan with aluminum foil. Bake in preheated 325-degree oven 45 minutes.

EASY BRISKET

SERVES 8 TO 10

1/2	cup yellow mustard
1/2	cup ketchup
1/2	cup chili sauce
6-7	pound lean beef brisket
2	large Spanish onions, thickly sliced

In small bowl combine mustard, ketchup, and chili sauce. Mix well. Place brisket in roasting pan. Spread condiment mixture liberally over meat. Add 2 inches water to roasting pan. Distribute onions around meat.

Bake uncovered in preheated 300-degree oven 5 to 6 hours or until tender, basting occasionally. Add water if liquid evaporates. Cover pan if meat browns too quickly.

VIENNESE BEEF STEW

3 pounds beef rump or chuck, in 2-inch cubes
4 tablespoons butter or margarine
2 tablespoons vegetable oil
6 medium onions, peeled, thinly sliced
1/4 cup Hungarian paprika
1/4 cup cider vinegar
    salt to taste
    pepper to taste
1 teaspoon thyme
1/2 cup tomato sauce
3-4 tablespoons flour
2 cups beef broth, divided
1 tablespoon caraway seed
    grated rind of 1 lemon
2 cloves garlic
10-12 ounces cooked spätzle or noodles

In large heavy pot brown beef in butter and oil. Remove beef and set aside. Add onions to pot and sauté until golden, adding more butter and oil if necessary. Stir in paprika and vinegar. Cook 5 minutes. Add reserved beef, salt, pepper, thyme, and tomato sauce.

In small bowl whisk flour into 1/2 cup beef broth and stir with remaining 1 1/2 cups beef broth into meat mixture. Simmer partially covered about 1 hour until meat is tender.

In food processor or blender or with mortar and pestle combine caraway seed, lemon rind, and garlic. Blend well. Stir into stew. Simmer 10 minutes. Serve with spätzle or noodles.

STUFFED ZUCCHINI SUPPER

SERVES 6

Great family fare.

TOMATO SAUCE:

1   medium onion, coarsely chopped
4   ribs celery, chopped
1/2 cup chopped parsley
4   tablespoons butter or margarine
     salt to taste
     pepper to taste
30   ounces tomato sauce

6   medium zucchini, each 5 inches long
1/2 teaspoon seasoned salt
1   pound ground beef
1   medium onion, coarsely chopped
2   tablespoons butter or margarine
1/4 pound ham, in cubes
2   slices white bread, in small pieces
8   ounces cream cheese, softened, divided
2   eggs, divided
1/2 cup chopped parsley, divided
     salt to taste
     pepper to taste

For tomato sauce, sauté onion, celery, and parsley in butter in large skillet about 5 minutes until golden. Add salt, pepper, and tomato sauce. Simmer covered 45 minutes. Pour into bottom of 9- by 13-inch glass baking dish, reserving 1½ cups sauce. Set aside prepared dish.

In large pot boil zucchini in salted water until tender. Cut in half lengthwise. Scoop out center and reserve. Sprinkle zucchini shells with seasoned salt. Place shells upside down on paper towels.

In skillet brown beef. Remove from skillet. In same skillet combine onion and butter. Cook slightly. Add ham, reserved beef, zucchini pulp, and bread. Cook 2 minutes.

Transfer half of meat mixture to food processor. Add 4 ounces cream cheese, 1 egg, and ¼ cup parsley. Process until coarsely chopped. Season to taste. Fill 6 zucchini shells with mixture. Repeat procedure with remaining meat mixture, cream cheese, egg, and parsley. Place zucchini shells in baking dish with tomato sauce. Bake in preheated 350-degree oven 20 to 35 minutes or until filling is firm, basting 2 or 3 times with reserved tomato sauce.

ITALIAN CHILI

SERVES 8

3   large onions, halved, thinly sliced
2   green peppers, seeded, in large chunks
4   cloves garlic, minced
1/3   cup olive oil
1½   pounds Italian sausage, in casings
56   ounces canned Italian whole tomatoes, drained
30   ounces canned kidney beans, drained
15   ounces tomato sauce
2   cups red wine
2   tablespoons chopped fresh oregano or
     2 teaspoons dried oregano
2   tablespoons chopped fresh basil or 2 teaspoons dried basil
¾   teaspoon salt
¾   teaspoon freshly ground pepper
1½   cups freshly grated Parmesan cheese

In large skillet sauté onions, peppers, and garlic in olive oil over medium heat until limp. Transfer to large pot. Set aside.

In same skillet sauté sausage 2 to 3 minutes or until very lightly browned. Remove from skillet. Slice into ¼-inch pieces, removing casings, if desired. Add sausage to pot. Stir in tomatoes, kidney beans, tomato sauce, wine, oregano, basil, salt, and pepper. Simmer uncovered 1 to 2 hours or until thickened. Just before serving stir in cheese.

CHUTNEY CHOP

SERVES 1

2   tablespoons fresh fine bread crumbs
¼   teaspoon dried rosemary, crumbled
     salt to taste
     pepper to taste
1   tablespoon premium mango chutney, divided
1   2-inch-thick loin lamb chop, well trimmed

In small shallow dish combine bread crumbs, rosemary, salt, and pepper. Mix well. Spread ½ tablespoon chutney on 1 side of chop. Dip chop chutney side down into crumb mixture. Spread remaining ½ tablespoon chutney on uncovered side of chop. Dip second side into mixture. Place chop in ungreased baking dish. Sprinkle with remaining crumb mixture. Bake in preheated 450-degree oven 20 to 25 minutes for medium-rare.

BUTTERFLIED LEG OF LAMB ON THE GRILL

SERVES 8

1	**clove garlic, crushed**
¾	**cup vegetable oil**
¼	**cup red wine vinegar**
½	**cup chopped onion**
2	**teaspoons Dijon mustard**
2	**teaspoons salt**
½	**teaspoon pepper**
½	**teaspoon oregano**
½	**teaspoon basil**
1	**bay leaf, crumbled**
6-7	**pound leg of lamb, boned, butterflied**

In jar with tight-fitting lid combine all ingredients except lamb. Shake to mix well. Place meat fat side down in large shallow pan. Pour marinade over lamb. Cover tightly. Refrigerate overnight, turning at least once.

Remove meat from refrigerator 1 hour before cooking. Broil fat side up 10 minutes, basting with marinade. Turn, baste, and broil 10 minutes. Grill over hot coals 15 to 20 minutes, testing for doneness. Meat should be pink. In small saucepan simmer remaining marinade 5 minutes and serve with meat.

RACK OF LAMB WITH ROSEMARY SAUCE

SERVES 8

12	**ounces Dijon mustard**
3	**tablespoons soy sauce**
3	**cloves garlic, minced**
3	**teaspoons rosemary**
3	**teaspoons thyme**
¾	**teaspoon ginger**
6	**tablespoons vegetable oil**
2	**teaspoons cracked peppercorns**
3	**racks of lamb**

In food processor or blender combine all ingredients except peppercorns and lamb. Blend well. Add peppercorns. In large bowl marinate lamb in sauce in refrigerator overnight.

Bring lamb to room temperature before cooking. Drain lamb, reserving sauce. In roasting pan bake lamb in preheated 500-degree oven 10 minutes. Reduce heat to 300 degrees and bake 25 to 35 minutes or to desired doneness, preferably pink, basting with sauce every 10 minutes. In small saucepan simmer remaining sauce 5 minutes. Serve sauce on side. See photo page 188.

BARBECUED LEG OF LAMB

SERVES 8 TO 10

4   **tablespoons Dijon mustard**
4   **tablespoons tarragon vinegar**
5   **tablespoons olive oil, divided**
8   **pound leg of lamb, butterflied**
4   **cups tomato sauce**
2   **tablespoons Worcestershire sauce**
1/4   **teaspoon celery salt**
1   **clove garlic, minced**
1   **small onion, minced**
2   **tablespoons sherry**
2   **tablespoons red wine vinegar**
    salt and pepper to taste

In large bowl combine mustard, tarragon vinegar, and 4 tablespoons olive oil. Mix well. Marinate lamb in mixture covered overnight in refrigerator.

In medium saucepan combine tomato sauce, Worcestershire sauce, celery salt, garlic, onion, sherry, red wine vinegar, remaining 1 tablespoon olive oil, salt, and pepper. Mix well. Simmer mixture 5 minutes, stirring constantly.

Grill lamb 20 to 30 minutes, basting frequently with cooked sauce. Serve with sauce on side.

LEFTOVER LAMB CURRY

SERVES 4

1   **teaspoon butter or margarine**
1   **medium onion, chopped**
1½-2   **pounds cooked lamb, in 1-inch cubes**
    salt and pepper to taste
½   **teaspoon Dijon mustard**
1-1½   **teaspoons curry powder**
    leftover juices and/or gravy from lamb plus enough
      water to measure 1 cup
    cooked rice or couscous

CONDIMENTS:
    currants, flaked coconut, chopped salted nuts, and chutney

In large skillet melt butter. Add onion. Sauté 2 to 3 minutes. Add lamb. Brown on all sides. Stir in salt, pepper, mustard, curry powder, and gravy mixture. Bring to boil. Reduce heat. Simmer 3 minutes. Serve over rice or couscous with condiments.

POULTRY

CHICKEN IN BALSAMIC VINEGAR SAUCE

SERVES 4

10	ounces eggplant, peeled, in 1/2-inch pieces
	salt to taste
2	chicken breasts, skinned, halved
	pepper to taste
3	tablespoons unsalted butter, divided
2	tablespoons olive oil, divided
8	cloves garlic, unpeeled
1 1/3	cups water, divided
1	cup chopped red onion
6	tablespoons balsamic vinegar, divided
1	tablespoon tomato paste
1	teaspoon chopped fresh thyme or 1/2 teaspoon dried thyme
1	tomato, peeled, seeded, diced
1-2	tablespoons chopped parsley
	cooked pasta

Sprinkle eggplant with salt. Let stand 30 minutes to remove bitterness. Rinse and pat dry with paper towel. Set aside.

Sprinkle chicken with salt and pepper. In large skillet heat 1 tablespoon butter and 1 tablespoon olive oil. Sauté chicken over medium heat until brown on both sides. Remove from skillet, reserving drippings in skillet.

In small saucepan combine garlic and 1 cup water. Bring to boil. Cook 10 minutes. Drain and peel garlic, cutting cloves in half.

Sauté onion and reserved eggplant in chicken drippings until soft. Stir in 5 tablespoons vinegar. Bring to boil. Simmer 3 minutes to reduce slightly. Stir in tomato paste. Add chicken, garlic, thyme, and remaining 1/3 cup water. Simmer 15 to 20 minutes until chicken is tender.

While chicken cooks marinate tomato in remaining 1 tablespoon olive oil and 1 tablespoon vinegar. To serve, transfer chicken to serving platter. Add remaining 2 tablespoons butter to skillet. Cook sauce over low heat, stirring constantly. Stir in tomato and parsley. Spoon sauce over chicken. Serve with pasta.

CHICKEN SMOTHERED IN VEGETABLES

SERVES 8

½ cup flour
1 teaspoon salt
½ teaspoon freshly ground pepper
4 chicken breasts, boned, skinned, halved
2 cloves garlic, minced
1½ cups sliced onion
¼ cup olive oil
*1 green pepper, seeded, sliced
2 cups sliced fresh mushrooms
2 teaspoons chopped fresh oregano
10 cherry tomatoes or 3 whole tomatoes, sliced

In large plastic bag combine flour, salt, and pepper. Coat chicken by shaking in bag. Arrange chicken in greased shallow baking pan. Grind additional pepper over chicken.

In large skillet sauté garlic and onion in olive oil until soft. Stir in green pepper, mushrooms, and oregano. Cook 1 minute. Add tomatoes. Pour vegetables over chicken. Bake in preheated 375-degree oven 45 minutes.

*1 cup broccoli flowerets may be substituted for green pepper.

SAUTÉED CHICKEN BREASTS WITH LEMON AND CAPERS

SERVES 6 TO 8

4 chicken breasts, boned, skinned, halved
½ cup flour
1 teaspoon salt
½ teaspoon paprika
¼ teaspoon pepper
4 tablespoons margarine, melted
2 tablespoons olive oil
4 tablespoons white wine
3 tablespoons fresh lemon juice
3-4 tablespoons capers

continued

Flatten chicken breasts between sheets of wax paper. In medium bowl combine flour, salt, paprika, and pepper. Mix well. Dredge each chicken piece in mixture, shaking off excess.

In large skillet heat margarine and olive oil until bubbly. Sauté chicken breasts on both sides about 3 to 4 minutes per side until lightly browned. Remove chicken to ovenproof platter. Place in preheated 250-degree oven.

Add wine to hot skillet, scraping any browned pieces. Stir in lemon juice. Simmer 1 minute. Return chicken to skillet. Add capers. Simmer 2 minutes. Transfer chicken to serving platter and cover with sauce.

CHICKEN WITH SHIITAKE MUSHROOMS AND SUN-DRIED TOMATOES

SERVES 4 TO 6

- ½ **cup flour**
- ½ **teaspoon salt**
- ¼ **teaspoon pepper**
- ¼ **teaspoon onion salt**
- 3 **chicken breasts, boned, skinned, halved**
- 4 **tablespoons olive oil, divided**
- 1 **ounce dried shiitake mushrooms**
- 2 **cloves garlic, chopped**
- ½ **cup sun-dried tomatoes (in oil), drained, in strips**
- ½ **cup sherry**
- 3 **tablespoons whipping cream**
- ¼ **teaspoon Herbes de Provence**

In large plastic bag combine flour, salt, pepper, and onion salt. Mix well. Add chicken. Coat well. Shake off excess flour.

In large skillet sauté chicken in 2 tablespoons olive oil until lightly browned on both sides. Remove from skillet.

Soak dried mushrooms in hot water until soft. Squeeze dry. Remove stems and slice caps.

Add remaining 2 tablespoons olive oil to skillet. Sauté mushrooms and garlic until golden. Add tomato strips and sherry. Bring to boil. Add cream and herbs. Reduce heat. Simmer until sauce thickens. Add chicken. Cover. Cook until thoroughly heated.

PARMESAN CHICKEN BREASTS

SERVES 8

1   cup bread crumbs
1   cup freshly grated Parmesan cheese
1   tablespoon finely chopped parsley
1   teaspoon paprika
6   chicken breasts, boned, skinned, halved
6   tablespoons butter or margarine, melted

In large bowl combine bread crumbs, Parmesan cheese, parsley, and paprika. Mix well. Dip chicken in melted butter, covering thoroughly. Dredge chicken in crumb mixture, coating well.

Arrange chicken in lightly greased 9- by 13-inch baking pan. Bake in preheated 350-degree oven 45 minutes.

CHICKEN WITH DATES

SERVES 6 TO 8

2   broiler-fryers, skinned if desired, quartered
4   tablespoons butter
2   cups chicken broth
1   cup orange juice
3   tablespoons cornstarch
1   teaspoon curry powder
1   teaspoon salt
1/2 teaspoon pepper
1   medium onion, chopped
    juice of 1 lemon
12-18 dates, pitted, halved
1   green pepper, chopped
    hot cooked rice
1   orange, peeled, sliced, halved

In large skillet brown chicken in butter. Transfer to 9- by 13-inch glass baking dish.

In medium saucepan combine chicken broth, orange juice, cornstarch, curry powder, salt, pepper, onion, and lemon juice. Cook over high heat until sauce thickens, stirring constantly. Pour over chicken.

Bake covered in preheated 350-degree oven 45 minutes. Arrange dates over chicken. Sprinkle with green pepper. Bake covered 15 minutes or until chicken is tender. Serve over hot rice. Garnish with orange slices.

CHICKEN WITH PINE NUTS

SERVES 4

1/2-1	**cup flour**
	salt to taste
	pepper to taste
4	**chicken breasts, boned**
2	**tablespoons olive oil**
1	**tablespoon chopped shallots**
1/2	**cup sliced fresh mushrooms**
1-2	**tablespoons finely chopped prosciutto**
1/2	**cup dry vermouth**
2	**medium tomatoes, chopped**
1	**teaspoon chopped fresh basil**
1	**teaspoon chopped fresh rosemary**
1-2	**teaspoons toasted pine nuts**
1 1/2	**tablespoons freshly grated Parmesan cheese**
1	**teaspoon chopped parsley**

In medium bowl mix flour, salt, and pepper. Dredge chicken in mixture. In large skillet sauté chicken in olive oil until browned on both sides. Remove from skillet.

In same skillet combine shallots, mushrooms, and prosciutto. Add vermouth, scraping browned bits from bottom of skillet. Simmer 2 to 3 minutes. Add tomatoes, basil, rosemary, and chicken. Cover. Cook slowly about 20 minutes until chicken is tender. Add pine nuts, cheese, and parsley.

SPICY THREE-PEPPER CHICKEN

2	tablespoons lemon juice
2	chicken breasts, boned, skinned, halved
4	teaspoons butter, divided
4	teaspoons vegetable oil, divided
1	clove garlic, minced
1	medium onion, coarsely chopped
1/2	red pepper, in 3/4-inch square pieces
1/2	green pepper, julienned
1/2	yellow pepper, cut in wide slices, then halved
1	large carrot, in 1/4-inch slices
1	tablespoon tomato paste
1	tablespoon white wine Worcestershire sauce
2 1/2	teaspoons Dijon mustard
2	tablespoons balsamic vinegar
2	tablespoons apple cider or dry white wine
2	tablespoons brown sugar
1/4	teaspoon cayenne pepper
	salt to taste
	pepper to taste

Sprinkle lemon juice on both sides of chicken. In large ovenproof skillet heat 2 teaspoons butter and 2 teaspoons oil. Add chicken. Sauté 2 minutes on each side or until lightly browned. Set aside.

In medium skillet heat remaining 2 teaspoons butter and 2 teaspoons oil. Add garlic and onion. Sauté until onion is soft. Add peppers and carrot. Sauté 2 minutes. Remove from heat.

In small bowl combine remaining ingredients. Mix well. Add mixture from small bowl to vegetables in skillet. Heat until sauce bubbles, stirring to coat vegetables with sauce.

Pour vegetable mixture over chicken. Cover skillet with lid or aluminum foil. Bake in preheated 350-degree oven 20 to 30 minutes.

CHICKEN SZECHWAN WITH PEANUTS

SERVES 2 TO 3

2   tablespoons cornstarch, divided
1   egg white, beaten
3   tablespoons light soy sauce, divided
1   tablespoon sherry
2   chicken breasts, boned, skinned, in small pieces
1/4-1/2   cup vegetable oil
1/2   teaspoon salt
3   tablespoons sugar
1   clove garlic, minced
1   tablespoon vinegar
1   tablespoon molasses
1/3   cup water
1-2   tablespoons sesame oil
2-3   dried red peppers, in small pieces
12   green onions with tops, in small pieces
1/3   cup unsalted or dry roasted peanuts
3   cups cooked white rice

In medium bowl combine 1 tablespoon cornstarch, egg white, 1 tablespoon soy sauce, and sherry. Beat until frothy. Marinate chicken in mixture at least 2 hours, turning occasionally and coating well.

In large skillet heat vegetable oil. Stir fry chicken pieces until white and just cooked through. Remove from skillet. Set aside.

In small bowl combine salt, sugar, garlic, vinegar, molasses, water, remaining 1 tablespoon cornstarch, and 2 tablespoons soy sauce. Mix well. In clean skillet heat sesame oil. Sauté red peppers until they turn black. Add green onions, reserved chicken, and molasses mixture. Cook 2 to 3 minutes until hot. Top with peanuts. Serve over rice.

LUAU CHICKEN

MARINADE:

1/2 **cup soy sauce**
1/2 **cup pineapple juice**
1/4 **cup vegetable oil**
1 **tablespoon brown sugar**
1 **tablespoon minced fresh ginger root**
1 **large clove garlic, finely chopped**
1 **teaspoon dry mustard**
1/2 **teaspoon freshly ground pepper**

4 **chicken breasts, boned, skinned, halved**
1/4 **pound butter, melted, optional**

In large bowl combine all marinade ingredients. Mix well. Add chicken to mixture. Cover and refrigerate at least 3 hours. Bring to room temperature.

Remove chicken from marinade. Broil chicken 4 to 5 inches from heat 10 minutes on each side or until golden brown, basting occasionally. May also be grilled, basting frequently. Serve with melted butter for "dunking" as with lobster, if desired.

JAPANESE FRIED CHICKEN

YIELD: 24 TO 36 PIECES

*2-3 **teaspoons ginger juice**
2 **tablespoons soy sauce**
2 **tablespoons sake (rice wine)**
2 **chicken breasts (1-1 1/2 pounds), boned, skinned, in 1- to 2-inch pieces**
1/4 **cup cornstarch**
vegetable oil as needed for frying

In large bowl combine ginger juice, soy sauce, and sake. Mix well. Add chicken pieces. Marinate 30 minutes, stirring occasionally. Drain chicken. Pat dry and dust with cornstarch.

In large skillet heat 3 inches oil to 350-degrees. Fry chicken 5 minutes or until cooked through. Serve as entree with rice or appetizer with Hot Orange Horseradish Sauce, page 15.

*Scrape brown skin from 2- to 3-inch piece of fresh ginger root. Grate ginger root. Squeeze pulp in hand to extract juice.

ITALIAN STUFFED CHICKEN BREASTS

SERVES 4

2   **ounces Parmesan cheese**
1/2 **cup fresh parsley leaves**
2   **ounces prosciutto, very thinly sliced, cut into strips**
3   **ounces mozzarella cheese, grated**
1   **ounce sun-dried tomatoes (in oil), drained**
14 **ounces fresh spinach, stems removed, or**
      8 ounces frozen spinach, thawed
1/2 **cup pine nuts**
     freshly ground pepper to taste
4   **chicken breasts, boned, halved**
1/4 **cup butter or margarine, melted (less if desired)**
     salt to taste

In food processor combine Parmesan and parsley. Blend well. Add prosciutto, mozzarella, and tomatoes. Mix well.

Wilt spinach in pot using only water clinging to leaves. If using frozen spinach, drain well. Add spinach and pine nuts to mixture in food processor. Process with quick on and off turns until combined. Add pepper to taste.

Stuff mixture under skin of each chicken breast and tuck ends of chicken under. Place skin side up in baking pan. Brush with butter. Season to taste.

Bake in preheated 375-degree oven 20 minutes. Transfer to broiler. Broil 5 minutes to brown.

CHICKEN IN A SKILLET

SERVES 4 TO 6

1 **cup flour**
1/2 **teaspoon salt**
1/8 **teaspoon pepper**
4 **chicken breasts, halved**
3 **tablespoons olive oil**
1 1/2 **tablespoons chopped shallots**
1 **cup sliced fresh mushrooms**
1-2 **tablespoons chopped prosciutto**
1/2 **cup dry vermouth**
2 **medium tomatoes, seeded, chopped**
1 **teaspoon chopped fresh basil**
1 **teaspoon chopped fresh rosemary**
1 **tablespoon toasted pine nuts**
1 1/2 **tablespoons grated Parmesan cheese**
2 **teaspoons chopped parsley**
  cooked noodles

In small bowl mix flour, salt, and pepper. Dredge chicken in mixture. In large skillet brown chicken in olive oil on both sides. Remove chicken from skillet.

Add shallots, mushrooms, prosciutto, and vermouth to skillet. Cook over medium heat 2 minutes. Add tomatoes, basil, rosemary, and chicken. Cover skillet. Simmer until chicken is cooked. Add pine nuts and cheese. Sprinkle with parsley. Serve over noodles.

CHICKEN IN A POUCH

SERVES 4

4 **tablespoons butter, divided**
4 **4- to 5-ounce chicken breasts, boned, skinned,**
   slightly flattened
8 **teaspoons Dijon mustard**
8 **large fresh mushrooms, stems removed, thinly sliced**
8 **carrots, julienned**
4 **medium zucchini, julienned**
4 **teaspoons finely chopped shallots**
4 **teaspoons chopped fresh thyme or 2 teaspoons dried thyme**
4 **tablespoons white wine**
4 **tablespoons finely chopped parsley**
  salt to taste
  freshly ground white pepper to taste

In small saucepan melt 2 tablespoons butter. Invert 12-inch or 14-inch round cake pan over aluminum foil. Trace edge with sharp knife. Repeat for a total of 4 circles. Brush foil with melted butter.

Place 1 chicken breast on each foil circle slightly below center. Brush top of each breast with 2 teaspoons mustard. Equally divide mushrooms, carrots, zucchini, shallots, and thyme around each breast. Sprinkle each with 1 tablespoon wine and 1 tablespoon parsley. Dot with remaining 2 tablespoons butter. Season to taste.

Fold foil to completely enclose contents, leaving room for expansion. Crimp seams tightly. Arrange packages on baking sheet. Bake in preheated 450-degree oven 20 minutes.

APPLE CHICKEN

SERVES 8 TO 10

2 **cups apple juice or apple cider**
2 **tablespoons Dijon mustard**
2 **cups whipping cream**
1/8 **teaspoon cayenne pepper**
1 3/4 **teaspoons salt, divided**
1 1/4 **teaspoons pepper, divided**
3/4 **cup flour**
6 **chicken breasts, boned, skinned, halved**
8 **tablespoons butter or margarine, divided**
3 **large tart apples, peeled, cored, in 1/4-inch circular slices**

In medium saucepan bring apple juice to boil. Cook until reduced to 1/2 cup. Stir in mustard and cream. Cook until thickened and reduced to 2 cups. Add cayenne, 1/4 teaspoon salt, and 1/4 teaspoon pepper. Mix well. Remove from heat. Set aside.

In shallow dish combine flour, remaining 1 1/2 teaspoons salt, and 1 teaspoon pepper. Mix well. Dredge chicken in mixture. In large skillet heat 6 tablespoons butter. Sauté chicken on both sides until brown and tender. Transfer chicken to platter. Keep warm.

Add remaining 2 tablespoons butter to skillet. Sauté apple slices 3 to 5 minutes. Transfer to chicken platter. Discard butter in skillet. Pour reserved cream sauce into skillet. Heat, stirring until smooth. If thicker gravy is desired, add flour. Spoon some gravy over chicken. Pass remaining gravy.

CHICKEN ALFREDO

SERVES 8 TO 10

1/2 cup flour

3 eggs, beaten

7 tablespoons water, divided

1 cup Romano cheese, divided

1/2 teaspoon salt

2 teaspoons chopped parsley

3/4 cup unseasoned bread crumbs

6 chicken breasts, boned, skinned, halved

7 tablespoons margarine, divided

2 tablespoons vegetable oil

1 cup whipping cream

1 pound mozzarella cheese, grated or thinly sliced

In small bowl place flour. In another small bowl combine eggs and 3 tablespoons water. Mix well. In medium bowl combine 1/2 cup Romano cheese, salt, parsley, and bread crumbs. Mix well. Dredge chicken in flour. Coat with egg and then bread crumb mixture.

In large skillet heat 3 tablespoons margarine and oil. Cook chicken 7 to 8 minutes on each side or until brown. Arrange chicken in 9- by 13-inch baking pan.

In medium saucepan combine cream and remaining 4 tablespoons margarine. Cook over low heat until margarine melts. Add remaining 4 tablespoons water and 1/2 cup Romano cheese. Cook 5 minutes, stirring constantly. Pour sauce over chicken. Top with mozzarella. Bake uncovered in preheated 425-degree oven 8 to 10 minutes.

OLD-FASHIONED CREAMED CHICKEN

SERVES 6 TO 8

4 tablespoons butter or margarine
6 tablespoons flour
1½ teaspoons salt, or to taste
  freshly ground pepper to taste
1 cup milk
1½ cups chicken broth
3 egg yolks, beaten
8 ounces fresh mushrooms, sliced, sautéed
6 chicken breasts, boned, skinned, cooked, in bite-size pieces
3 tablespoons coarsely chopped green pepper
3 tablespoons coarsely chopped pimiento
1 cup grated Parmesan cheese, optional
  white wine to taste, optional

In double boiler melt butter. Add flour. Mix well. Stir in salt and pepper. Add milk slowly, stirring constantly. Add chicken broth. Mix well. Cook 15 minutes, stirring frequently.

In small bowl combine egg yolks and small amount of chicken broth mixture. Mix well. Add to double boiler. Stir in mushrooms, chicken, green pepper, and pimiento. Heat well. Add cheese and/or wine, if desired. Do not heat longer than necessary. Chicken will overcook.

COLD POACHED CHICKEN WITH DILL

SERVES 8

6 chicken breasts, boned, skinned
1 cup safflower oil
½ cup tarragon vinegar
1 teaspoon salt
½ teaspoon garlic salt
½ teaspoon seasoned salt
2 green onions with tops, finely chopped
¼ cup chopped parsley
¼ cup chopped fresh dill plus sprigs dill, divided
  fresh fruit

Poach chicken gently 10 to 15 minutes or until tender. Cool.

In large plastic bag combine remaining ingredients except sprigs dill and fresh fruit. Mix well. Place chicken in bag. Seal. Refrigerate 3 hours or overnight, turning occasionally. Remove chicken from marinade. Arrange on platter, garnished with sprigs dill and fresh fruit.

MEDITERRANEAN GRILLED CHICKEN

SERVES 4

1	large ripe tomato, seeded, chopped
1	bulb fennel, chopped
1/4	cup minced red onion
6	calamata olives, pitted, coarsely chopped
1/4	cup plus 2 tablespoons fresh basil leaves, divided
3	tablespoons plus 1 teaspoon balsamic vinegar, divided
1	tablespoon olive oil
1/4	teaspoon salt
1/8	teaspoon sugar
	freshly ground pepper to taste
1/4	cup mayonnaise (may use lite)
1	large clove garlic, minced
2	chicken breasts, boned, skinned, halved

In medium bowl combine tomato, fennel, onion, olives, 1/4 cup basil, 3 tablespoons vinegar, olive oil, salt, sugar, and pepper. Toss lightly.*

In small bowl combine mayonnaise, 1 tablespoon basil, garlic, and remaining 1 teaspoon vinegar. Mix well. Coat chicken with mixture. Season to taste.

Grill chicken 4 minutes on each side. Serve hot or at room temperature covered with vegetable mixture. Garnish with remaining 1 tablespoon basil leaves.

*May be made several hours ahead. Refrigerate covered and bring to room temperature before serving.

TEQUILA CHICKEN WITH CITRUS SALSA

SERVES 4

MARINADE:

1/4 **cup tequila**
1 **tablespoon salt**
1 **tablespoon sugar**
3 **tablespoons chopped cilantro leaves**
4 **cloves garlic, minced**
1/2 **cup fresh lime juice**
1 **jalapeño pepper, seeded, sliced**
1 1/2 **cups extra virgin olive oil**

6 **chicken breasts, boned, skinned**

In food processor or blender combine all marinade ingredients. Process until well blended. Place chicken in large glass or ceramic bowl. Pour marinade over chicken. Refrigerate 3 hours.

Remove chicken from marinade. Grill 4 to 5 minutes on each side until browned, basting with marinade. Thinly slice cooked chicken. May be served hot or cold spread with cold salsa.

See photo page 187.

CITRUS SALSA

4 **oranges, peeled, sectioned**
2 **pink grapefruit, peeled, sectioned**
2 **cups diced fresh pineapple**
1 **medium red onion, thinly sliced**
1/2 **red pepper, seeded, chopped**
2 **tablespoons chopped cilantro leaves**
1 **tablespoon balsamic vinegar**
1 **tablespoon sugar**

In large bowl combine all salsa ingredients. Mix well. Refrigerate.

CHICKEN FAJITAS

SERVES 4

MARINADE:

2   tablespoons dry white wine
2   tablespoons white vinegar
2   tablespoons corn oil
2   tablespoons orange juice
1   teaspoon minced garlic
1/2 teaspoon salt
1/2 teaspoon pepper

1   pound boned, skinned chicken breasts
4   pita loaves or soft tortillas
3   tablespoons sour cream
4   thin slices onions
4   tablespoons seeded, chopped cucumber
4   tablespoons chopped tomatoes
4   tablespoons sliced black olives
4   tablespoons grated Cheddar cheese or feta cheese

In medium bowl combine all marinade ingredients. Mix well. Refrigerate chicken in marinade at least 12 hours.

Remove chicken from marinade. Grill 4 minutes on each side. Shred. Serve in pita loaves or rolled in soft tortillas with sour cream, onions, cucumber, tomatoes, olives, and cheese.

MARINATED CHICKEN KABOBS

SERVES 6

MARINADE:

¾   **cup dry white wine**

¾   **cup canola or safflower oil**

¾   **cup teriyaki sauce**

1-1½   **teaspoons dried rosemary or**
            1 tablespoon chopped fresh rosemary

2-3   **cloves garlic, crushed**

1   **tablespoon minced fresh ginger root**

1   **heaping tablespoon Dijon mustard**
       juice of ½ lemon

    wooden skewers

2¼   **pounds chicken breasts, boned, skinned, halved,**
           in 1½-inch pieces

1½   **green peppers, seeded, in 1½-inch pieces**

1½   **red peppers, seeded, in 1½-inch pieces**

1   **pound fresh mushrooms**

20   **stewing onions, peeled, optional**

1   **whole fresh pineapple, peeled, cored, in 1-inch pieces**
    cooked rice or couscous

In large bowl combine all marinade ingredients. Mix well. Add chicken, peppers, mushrooms, and onions, if desired. Marinate 3 to 4 hours. Drain, reserving marinade.

On each skewer alternate chicken, peppers, mushrooms, onions, and pineapple until skewer is filled.* Brush skewers with marinade before grilling or broiling. Cook 10 minutes or until chicken is done, turning frequently and brushing with marinade each time. Serve with rice or couscous.

Remaining marinade may be used as sauce after simmering 10 minutes.

*May be done several hours ahead and refrigerated.

HONEYED CORIANDER CHICKEN WITH SPICY PEANUT SAUCE

SERVES 4

MARINADE:

6	tablespoons soy sauce
1	tablespoon honey
1	tablespoon coriander seed
2	cloves garlic, minced
2	teaspoons peeled, finely grated fresh ginger root
1/4	teaspoon turmeric
1/4	teaspoon cayenne pepper, or to taste
21/2-3	pounds chicken parts, breasts halved, thighs and legs separated

In large bowl combine all marinade ingredients. Mix well. Add chicken. Coat well. Marinate at room temperature 3 hours or in refrigerator overnight. Remove chicken from marinade. Broil or grill chicken about 30 minutes until tender and browned, turning once.

SPICY PEANUT SAUCE

4	tablespoons peanut butter
4	tablespoons soy sauce
2	tablespoons fresh lemon juice
1/4	cup firmly packed brown sugar
11/2	teaspoons cayenne pepper, or to taste
1/4	cup vegetable oil

While chicken cooks combine all sauce ingredients in food processor or blender. Process until smooth. In small saucepan heat sauce briefly before serving with chicken.

CASTILIAN CHICKEN WITH OLIVES

SERVES 3 TO 4

2½-3	**pound chicken, quartered**
2	**tablespoons olive oil**
2	**tablespoons lemon juice**
2	**medium onions, chopped**
4	**large cloves garlic, minced**
1	**tablespoon oregano**
½	**teaspoon cumin**
½	**cup golden raisins**
½	**cup small pimiento-stuffed olives, halved**
1	**tablespoon capers with juice**
¼	**cup firmly packed brown sugar**
⅓	**cup dry white wine**
	salt to taste
	pepper to taste

In large shallow baking pan arrange chicken skin side up in single layer. In medium bowl combine olive oil, lemon juice, onions, garlic, oregano, cumin, raisins, olives, and capers. Mix well. Spread mixture over chicken. Cover. Refrigerate overnight. Sprinkle brown sugar over chicken. Pour white wine into pan. Season to taste.

Bake uncovered in preheated 350-degree oven 50 to 60 minutes or until brown and tender. Serve with small amount of pan juices. Pass remaining juices.

CHICKEN POT PIE

1½ cups plus 5 tablespoons flour, divided
2 teaspoons salt, divided
¼ pound plus 5 tablespoons unsalted butter, divided
¼ cup plus 1 tablespoon ice water, divided
4 chicken breasts, boned, skinned
1 cup whipping cream or half and half
4 carrots, in ½-inch pieces
2 zucchini, in ½-inch pieces
2 small yellow onions, coarsely chopped
1 cup chicken broth
¼ cup cognac or dry white wine
1 tablespoon tarragon
½ teaspoon freshly ground pepper
1 egg, beaten

In food processor combine 1½ cups sifted flour, ½ teaspoon salt, and ¼ pound butter. Process until mixture resembles coarse meal. Add ¼ cup ice water. Blend well. Transfer dough to lightly floured surface. Press large chunks of dough with heel of hand. Gather dough into ball. Repeat. Wrap in plastic wrap. Refrigerate 30 minutes before using.

Arrange chicken in large baking dish. Pour cream over chicken. Bake in pre-heated 425-degree oven 20 to 25 minutes. Remove chicken from cream, cool, and cut into 1-inch pieces. Reserve cream and cooking juices.

In medium saucepan boil carrots in salted water 3 minutes. Add zucchini. Boil 1 minute. Drain. Rinse under cold running water. Drain thoroughly.

In large saucepan melt remaining 5 tablespoons butter over medium heat. Add onions. Sauté about 5 minutes until soft. Add remaining 5 tablespoons flour. Cook 5 minutes, stirring constantly. Do not let flour brown. Add chicken broth. Cook until thickened, stirring constantly. Add reserved cream and cooking juices and cognac. Cook over low heat about 5 minutes until thick.

Stir in tarragon, remaining 1½ teaspoons salt, and pepper. Simmer 1 minute. Gently blend in chicken and vegetables. Remove from heat. Pour into deep 2-quart casserole or soufflé dish.

On lightly floured surface roll out dough to size several inches larger than casserole. Place pastry over top of casserole and trim, leaving 1-inch border.

In small bowl combine egg and remaining 1 tablespoon ice water. Mix well. Brush edge of casserole with egg mixture and press overhanging pastry into casserole. Brush top of pastry with egg mixture. Cut steam vent in center of pastry. Place casserole on baking sheet. Bake on center rack of preheated 425-degree oven until crust is golden.

CHICKEN TORTILLA CASSEROLE

SERVES 8

1/2   **cup chopped onion**
1/2   **cup chicken broth**
1/4   **cup chopped celery**
3   **cups cooked shredded chicken**
10-12   **6-inch corn tortillas, each cut into 12 wedges**
4   **ounces canned green chilies, drained, chopped**
10¾   **ounces canned cream of chicken soup**
1   **teaspoon pepper**
1   **cup grated Cheddar cheese, divided**
1   **cup grated Monterey Jack cheese, divided**
1   **cup salsa, mild, medium, or hot as desired**

In small saucepan combine onion, chicken broth, and celery. Bring to boil. Reduce heat. Cover. Simmer 3 to 4 minutes or until vegetables are just tender.

Transfer mixture to large bowl. Add chicken, tortilla wedges, chilies, cream of chicken soup, and pepper. Mix well. Stir in 1/2 cup Cheddar cheese and 1/2 cup Monterey Jack cheese. Spread mixture in lightly greased 9- by 13-inch baking pan. Top with salsa and remaining 1/2 cup Cheddar and 1/2 cup Monterey Jack cheeses.

Bake in preheated 350-degree oven 30 minutes. Let stand 5 minutes before serving.

CHICKEN AND PASTA CASSEROLE
WITH HOT PEPPER CHEESE

SERVES 6

8	ounces radiatore pasta or shells
3	tablespoons olive oil, divided
2	tablespoons butter, divided
2	medium zucchini, in 1/2-inch cubes
3	cloves garlic, finely chopped
1	medium red pepper, seeded, coarsely chopped
1	small green pepper, seeded, coarsely chopped
1/3	cup sliced green onions
2	large chicken breasts, boned, skinned, halved, in strips
1	teaspoon basil
1	cup chicken broth
2/3	cup drained, canned garbanzo beans
*10	ounces grated hot pepper cheese
2	tablespoons grated Parmesan cheese

Cook pasta according to package directions. Drain. Set aside. In large skillet or Dutch oven heat 1 tablespoon olive oil and 1 tablespoon butter. Add zucchini, garlic, peppers, and green onions. Cook 2 to 3 minutes or until vegetables are softened but not mushy, stirring constantly. With slotted spoon, remove to medium bowl.

Add chicken to skillet. Brown lightly, adding remaining 2 tablespoons olive oil and 1 tablespoon butter, if necessary. Sprinkle with basil. Cook 5 minutes or until chicken is cooked through.

Add chicken broth to skillet. Increase heat. Cook until broth simmers. Stir in garbanzo beans, cooked vegetables, and pasta. Mix well. Gradually add hot pepper cheese, blending well. Stir in Parmesan cheese. Cook only until cheese is melted and vegetables are thoroughly heated.

*Monterey Jack cheese may be substituted for milder flavor.

BAKED CHOW MEIN CHICKEN

SERVES 4

3-3½	pound broiler-fryer, cut up
1	onion, sliced
¼	cup flour
⅓	cup butter, melted
3	tablespoons soy sauce
¼	teaspoon pepper
⅛	teaspoon ginger
5	ounces chow mein noodles, finely crushed
¼	cup chopped almonds

Lightly coat chicken pieces and onion rings with flour. In medium bowl combine butter, soy sauce, pepper, and ginger. Mix well. Mix noodles and almonds. Dip chicken and onion in butter mixture. Roll chicken and onion in noodle mixture.

Arrange chicken in single layer in shallow baking dish. Top chicken with overlapping onion rings. Drizzle any remaining butter mixture over top. Bake covered in preheated 350-degree oven 30 minutes. Uncover. Bake 30 minutes.

CHICKEN AND LENTILS

SERVES 3 TO 4

1	tablespoon olive oil
1	large onion, in chunks
1	tablespoon finely minced fresh ginger root
¾	teaspoon cinnamon
½	teaspoon coriander
½	teaspoon cumin
4½	cups water, divided
2½-3	pound chicken, skinned, quartered
6	carrots, in 2-inch pieces
¼	cup raisins
1½	cups dried lentils, rinsed
10	ounces frozen chopped spinach, thawed, drained
	salt to taste
	pepper to taste

In Dutch oven heat olive oil. Sauté onion in oil until soft, stirring occasionally. Add ginger root, cinnamon, coriander, and cumin. Mix well. Add 3½ cups water, chicken, carrots, and raisins. Cover. Cook over medium heat 20 minutes. Add lentils and remaining 1 cup water. Cook 30 minutes. Add spinach. Cook 2 to 3 minutes. Season to taste.

PAELLA

1   **cup flour**
3   **teaspoons salt, divided**
1½   **teaspoons freshly ground pepper, divided**
½   **teaspoon garlic powder**
4-5   **pounds chicken legs and breasts**
½   **cup olive oil**
1   **pound hot Italian sausage**
4   **cloves garlic, chopped**
28   **ounces canned tomatoes, chopped**
3   **cups chicken broth**
2   **teaspoons oregano**
2   **cups chopped onions**
3   **cups long grain rice**
½   **teaspoon saffron**
2   **pounds cooked, shelled, deveined jumbo shrimp**
4   **ounces pimiento**
30   **ounces canned artichoke hearts**
24-36   **steamer clams, steamed 5 to 6 minutes**

In large plastic bag combine flour, 1 teaspoon salt, ½ teaspoon pepper, and garlic powder. Shake well to mix. Add chicken to bag, a few pieces at a time. Shake well to coat with mixture. In large skillet sauté chicken in olive oil until lightly browned.

In 8½-quart pot brown sausage. Pour off fat. Add chicken, garlic, tomatoes, chicken broth, oregano, onions, remaining 2 teaspoons salt, and 1 teaspoon pepper to pot. Simmer 15 minutes. Stir in rice and saffron. Cook 25 to 30 minutes or until rice is done. Add shrimp and pimiento. Mix well. Transfer to large greased baking dish. Arrange artichokes and clams on top.

Bake in preheated 350-degree oven until heated thoroughly.

JAMBALAYA

1 cup cubed ham steak
1 cup smoked Polish sausage, in pieces
2 tablespoons vegetable oil, divided
1½ cups chopped onions
1 cup chopped celery
¾ cup chopped green pepper
4 chicken legs or thighs
4 chicken breasts, halved
1½ teaspoons minced garlic
¾ teaspoon Tabasco
2 bay leaves
1½ teaspoons freshly ground pepper
¾ teaspoon thyme
28 ounces canned whole tomatoes, chopped
¾ cup tomato sauce
2 cups seafood stock or water
½ cup chopped green onions
2 cups rice
18 shrimp, shelled, deveined
18 oysters, shucked

In 4-quart ovenproof pot cook ham and sausage in 1 tablespoon oil 5 to 8 minutes. Add onions, celery, and green pepper. Sauté until tender but firm. With slotted spoon remove meat and vegetables to bowl.

Brown chicken in pot, adding remaining 1 tablespoon oil if necessary. Add garlic, Tabasco, bay leaves, pepper, and thyme. Cook 5 minutes. Add tomatoes and tomato sauce. Cook 5 minutes, stirring frequently. Blend in stock and green onions. Add rice, shrimp, oysters, meat, and vegetables. Mix well. Bake covered in preheated 350-degree oven 20 to 30 minutes or until rice is tender. Remove bay leaves and serve.

CHICKEN BLACKHAWK

SERVES 6 TO 8

3 tablespoons oregano
3 tablespoons thyme
1 tablespoon crushed red chilies
2 teaspoons black pepper
2 teaspoons salt
4 large cloves garlic, chopped
1 cup olive oil

2 3½- to 4-pound broiler-fryers, quartered
1 red pepper, julienned
1 green pepper, julienned
1 yellow pepper, julienned
12 pepperoncinis (imported mild green peppers)

For marinade, combine oregano, thyme, red chilies, black pepper, salt, garlic, and olive oil in large bowl. Mix well. Add chicken to marinade. Toss to coat evenly. Cover. Refrigerate 2 hours or overnight.

Remove chicken from marinade. Reserve marinade. Broil chicken 5 minutes or until browned. Transfer chicken to baking pan. Pour reserved marinade over chicken. Bake in preheated 350-degree oven 20 minutes or until tender. During last 15 minutes of cooking spread peppers and pepperoncinis over chicken.

HONEY GINGER CHICKEN

SERVES 4

*3½-4 pound broiler-fryer, quartered
1 teaspoon grated fresh ginger root, divided
juice of ½ lemon
salt and pepper to taste
¼ cup vegetable oil
¼ cup honey
½ teaspoon grated orange or lemon rind

Rub chicken with ½ teaspoon ginger root. Place chicken in foil-lined baking dish. Pour lemon juice over chicken. Sprinkle lightly with salt and pepper. In small bowl combine remaining ½ teaspoon ginger root, oil, and honey. Reserve for basting.

Bake chicken in preheated 325-degree oven 1 to 1½ hours until juices run clear when chicken is pierced with fork, basting with sauce every 15 minutes.

*Cornish hens, turkey breast, or turkey tenderloin may be substituted for chicken.

PERFECT ROAST CHICKEN

SERVES 4

1/2   **teaspoon salt**
5   **pound roasting chicken**
1/2   **teaspoon thyme**
1/2   **teaspoon sage**
1/2   **teaspoon rosemary**
1   **bay leaf**
1   **cup chopped onion**
1   **cup chopped celery, including leaves**
1   **cup chopped carrot**
  sprig parsley
1   **clove garlic, minced**
1/4   **cup hot water**

Rub salt into cavity of chicken. Add thyme, sage, rosemary, and bay leaf to cavity. Combine onion, celery, carrot, and parsley. Spread over bottom of large roasting pan. Place chicken breast side down on vegetables. Bake in preheated 450-degree oven 30 minutes. Turn chicken breast side up. Sprinkle garlic over breast and legs. Reduce heat to 400 degrees. Bake 1 hour.

Transfer chicken to serving platter. Remove fat and bay leaf from roasting pan. Add hot water to vegetables in pan. Heat until drippings and vegetables are loosened from pan. Transfer to food processor. Puree, adding additional water if necessary for gravy consistency. Serve with chicken.

GINGER GLAZED CHICKEN

SERVES 8

2/3   **cup soy sauce**
1/4   **cup sherry**
2   **cloves garlic, finely chopped**
2   **tablespoons grated fresh ginger root**
1   **tablespoon grated orange rind**

3-4   **pounds quartered chicken**

In small bowl combine soy sauce, sherry, garlic, ginger root, and orange rind. Mix well. Pour mixture into large plastic bag. Add chicken. Secure tightly. Marinate in refrigerator at least 24 hours, turning occasionally.

Transfer chicken and marinade to roasting pan. Bake in preheated 325-degree oven 1 hour, basting frequently.

ROSEMARY CHICKEN

SERVES 4

3½	**pound chicken**
1	**teaspoon salt**
2	**teaspoons dried rosemary, crumbled**
1½	**teaspoons ground or rubbed sage**
1½	**teaspoons thyme**
1	**teaspoon freshly ground pepper**
2	**bay leaves, divided**
5	**tablespoons olive oil, divided**
6	**small russet potatoes, quartered lengthwise, cut crosswise into ½-inch pieces**
12	**large shallots, peeled**
8	**medium carrots, in 2-inch pieces**
1¾	**cups chicken broth**
¼	**cup balsamic vinegar or 3 tablespoons red wine vinegar and ¼ teaspoon sugar**
4	**tablespoons unsalted butter**
2	**tablespoons minced parsley**

Rub chicken inside and out with salt. In small bowl combine rosemary, sage, thyme, and pepper. Mix well. Rub 2 teaspoons herb mixture into chicken cavity. Add 1 bay leaf to cavity. Tie chicken legs together. Brush chicken with 1 tablespoon olive oil. Transfer to baking pan.

Sprinkle chicken with half of remaining herb mixture. Surround with potatoes, shallots, and carrots. Sprinkle vegetables with remaining herb mixture and remaining 4 tablespoons olive oil. Add remaining bay leaf. Mix well.

Bake chicken in preheated 425-degree oven 45 minutes, basting occasionally and turning vegetables. Reduce heat to 350 degrees. Bake 45 minutes, continuing to baste and turn vegetables. Transfer chicken and vegetables to platter.

Pour pan juices into large glass measuring cup. Skim fat from top. Add enough chicken broth to measure 2 cups.

Add vinegar to baking pan. Bring to boil over medium heat, scraping up browned bits. Boil about 4 minutes until reduced to glaze.

Add broth mixture. Boil about 15 minutes until reduced to ½ cup. Reduce heat to low. Whisk in butter 1 tablespoon at a time. Stir in parsley. Pour sauce over chicken and vegetables.

CHILI LIME CHICKEN

SERVES 4

3   **dried ancho chilies, or any smoky dried chili**
3-4 **fresh hot chilies (jalapeño, pasilla)**
⅓   **cup fresh lime juice**
2-4 **cloves garlic, peeled**
¼   **cup vegetable oil**
     salt to taste, optional
2-3 **pound roasting chicken**
1   **lime**

Cut stems from dried chilies. Chop coarsely, retaining seeds. Cut stems from fresh chilies. For milder flavor remove seeds. For strong flavor retain seeds. Chop coarsely. In food processor or blender combine dried and fresh chilies, lime juice, and garlic. Process to paste.

In medium bowl mix paste, oil, and salt. Paste should be thick. Using fingers, spread paste on chicken inside and out. Loosen skin over chicken breast. Work paste under skin. Pierce lime with fork several times. Insert into chicken cavity.

Transfer chicken to rack in roasting pan. Place in preheated 450-degree oven. Immediately reduce heat to 350 degrees. Bake 45 to 60 minutes or until juices run clear when chicken is pierced with fork, basting every 15 minutes with pan drippings.

CORNISH HENS ORIENTAL

SERVES 2

MARINADE:
¼   **cup tamari or soy sauce**
¼   **cup soy oil or other vegetable oil**
¼   **cup cream sherry**

2   **Cornish hens**
10 **ounces grape jelly**
2   **cups cooked wild rice**

In medium bowl combine all marinade ingredients. Marinate hens in mixture 2 hours, turning and basting every 30 minutes.

In small saucepan melt grape jelly. Stuff hens with wild rice. Transfer to roasting pan. Coat hens with jelly and marinade. Bake in preheated 375-degree oven 15 to 20 minutes per pound.

GRILLED MARINATED CORNISH HENS

SERVES 3 TO 4

MARINADE:

1   small onion, coarsely chopped
8-10   cloves garlic, coarsely chopped
1⅓   cups orange juice
½   teaspoon thyme
½   teaspoon oregano
½   teaspoon marjoram
3-4   bay leaves, in small pieces
1   teaspoon salt
½   teaspoon freshly ground pepper

3-4   Cornish hens, halved
8-10   whole green onions, peeled

In large bowl combine all marinade ingredients. Mix well. Marinate hens in mixture overnight. Remove hens from marinade. Grill 25 to 30 minutes. Grill green onions during last 5 minutes of cooking. Serve hens garnished with grilled green onions.

CITRUS GRILLED CORNISH HENS

SERVES 6

MARINADE:

2   bulbs garlic, separated, peeled, crushed
¾   cup coarsely chopped fresh rosemary leaves
    juice of 8 limes or lemons
2   cups olive oil
⅔   cup honey
2   teaspoons salt
2   teaspoons cumin
1   teaspoon freshly ground pepper

6   Cornish hens, halved
    cooking spray

In large bowl combine all marinade ingredients. Mix well. Remove giblets from hen halves. Cover hens with marinade. Refrigerate covered overnight.

Remove hens from marinade. Arrange skin side up in large baking pans sprayed with cooking spray. Bake in preheated 375-degree oven 50 to 60 minutes or until tender and juices run clear. Brown on grill or under broiler 2 to 3 minutes.

ROCK CORNISH HENS WITH
GINGER CLEMENTINE SAUCE

	salt to taste
	pepper to taste
2	Rock Cornish hens
1	orange, halved, divided
3½	tablespoons butter, divided
2	tablespoons honey, divided
1	small shallot, minced
1	1-inch piece fresh ginger root, minced
1	tablespoon flour
¾	cup hot chicken broth
¼	cup Grand Marnier or other orange liqueur
1	clementine orange or tangerine, peeled, sectioned

Salt and pepper cavities of hens. Cut 1 orange half into 2 pieces. Place 1 orange quarter in cavity of each hen. Place hens in shallow roasting pan.

In small saucepan melt 2 tablespoons butter. Add 1 tablespoon honey, and 1 tablespoon juice squeezed from remaining orange half. Mix well. Brush mixture liberally over hens. Bake in preheated 350-degree oven 1 hour. Cover wing tips with foil if browning quickly.

In medium saucepan melt remaining 1½ tablespoons butter. Add shallot and ginger root. Sauté 5 minutes or until tender but not browned. Blend in flour. Gradually stir in hot chicken broth. Cook over low heat until mixture is thick and smooth, stirring constantly. Keep warm over very low heat.

Remove hens from oven. Transfer to ovenproof serving plate. Turn off oven. Return hens to oven to keep warm.

Pour off fat from roasting pan. Place roasting pan on stove top. Add Grand Marnier over very low heat. Stir well to scrape browned bits from pan. Pour into saucepan with chicken broth mixture. Add remaining 1 tablespoon honey and clementine. Heat well. Season to taste. Pour sauce over hens or serve separately.

See photo page 182.

TURKEY CHILI

1/2 **pound dried pinto beans, rinsed**
44 **ounces canned tomatoes**
1 **large green pepper, seeded, coarsely chopped**
1/2 **cup chopped celery with leaves**
1 **pound onions, coarsely chopped**
2 **tablespoons vegetable oil**
2 **cloves garlic, finely chopped**
1/2 **cup chopped parsley**
3 1/2 **pounds ground turkey**
1/4 **pound margarine**
2-4 **tablespoons chili powder**
1/2 **teaspoon cumin**
1 **tablespoon salt, or to taste**
freshly ground pepper to taste

In large pot soak beans overnight in water 2 inches above level of beans. Leaving beans in same water, simmer covered about 1 hour until tender, checking occasionally to make sure beans do not burn. Add tomatoes. Cook 5 minutes, breaking tomatoes into small pieces.

In medium skillet slowly sauté green pepper, celery, and onions in oil until tender, stirring frequently. Add garlic and parsley. Cook 3 minutes.

In large skillet sauté turkey in margarine until browned on all sides, breaking into small pieces. Add vegetable mixture to turkey. Stir in chili powder, cumin, salt, and pepper. Combine turkey mixture with beans. Cook uncovered 1 hour. Skim fat and serve.

SERVES 8

1½	pounds ground turkey
1	pound Italian turkey sausage, casing removed
1	large carrot, chopped
2	ribs celery, chopped
1	large green pepper, chopped
1	large onion, chopped
29	ounces canned tomatoes with juice, chopped
14	ounces canned stewed tomatoes
8	ounces tomato paste
1	tablespoon chili powder
½	teaspoon cumin
½	teaspoon salt
½	teaspoon oregano
¼	teaspoon cayenne pepper
⅛	teaspoon black pepper
1	large clove garlic, minced
¼	cup red wine
14	ounces canned kidney beans, optional

OPTIONAL:

sour cream
chopped onions
chopped lettuce
crushed tortilla chips
grated sharp Cheddar cheese

In 5- to 6-quart pot combine turkey, sausage, carrot, celery, green pepper, and onion. Cook over medium heat until tender. Break meat into small pieces.

Add remaining ingredients except optional ones to pot. Cover. Cook over low heat at least 2 hours. Serve with any or all optional ingredients, if desired.

TURKEY BREAST WITH COUNTRY VEGETABLES

SERVES 6

- 1/4 **pound margarine, melted**
- 1/2 **teaspoon thyme**
- 1/2 **teaspoon tarragon**
- 1/2 **teaspoon rosemary**
- 2 **cloves garlic, minced**
- 2 1/2-3 **pound turkey breast**
- 5-6 **Idaho potatoes, quartered**
- 6 **carrots, quartered**
- 2-3 **large onions, quartered**
- 6 **ribs celery, quartered**
- 14 1/2 **ounces chicken broth**

In small bowl combine margarine, herbs, and garlic. Mix well. Place turkey breast in roasting pan. Brush with half of margarine mixture.

Bake uncovered in preheated 375-degree oven 30 minutes. Add vegetables and chicken broth to pan. Pour remaining margarine mixture over all. Cover. Bake 1 hour.

TURKEY LOAF

SERVES 6

- 1 **cup soft bread crumbs**
- 1 **cup milk**
- 2 1/2-3 **pounds ground turkey**
- 1 **medium onion, finely chopped**
- 2 **eggs, lightly beaten**
- **salt to taste**
- **pepper to taste**
- 2 1/2 **tablespoons Worcestershire sauce**
- 1 **cup chili sauce**

In large bowl combine bread crumbs and milk. Mix well. Add turkey, onion, eggs, salt, pepper, and Worcestershire sauce. Blend well. Form into loaf.

Place in greased baking pan. Cover with chili sauce. Bake in preheated 400-degree oven 1 hour. Serve hot.

TURKEY LOAF WITH HERBS

SERVES 6 TO 8

1½	teaspoons olive oil
1	large onion, chopped
2	carrots, chopped
2	ribs celery with leaves, chopped
3	cloves garlic, minced
½	cup chopped parsley, divided
1	teaspoon sage
1	teaspoon thyme
1	teaspoon savory
16	ounces canned whole tomatoes, drained, seeded
1	tablespoon balsamic or red wine vinegar
1	tablespoon brown sugar
	Tabasco to taste
½	cup bread crumbs
1	egg, lightly beaten
2	tablespoons white wine Worcestershire sauce
1½	pounds ground turkey
2	teaspoons salt
1	teaspoon pepper plus freshly ground pepper, divided
	salsa, optional

In large skillet heat olive oil. Add onion, carrots, celery, garlic, ⅓ cup parsley, sage, thyme, and savory. Sauté 2 to 3 minutes, stirring constantly. Set aside.

In medium bowl combine tomatoes, vinegar, brown sugar, Tabasco, bread crumbs, egg, and white wine Worcestershire sauce. Mix well. In large bowl mix turkey, salt, and 1 teaspoon pepper. Add sautéed vegetables and tomato mixture. Mix well. Transfer to lightly oiled 8½- by 4½- by 2¾-inch loaf pan. Grind pepper over top.

Bake in preheated 375-degree oven 50 to 60 minutes or until loaf shrinks from pan and is lightly browned. Drain juices from pan. Let turkey loaf stand in pan 10 minutes. Remove and cut into slices of desired thickness. Sprinkle remaining parsley over slices. May be served hot, cold, or at room temperature with salsa, if desired.

See photo page 187.

ROAST DUCK WITH MANGO CHUTNEY SAUCE

2   **5-pound ducks**
     salt and freshly ground pepper to taste
1/4 **teaspoon nutmeg**
3   **ribs celery, in 1-inch pieces**
1   **large orange, peeled, in 1-inch pieces**
3   **tablespoons soy sauce**
1   **tablespoon plus 2 1/2 quarts water, divided**

On day before serving open duck cavities. Remove giblets and necks. Trim excess fat. Remove wings at second joint. Season inside of cavities with salt, pepper, and nutmeg. Stuff celery and orange into cavities.

Arrange necks, giblets, and wing pieces on bottom of large roasting pan. Place ducks on top and brush with mixture of soy sauce and 1 tablespoon water. Bake in preheated 375-degree oven 1 1/2 hours. Add 1 quart water to roasting pan. Bake 1 1/2 hours. Remove from oven. Transfer ducks to rack to cool.

Add 1 1/2 quarts water to roasting pan. Heat on top of stove over medium heat, scraping bottom of pan. Bring to slow boil. Remove from heat. Strain. Cool. Refrigerate strained stock and ducks separately overnight.

Carve each duck into quarters. Remove fat from under skin. Arrange carved duck skin side up on heavy sheet pan.

MANGO CHUTNEY SAUCE

1/2 **cup sugar**
1/4 **cup water**
1/2 **cup white vinegar**
3   **tablespoons flour**
1/3 **cup currants**
10   **ounces premium mango chutney**

Before reheating duck prepare sauce. Remove cold fat from top of stock, reserving 2 tablespoons. In medium saucepan bring 2 quarts of stock to boil. In small saucepan bring sugar and 1/4 cup water to boil. Cook until mixture caramelizes to golden brown. Add vinegar slowly. Cook until liquid is reduced by half. Add slowly to stock.

In another small saucepan mix flour and reserved 2 tablespoons fat. Cook over very low heat 1 to 2 minutes. Add to sauce. Cook slowly 10 minutes. Stir in currants and chutney.

Reheat duck in preheated 450-degree oven 15 to 18 minutes, draining fat several times. Place breast and thigh portion on each plate. Cover with sauce. Pass remaining sauce.

STUFFED DUCK WITH RICE COMPLEMENT

SERVES 3 TO 4

2	**4-pound ducks**
3-5	**apples, cored, quartered**
1	**cup Burgundy wine**
1/2	**cup water**
1/2	**pound butter, melted**
1/3	**cup lemon juice**
1/4	**cup chopped parsley**
1/4	**cup plus 2 tablespoons chopped green onions, divided**
1	**tablespoon Worcestershire sauce**
1/2	**teaspoon prepared mustard**
	salt to taste
	pepper to taste

Stuff ducks with apples. Place in large roasting pan. In small bowl mix Burgundy and water. Pour over ducks. Pierce skin of ducks. Cover.

Bake in preheated 325-degree oven 2 hours or until tender. Pour off juices. Chill thoroughly. Slice all meat. Place in baking dish. Chill again.

In medium saucepan mix butter and lemon juice. Heat until hot but not boiling. Add remaining ingredients, reserving 2 tablespoons chopped green onions. Mix well. Pour over chilled duck. Let stand at room temperature 30 minutes. Bake covered in preheated 325-degree oven 1 hour. Sprinkle with reserved green onions. Serve with Rice Complement.

RICE COMPLEMENT

1/2	**pound pork sausage**
3	**cups cooked white rice**
1	**tablespoon soy sauce, or to taste**
3/4	**cup chopped green onions**

In medium skillet brown sausage. Drain all but 3 tablespoons fat. Add rice. Heat thoroughly. Pour soy sauce over rice. Add half of green onions. Transfer to 1-quart casserole. Cover. Bake in preheated 350-degree oven 30 minutes. Top with remaining green onions.

CHINESE DUCK

SERVES 2 TO 4

4-5 **pound duck**
soy sauce as needed
1 **clove garlic, minced**
2 **teaspoons ginger**

Remove giblets from duck. Pierce duck lightly with fork to allow fat to drain during roasting. Rub duck generously inside and out with soy sauce followed by generous rubbing of combined garlic and ginger. Cover duck lightly with plastic wrap. Let stand at room temperature 1½ hours.

Remove plastic wrap. Rub another coat of soy sauce over duck. Place duck on greased rack in shallow roasting pan. Bake in preheated 300-degree oven 3 hours, piercing occasionally. If desired, increase heat to 400 degrees for last 30 minutes for additional crispness.

QUARTERED DUCK WITH ORANGE

SERVES 4 TO 6

3 **tablespoons brown sugar**
1½ **cups orange juice**
3 **tablespoons lemon juice**
1½ **tablespoons grated orange rind**
2 **5- to 7-pound ducks, quartered**
salt to taste
pepper to taste

In small bowl combine brown sugar, orange juice, lemon juice, and rind. Mix well. Season ducks to taste. Spread with orange mixture.

Place duck quarters skin side up on rack in shallow baking pan. Brush frequently with orange mixture. Do not pierce skin. Bake duck uncovered in preheated 325-degree oven 3 to 4 hours or until duck is tender. If duck is not brown place under broiler several minutes.

VEGETABLES

CRISPY ASPARAGUS WITH CHICKEN BROTH SAUCE

SERVES 4 TO 6

2 **tablespoons butter**
2 **tablespoons brown sugar**
4 **cups fresh asparagus, in 1-inch pieces**
1 **cup chicken broth**

In large heavy skillet melt butter. Stir in brown sugar. Add asparagus. Sauté 2 minutes. Add chicken broth. Bring to boil. Reduce heat. Cover. Simmer until asparagus is bright green and crisp.

Drain asparagus, reserving cooking liquid. Rinse asparagus under cold water 30 seconds to retain color. Cook reserved liquid until reduced to ½ cup.

To serve, toss asparagus quickly in hot liquid or reheat asparagus and liquid together in microwave.

SPINACH ARTICHOKE TIMBALES

SERVES 8

2 **tablespoons butter or margarine**
9 **ounces frozen artichoke hearts, thawed**
¼ **cup chopped onion**
1 **clove garlic, minced**
2 **eggs plus 2 egg yolks**
1 **cup whipping cream**
⅓ **cup grated Parmesan cheese**
½ **teaspoon salt**
   freshly ground pepper to taste
   pinch cayenne pepper
10 **ounces frozen chopped spinach, thawed, drained well**

In medium skillet melt butter. Sauté artichoke hearts, onion, and garlic until soft. Transfer to food processor. Puree. Add eggs, egg yolks, cream, cheese, salt, pepper, and cayenne. Blend well. Add spinach. Mix well.

Divide mixture among 8 greased individual ½-cup timbale molds or soufflé dishes. Place molds in shallow baking pan. Pour boiling water to halfway up sides of molds.

Bake uncovered in preheated 350-degree oven 20 to 30 minutes or until firm. Remove from oven. Let stand 10 minutes. Loosen sides with sharp knife. Invert onto serving plates.

May be prepared 1 day ahead, covered, refrigerated, and brought to room temperature before baking.

ARTICHOKES WITH AIOLI

6	**artichokes**
1½	**teaspoons salt**
3	**tablespoons olive oil**
2-3	**cloves garlic**
1	**teaspoon chopped fresh oregano or**
	½ teaspoon dried oregano
1½	**teaspoons chopped fresh rosemary or**
	½ teaspoon dried rosemary
1½	**teaspoons chopped fresh thyme or**
	½ teaspoon dried thyme

AIOLI:

1	**egg**
1	**teaspoon Dijon mustard**
2	**teaspoons tarragon or white vinegar**
2-3	**cloves garlic**
½	**teaspoon salt**
	pinch cayenne pepper
½	**cup olive oil**
½	**cup safflower oil**
	paprika

Snip ends of outer leaves of artichokes. Fill 3- to 4-quart saucepan with 2 inches water. Add salt, olive oil, garlic, oregano, rosemary, and thyme. Add artichokes. Cover. Simmer 45 minutes or until tender when pierced with fork. Remove artichokes and drain.

In food processor or blender combine all aioli ingredients except oils. Blend until smooth. With motor running add oils in slow steady stream until thick mayonnaise forms. Cover and refrigerate.

To serve, place each artichoke on individual serving plate. Add 2 tablespoons aioli on side. Sprinkle aioli with paprika.

SPINACH WITH RAISINS AND PINE NUTS

SERVES 4

2 **pounds fresh spinach, stems removed, coarsely chopped**
2 **cloves garlic, peeled, crushed**
1 **tablespoon extra virgin olive oil**
1/3 **cup raisins, soaked in warm water 10 minutes**
1/3 **cup pine nuts, lightly toasted**
    salt to taste
    white pepper to taste

In large saucepan of boiling water cook spinach 10 to 15 seconds. Drain and blot on paper towels.

In large skillet sauté garlic in olive oil until golden but not browned. Remove garlic. Sauté raisins and pine nuts in garlic oil 1 minute. Stir in spinach, salt, and white pepper. Sauté over low heat 3 minutes, stirring constantly.

See photo page 277.

SESAME BROCCOLI WITH PEPPERS

SERVES 6 TO 8

4-5 **cups broccoli flowerets**
1 **yellow pepper, seeded, in thick strips**
1 **red pepper, seeded, in thick strips**
1 **clove garlic, minced**
1 **teaspoon finely grated fresh ginger root**
1/4 **cup fat free chicken broth**
1 **tablespoon sherry**
1 **tablespoon butter**
1 **teaspoon cider vinegar**
1 **teaspoon cornstarch**
    salt to taste
    pepper to taste
1 **tablespoon sesame seed, toasted**

Microwave or blanch broccoli and peppers until tender-crisp. Rinse under cold water. Drain well. Set aside.

In small saucepan combine remaining ingredients except sesame seed. Boil 1 minute. Pour over vegetables. Blend well. Sprinkle with sesame seed.

BROCCOLI STRUDEL

YIELD: FOUR
16-INCH STRUDELS

1/2 cup sliced green onions
2 cloves garlic, minced
2 tablespoons plus 1/2 pound butter, divided
11/4 pounds broccoli
1/2 teaspoon salt
21/2 ounces boiled ham, diced
3 egg yolks, beaten
2 tablespoons chopped parsley
1/2 tablespoon chopped chives
16 ounces 1% small curd cottage cheese
3 tablespoons pesto sauce
3/4 cup grated Parmesan cheese
20 sheets frozen filo dough, thawed
1/2 cup bread crumbs

In medium skillet sauté green onions and garlic in 1 tablespoon butter. Remove and discard lower 3 inches of tough broccoli stems. In large saucepan of salted boiling water cook broccoli several minutes until bright green and still crisp. Chop cooked broccoli into 1/2-inch chunks.

In large bowl combine broccoli, green onions, garlic, ham, egg yolks, parsley, chives, cottage cheese, pesto, and Parmesan cheese. Mix well.

In small saucepan melt 1/2 pound butter. Unfold 1 filo sheet. Brush with melted butter. Sprinkle with 1 teaspoon bread crumbs. Place second filo sheet over first. Brush with butter and sprinkle with 1 teaspoon bread crumbs. Repeat until 5 filo sheets are stacked.

Spread a fourth of broccoli mixture across short end and down 3 inches of stacked filo sheets. Starting at top of short end, roll sheets into cylinder. Brush with remaining 1 tablespoon butter, melted. Cut 3 to 4 slits in top to let strudel vent while baking. Repeat procedure with remaining filo and broccoli mixture.

Arrange cylinders on dry baking sheet. Bake in preheated 350-degree oven 25 minutes or until golden brown. Cool before slicing.

See photo page 277.

BROCCOLI-CHEDDAR CUPS

SERVES 10

10   ounce package ready-to-bake refrigerated buttermilk flaky
     biscuits (10 biscuits)
2   cups chopped fresh broccoli or 10 ounces chopped frozen
     broccoli, cooked, drained
5   ounces Cheddar cheese, grated
1   large plum tomato, chopped
1/4 cup finely chopped green onions
1   tablespoon plus 2 teaspoons margarine, melted

Between 2 sheets of wax paper roll each biscuit into circle 4 inches in diameter. Place 1 biscuit into each of ten 2½-inch-diameter, non-stick muffin tins, pressing it into bottom and up sides to form crust.

In medium bowl combine remaining ingredients. Mix well. Spoon equal amounts of mixture into each biscuit-lined tin. Bake in preheated 400-degree oven 15 to 20 minutes or until biscuits are golden. Serve warm.

CAULIFLOWER PUREE

SERVES 6 TO 8

1   large cauliflower, in flowerets
1   medium onion, chopped
1/2-3/4 cup buttermilk
       salt to taste
       pepper to taste
3   tablespoons butter or margarine
2   tablespoons chopped parsley

In large saucepan combine cauliflower flowerets, onion, and water to cover. Cook 15 minutes or until tender. Drain.

Transfer to food processor. Puree until smooth, slowly adding buttermilk. Add salt, pepper, and butter. Blend well. Pour into greased 1-quart casserole or soufflé dish.

Bake in preheated 350-degree oven until thoroughly heated. Garnish with parsley.

SAUTÉED CAULIFLOWER

SERVES 4 TO 6

1   egg, slightly beaten
1/4   cup milk
1/2   cup flour
1/2   cup grated Parmesan or Romano cheese
1/2   cup vegetable oil, or as needed
1   large head cauliflower, in flowerets

In small bowl combine egg and milk. Mix well. In another small bowl combine flour and cheese. Mix well. In large skillet heat oil over medium heat.

Dip cauliflower flowerets in egg mixture, then in flour mixture. Sauté flowerets in oil until golden brown, turning once. Drain on paper towel.

BRAISED RED CABBAGE WITH CRANBERRIES

SERVES 12

1   tablespoon olive oil
7   tablespoons brown sugar, divided
2   tablespoons minced garlic (about 5 cloves)
3   cups fresh or frozen cranberries, divided
1/2   cup red wine vinegar
2   pounds red cabbage, grated
1   cup dry red wine
1/8-1/4   teaspoon cayenne pepper
      salt to taste

In large non-aluminum saucepan heat olive oil and 3 tablespoons brown sugar over medium heat. Add garlic. Sauté 2 minutes. Add 2 cups cranberries and vinegar. Cover. Cook 4 to 6 minutes or until cranberries begin to burst.

Add cabbage and wine. Cook about 15 minutes until cabbage is tender, stirring occasionally. Add remaining 4 tablespoons brown sugar and cayenne. Mix well. Stir in remaining 1 cup cranberries. Remove from heat. Cover. Let stand 5 minutes or until cranberries are tender. Salt to taste. Serve hot or cold.

See photo page 278.

CABBAGE AND FENNEL SAUTÉ

SERVES 4

2-3	slices bacon, coarsely chopped
1	small onion, chopped
1	pound cabbage, coarsely chopped
1/2	bulb fennel, sliced
1	tablespoon golden raisins
	salt to taste
	pepper to taste
1	tablespoon chopped fresh dill, optional

In large skillet fry bacon over medium heat until just beginning to crisp. Add onion. Cook until onion is soft.

Add cabbage, fennel, and raisins. Sauté 5 minutes or until cabbage and fennel are tender-crisp, stirring frequently. Season to taste. Remove from skillet with slotted spoon. Serve sprinkled with dill, if desired.

CARROT AND ROASTED PEPPER PUREE

SERVES 4

6	medium carrots, in 1-inch slices
1	red pepper, roasted, seeded, coarsely chopped
2	teaspoons unsalted butter, room temperature, or
	4 teaspoons lowfat yogurt
3	tablespoons brown sugar
1/2	teaspoon salt
1/4	teaspoon mace

In medium saucepan combine carrots with water to cover. Bring to boil over medium heat. Reduce heat. Simmer about 10 minutes until tender. Drain well.

In food processor combine carrots and pepper. Process until smooth. Add butter or yogurt, brown sugar, salt, and mace. Process until well blended.

LEMON GLAZED CARROTS

SERVES 4

6   **large carrots, sliced**
1/2   **cup water**
1   **teaspoon salt**
4   **tablespoons butter**
1/4   **cup sugar**
1   **tablespoon lemon juice**
1   **teaspoon grated lemon rind**
2   **tablespoons chopped parsley**

In medium saucepan combine carrots with water and salt. Cover. Bring to boil. Reduce heat. Cook 10 minutes. Drain.

In medium skillet melt butter. Stir in sugar, lemon juice, and lemon rind. Cook over low heat until sugar dissolves. Add carrots. Cook over low heat, stirring until carrots are glazed. Serve warm sprinkled with parsley.

CARROTS GRAND MARNIER

SERVES 8 TO 10

6   **cups finely grated carrots**
2   **cups finely sliced green onions**
1   **cup chicken broth**
4   **tablespoons butter or margarine**
1   **teaspoon finely chopped fresh fennel**
2   **tablespoons Grand Marnier or other orange liqueur**
1 1/2   **tablespoons chopped parsley**
3   **tablespoons grated orange rind**

In large saucepan combine carrots, green onions, and chicken broth. Simmer 2 to 4 minutes or until liquid is completely absorbed. Add butter and fennel. Mix well.

Just before serving stir in liqueur. Garnish with parsley and orange rind.

CARROT PUDDING

SERVES 4 TO 6

¼   **pound butter, softened**
½   **cup brown sugar**
2   **eggs**
1¼   **cups plus 1 tablespoon flour, divided**
1   **teaspoon baking powder**
½   **teaspoon salt, optional**
5   **large carrots, grated**
1   **teaspoon fresh lemon juice**
½   **cup sour cream**
2   **tablespoons margarine, melted**

In large bowl cream butter. Add brown sugar gradually. Mix well. Add eggs 1 at a time, beating well after each addition.

In small bowl sift together 1¼ cups flour, baking powder, and salt, if desired. Add to butter mixture with carrots, lemon juice, and sour cream. Mix well.

Blend melted margarine and remaining 1 tablespoon flour. Coat 6-cup ring mold with mixture. Spoon carrot pudding into mold. Bake in preheated 350-degree oven 30 to 40 minutes.

CARROT CASSEROLE

SERVES 4

1½   **pounds carrots, sliced diagonally into ¾- to 1-inch pieces**
¾   **cup lite mayonnaise**
3   **tablespoons finely grated onion**
2-3   **tablespoons prepared horseradish**
¼   **teaspoon pepper**
¾   **cup herbed stuffing mix**
1   **tablespoon butter or margarine, melted**

In large saucepan cook carrots in water to cover 12 to 14 minutes or until barely softened. Drain, reserving 2 tablespoons cooking liquid. Set aside.

In small bowl combine mayonnaise, onion, horseradish, and pepper. Mix well. Set aside. In another small bowl toss stuffing mix with butter.

Arrange carrots in single layer in lightly greased 8-inch square baking dish. Sprinkle with reserved cooking liquid. Spread mayonnaise mixture over carrots. Sprinkle with stuffing mixture. Bake in preheated 350-degree oven 30 minutes.

May be assembled 6 to 8 hours before serving and refrigerated. Bring to room temperature. Bake 35 minutes.

VENEZUELAN CARROT SOUFFLÉ

SAUCE:

1/2 **medium onion, chopped**
2 **tablespoons chicken broth**
1/2 **green pepper, chopped**
1/2 **red pepper, chopped**
2 **cups plain yogurt**
3 **cloves garlic, minced**
1 **teaspoon Dijon mustard**
2 **teaspoons sugar**
 salt to taste
 pepper to taste

SOUFFLÉ:

2 **pounds carrots, grated**
1 **small onion, grated**
1 **tablespoon butter**
6 **large eggs, slightly beaten**
2 **slices white bread, crusts removed, crumbled**
1/2 **cup milk**
2 **teaspoons flour**
1 **pound Pecorino cheese, grated**
1/2 **pound Swiss or baby Swiss cheese, grated**
1/2 **pound Parmesan cheese, grated**
1/2 **pound mozzarella cheese, grated**
1/2 **red pepper, finely chopped**
1/2 **green pepper, finely chopped**
1 **teaspoon Dijon mustard**
1 **teaspoon Worcestershire sauce**
1 **teaspoon soy sauce**
1/2 **cup chicken broth**
 salt to taste
 pepper to taste

SAUCE:

In small skillet sauté onion in chicken broth. Add peppers. Cook 1 minute.

In medium bowl combine onion and peppers with remaining sauce ingredients. Mix well. Cover. Refrigerate overnight.

SOUFFLÉ:

In large saucepan cook carrots in 1 inch water until slightly softened. In small skillet sauté onion in butter.

continued

In large bowl combine eggs, bread, milk, and flour. Mix well. Add carrots, onion, cheeses, peppers, mustard, Worcestershire sauce, soy sauce, chicken broth, salt, and pepper. Mix well. Pour into greased 10- to 12-inch soufflé dish lined, sides and bottom, with greased aluminum foil.

Bake in preheated 400-degree oven 1 hour or until inserted tester comes out clean. Check during final 15 minutes of baking. Cool 10 to 15 minutes. Invert soufflé onto serving plate and carefully remove foil. Serve warm or cold with or without sauce.

See photo page 279.

PARSNIP POTATO PUREE

SERVES 4

2 **pounds parsnips, peeled, in 1½-inch chunks**
1 **pound Idaho or russet potatoes, peeled, in 1½-inch chunks**
4 **tablespoons butter**
4 **tablespoons margarine**
1 **teaspoon minced green onion**
½ **teaspoon salt, or to taste**
 chopped parsley, optional

In large saucepan cook parsnips and potatoes in water to cover until very soft. Transfer to colander. Drain well.

In same saucepan melt butter and margarine. Add parsnips, potatoes, green onion, and salt. Using hand mixer beat until fluffy. Serve in heated bowl garnished with parsley, if desired.

ONION BLUE CHEESE BUBBLE

SERVES 6

A savory accompaniment to grilled meats or poultry.

*10   1/2-inch-thick slices Italian bread
1 1/4   pounds red onions, thinly sliced
  1/2   pound blue cheese, crumbled
    6   tablespoons unsalted butter, softened
    1   tablespoon Worcestershire sauce
1 1/2   teaspoons basil
    1   teaspoon dill weed
  1/2   teaspoon cracked pepper

Arrange bread on dry baking sheet. Bake in preheated 400-degree oven 4 to 6 minutes or until slightly crisp and lightly toasted. Line bottom of lightly greased 8 1/2- by 11-inch baking dish with toasted bread without overlapping.

Separate onion slices into rings. Cover bread with onions. In small bowl combine remaining ingredients. Spread over onions. Mixture will be lumpy and some onions will remain uncovered.

Bake in preheated 400-degree oven 20 to 25 minutes or until top is bubbly and lightly browned. Watch carefully during final 5 minutes to avoid burning onions.

*If bread slices are especially large or small use as many as necessary to line bottom of baking dish without overlapping.

BAKED ONIONS WITH YOGURT

SERVES 4

    4   onions, 2 to 3 inches in diameter
    2   tablespoons butter or margarine, melted
  1/2   cup plain yogurt
    1   tablespoon lemon juice
    1   tablespoon brown sugar
  1/4   teaspoon salt
  1/4   teaspoon pepper
    2   tablespoons finely chopped parsley

Place unpeeled onions in foil-lined shallow baking dish. Bake in preheated 375-degree oven 1 1/2 hours or until tender.

Spear onions with fork. Cut off both ends and remove skin. Place onions in warmed 1-quart shallow serving dish. Pour butter and yogurt over onions. Sprinkle with lemon juice, brown sugar, salt, and pepper. Top with parsley.

POACHED LEEKS WITH LEMON AND PARSLEY

SERVES 4

8	medium leeks, split, rinsed, white and light green parts only
1/2	bunch Italian parsley
2	teaspoons lemon zest pieces
5	tablespoons olive oil
1/2	teaspoon salt, or to taste
	freshly ground pepper to taste
1	tablespoon fresh lemon juice

In large saucepan of simmering water cook leeks about 20 minutes until tender. Drain. In small saucepan of boiling water cook parsley 30 seconds. Drain and rinse under cold water. Pat dry.

In food processor puree parsley, lemon zest, olive oil, salt, and pepper. Arrange leeks on serving dish. Drizzle lightly with parsley mixture. Sprinkle with lemon juice. Season to taste. Serve cold or at room temperature.

See photo page 277.

PEAS IN LETTUCE

SERVES 4 TO 6

Cooking frozen peas in lettuce leaves makes them taste fresh.

	outside leaves from head of iceberg or romaine lettuce
1	pound frozen peas
2	tablespoons butter, divided
1/2	teaspoon salt
1/2	teaspoon freshly ground pepper
1/4	teaspoon freshly grated nutmeg
8-10	fresh mushrooms, sliced
2	tablespoons diced onion

In large heavy saucepan with tight-fitting lid arrange nest of washed lettuce leaves dripping water. Mound peas in center. Add 1 tablespoon butter, salt, pepper, and nutmeg. Cover with additional lettuce leaves. Cook covered over low heat 15 minutes.

In medium skillet sauté mushrooms and onion in remaining 1 tablespoon butter. Discard lettuce leaves and stir peas into mushrooms and onion.

CORN AND TOMATO SAUTÉ

SERVES 4

2   **tablespoons butter**
3   **cups corn**
1   **small onion, chopped**
     salt to taste
     pepper to taste
1/2   **cup chopped celery or red or green pepper**
1-2   **tomatoes, sliced**
1/3   **cup sour half and half**
1/4   **cup lowfat cream style cottage cheese**
1   **tablespoon chopped fresh basil or 1 teaspoon dried basil**
1/2   **teaspoon dill weed**

In large skillet melt butter. Add corn, onion, salt, and pepper. Cook covered over medium heat 3 to 4 minutes. Add celery, or red or green pepper. Cook covered 3 to 4 minutes. Mound mixture in center of skillet. Arrange tomato slices around edges of skillet.

In small bowl combine remaining ingredients. Mix well. Spread 1 tablespoon cottage cheese mixture over each tomato slice. Cook covered over low heat until tomato slices are warm. Serve each portion of corn mixture topped with tomato slice.

FRESH CORN PUDDING

SERVES 8

4   **cups cooked fresh corn (about 6 ears)**
4   **eggs, well beaten**
2   **tablespoons butter, melted**
2   **teaspoons sugar**
2   **teaspoons salt**
1/2   **teaspoon freshly ground pepper**
3   **drops Tabasco**
2   **cups milk**
1/4   **cup grated Parmesan, Swiss, or Cheddar cheese**

In large bowl combine all ingredients except cheese. Mix well. Pour into greased 2-quart baking dish. Top with cheese. Set baking dish into shallow baking pan partially filled with hot water.

Bake in preheated 350-degree oven 60 to 70 minutes or until inserted tester comes out clean.

ZUCCHINI PANCAKES

YIELD:
TWENTY-FOUR
2¹/₂-INCH
PANCAKES

4 cups shredded zucchini
1 teaspoon salt
¼ cup finely chopped yellow pepper
¼ cup finely chopped red pepper
¼ cup minced green onions
½ teaspoon freshly ground pepper
2 egg whites, beaten
4 tablespoons freshly grated Parmesan cheese
5 dashes Tabasco
4-5 tablespoons flour
3 tablespoons margarine

Place shredded zucchini in colander. Toss with salt. Let stand 10 minutes. Press out excess moisture. Squeeze dry in paper towel.

In medium bowl combine zucchini, peppers, green onions, ground pepper, egg whites, Parmesan cheese, Tabasco, and enough flour to hold mixture together. Blend well. In large skillet melt margarine. Spoon zucchini mixture by tablespoonfuls into hot skillet, flattening slightly. Turn when golden brown on bottom. Brown other side. Drain on paper towel. Serve warm or at room temperature with creamy caviar topping, if desired.

CREAMY CAVIAR TOPPING: (optional)
¾ cup lowfat cottage cheese
1 tablespoon skim milk
2 teaspoons fresh lemon juice
5 cloves garlic, roasted
1 ounce caviar

In food processor or blender combine cottage cheese, milk, and lemon juice. Blend well. Add garlic. Process well. Stir in caviar. Chill.

See photo page 284.

CONFETTI SUPPER PANCAKES

YIELD: TWELVE
TO FIFTEEN
3½-INCH OR
TWENTY-FOUR
2½-INCH
PANCAKES

10 ounces frozen corn, thawed, divided
1   egg yolk
3½ tablespoons yellow cornmeal
3   tablespoons flour
2   tablespoons milk
1   tablespoon chopped chives
¼   teaspoon dried thyme
⅛-½ teaspoon dried crushed red pepper, or to taste
    salt to taste
    pepper to taste
1   cup chopped red pepper
3   egg whites
    melted butter or vegetable oil
16 ounces sour cream or plain yogurt

In food processor or blender puree two-thirds of corn. In large bowl combine puree, remaining whole corn, egg yolk, cornmeal, flour, milk, chives, thyme, dried red pepper, salt, pepper, and chopped red pepper. Mix well. In medium bowl beat egg whites until stiff peaks form. Stir a third beaten egg whites into corn mixture. Gently fold in remaining whites.

Drop batter by ¼ cup (for larger) or ⅛ cup onto hot greased griddle. Pat down slightly with spatula. Cook on both sides until golden. Serve with sour cream or yogurt.

See photo page 284.

ZUCCHINI CASSEROLE

SERVES 12

2   cups cooked rice
7   ounces canned green chilies, chopped, drained
1   pound Monterey Jack cheese, grated, divided
3   medium zucchini, boiled 3 minutes, sliced
2   large tomatoes, sliced
16 ounces sour cream
1   tablespoon finely chopped parsley
1   teaspoon oregano
1   teaspoon salt
2   tablespoons finely chopped green pepper
2   tablespoons finely chopped onion

In greased 9- by 13-inch baking pan evenly spread rice. Layer chilies over rice. Sprinkle two-thirds of cheese over top followed by zucchini and then tomatoes.

In small bowl combine sour cream, parsley, oregano, salt, green pepper, and onion. Mix well. Spread mixture over layer of tomatoes, lifting tomatoes lightly with fork to allow some sour cream to seep in. Top with remaining cheese. Bake in preheated 350-degree oven 30 minutes.

BAKED ZUCCHINI AND TOMATOES WITH OREGANO

SERVES 4

3	**¼-pound zucchini, in ¼-inch rounds**
3	**medium plum tomatoes, in ¼-inch rounds**
	salt to taste
	pepper to taste
1	**medium green pepper, seeded, coarsely chopped**
½	**cup coarsely chopped red onion**
1	**teaspoon finely minced garlic**
1	**tablespoon chopped fresh oregano or 1 to 2 teaspoons dried oregano**
2	**tablespoons grated Parmesan cheese**
2	**tablespoons olive or canola oil**
2-3	**small sprigs oregano, optional (may substitute basil or parsley)**

Starting at outer edge of lightly greased 8- to 9-inch round baking dish, arrange zucchini and tomato rounds alternately. Overlap each by one-half. Reserve 1 tomato round. Season arranged vegetables to taste.

In small bowl combine green pepper, onion, garlic, oregano, and cheese. Mix well. Sprinkle over vegetables. Drizzle with oil. Bake uncovered in preheated 425-degree oven 25 minutes. Arrange reserved tomato round and sprigs oregano, if desired, decoratively on vegetables.

SPAGHETTI SQUASH CASSEROLE

SERVES 6 TO 8

1   **8-inch spaghetti squash**
2-3   **tablespoons butter or margarine**
1/2   **pound fresh mushrooms, sliced**
1   **cup chopped onion**
2   **cloves garlic, crushed**
1/2   **green or red pepper, seeded, chopped**
     salt to taste
     pepper to taste
1   **teaspoon basil**
1/2   **teaspoon oregano**
     pinch thyme
1/4   **cup chopped parsley**
14   **ounces prepared spaghetti sauce**
8   **ounces cottage or ricotta cheese**
1   **cup grated mozzarella cheese**
1   **cup grated Parmesan cheese**

Pierce squash several times with fork. Place on paper towel in microwave oven. Microwave 6 minutes. Turn and microwave 6 to 8 minutes. Cool. Scoop squash meat from outer skin and transfer to large bowl.

In large skillet melt butter. Sauté mushrooms, onion, garlic, and green or red pepper. Add salt, pepper, basil, oregano, thyme, and parsley. Cook until onion is soft. Combine with squash in large bowl.

Add spaghetti sauce, cottage cheese, and mozzarella cheese. Mix well. Pour into greased 2-quart casserole. Top with Parmesan cheese. Bake uncovered in pre-heated 375-degree oven 40 minutes.

SQUASH-APPLE BAKE

SERVES 4 TO 6

4-5   **cups peeled, sliced butternut squash**
1   **medium Granny Smith apple, cored, thinly sliced**
6   **tablespoons brown sugar**
2   **tablespoons butter or margarine**
1/4   **teaspoon cinnamon**
  pinch salt, optional
1/2   **cup orange juice**
1   **teaspoon grated orange rind**

In large saucepan combine sliced squash with boiling salted water. Cook until just tender. Drain.

In greased 1-quart casserole layer squash and apple slices alternately, sprinkling each layer with small amount of brown sugar, dots of butter, a little cinnamon, and salt, if desired. Pour orange juice over all. Sprinkle top with orange rind. Bake covered in preheated 350-degree oven 30 minutes.

CRANBERRY SQUASH

SERVES 8

4   **pounds spaghetti squash, halved, seeded**
1/4   **cup water**
1 1/2   **cups fresh or frozen cranberries, divided**
6   **tablespoons orange juice**
3   **tablespoons sugar**

In large shallow microwavable dish place squash cut side up. Add water. Cover with plastic wrap. Microwave about 12 minutes until soft, checking frequently.* Use fork to scrape cooked squash into large bowl.

In medium saucepan combine 1 1/4 cups cranberries, orange juice, and sugar. Cook over high heat until berries pop, stirring constantly. Reduce heat. Cook 2 to 3 minutes, stirring occasionally. Coarsely chop remaining 1/4 cup cranberries. Add cooked and chopped cranberries to squash in large bowl. Toss lightly.

*If microwave is not available place cut squash in large pot with water 2 inches above top of squash. Bring to boil. Reduce heat. Simmer covered about 15 minutes until soft. Drain.

PORTOBELLO MUSHROOMS STUFFED WITH EGGPLANT

SERVES 5

5   **portobello mushrooms, stems removed and chopped**
2   **tablespoons butter**
1   **medium eggplant, peeled**
1   **teaspoon salt, divided**
3   **tablespoons olive oil**
1   **medium onion, finely chopped**
1   **large tomato, peeled, seeded, chopped**
    freshly ground pepper to taste
1/4   **teaspoon cumin**
4   **tablespoons grated Parmesan cheese, divided**
1   **teaspoon lemon juice**
1   **teaspoon finely chopped parsley**
3   **large fresh basil leaves, chopped**
12   **black olives, pitted, sliced**

Reserving stems, sauté mushrooms in butter in large skillet 5 minutes on each side. Set aside. Slice eggplant lengthwise into 1/4-inch strips. Cut strips into 1-inch-long pieces. Sprinkle eggplant with 1/2 teaspoon salt and let drain in colander 10 minutes.

In large skillet heat olive oil. Sauté onion until golden. Do not brown. Add eggplant and reserved mushroom stems. Sauté until almost tender. Add tomato, pepper, cumin, 3 tablespoons Parmesan cheese, lemon juice, parsley, basil, remaining 1/2 teaspoon salt, and olives. Mix well. Heat thoroughly.

Fill mushrooms evenly with eggplant mixture, rounding well. Sprinkle with remaining 1 tablespoon Parmesan cheese. Transfer to large greased baking dish. Bake in preheated 350-degree oven 20 to 25 minutes.

See photo page 277.

MUSHROOM STRUDEL

YIELD: 12 SLICES

5-6	green onions with tops, finely chopped
1/4	pound plus 6 tablespoons butter, divided
1	pound fresh mushrooms, finely chopped
1/4	pound prosciutto, finely chopped
3	tablespoons chopped parsley
2 1/2	ounces Boursin cheese with garlic and herbs
8	ounces cream cheese
1/4	teaspoon fresh thyme
2-3	tablespoons white wine
3	egg yolks
1	egg, beaten
1	teaspoon salt
	pepper to taste
8	sheets frozen filo dough, thawed

In large skillet sauté green onions in 1/4 pound butter 2 minutes. Add mushrooms. Cook 2 to 3 minutes, stirring constantly. Remove from heat. Add prosciutto, parsley, and cheeses. Stir until cheeses are melted and well blended. Add thyme, wine, egg yolks, salt, and pepper. Mix well. Refrigerate until cool.

Place 1 filo sheet on towel or wax paper. Brush with 1 tablespoon melted butter. Place second filo sheet over first. Brush with 1 tablespoon melted butter. Repeat until 4 filo sheets are stacked.

Spread half of mushroom mixture over top of filo sheets, leaving 2-inch margin along 1 long side. Lift towel or wax paper, using it to roll sheets over filling, jelly-roll fashion, starting from long end spread with mushroom filling. Roll into cylinder 2 inches in diameter. Place cylinder on buttered 10- by 15-inch baking pan.

Repeat procedure with remaining filo sheets and mushroom filling. Brush tops of cylinders with remaining butter melted and beaten egg. Bake in preheated 350-degree oven 15 minutes. Increase heat to 450 degrees. Bake 5 to 10 minutes. Cut into slices. Serve warm.

EGGPLANT PUREE PIE

SERVES 8

1 pound eggplant, peeled, in 1/4-inch slices
  cooking spray
3 eggs
1 1/2 cups ricotta cheese
6 ounces cream cheese (may substitute lite)
1 cup grated Parmesan cheese, divided
1/2 cup bread crumbs
  salt and pepper to taste
5 green onions, sliced
1 tomato, chopped, optional

Arrange eggplant slices on baking sheet sprayed with cooking spray. Bake in preheated 400-degree oven 20 minutes.

In large bowl combine baked eggplant, eggs, ricotta cheese, cream cheese, 3/4 cup Parmesan cheese, bread crumbs, salt, pepper, and green onions. Puree mixture in 2 batches in food processor. Pour into lightly greased 8-inch pie pan.

Bake in preheated 350-degree oven 25 minutes. Sprinkle remaining 1/4 cup Parmesan cheese over top. Bake 20 minutes. Place under broiler to brown, if desired. Serve with tomato sprinkled over top, if desired.

BAKED EGGPLANT, TOMATO, AND CHÈVRE CHEESE

SERVES 4

4 1/2-inch slices eggplant, peeled
4 tablespoons margarine, or as needed
  salt to taste
4 1/2-inch slices large tomato
4 1/2-inch slices chèvre cheese
2 tablespoons olive oil
1/2 cup coarse bread crumbs, toasted

In large skillet sauté eggplant in margarine 5 to 6 minutes until softened and lightly browned on both sides. Salt to taste. Place 1 slice in each of 4 small individual baking dishes. Cover each with tomato slice.

Dip cheese slices in olive oil on both sides. Dredge cheese in bread crumbs to coat. Place 1 cheese slice over each tomato slice in each baking dish.

Bake in preheated 350-degree oven 10 minutes or until cheese is slightly melted and browned. Place under broiler to brown, if desired.

SZECHWAN EGGPLANT

SERVES 4

1½ **pounds eggplant, peeled, in ¾-inch cubes**
1 **teaspoon salt**
2 **tablespoons vegetable oil**
1 **tablespoon minced fresh ginger root**
2 **cloves garlic, minced**
4 **ounces ground pork, optional**
½ **cup water**
2 **tablespoons soy sauce**
1 **tablespoon dry sherry or Scotch**
2 **teaspoons cornstarch**
½ **teaspoon sugar**
¼-½ **teaspoon Tabasco**
2 **tablespoons chopped fresh coriander or parsley**

In colander toss eggplant cubes with salt. Let stand 1 hour. Press out excess liquid between layers of paper towels.

In wok or large skillet heat oil. Add ginger root and garlic. Stir fry 30 seconds. Add pork, if desired. Stir fry 2 minutes or until no longer pink. Add eggplant. Toss and cook until coated with oil.

In small bowl combine water, soy sauce, sherry, cornstarch, sugar, and Tabasco. Mix well. Stir into wok. Cover. Reduce heat to medium. Cook 5 minutes or until eggplant is tender, stirring occasionally. Serve sprinkled with coriander or parsley.

EGGPLANT LASAGNA

SERVES 6

2 pounds eggplant, peeled, in ¼-inch slices
2-3 tablespoons olive oil
*2 cups tomato sauce, page 127
8 ounces skim milk ricotta cheese
2 tablespoons finely chopped parsley
4 ounces mozzarella cheese, thinly sliced
3 tablespoons grated Parmesan cheese

Arrange eggplant slices on large baking sheet. Brush with olive oil. Broil 5 minutes on each side.

In large casserole spoon layer of tomato sauce. Place single layer of eggplant on sauce. Follow with layer of ricotta mixed with parsley. Top with layer of mozzarella cheese, tomato sauce, and Parmesan cheese. Repeat layers in same order until all ingredients are used, ending with mozzarella sprinkled with Parmesan.

Bake in preheated 350-degree oven 25 minutes or until cheese is melted.

*May substitute tomato sauce of choice.

CHILI-CHEESE TOMATOES

SERVES 6

3 large or 4 medium tomatoes, peeled
1 cup sour cream
1 tablespoon flour
1 teaspoon sugar
½ teaspoon salt
¼ teaspoon freshly ground pepper
3 tablespoons mild, canned, chopped green chilies, or to taste
1 cup grated longhorn Cheddar cheese

Slice large tomatoes in 3 thick slices or medium tomatoes in half horizontally. Squeeze gently to remove some seeds. Arrange tomatoes on broiler pan.

In small bowl combine remaining ingredients except cheese. Mix well. Spoon mixture over tomatoes. Sprinkle with cheese. Just before serving place in preheated broiler 4 inches from heat. Broil 4 minutes or until cheese is bubbly and golden brown.

GREEN TOMATO CASSEROLE

SERVES 8

2   **large onions, sliced**
2-3   **tablespoons butter or olive oil**
8   **green tomatoes, in ¹/₂-inch pieces**
1   **teaspoon salt**
1   **teaspoon curry powder**
¹/₂   **teaspoon paprika**
¹/₄   **teaspoon pepper**
1   **cup dark brown sugar**
¹/₂   **cup water**
    bread crumbs
    grated Parmesan cheese

In large skillet sauté onions in butter until opaque. Remove onions with slotted spoon, reserving liquid in skillet. Set aside onions. Sauté tomatoes in onion liquid. Remove tomatoes with slotted spoon, reserving liquid. Set aside tomatoes. Add salt, curry powder, paprika, pepper, brown sugar, and water to liquid. Simmer 5 minutes.

Spread layer of onions in 2-quart casserole. Cover with layer of tomatoes. Repeat layers until all onions and tomatoes are used. Add simmered liquid to within 1 inch of top of casserole. Top with bread crumbs and/or Parmesan cheese. Bake in preheated 300-degree oven until crumbs and/or cheese brown and juice simmers.

SUMMER GARDEN TART

SERVES 6 TO 8

PASTRY:
- 1/4 **pound butter, in pieces**
- 13/4 **cups flour**
- **salt to taste, optional**
- 1 **egg yolk**
- 1 **tablespoon plus 1 teaspoon vegetable oil**
- 4 **tablespoons ice water**

FILLING:
- 1 1/2 **cups peeled, cubed eggplant**
- **salt**
- 2 **tablespoons olive oil**
- 1 **tablespoon margarine**
- 1 **large onion, chopped**
- 1 1/2 **cups sliced fresh mushrooms**
- 3 **large ripe tomatoes, peeled, seeded, coarsely chopped**
- 2 **heaping tablespoons tomato paste**
- 1 **tablespoon chopped fresh basil**
- 1 **teaspoon chopped fresh thyme**
- 1/4 **teaspoon oregano**
- **pepper to taste**
- 3 **eggs, beaten**

- 3 **tablespoons Dijon mustard**
- 1 **cup grated Gruyère cheese, divided**

For pastry, in food processor combine butter and flour. Process until mixture resembles coarse meal. Add salt, if desired, egg yolk, oil, and ice water. Process until dough forms ball. Flatten dough and place between 2 sheets of plastic wrap. Refrigerate 1 hour.

Place eggplant in colander and salt well. Set aside to drain.

In large skillet heat olive oil and margarine. Add onion. Cook 2 minutes. Add mushrooms and drained eggplant. Cook until lightly browned. Remove from skillet and set aside.

Add tomatoes and tomato paste to skillet. Mix well. Heat thoroughly. Stir in basil, thyme, oregano, and salt and pepper to taste. Add eggplant mixture to skillet. Mix well. Remove from heat. Stir in eggs.

Roll out pastry and fit into 9-inch pie pan. Spread mustard over pastry. Sprinkle 1/2 cup cheese over mustard. Pour eggplant mixture into crust and cover with remaining 1/2 cup cheese. Bake in preheated 375-degree oven 45 minutes or until top is set.

VEGETABLE MEDLEY

SERVES 8 TO 10

1 **pound green beans, trimmed, in 2$\frac{1}{2}$- to 3-inch slices**
2 **tablespoons margarine**
2 **tablespoons olive oil**
1 **clove garlic, minced**
1 **pound portobello mushrooms, 3 inches or more in diameter, in $\frac{1}{3}$-inch slices**
1 **medium eggplant, peeled, in $\frac{1}{2}$-inch slices**
1 **tablespoon chopped parsley**
1 **teaspoon thyme**
  salt and pepper to taste

In medium saucepan cook or steam green beans 4 to 6 minutes. Drain. Rinse under cold water. Set aside.

In large skillet heat margarine and olive oil. Add garlic and sauté until softened. Add mushrooms and eggplant. Sauté over low heat 5 to 10 minutes. Add reserved beans, parsley, thyme, salt, and pepper. Mix well. Serve warm or at room temperature. See photo page 278.

ROASTED VEGETABLES

SERVES 6 TO 8

4 **tablespoons olive oil, or as needed, divided**
1 **large red onion, in $\frac{1}{4}$-inch slices**
3 **tablespoons balsamic vinegar, divided**
6-7 **plum tomatoes, in $\frac{1}{4}$- to $\frac{1}{2}$-inch slices**
3 **large fresh basil leaves, in $\frac{1}{4}$- to $\frac{1}{2}$-inch strips**
  salt and pepper to taste
1 **large eggplant, peeled, in $\frac{1}{4}$- to $\frac{1}{2}$-inch slices**
$\frac{1}{2}$ **medium red pepper, in strips**
$\frac{1}{2}$ **yellow pepper, in strips**
  sprigs rosemary and sprigs thyme

In 9- by 13-inch baking dish spread thin layer of olive oil. Separate onion slices into rings and layer over bottom of dish. Brush rings with thin layer of vinegar and drizzle with olive oil. Layer tomatoes over onions. Brush with vinegar and olive oil. Sprinkle with basil, salt, and pepper.

Bake in preheated 450-degree oven 30 minutes. Remove from oven. Add layer of eggplant. Cover with pepper strips. Brush with remaining vinegar and olive oil. Top with rosemary and thyme. Season to taste.

Return to 450-degree oven for 30 minutes. Serve hot or at room temperature.

MARINATED VEGETABLES

SERVES 4

MARINADE:

4 tablespoons white wine vinegar
2 tablespoons balsamic vinegar
1 teaspoon salt
1/2 teaspoon chopped parsley
1/4 teaspoon dried thyme
1/4 teaspoon dried basil or 1 teaspoon fresh basil, in thin strips
1/4 teaspoon freshly ground pepper
1 clove garlic, slivered
1/2 cup olive oil or 6 tablespoons vegetable oil plus
    2 tablespoons olive oil

1 pound fresh asparagus, cooked tender-crisp
1 medium green pepper, in 1/4-inch strips
1 medium red pepper, in 1/4-inch strips
1 medium yellow pepper, in 1/4-inch strips

In small bowl combine all marinade ingredients. Mix well. Pour into large plastic storage bag. Add asparagus and pepper strips. Seal bag. Transfer bag to refrigerator.

Marinate vegetables several hours or overnight, turning occasionally. Serve chilled or at room temperature.

CURRIED VEGETABLES

SERVES 4 TO 6

2 tablespoons vegetable oil
1 medium onion, sliced
1 clove garlic, minced
1 teaspoon grated fresh ginger root
2-3 teaspoons curry powder
4 cups sliced zucchini or 2 cups sliced zucchini and
    2 cups sliced yellow squash
*2 cups sliced Japanese eggplant
1/4 cup slivered almonds, toasted, chopped
1/4 cup raisins
1/4 cup plus 1 tablespoon water, divided
1 tablespoon cornstarch
1/2 teaspoon salt
1 cup plain yogurt
    cooked rice or couscous

In large skillet heat oil. Sauté onion, garlic, and ginger root 2 minutes. Add curry powder, zucchini, and eggplant. Cook 5 minutes, stirring constantly. Add almonds, raisins, and 1/4 cup water. Cover. Reduce heat and simmer 5 minutes or until tender.

In small bowl combine cornstarch, salt, and remaining 1 tablespoon water. Mix well. Stir into vegetables. Cook until vegetables are glazed. Remove from heat. Let stand 3 minutes. Stir in yogurt. Serve over rice or couscous.

*May substitute small slices domestic eggplant, if desired.

VEGETABLE STEW

SERVES 6

2	**large tomatoes, peeled, sliced**
2	**medium onions, thinly sliced**
1	**clove garlic, minced**
2	**large zucchini, sliced**
1	**medium head romaine lettuce, shredded**
10	**ounces frozen peas**
1	**cup minced parsley, divided**
2	**tablespoons minced fresh basil leaves**
10	**ounces frozen lima beans or fava beans**
1/3-1/2	**cup olive oil**
	salt to taste
	freshly ground pepper to taste
	grated Parmesan cheese

Spread tomatoes over bottom of large saucepan. Top with onions and garlic. Layer with zucchini. Add lettuce. Top with peas. Sprinkle 1/2 cup parsley and basil over peas. Add beans. Sprinkle remaining 1/2 cup parsley and olive oil over all. Be sure to follow this order. *Do not stir or mix vegetables.*

Cook covered over medium heat 10 minutes or until vegetables at bottom of saucepan release their liquid. Season to taste. Stir vegetables and mix well. Cook covered over low heat 30 minutes or until beans are tender, stirring frequently. Serve sprinkled with Parmesan cheese.

FIVE-VEGETABLE TORTE

SERVES 8 TO 10

4-5	**tablespoons olive oil**
1	**large Spanish onion, sliced ¼ inch thick**
3	**medium yellow squash, sliced ¼ inch thick**
3	**medium zucchini, sliced ¼ inch thick**
1	**medium red pepper, sliced ¼ inch thick**
1	**yellow pepper, sliced ¼ inch thick**
1	**green pepper, sliced ¼ inch thick**
½	**pound fresh mushrooms, including stems, sliced ¼ inch thick**
6	**large eggs**
¼	**cup whipping cream**
2	**cups stale bread, in ½-inch cubes**
8	**ounces cream cheese, in small pieces**
2	**cups grated Swiss cheese**
2	**teaspoons salt**
2	**teaspoons pepper**
	rosemary to taste, optional
	thyme to taste, optional

In large pot heat olive oil. Add onion, squash, zucchini, peppers, and mushrooms. Cook over medium-high heat about 15 minutes until vegetables are slightly cooked but still crisp, stirring constantly. Drain.

In large bowl beat eggs and cream. Add remaining ingredients. Stir vegetables into egg mixture. Mix well. Pour into greased 9-inch springform pan, packing mixture tightly. Place on baking sheet.

Bake in preheated 350-degree oven 1 to 1½ hours or until firm to touch, puffed, and brown. If top browns too quickly during baking, cover with aluminum foil. Serve hot, at room temperature, or cold.

May be reheated in preheated 350-degree oven for about 30 minutes.

PASTA, RICE, & POTATOES

SEVEN VEGETABLE PASTA

SERVES 6 TO 8

½   **teaspoon salt**
1   **medium eggplant, cubed**
1   **rib celery, finely chopped**
1   **large clove garlic, minced**
1   **medium onion, thinly sliced**
⅓   **cup finely chopped Italian parsley**
⅓   **cup olive oil**
2   **medium zucchini, cubed**
¼   **cup water**
½   **pound fresh mushrooms, sliced**
28   **ounces canned crushed tomatoes**
1   **cup dry white wine**
1   **tablespoon dried oregano, crushed**
   salt to taste
   freshly ground pepper to taste
1½   **pounds penne pasta or pasta of choice, cooked**
½   **cup freshly grated Parmesan cheese**

Salt eggplant and let stand 1 hour. Rinse and squeeze out all liquid. Set aside.

In large skillet combine celery, garlic, onion, and parsley. Sauté in olive oil until soft. Add zucchini, eggplant, and water. Cover. Cook 10 minutes. Uncover. Add mushrooms, tomatoes, wine, oregano, salt, and pepper. Cover. Simmer 15 minutes or until desired doneness. Serve sauce over hot pasta with freshly grated Parmesan cheese.

ARUGULA PESTO PASTA

SERVES 2

2 medium cloves garlic
2 tablespoons pine nuts, toasted
1 cup arugula
2 tablespoons chopped fresh basil
½ cup olivada San Remo (olive spread)
2 teaspoons lemon juice
   salt and pepper to taste
¾ cup olive oil
½ cup grated Parmesan cheese
8 ounces fettucine or linguine

For pesto combine garlic and pine nuts in food processor. Process until chopped. Add arugula and basil. Process until paste forms. Add olivada, lemon juice, salt, and pepper. Blend well. With motor running slowly add olive oil, processing until thoroughly blended. Add Parmesan cheese. Mix well.

Cook pasta according to package directions. Drain. Add as much pesto as desired. Mix well. Serve at room temperature.

PASTA WITH FRESH BASIL

SERVES 4

3 tablespoons extra virgin olive oil
1 tablespoon butter or margarine
4 medium cloves garlic, crushed
6-8 Italian plum tomatoes
½ cup water
1 teaspoon salt
½ teaspoon pepper
⅔ pound penne pasta
10 fresh basil leaves, chopped
½ cup grated Parmesan cheese

In medium saucepan heat olive oil and butter over medium heat. Add garlic. Sauté 2 minutes. Plunge tomatoes in boiling water for 20 seconds. Drain. Remove skins. Cut up and add to saucepan. Stir in water, salt, and pepper. Cook over medium heat 15 to 20 minutes, stirring occasionally.

Cook pasta according to package directions. Drain. Just before serving add basil to sauce, stir, and serve over pasta. Sprinkle Parmesan cheese over each serving.

FETTUCINE WITH CREAMY TOMATO SAUCE

SERVES 2

8   tablespoons butter or margarine, divided
6   ounces tomatoes, peeled, seeded, chopped
     salt to taste
     pepper to taste
1/4 pound prosciutto, chopped
1/2 red or green pepper, roasted, peeled, in strips
1/2 cup frozen peas
8   ounces fettucine
1/2 cup whipping cream
1/3 cup freshly grated Parmesan cheese

For creamy tomato sauce, melt 4 tablespoons butter in medium saucepan. Add tomatoes, salt, and pepper. Simmer 10 minutes. Stir in prosciutto, pepper strips, and peas. Hold over low heat.

In large saucepan of boiling water cook fettucine until "al dente" (slightly under-done). Drain pasta. Transfer to warmed serving bowl. Top with cream and Parmesan cheese. Dot with remaining 4 tablespoons butter. Add tomato sauce. Toss lightly.

See photo page 278.

PASTA WITH SPINACH-GORGONZOLA SAUCE

SERVES 2

2   tablespoons butter
4   ounces imported Gorgonzola cheese
1   pound fresh spinach, cooked, drained, pureed
1   tablespoon beef broth
1¼   cups dry Marsala
3/4   cup whipping cream
1   clove garlic, minced
      freshly ground pepper to taste
8   ounces fettucine
      freshly grated Parmesan cheese

For spinach-Gorgonzola sauce, combine butter and Gorgonzola cheese in large saucepan. Cook over low heat until smooth, stirring constantly. Add spinach, beef broth, and Marsala. Mix well. Cook 5 minutes. Gradually add cream, garlic, and pepper. Cook 3 to 4 minutes.

Cook fettucine according to package directions. Drain. Transfer to serving platter. Pour sauce over pasta. Sprinkle Parmesan cheese over top. Serve immediately.

GRILLED VEGETABLE PASTA WITH PISTACHIO BASIL PESTO

SERVES 6

7-10	**cloves garlic, minced**
¼	**cup chopped fresh basil**
¾	**cup olive oil**
1	**cup grated Romano or Parmesan cheese**
¾	**cup chopped pistachios**
1	**pint cherry tomatoes**
1	**red pepper, in ¾- to 1-inch cubes**
1	**yellow pepper, in ¾- to 1-inch cubes**
1	**medium onion, in 1-inch cubes**
1	**whole elephant garlic, equivalent to 3 large cloves, in ⅛-inch slices**
3	**small zucchini, in ½-inch slices**
1	**pound fresh mushrooms, halved**
1	**package bamboo skewers, soaked**
1½	**pounds fettucine**

For pistachio basil pesto sauce, process garlic and basil in food processor or blender until smooth. With motor running add olive oil gradually. Stir in cheese and pistachios. Set aside.

Place vegetables on skewers. Grill 10 to 15 minutes, turning halfway through cooking time. Cook pasta according to package directions. Drain. Transfer to large serving bowl. Add half of vegetables and pesto sauce and toss. Top with remaining vegetables.

CLOCKWISE FROM UPPER LEFT: PORTOBELLO MUSHROOMS STUFFED WITH EGGPLANT, POACHED LEEKS WITH LEMON AND PARSLEY, BROCCOLI STRUDEL, AND SPINACH WITH RAISINS AND PINE NUTS

CLOCKWISE FROM UPPER LEFT: VEGETABLE MEDLEY, BRAISED RED CABBAGE WITH CRANBERRIES, RICE SALAD WITH CUCUMBERS AND SHRIMP, AND FETTUCCINI WITH CREAMY TOMATO SAUCE

VENEZUELAN CARROT SOUFFLÉ AND CHILLED ASPARAGUS ORIENTAL

LEFT TO RIGHT: OLD-FASHIONED SWEET POTATOES, RED CHILI PASTA, AND A FEAST OF RICE

PASTA NESTS WITH CREAMED SPINACH

SERVES 10 TO 12

PASTA NESTS:

8   **ounces angel hair pasta**
    canola oil as needed
    salt to taste

CREAMED SPINACH:

20 **ounces frozen chopped spinach**
3   **tablespoons butter**
3   **tablespoons flour**
1   **cup milk**
1/8 **teaspoon nutmeg**
1/2-1 **teaspoon salt, or to taste**
    pepper to taste
1/4 **teaspoon A-1 sauce**
1/4 **teaspoon Maggi seasoning**
    pinch garlic powder
1/4 **pound fresh mushrooms, sliced, sautéed, optional**
1   **large onion, chopped, sautéed, optional**

PASTA NESTS:

Cook pasta according to package directions. Drain well. Mix with small amount of canola oil to prevent sticking.

Shape 1/3 cup noodles into 2-inch round mass with fork pressing into bowl of large spoon. Indent center to form nest. Repeat until all noodles have been assembled into nests. Place nests 1 at a time on large slotted spoon. In skillet lower each nest in hot oil and cook until nest begins to brown and holds shape. Turn over and brown other side. Remove with slotted spoon. Drain on paper towel. Salt to taste.

CREAMED SPINACH:

Cook spinach according to package directions. Drain and squeeze dry. In double boiler melt butter. Gradually stir in flour. Add milk. Mix well. In food processor combine spinach, butter mixture, nutmeg, salt, pepper, A-1 sauce, Maggi seasoning, and garlic powder. Process until well blended. Stir in mushrooms and/or onion, if desired.

Fill pasta nests with spinach mixture. Arrange on baking sheet. Bake in preheated 350-degree oven 15 to 20 minutes.

LEFT TO RIGHT:
CONFETTI SUPPER
PANCAKES AND
ZUCCHINI PANCAKES

LASAGNA WITH SPINACH PESTO

SERVES 8

*SPINACH PESTO:

10 ounces frozen chopped spinach, thawed, well drained,
       juice reserved
1   cup chopped parsley
²⁄₃ cup grated Parmesan cheese
½   cup walnut pieces
4   flat anchovies
2   cloves garlic, minced
1   tablespoon dried basil
¼   teaspoon ground fennel seed
    salt to taste
¼   cup olive oil

WHITE SAUCE:

¼   pound butter
½   cup flour
3   cups milk
½   teaspoon salt
½   teaspoon white pepper
½   teaspoon freshly grated nutmeg, optional

1   pound lasagna noodles
½   cup pine nuts, optional
3   cups grated Fontina or mozzarella cheese
1   cup grated Parmesan cheese

For spinach pesto, combine all pesto ingredients except olive oil and spinach juice in food processor. Process until smooth. Add olive oil gradually, continuing to process. Add ⅓ cup reserved spinach juice. Process briefly.

For white sauce, melt butter in medium saucepan over medium heat. Stir in flour. Cook 1 minute, stirring constantly. Add milk gradually, continuing to stir. Cook and stir until sauce thickens. Add salt, white pepper, and nutmeg, if desired.

Cook lasagna noodles according to package directions. Rinse with cold water. Drain.

Spread a third of sauce in bottom of 9- by 13-inch baking pan. Layer a third of noodles over sauce. Sprinkle with pine nuts, if desired. Divide 2 cups pesto into thirds. Spread ⅔ cup of pesto over pine nuts. Follow with a third of each cheese. Repeat layering, finishing with cheese. Bake in preheated 350-degree oven 30 to 40 minutes or until bubbling and lightly browned. Cool 10 minutes before cutting.

*May be made several days ahead and refrigerated. Bring to room temperature for easier spreading.

VEGETARIAN PASTA

½ cup dried mushrooms

1 cup boiling water

olive oil

2 pounds fresh mushrooms, coarsely chopped

8 cloves garlic, minced

juice of 1 lemon

1 tablespoon Worcestershire sauce

5 tablespoons chopped fresh basil or 2 tablespoons dried basil

2 teaspoons dried oregano

1 teaspoon dried chilies or cayenne pepper, or to taste

1 teaspoon freshly ground pepper

1 cup dry red wine

3 pieces lemon rind, 1 by 3 inches, yellow part only

12 ounces tomato paste

28 ounces canned tomato puree

28 ounces canned crushed tomatoes

2 tablespoons honey or molasses

10 ounces beef bouillon

2 cups water

1½ pounds pasta of choice

In small bowl soak dried mushrooms in 1 cup boiling water 30 minutes or until softened. Drain, reserving liquid. Strain liquid through cheesecloth or paper towel. Reserve. Wash mushrooms and chop.

Heat large skillet over medium heat 1 minute. Add enough olive oil just to cover bottom of skillet. Sauté fresh mushrooms until they start to brown. Add garlic and dried mushrooms. Cook 5 minutes. Add lemon juice and Worcestershire sauce. Cook 1 minute. Add basil, oregano, chilies, and pepper. Cook 1 minute. Stir in reserved mushroom liquid, wine, and lemon rind. Add tomato paste, puree, crushed tomatoes, honey, and beef bouillon. Mix well. Blend in 2 cups water. Simmer partially covered at least 1 hour, stirring occasionally. Mixture should thicken. Add water if too thick. Cook pasta according to package directions. Drain. Serve sauce over pasta.

SPINACH LINGUINE WITH SUN-DRIED TOMATOES

SERVES 6 TO 8

8 ounces spinach linguine
3-4 tablespoons olive oil
4 large plum tomatoes, coarsely chopped
1 red pepper, coarsely chopped
3 large cloves garlic, minced
1 bunch green onions with tops, thinly sliced
12 sun-dried tomatoes (in oil), drained, chopped
1 teaspoon dried basil
1/2 teaspoon dried oregano
1 teaspoon salt
1/2 teaspoon pepper
4 tablespoons chopped parsley, divided

In large saucepan cook linguine in salted water over medium heat until tender but firm. Drain. Set aside.

In large heavy skillet heat olive oil. Add remaining ingredients except 2 tablespoons parsley. Sauté 3 to 4 minutes, stirring constantly. Add linguine. Toss thoroughly over medium-high heat until hot. Transfer to serving bowl. Garnish with remaining 2 tablespoons parsley. Serve immediately.

SPINACH AND RED PEPPER PASTA

SERVES 4 TO 6

1/2 cup olive oil
1 large clove garlic, minced
1 tablespoon fresh basil leaves, in narrow strips
1 tablespoon chopped parsley
12 ounces penne pasta
1 pound fresh spinach, stems removed
1/2 cup seeded, diced red pepper
salt to taste
pepper to taste
1/2 cup grated Parmesan cheese

continued

288

In large pot heat olive oil. Add garlic, basil, and parsley. Cook 3 minutes. Set aside.

Cook pasta according to package directions. Drain. Add just enough of the olive oil mixture to coat pasta. Add spinach and red pepper to reserved oil mixture. Return to heat and cook until spinach wilts and both vegetables are heated through. Add pasta. Mix well. Season to taste. Transfer to serving dish. Add as much Parmesan cheese as desired. Pass any remaining cheese.

PASTA WITH RED PEPPER-LENTIL SAUCE

SERVES 6 TO 7

1	**cup dried lentils**
5	**cups water**
2	**bay leaves**
2	**cups diced onions**
2	**cloves garlic, minced**
1	**tablespoon dried basil**
1	**cup dry red wine, divided**
2	**cups red peppers, seeded, chopped**
1	**teaspoon balsamic vinegar**
	salt to taste
	freshly ground pepper to taste
2	**tablespoons tomato paste**
1-1½	**pounds pasta of choice, cooked**
	chopped fresh basil

Rinse lentils in colander. In large saucepan boil water. Add lentils and bay leaves. Simmer 20 to 30 minutes until lentils are tender but not mushy. Drain and remove bay leaves.

In large non-stick pot or skillet combine onions, garlic, dried basil, and ½ cup wine. Cook covered over medium heat. Add peppers. Cook about 25 minutes until soft.

Transfer vegetable mixture to food processor. Puree. Return to pot. Stir in lentils. Stir in remaining ½ cup wine, vinegar, salt, pepper, and tomato paste. Cook gently 10 minutes. Serve sauce over hot pasta. Garnish with fresh basil.

RED CHILI PASTA

For those who enjoy highly seasoned food.

½ pound fresh mushrooms, sliced
3 tablespoons garlic oil, divided
7¼ ounces roasted red peppers, drained, sliced
6 ounces marinated artichoke hearts, drained, sliced
2½ ounces canned, sliced black olives, drained
1 pound red chili pasta
½ cup grated Parmesan cheese
salt to taste
pepper to taste

In medium skillet sauté mushrooms in 1 tablespoon garlic oil. In medium bowl combine mushrooms, peppers, artichoke hearts, and olives. Mix well.

Cook pasta according to package directions. Drain. In large bowl toss remaining 2 tablespoons garlic oil with pasta. Stir mushroom mixture into pasta. Sprinkle with cheese. Season to taste.

See photo page 280.

SHRIMP CREOLE PASTA

2   cups chopped celery
1   large yellow onion, chopped
1   green pepper, chopped
¼   cup olive oil
½   teaspoon black pepper
½   teaspoon white pepper
¼   teaspoon cayenne pepper
1   teaspoon dried thyme
1   teaspoon dried basil
3   bay leaves
1   teaspoon salt
28 ounces canned crushed tomatoes
6   ounces tomato paste
7   cups water or shrimp stock
2   teaspoons sugar
2   chicken bouillon cubes
1½-2 pounds cooked, shelled, deveined shrimp
½   cup chopped parsley
½   cup chopped green onions
1   pound fettucine, cooked, or 2 cups cooked rice

In Dutch oven combine celery, onion, green pepper, olive oil, peppers, thyme, basil, bay leaves, and salt. Cook 10 minutes. Add tomatoes, tomato paste, water, sugar, and bouillon cubes. Bake covered in preheated 350-degree oven 2 to 2½ hours. Turn off oven. Stir in shrimp, parsley, and green onions. Let stand covered in oven 10 to 15 minutes. Serve over fettucine or rice.

PESTO PRIMO

SERVES 2

2-3 cloves garlic, minced
½ cup tightly packed fresh basil leaves
½ cup chopped parsley leaves
¼ cup freshly grated Parmesan cheese
1 tablespoon butter, melted
¼ cup olive oil
¼ cup boiling water
¼ cup chopped toasted walnuts
½ teaspoon salt
10 ounces canned chopped clams, drained, or chopped cooked shrimp
8 ounces thin spaghetti

In food processor or blender combine garlic, basil, parsley, cheese, butter, olive oil, boiling water, walnuts, and salt. Process until pureed. Pour into large bowl. Fold in clams or shrimp. Let stand at room temperature 30 minutes. Cook spaghetti until "al dente" (slightly underdone). Drain. Add to pesto mixture. Serve immediately.

TORTELACCI CASSEROLE

SERVES 8

27 ounces tortelacci
3 quarts boiling water
2 cups milk
½ cup half and half
6 tablespoons spaghetti sauce
2 ounces mushroom or wild mushroom soup mix
½ cup grated Parmesan cheese

In large pot cook tortelacci in boiling water until "al dente" (slightly underdone). Drain. Rinse in cold water. Drain.

In medium saucepan combine milk, half and half, and spaghetti sauce. Mix well. Stir in mushroom soup mix. Heat mixture over medium heat, stirring frequently. Simmer 10 minutes until mixture thickens, continuing to stir frequently.

In casserole combine noodles and sauce. Mix well. Sprinkle top with Parmesan cheese. Cover with foil. Bake in preheated 350-degree oven 20 minutes. Remove foil. Bake 10 minutes or until bubbly.

FIREWORKS LINGUINE

SERVES 6 TO 8

1	yellow onion, chopped
4	large cloves garlic, minced
4	slices bacon, in small pieces
2	tablespoons olive oil
1	cup freshly grated Parmesan cheese, divided
56	ounces canned Italian style tomatoes with juice, in small pieces
12	ounces tomato paste
13	ounces canned chopped clams, drained, ¼ cup juice reserved
2	tablespoons chopped fresh basil or 1 teaspoon dried basil
2	tablespoons brown sugar
1	teaspoon freshly ground pepper
1-1½	tablespoons Italian seasoning
1-2	teaspoons dried crushed red pepper
1	pound shelled, deveined small shrimp
1½	pounds linguine, cooked

In Dutch oven or large saucepan sauté onion, garlic, and bacon in olive oil about 10 minutes until onion is nearly transparent and bacon almost cooked. Add ⅓ cup Parmesan cheese, tomatoes with juice, tomato paste, clams and juice, basil, brown sugar, and pepper. Mix well. Add Italian seasoning and red pepper gradually, to taste. Simmer at least 2 hours. (Improves in flavor if cooked, cooled, refrigerated overnight, and reheated.)

Five to ten minutes before serving add shrimp. Increase heat to fast simmer. Cook until shrimp are no longer transparent. Shrimp will toughen if overcooked. Serve over hot linguine. Pass remaining ⅔ cup Parmesan cheese.

SPAGHETTI PIE

SERVES 6

6   **ounces spaghetti or linguine**
2   **eggs, beaten**
⅓   **cup grated Parmesan cheese**
12   **ounces drained skim milk ricotta cheese or mashed tofu**
10   **ounces frozen chopped spinach, thawed, drained**
16   **ounces low sodium spaghetti sauce**
4   **ounces skim milk mozzarella cheese, grated**

Cook pasta according to package directions. Drain. Cool.

In medium bowl combine pasta, eggs, and Parmesan cheese. Toss well. Press mixture into bottom and up sides of 9-inch pie pan, forming a "shell." Spread ricotta cheese over "shell." Top with spinach. Pour spaghetti sauce over spinach. Top with mozzarella cheese.

Bake in preheated 350-degree oven 30 minutes or until sauce is bubbly and cheese is golden. Cool 5 minutes before cutting.

SHANGHAI PASTA

SERVES 2

MARINADE:
1   **tablespoon soy sauce**
1   **tablespoon oyster sauce**
1   **tablespoon tomato paste**
1   **tablespoon water**
1   **tablespoon dried prepared French dressing mix**
1   **large clove garlic**

2   **chicken breasts, boned, skinned, halved, in ¾-inch cubes**
3   **tablespoons plus 1 teaspoon vegetable oil, divided**
1   **large carrot, sliced**
1   **medium red pepper, seeded, in ¾-inch pieces**
1   **cup corn**
1   **medium onion, in wedges**
1   **rib celery, sliced**
4   **ounces pea pods**
3   **tablespoons water, divided**
8   **ounces pasta of choice, cooked**
1   **tablespoon soy sauce**
1   **tablespoon oyster sauce**
1   **cup chicken broth**
2   **tablespoons cornstarch**

In large bowl combine all marinade ingredients. Mix well. Add chicken. Cover. Refrigerate 1½ hours.

Heat wok over high heat. Add 2 tablespoons oil. Stir fry chicken until cooked. Using slotted spoon, transfer chicken to serving dish.

Add 1 tablespoon oil to heated wok. Cook carrot 2 minutes. Add red pepper, corn, onion, celery, pea pods, and 2 tablespoons water. Cover. Cook 4 minutes. Add cooked pasta, soy sauce, oyster sauce, and remaining 1 teaspoon oil. Stir fry 10 seconds. Add chicken, chicken broth, and cornstarch blended with remaining 1 tablespoon water. Cook until sauce thickens.

PASTA WITH BASIL MARINARA SAUCE

SERVES 8

¼	**medium onion, finely chopped**
½-¾	**cup olive oil**
2	**medium cloves garlic, minced**
¼	**cup ground prosciutto or salt pork**
28	**ounces canned crushed tomatoes with juice**
6	**ounces tomato paste**
4	**fresh basil leaves**
2	**tablespoons dried basil**
½	**tablespoon salt**
¾	**teaspoon pepper**
1	**pound rigatoni or other pasta**
1-1½	**cups freshly grated Parmesan cheese**

In large skillet sauté onion in olive oil until transparent. Add garlic and prosciutto. Cook 3 to 5 minutes, stirring to prevent burning. Stir in tomatoes with juice and tomato paste. Add fresh basil, dried basil, salt, and pepper. Bring to boil. Reduce heat. Simmer 15 to 20 minutes, stirring occasionally.

Cook rigatoni according to package directions. Drain. Mix with sauce. Top with Parmesan cheese.

ELEVEN LAYER LASAGNA

TOMATO SAUCE:

3	carrots, finely chopped
2-3	onions, finely chopped
3	ribs celery, finely chopped
¾	cup vegetable oil
84	ounces canned, peeled Italian tomatoes, seeds strained out

BOLOGNESE SAUCE:

1	pound lean ground beef
2	tablespoons butter or margarine
	tomato sauce (above)
½	teaspoon salt
¼	teaspoon freshly ground pepper

GREEN PEA LAYER:

¼	cup vegetable oil
2	onions, chopped
20	ounces frozen small green peas
½	cup chopped parsley
½	teaspoon salt
¼	teaspoon freshly ground pepper

MUSHROOM LAYER:

¼	cup vegetable oil
2	cloves garlic, crushed
1	pound fresh mushrooms, sliced
½	cup chopped parsley
½	teaspoon salt
¼	teaspoon freshly ground pepper

WHITE SAUCE:

½	pound plus 2 tablespoons butter or margarine
1	cup plus 2 tablespoons flour
6	cups milk
1	cup grated Parmesan cheese
½	teaspoon freshly grated nutmeg
1-2	teaspoons salt
½-1	teaspoon freshly ground pepper

2	pounds lasagna noodles, cooked
1	pound sliced ham

continued

TOMATO SAUCE:

In large skillet sauté carrots, onions, and celery in oil until softened. Add tomatoes. Simmer until vegetables are tender. Cool. In food processor puree vegetables. Return to skillet. Cook until thickened. May be made ahead and refrigerated or frozen.

BOLOGNESE SAUCE:

In medium skillet brown beef in butter. Drain well. Reserving 3 cups tomato sauce (above) add remainder to beef with salt and pepper. Mix well.

GREEN PEA LAYER:

In large skillet heat oil. Add onions. Cook until softened. Add peas. Cook until peas are warmed thoroughly but still crisp and bright green. Remove skillet from heat. Stir in parsley, salt, and pepper.

MUSHROOM LAYER:

In large skillet heat oil. Brown garlic and remove. Quickly sauté mushrooms until they just turn color but are not yet emitting juice. Transfer to medium bowl. Stir in parsley, salt, and pepper.

WHITE SAUCE:

In large saucepan melt butter. Stir in flour until smooth. Cook 1 minute. Remove from heat. Gradually add milk. Blend well. Return to medium heat. Cook until thickened, stirring constantly. Add cheese, stirring constantly until blended. Add nutmeg, salt, and pepper. Mix well.

TO ASSEMBLE:

Cover bottom of 12- by 18-inch baking pan with 1 cup tomato sauce. Arrange single layer of noodles lengthwise in pan. Cover noodles with 3 to 4 cups bolognese sauce. Follow with single layer of noodles arranged crosswise. Cover with green pea mixture. Cover with single layer of noodles arranged lengthwise. Cover with ham. Follow with crosswise layer of noodles.

Combine mushroom mixture with 2 cups white sauce. Spread over noodles. Follow with lengthwise layer of noodles. Mix 4 cups white sauce with 1 to 2 cups bolognese sauce. Cover noodles with mixture. Follow with crosswise layer of noodles. Spread with remaining tomato sauce. Cover with foil. Bake in preheated 350-degree oven 40 minutes or until thoroughly heated. Remove foil. Bake 20 minutes or until lightly browned. Serve in 3- to 4-inch squares.

Great dish for large group. May be assembled ahead and refrigerated or frozen and brought to room temperature or thawed before baking.

MONTEREY LASAGNA

SERVES 6 TO 8

1¾ pounds lean ground beef
¼ cup chopped green onions
1¼ ounce package taco seasoning mix
1 cup water
8 ounces tomato sauce
4 ounces tomato paste
1 egg, slightly beaten
2 cups lite sour cream
½ cup sliced black olives
10-12 flour tortillas, halved, divided
8 ounces grated sharp Cheddar cheese
8 ounces grated Monterey Jack cheese
4 ounces mild or medium green chilies, chopped
chopped tomatoes, optional
avocado slices, optional
taco sauce, optional
sour cream, optional

In large non-stick skillet brown beef and green onions. Drain. Stir in taco seasoning and water. Simmer 5 minutes. Blend in tomato sauce and tomato paste. Simmer 3 to 4 minutes or until slightly thickened. Set aside. In small bowl combine egg, sour cream, and olives. Mix well. Set aside.

Pour just enough meat mixture into 9- by 13-inch baking dish to cover bottom lightly. Arrange a third of tortillas over meat sauce, overlapping slightly. Cover with half of remaining meat sauce followed by half of sour cream sauce. Sprinkle with a third of Cheddar cheese and a third of Monterey Jack cheese. Repeat tortilla, meat sauce, sour cream sauce, and cheese layers. Spread chilies over cheese. Cover with remaining tortillas. Sprinkle with remaining cheese.

Bake in preheated 350-degree oven 30 to 35 minutes or until bubbly and lightly browned. Let stand 5 minutes before slicing. Accompany each serving with some or all of optional ingredients, if desired.

PASTA MEZZANOTTE

SERVES 6 TO 8

¾   **cup finely chopped onion**
½   **cup finely chopped carrot**
½   **cup finely chopped celery**
¼   **cup plus 1 teaspoon olive oil, divided**
1   **tablespoon minced garlic**
⅓   **teaspoon dried rosemary**
⅓   **teaspoon dried sage**
⅓   **teaspoon dried thyme**
½   **pound lean ground veal**
½   **pound lean ground pork**
½   **cup red wine**
1½   **cups tomato sauce**
2   **cups chicken broth**
1   **bay leaf**
1   **clove**
1   **inch sprig rosemary**
1   **teaspoon salt, or to taste**
    freshly ground pepper to taste
1   **pound fettucine**

In Dutch oven sauté onion, carrot, and celery in ¼ cup olive oil until golden. Add garlic, rosemary, sage, and thyme. Cook 5 minutes.

In medium skillet brown veal and pork in 1 teaspoon olive oil. Add wine. Cook 5 minutes. Add meat to vegetables. Add tomato sauce and chicken broth. Bring to boil. Reduce heat. Add bay leaf, clove, sprig rosemary, salt, and pepper. Simmer uncovered 2 hours, stirring frequently. Remove bay leaf.

Cook fettucine according to package directions. Drain. Serve sauce over fettucine.

COUSCOUS

SERVES 6

2   **tablespoons vegetable oil**
½   **red pepper, diced**
½   **yellow pepper, diced**
4   **green onions, thinly sliced**
½   **cup currants**
3   **cups water or chicken broth**
½   **teaspoon turmeric**
2   **cups couscous**
2   **tablespoons chopped parsley**

In large saucepan heat oil. Add peppers and green onions. Sauté 2 minutes. Stir in currants, water or chicken broth, and turmeric. Bring to boil. Stir in couscous. Cover pan and remove from heat. Let stand 10 minutes. Fluff mixture with fork. Serve sprinkled with parsley.

RISOTTO WITH MUSHROOMS AND PEA PODS

SERVES 4

¼   **pound fresh mushrooms, sliced (preferably shiitake or chanterelle)**
4   **green onions, including some green tops, diced**
¼   **cup virgin olive oil**
1   **cup Arborio (Italian rice)**
¼   **cup dry white wine**
4   **cups warm chicken broth, divided**
¼   **pound shelled, deveined medium shrimp**
¼   **cup grated Parmesan cheese**
¼   **cup grated mozzarella cheese**
¼   **cup julienned pea pods, blanched**

In large skillet sauté mushrooms and green onions in olive oil 5 minutes. Add rice. Cook 2 minutes, taking care not to burn. Add wine and ⅓ cup chicken broth, simmering slowly and stirring frequently until broth is almost completely absorbed. Add ⅓ cup broth. Repeat procedure until ⅓ cup broth remains, about 30 minutes. Add shrimp and remaining ⅓ cup broth. Simmer 5 minutes. Remove from heat. Stir in cheeses and pea pods.

See photo page 283.

CHICKEN LIVER RISOTTO

SERVES 4

½ **pound chicken livers**
2 **cups milk**
5 **tablespoons butter or margarine, divided**
½-1 **green pepper, seeded, julienned**
1 **medium onion, finely chopped**
1 **cup Arborio (Italian rice)**
2 **cups chicken broth, heated, divided**
4 **ounces fresh mushrooms, sliced**
2-3 **tablespoons flour**
salt to taste
pepper to taste
4 **lean slices bacon, crisply cooked, drained, crumbled**
grated Parmesan cheese

In medium bowl soak chicken livers in milk 20 minutes. Drain and set aside. In large heavy skillet melt 2 tablespoons butter. Add green pepper and onion. Sauté gently until vegetables are soft but not brown.

Add rice to skillet. Mix well. Blend in ¾ cup chicken broth. Bring to boil, stirring constantly. Reduce heat and simmer. Gradually add remaining 1¼ cups chicken broth, stirring with each addition until rice is tender and all liquid is absorbed. If more liquid is needed, add boiling water.

In medium skillet sauté mushrooms in 1 tablespoon butter just until mushrooms change color. Remove mushrooms to plate.

Season flour with salt and pepper. Dredge chicken livers in flour, coating well. Add remaining 2 tablespoons butter to medium skillet. Cook livers 6 to 10 minutes, browning on all sides. Slice cooked livers into small pieces. Add mushrooms, livers, and bacon to rice mixture, tossing with fork. Heat quickly. Transfer to serving dish and top generously with Parmesan cheese.

VEGETABLE RISOTTO

¼ **cup plus 1 tablespoon chopped onion, divided**
½ **cup orange or red pepper, sliced**
½ **cup diced zucchini**
3 **tablespoons olive oil, divided**
2 **tablespoons butter, divided**
1 **clove garlic, minced, optional**
1 **teaspoon chopped fresh rosemary or**
   ¼ **teaspoon dried rosemary, crumbled**
½ **cup Arborio (Italian rice)**
2 **tablespoons white wine or dry vermouth**
2 **cups nonfat chicken broth or bouillon**
2-3 **tablespoons grated Parmesan cheese**
1 **cup shredded radicchio**

In large saucepan sauté ¼ cup onion, pepper, and zucchini in 1 tablespoon olive oil until onion is slightly brown. Remove vegetables with slotted spoon. Set aside.

Add remaining 2 tablespoons olive oil and 1 tablespoon butter to saucepan. Sauté remaining 1 tablespoon onion, garlic, if desired, and rosemary 5 minutes. Stir in rice. Cook 2 to 3 minutes or until rice changes color. Add wine. Cook 1 minute or until rice absorbs liquid.

In small saucepan bring chicken broth to simmer. Add ½ cup hot broth to rice mixture. Cook over medium heat until rice absorbs liquid. Continue adding broth by half cupfuls until each addition is absorbed and rice appears creamy. Add remaining 1 tablespoon butter, if desired. Stir in Parmesan cheese. Add sautéed vegetables. Mix well. Stir in radicchio. Serve immediately.

FRUITED WILD RICE

SERVES 12

1½ cups wild rice
1 cup chopped pecans, divided
¼ pound unsalted butter
2 large onions, finely chopped
2 large leeks, white and light green only, finely chopped
2 teaspoons dried thyme, crumbled
2 bay leaves
1½ cups long grain white rice
4 cups chicken broth
salt to taste
pepper to taste
1½ cups fresh cranberries
1¼ cups coarsely chopped dried apricots
⅔ cup golden raisins

In large bowl combine wild rice with hot water to cover. Soak 30 minutes. Drain. In large ovenproof pot sauté ¾ cup pecans in butter until lightly browned, stirring occasionally. Remove nuts with slotted spoon. Set aside.

Add onions, leeks, thyme, and bay leaves to pot. Cook covered over low heat about 15 minutes until vegetables are almost tender, stirring occasionally. Add wild rice, white rice, chicken broth, salt, and pepper. Bring to boil. Cover. Reduce heat and simmer about 30 minutes until liquid is absorbed. Blend in cranberries, apricots, and raisins.*

Bake covered in preheated 350-degree oven 15 minutes. Discard bay leaves. Stir in sautéed pecans. Bake uncovered 15 minutes. Let stand 5 minutes. Sprinkle with remaining ¼ cup pecans.

May be used for stuffing.

*May be prepared 1 day ahead up to this point and refrigerated.

SERVES 6

3	**tablespoons vegetable oil**
1	**large onion, thinly sliced**
2	**large carrots, thinly sliced**
1¼	**cups brown rice, cooked**
4	**cloves garlic, minced**
2-3	**tablespoons minced fresh ginger root**
	pinch cayenne pepper
3	**tablespoons soy sauce, or to taste**
4	**cups vegetables of choice: chopped or sliced broccoli flowerets, seeded sliced red or green peppers, bean sprouts, peas, sliced mushrooms, pea pods, or sliced water chestnuts**
¼	**cup pine nuts, optional**

In large deep skillet or wok heat oil. Stir fry onion and carrots until onion is translucent. Add cooked brown rice, garlic, ginger root, cayenne, and soy sauce. Mix well. Add 4 cups assorted vegetables. Stir over medium-high heat until hot and vegetables are tender-crisp. Add pine nuts, if desired.

To make this a "one-pot dinner," cooked chicken, shrimp, or beef strips may be added.

See photo page 281.

THAI FRIED RICE

SERVES 6
AS MAIN DISH;
10 AS SIDE DISH

Spicy!

- ¼ **cup vegetable oil**
- 5 **medium onions, finely chopped**
- 5 **cloves garlic, finely chopped**
- 1½ **teaspoons sugar**
- *1 **tablespoon Tabasco or chili paste with garlic**
- 1-1½ **pounds cooked, shelled, deveined shrimp, beef, or pork, (or combination), in small pieces**
- 3 **eggs, slightly beaten**
- 3 **cups cooked rice**
- ¼ **cup fish sauce**
- 1½ **green, yellow, or red peppers, finely sliced**
- 2 **tomatoes, chopped**
- 4 **ounces bamboo shoots**
  thin cucumber slices
  green onions, sliced decoratively

In wok or large skillet heat oil. Add onions and garlic. Stir fry over medium heat. Stir in sugar and Tabasco. Add shrimp or meat. Mix well.

Push mixture to side and add eggs, using additional oil, if necessary. When eggs start to set, scramble lightly. Add rice. Stir fry until heated. Add fish sauce, peppers, tomatoes, and bamboo shoots. Stir fry until heated. Do not overcook. Adjust seasoning, if desired. Garnish with cucumber slices and green onions. Serve hot or cold.

*Chili paste (extremely hot) is available in Oriental section of some supermarkets and Oriental markets.

RICH POTATOES

8   medium red potatoes
8   ounces soft garlic and spice cheese or
      garlic and herb cheese
¾   cup finely grated mild yellow Cheddar cheese, divided
4   tablespoons butter
⅓   cup crumbled crisply cooked bacon
¼   cup chopped chives
¼   cup grated Parmesan cheese
¼   cup finely chopped parsley
    butter flavored cooking spray
¼   cup finely grated white Cheddar cheese
½   teaspoon paprika

Fill 4-quart pot with water. Bring to boil. Add potatoes. Cook over medium heat 40 minutes. Drain. Peel potatoes.

In large bowl combine potatoes and soft garlic and spice or herb cheese. Beat at low speed 1 minute. Add ½ cup yellow Cheddar cheese, butter, bacon, chives, Parmesan cheese, and parsley. Beat at medium speed 2 minutes or until mixture is well blended and smooth. Pour into 10-inch casserole sprayed with butter flavored cooking spray. Top with remaining ¼ cup yellow Cheddar cheese, white Cheddar cheese, and paprika.

Bake in preheated 400-degree oven 25 minutes. Transfer to broiler 1 minute or until top is browned.

MASHED POTATOES WITH HORSERADISH

SERVES 4

1½   pounds red potatoes, peeled
3-4   tablespoons margarine
¼   cup hot milk
    salt to taste
1   teaspoon prepared white horseradish, or to taste

In medium pot boil potatoes about 20 minutes until just done. Put potatoes through ricer 2 or 3 at a time. In large bowl combine riced potatoes, margarine, and hot milk. Mix well. Stir in salt and horseradish. Serve immediately.

See photo page 187.

OLIVE-CAPER POTATO SLICES

SERVES 4 TO 6

2 **large Idaho potatoes, unpeeled, sliced lengthwise**
    ⅓ inch thick
    olive oil as needed
4 **ounces canned, chopped black olives**
4 **ounces capers, drained**
    salt to taste
    pepper to taste

Sprinkle potato slices with olive oil. Cover with layer of olives followed by layer of capers. Arrange potato slices on baking sheet. Bake in preheated 450-degree oven 20 to 25 minutes or until potato edges are brown and crisp.

CRISPY POTATOES

SERVES 4

1 **pound small red potatoes, halved**
    olive oil
    salt to taste
    pepper to taste
6 **shallots, sliced**

Arrange potatoes in large glass baking dish. Drizzle olive oil over potatoes. Season to taste. Scatter shallot slices among potatoes.

Bake in preheated 325-degree oven 3 to 5 hours, stirring occasionally.

PAN-FRIED GARLIC POTATOES

SERVES 6 TO 8

    olive oil
5   **Idaho potatoes, each in 6 lengthwise wedges, patted dry**
5-10   **unpeeled cloves garlic**
1/2-1   **teaspoon finely chopped fresh rosemary**
    salt to taste
    freshly ground pepper to taste

In large non-stick skillet pour enough olive oil to cover bottom. Heat until bubbly. Add potatoes. Sauté on all sides until browned. Add garlic, rosemary, salt, and pepper. Reduce heat. Cover skillet and cook until potatoes are fork tender. Place 1 to 2 cloves garlic on each serving of potatoes.

If not serving immediately, uncover and keep warm. Potatoes will steam and lose crisp texture if cover remains.

See photo page 182.

PISTACHIO CRUSTED SWEET POTATOES

SERVES 6 TO 8
YIELD: 24 OVALS

4   **medium sweet potatoes**
1   **egg white**
2   **teaspoons coriander**
1/2   **teaspoon turmeric**
*1/2-1   **teaspoon salt**
1/4   **teaspoon cayenne pepper**
1/4-1/2   **teaspoon freshly ground pepper to taste**
4   **tablespoons plain yogurt**
1   **cup shelled, coarsely chopped pistachios,**
    unsalted preferred

Bake sweet potatoes in oven or microwave until just tender. Peel potatoes. In medium bowl combine potatoes, egg white, coriander, turmeric, salt, cayenne, and pepper. Mix well. Stir in yogurt. Using 2 tablespoons, shape rounded tablespoonfuls of mixture to form ovals. (May be prepared ahead to this point, covered, and refrigerated.) Roll potato ovals in pistachios, coating well. Arrange on foil-lined baking sheet. Bake in preheated 400-degree oven 10 minutes or until hot.

*1/2 teaspoon if salted pistachios are used.

See photo page 188.

OLD-FASHIONED SWEET POTATOES

SERVES 10

5 medium sweet potatoes
¼ cup half and half
¼ pound butter or margarine, in pieces
2 eggs
3 tablespoons sugar
1 tablespoon dark brown sugar
1 teaspoon flour
1 teaspoon cream of tartar
¼ cup orange juice
2 teaspoons lemon juice
2 teaspoons vanilla
½ teaspoon cinnamon
pinch nutmeg
marshmallows, optional

In large pot cook sweet potatoes in skins in rapidly boiling, salted water until very soft. Drain. Cool slightly. Peel potatoes.

In large bowl combine potatoes and remaining ingredients except marshmallows. Beat at low speed until blended. Increase speed to medium. Beat until very smooth. Transfer mixture to 1½-quart casserole or individual ramekins. Cover with aluminum foil.

Bake in preheated 325-degree oven 30 minutes or until hot. Decrease baking time if using ramekins. Remove foil. Cover top of casserole with marshmallows, if desired, pushing them down slightly. Return to oven. Bake 15 minutes or until marshmallows are golden brown. Serve immediately.

See photo page 280.

POLENTA WITH EGGPLANT SAUCE

SERVES 6 TO 8

EGGPLANT SAUCE:

2	tablespoons vegetable oil
2	tablespoons butter
1/2	clove garlic, minced
1	medium onion, coarsely chopped
1	medium eggplant, in 1/2-inch slices
5-6	plum tomatoes or 16 ounces canned plum tomatoes, drained
	salt to taste
	pepper to taste

CHOICE OF 3 OF FOLLOWING:

1/2	teaspoon basil
1/2	teaspoon thyme
1/2	teaspoon parsley
1/2	teaspoon marjoram
1/2	teaspoon rosemary

In large skillet heat oil and butter. Sauté garlic and onion until golden. Add eggplant. Cook until browned and softened. Stir in tomatoes, salt, pepper, and choice of herbs. Cook covered 15 to 20 minutes, stirring occasionally. Set aside.

*MEAT SAUCE:

1/4	cup dried mushrooms
2	tablespoons vegetable oil
1	medium onion, chopped
1	clove garlic, minced
1/2	small green pepper, chopped
1	rib celery with leaves, chopped
1	tablespoon chopped parsley
1 1/2	pounds ground chuck
1/3	pound ground pork
1/3	pound ground veal
6	ounces tomato paste
6	tablespoons chili sauce
1	cup plus 2 tablespoons water
1/4	cup white wine
	salt to taste
	pepper to taste
2	tablespoons butter

continued

In small bowl soak mushrooms in hot water to cover 20 to 30 minutes. Drain, reserving water. Chop mushrooms. Set aside.

In large heavy pot heat oil. Add onion, garlic, green pepper, celery, and parsley. Sauté until browned. Add meat, stirring frequently to break into small pieces. Cook about 15 minutes until meat is brown. Add tomato paste, chili sauce, water, wine, salt, pepper, mushrooms, and reserved water from mushrooms. Simmer covered 1 hour, stirring occasionally. Add more water if needed. Remove from heat. Stir in butter. Set aside.

POLENTA:

6   cups water
2   cups polenta (yellow cornmeal)
1   teaspoon salt

In large heavy pot heat water until lukewarm. Add polenta in steady stream, stirring constantly. Add salt. Cook over high heat until water boils, continuing to stir. Reduce heat. Simmer covered 30 to 45 minutes, stirring occasionally.

TO ASSEMBLE:

⅓   cup grated Parmesan cheese

Spoon a third of polenta into buttered 12-inch round shallow serving dish or casserole. Keep remaining polenta heated in pot. Cover polenta layer with half of eggplant sauce. Sprinkle with a third of Parmesan cheese. Follow with another third of polenta. Cover with meat sauce. Sprinkle with a third of Parmesan cheese. Spread final layer of polenta over top. Cover with remaining eggplant sauce and sprinkle with remaining Parmesan cheese. Serve immediately.

*All of meat sauce is not needed for this recipe. Remaining meat sauce may be frozen.

POLENTA WITH CHEESE

SERVES 6

4   **cups chicken broth**
1   **teaspoon salt**
1   **cup polenta (yellow cornmeal)**
2   **tablespoons grated mozzarella cheese**
6   **tablespoons grated Parmesan cheese, divided**
1½   **ounces Montrachet cheese, grated**
8   **ounces Fontina cheese, thinly sliced**
1   **tablespoon fresh sage leaves**
4   **tablespoons butter**

In large saucepan bring chicken broth to boil. Add salt and cornmeal slowly, stirring constantly. Mix well. Reduce heat. Cook 15 minutes, stirring occasionally. Add mozzarella, 4 tablespoons Parmesan, and Montrachet. Mix well. Cook 10 minutes, stirring occasionally.

Spoon mixture onto wet surface. Cool. With biscuit cutter or inverted glass cut mixture into rounds. Place rounds in greased casserole. Top rounds with Fontina slices. Sprinkle with remaining 2 tablespoons Parmesan cheese.

In small skillet sauté sage leaves in butter. Drizzle over casserole. Bake in preheated 375-degree oven 15 to 20 minutes or until thoroughly heated.

BURRITOS

SERVES 2

2   **12-inch flour tortillas**
4   **tablespoons refried beans**
2   **tablespoons salsa**
2   **tablespoons pitted, sliced black olives**
2   **tablespoons chopped red onion**
2   **tablespoons shredded Cheddar cheese**
4-6   **slices avocado**
2   **teaspoons sliced jalapeño peppers**
    additional salsa and sour cream, optional

Spread each tortilla with 2 tablespoons refried beans. Top each with 1 tablespoon of salsa, olives, onion, and cheese. Place 2 to 3 slices avocado over mixture and sprinkle with 1 teaspoon jalapeños. Fold tortilla in 1 inch on sides. Roll up from bottom to top. Place seam side down on plate.

Microwave on high 1 minute 30 seconds or bake in preheated 350-degree oven 8 to 10 minutes.

Serve with additional salsa and sour cream, if desired.

BREADS

LEMON BLUEBERRY CORNMEAL MUFFINS

**YIELD: 18 LARGE
OR 36 MINIATURE**

rind (yellow part only) of 2 lemons, grated
1   cup sugar
1/2   cup vegetable oil
1   large egg, beaten
1   cup buttermilk
1 1/2   cups flour
1/3   cup cornmeal
1   teaspoon baking soda
1/4   teaspoon salt
1 1/2-2   cups fresh blueberries

GLAZE:
6   tablespoons lemon juice
1 1/2   tablespoons sugar

In large bowl combine lemon rind, sugar, oil, and egg. Mix well. Stir in buttermilk. Add flour, cornmeal, baking soda, and salt. Mix well. Gently fold in blueberries. Let batter stand 15 minutes.

Pour batter into greased or paper-lined muffin tins, filling them three-fourths full. Bake in preheated 375-degree oven 22 minutes for large and 15 to 17 minutes for miniature muffins or until inserted tester comes out clean.

In small bowl combine glaze ingredients. Mix well. Dip inverted, warm muffins into glaze. Cool before serving.

See photo page 181.

LEMON YOGURT MUFFINS

YIELD: 12

2 cups flour
1 teaspoon baking powder
1 teaspoon baking soda
1/4 teaspoon salt
1/4 cup sugar
2 tablespoons honey
2 eggs
1 1/4 cups plain yogurt
4 tablespoons butter or margarine, melted
1 tablespoon grated lemon rind

LEMON SYRUP:
1/3 cup lemon juice
1/3 cup sugar
3 tablespoons water

In medium bowl sift together flour, baking powder, baking soda, and salt. In large bowl combine sugar, honey, eggs, yogurt, butter, and lemon rind. Mix well. Add dry ingredients. Stir until just mixed. Do not overbeat. Pour into 12 greased muffin tins. Bake in preheated 375-degree oven 15 minutes.

While muffins bake combine all syrup ingredients in small saucepan. Boil 1 minute. Pierce baked muffins with fork. Drizzle syrup over each muffin. Remove muffins from tins. Serve warm.

MORNING GLORY MUFFINS

YIELD: 20

2 cups flour
1 1/4 cups sugar
2 teaspoons baking soda
2 teaspoons cinnamon
1/2 teaspoon salt
1 1/2 cups finely grated carrots
1 1/2 cups peeled, finely grated apples
3/4 cup grated coconut
1/2 cup chopped dates
1/2 cup chopped pecans
3 eggs, beaten
1 cup vegetable oil
1/2 teaspoon vanilla

In large bowl sift together flour, sugar, baking soda, cinnamon, and salt. In another large bowl combine carrots, apples, coconut, dates, and pecans. Mix well. Add eggs, oil, and vanilla to carrot mixture. Mix well. Stir into dry ingredients until moistened. Spoon into greased muffin tins.

Bake in preheated 375-degree oven 20 to 25 minutes or until inserted tester comes out clean.

See photo page 181.

BANANA APPLE MUFFINS

YIELD: 12

1	**cup all-purpose white flour**
3/4	**cup whole wheat flour**
3/4	**cup oats**
1/4	**cup wheat germ**
1/3	**cup sugar**
1/2	**teaspoon salt**
4	**teaspoons baking powder**
1	**banana, mashed (about 1/2 cup)**
1	**egg**
1/4	**cup vegetable oil**
1/2	**cup milk**
1/2	**cup orange juice**
1	**unpeeled apple, finely diced (about 1/2 cup)**
1/2	**cup raisins**

In medium bowl combine flours, oats, wheat germ, sugar, salt, and baking powder. Mix well. In large bowl combine banana, egg, oil, milk, and orange juice. Mix well. Add dry ingredients to banana mixture. Stir until dry ingredients are just absorbed. Blend in apple and raisins.

Spoon batter into 12 greased or paper-lined muffin tins. Bake in preheated 400-degree oven 20 minutes.

PINEAPPLE CARROT MUFFINS

YIELD: 12

2   **eggs**
1/4   **cup vegetable oil**
3/4   **cup milk**
1/2   **cup grated carrots**
8   **ounces crushed pineapple with juice**
1   **teaspoon vanilla**
1 1/4   **cups flour**
1/2   **cup plus 1 tablespoon wheat germ, divided**
1/4   **cup oat bran**
1/2   **cup brown sugar**
1/2   **teaspoon salt**
1   **teaspoon baking soda**
2   **tablespoons sugar**

In large bowl combine eggs, oil, milk, carrots, pineapple, and vanilla. Beat well. In medium bowl combine flour, 1/2 cup wheat germ, oat bran, brown sugar, salt, and baking soda. Mix well. Add to egg mixture. Blend well. Spoon into 12 greased or paper-lined muffin tins.

In small bowl mix remaining 1 tablespoon wheat germ and sugar. Sprinkle over batter. Bake in preheated 400-degree oven 20 minutes or until inserted tester comes out clean.

DILLED CHEDDAR CORN MUFFINS

YIELD: 12

1   **cup yellow cornmeal**
1   **cup flour**
1/3   **cup sugar**
2 1/2   **teaspoons baking powder**
1/2   **teaspoon baking soda**
3/4   **teaspoon salt**
1   **large egg**
3/4   **cup milk**
1 1/2   **cups grated extra sharp Cheddar cheese**
1   **cup cooked corn**
4   **tablespoons butter, melted**
1   **tablespoon dill weed**

continued

In large bowl combine cornmeal, flour, sugar, baking powder, baking soda, and salt. Mix well. In medium bowl blend egg and milk. Stir cheese, corn, butter, and dill weed into egg mixture. Add to dry ingredients. Stir until dry mixture is just moistened. Do not overmix. Batter will be stiff.

Line 12 muffin tins with paper baking cups. Spoon batter into cups, filling almost entirely. Bake in preheated 400-degree oven 20 to 22 minutes or until golden and inserted tester comes out clean. Cool in tins on rack 10 minutes. Remove from tins.

MINIATURE CORNMEAL MUFFINS WITH PEPPERS

YIELD: 44 TO 48 MINIATURE

1 **cup sugar**
1/4 **pound unsalted butter, softened**
2 **large eggs**
1 1/4 **cups flour**
1/4 **cup cornmeal**
1 **teaspoon baking soda**
1/8 **teaspoon salt**
1/2 **cup cooked corn**
1/2 **cup mixed finely diced red and green peppers**
1 **cup buttermilk**

In large bowl cream sugar and butter until light and fluffy. Add eggs 1 at a time, beating well after each addition. In small bowl combine flour, cornmeal, baking soda, salt, corn, and peppers. Mix well. Add flour mixture to creamed mixture alternately with buttermilk.

Spoon batter into lightly greased miniature muffin tins. Bake in preheated 400-degree oven 12 minutes or until browned. Cool in tins on rack 15 minutes. Remove from tins.

ZUCCHINI MUFFINS

YIELD: 12

- 3 eggs, beaten
- 2 cups sugar
- 1 cup vegetable oil
- 3 teaspoons vanilla
- 3 cups flour
- 1 teaspoon baking soda
- 1/4 teaspoon baking powder
- 1 teaspoon salt
- 1/2 cup chopped dates
- 1/2 cup raisins
- 1 cup chopped walnuts
- 2 cups grated zucchini
- 1 unpeeled orange, seeded, coarsely chopped

In large bowl combine eggs, sugar, oil, and vanilla. Mix well. In another large bowl sift together flour, baking soda, baking powder, and salt. Add dates and raisins to dry ingredients, blending with fingers. Stir in walnuts, zucchini, and orange. Mix well. Add dry ingredients to egg mixture, mixing until just moistened.

Spoon batter into 12 greased or paper-lined muffin tins, filling them three-fourths full. Bake in preheated 350-degree oven 30 minutes.

PEANUT BUTTER OATMEAL MUFFINS

YIELD: 12

- 3/4 cup chunky peanut butter
- 1 tablespoon sesame oil
- 1/4 cup sugar
- 1/4 cup packed dark brown sugar
- 2 egg whites, lightly beaten
- 1 cup skim milk
- 2 teaspoons vanilla
- 1 1/2 cups whole wheat flour
- 3/4 cup quick-cooking oats
- 1 tablespoon baking powder
- 1/2 teaspoon salt
  cooking spray

continued

In medium bowl combine peanut butter, sesame oil, and sugars. Mix well. Stir in egg whites. Add milk in small amounts, blending well after each addition. Add vanilla.

In large bowl mix whole wheat flour, oats, baking powder, and salt. Pour peanut butter mixture into dry ingredients. Mix until dry ingredients are just moistened. Spoon batter into 12 muffin tins coated with cooking spray or lined with paper baking cups.

Bake in preheated 375-degree oven 20 minutes or until golden brown. Cool in tins on rack 10 minutes. Remove from tins.

CURRANT GINGER SCONES

YIELD: 10 TO 12

- ¼ **pound unsalted butter, softened**
- ¼ **cup sugar**
- 2½ **cups flour**
- 1 **tablespoon baking powder**
- 1 **teaspoon cinnamon**
- ¼ **teaspoon allspice**
- ¼ **teaspoon ground cloves**
- ½ **teaspoon salt**
- ⅔ **cup milk**
- ½ **cup currants**
- 2 **teaspoons finely chopped crystallized ginger**

In large bowl cream butter and sugar. In medium bowl sift together flour, baking powder, cinnamon, allspice, cloves, and salt. Add dry ingredients to creamed mixture alternately with milk, ending with dry ingredients. Blend in currants and ginger.

Roll dough into ball. Flatten into circle 1 inch thick. Cut into 10 to 12 triangular wedges. Transfer to ungreased baking sheet. Bake in preheated 375-degree oven 12 to 15 minutes or until golden brown.

May be served with Lemon Butter page 447.

OLD-FASHIONED CREAM SCONES

YIELD: 8

2 cups flour
1 tablespoon baking powder
3 tablespoons sugar, divided
1/2 teaspoon salt
6 tablespoons butter or margarine, divided
1/3 cup whipping cream or milk
2 eggs, beaten
1/2 cup raisins or currants, optional

In large bowl combine flour, baking powder, 2 tablespoons sugar, and salt. Mix well. Blend in 4 tablespoons butter. Add cream and eggs. Mix well. Fold in raisins or currants, if desired.

Knead dough briefly. Divide in half. Roll or pat each half into 6-inch circle. Cut each circle into fourths. Brush each fourth with remaining 2 tablespoons butter, melted, and sprinkle with remaining 1 tablespoon sugar. Bake in preheated 400-degree oven 10 minutes.

SUN-DRIED TOMATO AND FETA SCONES

YIELD: 12

1/2 cup sun-dried tomatoes, in small pieces
1 1/2 cups boiling water
2 cups flour
2 teaspoons baking powder
2 teaspoons dried basil
3/4 teaspoon salt
2 tablespoons margarine
6 ounces feta cheese, crumbled
1/2 cup skim milk
1 teaspoon Tabasco
1 egg, lightly beaten
    cooking spray

In medium bowl combine tomatoes and boiling water. Let stand 10 minutes. In large bowl combine flour, baking powder, basil, and salt. Cut in margarine with pastry blender until mixture resembles coarse meal. Add cheese, milk, Tabasco, and egg to tomatoes. Mix well. Add to dry ingredients, stirring until just moistened. Dough will be sticky.

With floured hands pat dough into circle 1/2 inch thick. Cut into 12 triangular wedges. Arrange on baking sheet coated with cooking spray. Bake in preheated 400-degree oven 12 minutes or until golden. Serve warm. See photo page 79.

SWIRLED APRICOT CREAM CHEESE BREAD

YIELD: 1 LOAF

1   cup dried apricots, in thin strips
1/2   cup golden raisins
4   tablespoons butter, softened
1/2   cup packed brown sugar
1/2   cup sugar
1   large egg
2   cups flour
2   teaspoons baking powder
1/2   teaspoon baking soda
1/2   teaspoon salt
3/4   cup orange juice
1/2   cup sliced almonds, divided

FILLING:

4   ounces cream cheese, softened
2   tablespoons sugar
1   egg yolk
1 1/2 teaspoons finely grated orange zest

In small bowl combine apricots and raisins. Add boiling water to cover. Let stand 30 minutes.

In large bowl cream butter and sugars. Beat in egg. In medium bowl sift together flour, baking powder, baking soda, and salt. Add to creamed mixture alternately with orange juice. Batter will be thick. Stir in drained apricots, raisins, and 1/4 cup almonds.

In food processor or blender combine all filling ingredients. Process until smooth. Pour two-thirds of batter into greased, lightly floured 9- by 5-inch loaf pan. Spread all filling evenly over batter. Top with remaining batter. Lightly swirl with knife. Sprinkle with remaining 1/4 cup almonds.

Bake in preheated 350-degree oven 55 to 60 minutes or until golden and firm. Cool in pan 10 minutes. Remove to rack. Cool completely. Refrigerate tightly wrapped in foil or plastic wrap.

See photo page 181.

BANANA ZUCCHINI NUT BREAD

YIELD: 2 LOAVES

3   **eggs**
2   **cups sugar**
1   **cup vegetable oil**
2   **teaspoons vanilla**
2   **cups unpeeled, grated zucchini, drained**
2   **cups flour**
3   **teaspoons cinnamon**
2   **teaspoons baking soda**
1/2   **teaspoon baking powder**
1   **teaspoon salt**
1   **cup chopped walnuts or pecans**
3   **very ripe bananas, mashed**

In large bowl combine eggs, sugar, oil, and vanilla. Beat well. Stir in zucchini. Sift together flour, cinnamon, baking soda, baking powder, and salt. Fold dry ingredients and nuts into egg mixture. Stir in bananas. Pour into 2 greased, lightly floured 9- by 5-inch loaf pans.

Bake in preheated 350-degree oven 1 hour or until inserted tester comes out clean. (If more time is needed and bread is browning quickly, reduce heat to 300 degrees.) Remove loaves from oven. Cool in pans 30 minutes. Remove to rack. When cool wrap in foil until served. Freezes well.

BLUEBERRY BREAD

YIELD: 2 LOAVES

1/2   **pound butter, softened**
2   **cups sugar**
1   **teaspoon vanilla**
4   **eggs**
3   **cups plus 2 tablespoons flour, divided**
1   **teaspoon salt**
1   **teaspoon cream of tartar**
1/2   **teaspoon baking soda**
8   **ounces lemon yogurt**
    rind of 1 lemon, grated
2   **cups fresh blueberries**
1   **cup chopped pecans or walnuts, optional**

continued

In large bowl cream butter, sugar, and vanilla until fluffy. Add eggs 1 at a time, beating well after each addition.

In medium bowl sift together 3 cups flour, salt, cream of tartar, and baking soda. In small bowl combine yogurt and rind. Mix well. Add to creamed mixture alternately with dry ingredients.

Dust blueberries with remaining 2 tablespoons flour. Stir berries and nuts, if desired, into batter. Pour batter into 2 greased, floured 9- by 5-inch loaf pans. Bake in preheated 350-degree oven 50 to 55 minutes or until inserted tester comes out clean.

FLORIDA LIME BREAD

YIELD: 1 LOAF

1/4 **pound butter, softened**
1 **cup sugar**
2 **eggs**
1 1/2 **cups flour**
1 **tablespoon baking powder**
 pinch salt
1/4 **cup milk**
1/4 **cup lime juice**
 grated rind of 1 lime

GLAZE:
 juice of 1 lime
1/2 **cup confectioners sugar**

In large bowl cream butter and sugar. Add eggs 1 at a time, beating well after each addition. In small bowl sift together flour, baking powder, and salt. Add to creamed mixture alternately with milk. Add lime juice and rind. Mix well. Pour into greased 9- by 5-inch loaf pan. Bake in preheated 350-degree oven 45 to 60 minutes or until inserted tester comes out clean.

In small bowl combine glaze ingredients. Mix well. Pour mixture over bread. Cool in pan on rack 30 minutes. Remove from pan.

CRANBERRY NUT BREAD

YIELD: 1 LOAF

2 cups sifted flour
1 cup sugar
1½ teaspoons baking powder
½ teaspoon baking soda
1 teaspoon salt
4 tablespoons butter or margarine
1 egg, beaten
¾ cup orange juice
1 tablespoon finely grated orange rind
1 cup coarsely chopped fresh cranberries
½ cup chopped walnuts or pecans

In large bowl sift together flour, sugar, baking powder, baking soda, and salt. Cut in butter with pastry blender. Blend well.

In small bowl combine egg, orange juice, and orange rind. Mix well. Add to dry ingredients. Mix well. Fold in cranberries and nuts. Pour into greased 9- by 5-inch loaf pan.

Bake in preheated 350-degree oven 55 to 60 minutes or until inserted tester comes out clean. Cool in pan 10 minutes. Remove from pan. Cool on rack.

PEAR BREAD

YIELD: 1 LOAF

4 tablespoons butter, softened
4 tablespoons margarine, softened
1 cup sugar
2 eggs
1½-2 teaspoons vanilla
½ teaspoon almond extract
2 cups flour
1 teaspoon baking powder
½ teaspoon baking soda
¼ teaspoon nutmeg
4 tablespoons plain yogurt
1½ cups coarsely chopped, peeled pears (barely ripe)
½ pear, peeled, cored, thinly sliced lengthwise

continued

In large bowl cream butter, margarine, and sugar until light and fluffy. Add eggs 1 at a time, beating after each addition. Add vanilla and almond extract. Mix well.

In medium bowl sift together flour, baking powder, baking soda, and nutmeg. Add to creamed mixture in thirds alternating with yogurt blending after each addition. Stir in chopped pears. Pour into greased 9- by 5-inch loaf pan. Arrange pear slices on top decoratively, pushing slightly into batter without submerging.

Bake in preheated 350-degree oven 1 hour or until inserted tester comes out clean. Cool in pan on rack 1 to 2 minutes. Remove from pan. Cool completely on rack.

SWEET-SOUR LOAF

YIELD: 1 LOAF

6	**tablespoons butter or margarine, softened**
1⅓	**cups sugar, divided**
2	**eggs**
½	**cup milk**
	rind of 1 lemon, grated
1½	**cups flour**
1	**teaspoon baking powder**
¼	**teaspoon salt**
1½	**cups finely chopped walnuts or pecans**
	juice of 1 lemon

In large bowl cream butter and 1 cup sugar. In small bowl beat eggs. Add milk and lemon rind. Mix well. Add to creamed mixture.

In medium bowl sift together flour, baking powder, and salt. Blend into butter mixture. Stir in nuts. Pour into greased 9- by 5-inch loaf pan. Bake in preheated 350-degree oven 1 hour or until inserted tester comes out clean. Pierce top of hot loaf with two-tined fork in 10 to 15 places.

In small bowl mix lemon juice and remaining ⅓ cup sugar. Pour lemon mixture over hot loaf. Cool before removing from pan.

COCONUT BREAD

2 **cups grated coconut, divided**
2²/₃ **cups flour**
1 **cup sugar**
4 **teaspoons baking powder**
¹/₂ **teaspoon salt**
1¹/₂ **cups plus 2 tablespoons milk, divided**
1 **egg, slightly beaten**
2 **tablespoons vegetable oil**
2¹/₂ **teaspoons coconut extract, divided**
¹/₂ **cup confectioners sugar**

Spread 1¹/₂ cups coconut on baking sheet. Bake in preheated 325-degree oven 3 minutes. Toss. Bake 2 minutes. Remove from oven. Cool. Increase heat to 350 degrees.

In medium bowl sift together flour, sugar, baking powder, and salt. In large bowl combine 1¹/₂ cups milk, egg, oil, and 1¹/₂ teaspoons coconut extract. Mix well. Add toasted coconut to dry ingredients. Stir dry ingredients into milk mixture. Add remaining ¹/₂ cup coconut. Mix well. Pour into lightly greased 9- by 5-inch loaf pan. Bake in preheated 350-degree oven 1 hour or until lightly browned and inserted tester comes out clean.

While bread bakes combine remaining 2 tablespoons milk and 1 teaspoon coconut extract in small bowl. Add confectioners sugar. Mix well.

Cool bread in pan 1 to 2 minutes. Remove from pan to rack, keeping top side up. Drizzle sugar-milk mixture over top, allowing some to run down sides. Cool before slicing.

CHOCOLATE CHIP TEA BREAD

YIELD: 1 LOAF

4   **tablespoons unsalted butter or margarine, softened**
1/3 **cup sugar**
1   **teaspoon vanilla**
1   **egg**
1/2 **cup cocoa**
1   **teaspoon instant espresso powder**
1 1/2 **cups flour**
1   **teaspoon baking soda**
1/2 **teaspoon salt**
1   **cup buttermilk**
1/2 **cup golden raisins**
1/2 **cup dark raisins**
1   **cup chopped walnuts**
1   **cup semi-sweet chocolate chips**

In large bowl cream butter, sugar, and vanilla 5 minutes. Beat in egg. Add cocoa and espresso powder. Mix well at low speed.

In medium bowl sift together flour, baking soda, and salt. Add to butter mixture alternately with buttermilk. Stir in raisins, walnuts, and chocolate chips. Pour into greased 9- by 5-inch loaf pan.

Bake in preheated 375-degree oven 55 to 60 minutes or until inserted tester comes out clean, checking after 40 to 45 minutes. If loaf browns too quickly cover with foil for duration of baking. Cool in pan 10 minutes. Remove from pan. Cool on rack. Refrigerate before serving.

QUICK CUMIN BREAD

YIELD: 1 LOAF

An unusual taste for those who enjoy spicy food.

1½   **cups flour**
2   **tablespoons sugar**
1   **tablespoon baking powder**
2   **teaspoons cumin**
½   **teaspoon cumin seed, lightly crushed**
¼   **teaspoon dry mustard**
2   **teaspoons parsley flakes**
1   **teaspoon dried crushed red pepper**
1   **teaspoon salt**
2   **large eggs, beaten**
¾   **cup milk**
3   **tablespoons vegetable oil**

In large bowl combine flour, sugar, baking powder, cumin, cumin seed, mustard, parsley flakes, dried red pepper, and salt. Mix well. In small bowl mix eggs, milk, and oil. Add to dry ingredients, stirring until just moistened. Pour into greased 8½- by 4½- by 2¾-inch loaf pan.

Bake in center of preheated 350-degree oven 40 to 45 minutes or until inserted tester comes out clean. Cool in pan on rack 15 minutes. Remove from pan. Cool completely on rack.

WHEAT BREAD WITH WALNUTS, APPLES, AND CHEESE

YIELD: 1 LOAF

1/4 **pound butter or margarine, softened**
1/3 **cup sugar**
1/3 **cup honey**
2 **large eggs**
1 **cup whole wheat flour**
1 **cup all-purpose white flour**
1 **teaspoon baking powder**
1/2 **teaspoon baking soda**
1/2 **teaspoon salt**
1 1/2 **cups grated Granny Smith apples**
1 **cup grated Swiss cheese**
3/4 **cup coarsely chopped walnuts**

In large bowl cream butter and sugar. Add honey. Mix well. Beat in eggs 1 at a time. In medium bowl sift together flours, baking powder, baking soda, and salt. Add to creamed mixture gradually, beating until well mixed. Stir in apples, cheese, and walnuts. Pour into greased 8 1/2- by 4 1/2- by 2 3/4-inch loaf pan.

Bake in preheated 350-degree oven 55 to 60 minutes until browned and inserted tester comes out clean. Cool in pan on rack 5 minutes. Remove from pan. Cool completely on rack.

RAISIN NUT BREAD

YIELD: 6
MINIATURE LOAVES

1	cup raisins
2	cups boiling water
2	teaspoons baking soda
1/4	pound butter or margarine, softened
2	cups sugar
2	teaspoons vanilla
2	eggs, beaten
1	teaspoon salt
4	cups flour
1	cup chopped walnuts or pecans
	cooking spray

In small bowl combine raisins, boiling water, and baking soda. Mix well. Cool. In large bowl cream butter and sugar. Add vanilla, eggs, and salt to creamed mixture. Mix well. Add flour alternately with raisin mixture to creamed mixture. Mix well. Stir in nuts.

Spray 6 miniature loaf pans with cooking spray. Fill pans half full with batter. Bake in preheated 350-degree oven 1 hour or until inserted tester comes out clean.

IRISH SODA BREAD WITH CURRANTS

YIELD:
1 LARGE LOAF

4	cups flour
2	tablespoons sugar
2	teaspoons baking soda
1 1/2	teaspoons salt
4	tablespoons butter or margarine
2/3	cup currants
1	cup milk
1/2	cup white vinegar

In large bowl sift together flour, sugar, baking soda, and salt. Cut in butter with pastry blender until mixture resembles coarse meal. Stir in currants. In small bowl combine milk and vinegar. Mix well. Add half of liquid to flour mixture. Blend well. Add remaining liquid. Mix well.

On lightly floured surface knead dough until smooth. Shape into round loaf. Place on greased baking sheet. Bake in preheated 375-degree oven 35 to 40 minutes or until inserted tester comes out clean.

DUBLIN SODA BREAD

YIELD:
1 LARGE LOAF

2   cups whole wheat flour
2   cups all-purpose white flour
1   teaspoon salt
1   teaspoon baking powder
2   tablespoons caraway seed, optional
4   tablespoons butter
2   cups raisins
1⅓ cups buttermilk
1   egg, beaten
1   teaspoon baking soda
1   tablespoon honey
2   tablespoons milk

In large bowl sift together flours, salt, and baking powder. Add caraway seed, if desired. Cut in butter with pastry blender until mixture resembles coarse meal. Stir in raisins.

In medium bowl combine buttermilk, egg, baking soda, and honey. Mix well. Add to flour mixture. Blend until just moistened. On lightly floured surface knead dough briefly until smooth. Shape into ball. Place on greased baking sheet. Slice a 4-inch cross over top. Brush with milk.

Bake in preheated 350-degree oven 1¼ hours or until inserted tester comes out clean. Cool completely before slicing.

Best eaten within 1 to 2 days. Wrap in foil and store in refrigerator.

BEER BREAD

YIELD: 1 LOAF

3   cups self-rising flour
½   cup sugar
12 ounces flat beer
¼   pound butter or margarine, melted

In medium bowl combine flour and sugar. Mix well. Stir in beer. Mix well. Pour mixture into greased, floured 9- by 5-inch loaf pan.

Bake in preheated 350-degree oven 45 minutes. Pour melted butter over bread. Return to oven. Bake 15 minutes. Remove from oven. Cool in pan on rack 30 minutes. Remove from pan.

APPLE COFFEE CAKE

SERVES 12 TO 16

1½ cups vegetable oil
2 cups sugar
2 eggs, well beaten
2 teaspoons vanilla
3 cups sifted flour
1 teaspoon cinnamon
1 teaspoon baking soda
½ teaspoon salt
3 cups diced, peeled Granny Smith apples
1 cup chopped walnuts or pecans

In large bowl combine oil, sugar, eggs, and vanilla. Mix well. In medium bowl sift together flour, cinnamon, baking soda, and salt. Add dry ingredients to oil mixture. Blend well. Mix in apples and nuts. Batter will be thick.

Spoon batter into lightly floured 10-inch tube pan. Bake in preheated 350-degree oven 1 to 1½ hours, checking final 30 minutes and covering with foil if too brown. Cool in pan on rack. Remove from pan to serving plate, keeping top side up.

CHERRY TWISTS

YIELD: 8

2 tablespoons butter, melted
½ teaspoon vanilla
8 ounces refrigerated crescent rolls
3 tablespoons chopped slivered almonds, divided
3 tablespoons chopped dried cherries, divided
3 teaspoons sugar, divided

In small bowl combine butter and vanilla. Mix well. Unroll crescent roll dough. Pinch seams together to make 2 rectangles. Brush with butter mixture.

Starting from short end of each rectangle sprinkle half with 1½ tablespoons almonds, 1½ tablespoons cherries, and 1½ teaspoons sugar. Fold top half of rectangle over filling and cut into 4 strips. Twist each strip 2 or 3 times in opposite directions. Place strips on ungreased baking sheet. Press ends onto sheet to hold in place.

Bake in preheated 375-degree oven 10 to 12 minutes or until golden brown. Remove from baking sheet. Cool on rack.

See photo page 282.

CHEATER SCHNECKEN

SYRUP:

¹/₂ **pound unsalted butter**
¹/₂ **cup packed dark brown sugar**
¹/₂ **cup packed light brown sugar**
2   **tablespoons water**

¹/₂ **pound unsalted butter, melted**
144 **small pecan halves**
24   **ounces refrigerated crescent rolls**
2   **cups light brown sugar (approximate)**
     cinnamon

For syrup, melt butter in medium saucepan. Add brown sugars and water. Boil gently 3 minutes or until slightly thickened. Remove from heat. Set aside.

In miniature muffin tins brush each section with melted butter. Place 3 pecans top side down in each section. Spoon 1 generous teaspoon of syrup over nuts.

On floured surface roll out 2 triangles of dough to make rectangle. Press together at seams. Smooth lightly with rolling pin. Brush surface with melted butter and sprinkle with heaping tablespoon brown sugar followed by generous amount of cinnamon. Starting at short end, roll up carefully. Brush again with melted butter. Slice into 4 equal pieces. Place each piece cut side down in muffin tin. Repeat procedure until all dough is used. Brush again with melted butter.

Bake in preheated 350-degree oven 17 minutes. (Place sheet of foil under muffin tins to catch spillover.) Cool in tins on rack. With knife and spoon gently push extra syrup around each schnecken. Place sheet of wax paper larger than tins over schnecken. Carefully invert tins, holding until most of syrup drips out. Cool. Serve syrup side up.

See photo page 181.

SWEET SPIRALS

YIELD: 48 SPIRALS

1/2 **pound butter, softened**
1 **cup sugar**
3 **large eggs**
1 **teaspoon vanilla**
   rind of 1 lemon, grated
2 **tablespoons lemon juice, divided**
3 **cups flour**
3 **teaspoons baking powder**
1/2 **teaspoon salt**
2 **pounds fruit preserves (e.g., apricot, strawberry)**
1 **cup chopped pecans**
1 **cup golden raisins**
   cinnamon to taste
   sugar to taste

In large bowl cream butter and sugar. Add eggs 1 at a time, beating well after each addition. Add vanilla, lemon rind, and 1 tablespoon lemon juice.

In medium bowl sift together flour, baking powder, and salt. Blend into butter mixture. Cover dough. Refrigerate 3 hours or overnight.

Divide dough into fourths. Using rolling pin roll each portion on floured surface to 1/4-inch-thick rectangle. Spread with preserves. Sprinkle with pecans, raisins, cinnamon, sugar to taste, and remaining 1 tablespoon lemon juice. Roll up dough.

Transfer dough seam side down to greased, floured baking sheet. Bake in pre-heated 350-degree oven 50 minutes or until brown. Slice into 1-inch pieces while still warm.

BEST EVER CORN BREAD

YIELD:
SIXTEEN 2-INCH
SQUARES OR
24 CORNSTICKS

3 **eggs**
1/2 **cup vegetable oil**
1/2 **teaspoon salt**
8 **ounces sour cream**
8.5 **ounces canned creamed corn**
12 **ounces corn muffin mix**

In large bowl combine eggs, oil, and salt. Mix well. Add sour cream and corn. Mix well. Add muffin mix. Mix well. Pour into greased 8-inch square glass baking dish. Bake in preheated 375-degree oven 45 minutes.

VARIATION:
To prepare cornsticks, brush cornstick pans with melted butter or margarine. Heat pans in preheated 500-degree oven 5 minutes. Spoon batter into pans. Bake about 10 minutes until golden. Repeat with remaining batter.

See photo page 187.

GREEN CHILI AND CHEESE CORN BREAD

SERVES 12 TO 15

1/4 **pound butter, softened**
1/2 **cup sugar**
4 **eggs**
4 **ounces canned green chilies, chopped**
1 **pound canned creamed corn**
1/2 **cup grated Monterey Jack cheese**
1/2 **cup grated mild Cheddar cheese**
1 **cup flour**
1 **cup yellow cornmeal**
4 **teaspoons baking powder**
1/4 **teaspoon salt**

In large bowl cream butter and sugar until light and fluffy. Add eggs 1 at a time, beating well after each addition. Stir in chilies, corn, and cheeses.

In medium bowl sift together flour, cornmeal, baking powder, and salt. Add to corn mixture. Blend well. Pour into greased 9- by 13-inch baking pan. Place in preheated 350-degree oven. Immediately reduce heat to 300 degrees. Bake 55 minutes or until golden brown and bread begins to pull away from sides of pan.

May be baked 1 week in advance and frozen. Thaw completely and reheat in foil in preheated 325-degree oven 20 minutes.

ONION SHALLOT RYE ROLLS

YIELD:

12 VERY LARGE,

24 LARGE, OR

36 DINNER

2 **tablespoons brown sugar**

1 **cup warm water (105 to 115 degrees)**

1 **package active dry yeast**

3/4 **cup whole grain rye flour or medium rye flour**

1/4 **cup olive oil**

1 **large egg**

1 1/2 **teaspoons salt**

2 3/4 **cups all-purpose white flour**

TOPPING:

1/4 **cup olive oil**

1 **large onion, chopped**

2 **medium shallots, minced**

freshly ground white pepper, optional

1/4 **teaspoon garlic powder, optional**

1/4 **cup plain yogurt**

2 **teaspoons caraway seed**

In small bowl dissolve brown sugar in warm water. Sprinkle in yeast. Blend well. Let stand until foamy.

In food processor combine rye flour, olive oil, egg, salt, and white flour. Process briefly until mixed. With motor running add yeast mixture through tube. Process until ball forms on blade plus 40 seconds. If ball does not form add 1 teaspoon water at a time, processing after each addition. If too sticky add white flour 1 tablespoon at a time, processing after each addition, to form a soft dough.

On floured surface knead dough briefly. Shape into ball. Transfer dough to warm, greased bowl, turning to coat all sides. Cover with plastic wrap. Let rise in warm place for 1 hour or until double in size.

On floured surface punch down dough gently. Knead briefly. Divide dough into 12, 24, or 36 pieces, as desired. With floured hands shape into oblong rolls. Arrange rolls barely touching in greased, non-glass 9- by 13-inch baking pan. Cover with plastic wrap. Let rise in warm place about 40 minutes.

TOPPING:

While rolls rise heat olive oil in medium skillet over medium heat. Add onion, shallots, and a few grinds of white pepper and garlic powder, if desired. Sauté 10 minutes or until softened, stirring frequently. Add yogurt. Increase heat. Boil 3 minutes or until liquid is reduced by half, stirring constantly. Transfer to small bowl. Stir in caraway seed. Cool.

Gently spoon topping evenly over tops of risen rolls. Bake in preheated 375-degree oven 25 minutes or until golden brown for dinner size. Cool on rack.

SWEET POTATO ROLLS

YIELD: 30 TO 40

2   **packages active dry yeast**
4   **tablespoons sugar, divided**
1/4   **cup warm water (105 to 115 degrees)**
1 1/2   **cups fresh or canned mashed sweet potato or yam**
3   **tablespoons butter, softened**
1   **teaspoon salt**
3   **eggs, divided (1 egg optional)**
3 1/2   **cups flour, divided**
1   **tablespoon vegetable oil, or as needed**
1   **tablespoon water, optional**

In large bowl combine yeast, 1 tablespoon sugar, and warm water. Mix well. Let stand 5 minutes. Add remaining 3 tablespoons sugar, sweet potato, butter, salt, and 2 eggs. Mix well. Stir in 3 cups flour.

On lightly floured surface knead dough gently 2 to 3 minutes, adding just enough flour to prevent sticking. When dough is smooth and resilient to light pressure, shape into ball. Transfer to oiled bowl, turning to coat all sides. Cover with towel. Let rise in warm place 1 1/4 to 1 1/2 hours or until double in size. Punch down dough. Reshape in ball. Let stand 2 minutes.

Pull off pieces of dough to form balls 1 1/2 inches in diameter. Arrange 2 inches apart on greased baking sheet. Cover lightly with cloth towel. Let rise 30 minutes or until double in size. Rolls may be dusted with flour before baking or brushed with egg mixed with water for glazed finish. Bake in preheated 375-degree oven 12 to 15 minutes or until lightly browned.

SPOON ROLLS

YIELD: 24

1   **package active dry yeast**
2   **cups warm water (105 to 115 degrees)**
1/4   **pound butter, melted**
1/4   **cup sugar**
1   **egg, beaten**
4   **cups self-rising flour**

In large bowl dissolve yeast in warm water. In medium bowl combine melted butter, sugar, egg, and self-rising flour. Mix well. Stir into yeast mixture.

In large airtight container or plastic bag refrigerate dough 3 hours. Spoon 1 heaping tablespoon dough into each of 24 greased muffin tins. Bake in preheated 425-degree oven 20 minutes.

CRUSTY GARLIC ROLLS

YIELD: 18

2 **packages active dry yeast**
1 **tablespoon sugar**
1¼ **cups warm water (105 to 115 degrees)**
3 **tablespoons extra virgin olive oil, divided**
8 **cloves garlic, minced**
¼ **teaspoon freshly ground pepper**
2 **tablespoons unsalted butter**
3½ **cups flour**
2 **teaspoons salt**

In small bowl combine yeast, sugar, and warm water. Mix well. Let stand 10 to 15 minutes until foamy. Stir in 1 tablespoon olive oil. In small skillet sauté garlic and pepper in butter and remaining 2 tablespoons olive oil 2 minutes. Cool slightly. In large bowl combine flour and salt. Mix well. Add garlic and yeast mixtures. Blend well.

On lightly floured surface knead dough until firm. Transfer to oiled bowl, turning to coat all sides. Cover. Let rise in warm place 1 hour. Knead dough slightly.

On floured surface roll dough to ¼-inch thickness. Cut into rounds with 2½-inch cookie cutter. Transfer to greased baking sheet. Let rise 45 minutes. Bake in preheated 425-degree oven 15 minutes or until golden brown. Serve warm.

MONKEY BREAD

SERVES 12 TO 16

½ **pound margarine, melted**
2 **tablespoons finely chopped fresh dill**
2 **teaspoons fines herbes**
4 **tubes refrigerated buttermilk biscuits**

In small bowl combine margarine, dill, and fines herbes. Mix well. Roll biscuits into balls. Dip balls into margarine mixture. Layer in ungreased angel food cake pan. Bake in preheated 350-degree oven 45 minutes. Serve warm.

POLISH NUT BREAD

YIELD:

2 LARGE LOAVES

2   packages active dry yeast

1/4   cup warm water (105 to 115 degrees)

5   cups flour

5   tablespoons sugar

1   teaspoon salt

1/4   pound butter

3   egg yolks, beaten

1   cup milk

FILLING:

1/2   pound ground pecans

1/2   pound ground walnuts

1/4   pound butter

1   cup sugar

1   cup whipping cream

1   egg

1   teaspoon cinnamon

1   teaspoon cardamom

1   egg

1   tablespoon water

In small bowl dissolve yeast in warm water. Let stand in warm place 15 to 20 minutes until foamy. In large bowl combine flour, sugar, and salt. Mix well. Stir in yeast mixture.

Cut in butter with pastry blender. Add egg yolks and milk. Mix well. Knead in bowl until fairly smooth. Transfer dough to greased bowl. Cover and let rise in warm place until double in size.

While dough rises combine all filling ingredients in large saucepan. Mix well. Cook over medium heat 5 to 10 minutes or until thickened. Cool.

Punch down dough. Cover and let rise 20 minutes. Divide dough in half. Roll each half into 8- by 12-inch rectangle. Spread each rectangle with half of filling mixture. Roll each from long side, sealing ends. Cover and let rise 15 minutes. In small bowl mix 1 egg with water. Brush loaves with egg mixture. Transfer loaves to baking sheet. Bake in preheated 350-degree oven 45 to 50 minutes.

Bread freezes well.

See photo page 186.

WALNUT HERB BREAD

YIELD:
1 LARGE LOAF

1 package active dry yeast
1/4 cup light brown sugar
1 1/2 cups warm water (105 to 115 degrees)
3 cups whole wheat flour, divided
1 1/2 cups all-purpose white flour, divided
1/2 tablespoon salt
1/2 cup dry milk
1/4 cup walnut oil
2 tablespoons chopped parsley
1 tablespoon chopped fresh rosemary
1 1/2 cups coarsely chopped walnuts

In large bowl combine yeast, brown sugar, and warm water. Let stand 10 minutes. Add 1 1/2 cups whole wheat flour, 1 cup white flour, salt, dry milk, walnut oil, parsley, and rosemary. Beat until smooth. Add remaining 1 1/2 cups whole wheat flour and 1/2 cup white flour. Beat vigorously or blend in food processor until dough forms ball. Add walnuts. Mix well.

Transfer dough to greased bowl, turning to coat all sides. Cover with damp towel. Let rise in warm place until double in size. Transfer dough to floured surface. Punch down dough. Form loaf shape. Place in greased 11- by 5 1/4-inch loaf pan. Let rise 40 minutes.

Bake in preheated 350-degree oven 40 minutes. Remove from pan. Cool on rack.

WALNUT WHEATBERRY BREAD

YIELD: 2 LOAVES

2   **packages active dry yeast**
2   **cups warm water (105 to 115 degrees)**
1/2 **cup honey, divided**
1/4 **cup oat bran**
1/4 **cup wheat germ**
*1   **cup cooked wheatberries**
1   **cup oats**
1   **teaspoon salt**
1   **cup coarsely broken walnuts**
3   **cups whole wheat flour, divided**
3   **cups all-purpose white flour**
1   **tablespoon vegetable oil**

In small bowl combine yeast, warm water, and 1 tablespoon honey. In large bowl combine remaining honey, oat bran, wheat germ, wheatberries, oats, salt, and walnuts. Add yeast mixture. Stir in 1½ cups whole wheat flour. Mix well. Add remaining 1½ cups whole wheat flour. Slowly blend in white flour until dough is stiff.

Transfer dough to floured surface. Knead until smooth and dough no longer sticks to hands. Place in oiled bowl, turning to coat all sides. Cover with dry towel. Let rise at room temperature at least 1 hour. Punch down dough. Divide in half. Knead out bubbles and shape into 2 loaves.

Place loaves in 2 greased 9- by 5-inch loaf pans. Slit loaves lengthwise across top with sharp knife. Cover with dry towel. Let rise 30 minutes. Bake in preheated 350-degree oven 35 to 45 minutes or until golden brown. Remove loaves from pans. Cool on rack.

May be baked 1 to 2 days in advance or up to 1 month if frozen.

*Wheatberries take 3 hours to cook. Available in health food stores.

WHOLE WHEAT BREAD

YIELD: 2 LOAVES

2	tablespoons active dry yeast
3	cups warm water (105 to 115 degrees)
1/2	cup corn oil
1/2	cup honey
2	teaspoons salt
1	egg, beaten
9-10	cups whole wheat flour, divided

In large bowl sprinkle yeast into warm water. Let stand 5 to 10 minutes until foamy. Stir to mix. Add corn oil, honey, salt, and egg. Mix well. Stir in 4 cups flour. Beat 100 times with wooden spoon until smooth. Let stand 15 to 45 minutes until bubbly and starting to rise. Add 5 cups flour, stirring in 1 direction until well mixed.

On lightly floured surface knead dough 5 to 10 minutes, adding more flour as needed. Transfer dough smooth side down to large greased bowl. Invert dough so greased side is up. Cover.

Let rise in warm place until double in size. Punch down dough. Let rise another hour or until double in size. Punch down. Divide dough in half. Knead several times. Transfer to 2 greased 9- by 5-inch loaf pans. Let rise until double in size. Bake in preheated 400-degree oven 20 to 25 minutes. Remove from pans. Cool on rack.

CHEESE-CRUSTED RYE BREAD

YIELD: 1 LOAF

2	cloves garlic
1/4	cup loosely packed sprigs parsley
2	green onions with tops, in 1-inch pieces
12	tablespoons butter or margarine, softened
1/2	teaspoon basil
1 1/2	cups grated Swiss cheese
1 1/2-1 3/4	pound oval loaf rye bread, unsliced

In food processor mince garlic and parsley. Add green onions, butter, and basil. Blend well. Remove two-thirds of mixture to small bowl. Add cheese to one-third mixture in processor. Blend well.

Slice diagonal cuts 2 inches apart through rye bread, slicing almost to bottom but leaving bottom crust intact. Spread herbed butter from bowl between slices. Spread butter-cheese mixture from processor over top and sides. Wrap bread in foil. Place on baking sheet.

Bake in preheated 400-degree oven 25 minutes. Remove from foil. Bake 10 minutes or until top is crusty. Transfer bread to cutting board. Slice through bottom crust.

BALLYMALOE BROWN BREAD

YIELD: 2 LOAVES

1/4	cup molasses
3	cups warm water (105 to 115 degrees)
3	packages active dry yeast or 2 ounces cake yeast
7 1/2	cups coarse-ground whole wheat flour
4	teaspoons salt

In small bowl combine molasses and warm water. Mix well. Sprinkle or crumble yeast into molasses-water mixture. Let stand 5 minutes or until foamy on top. In large bowl combine whole wheat flour and salt. Mix well. Add yeast mixture to flour. Blend well. Divide dough between 2 greased 9- by 5-inch loaf pans. Cover each with towel. Let rise in warm place until dough reaches tops of pans.

Transfer to preheated 450-degree oven. Bake 10 minutes. Reduce heat to 400 degrees. Bake 20 minutes or until browned. Remove bread from pans and invert onto greased baking sheets. Bake 5 to 7 minutes or until bottoms are brown. Cool on rack.

AFGHAN BREAD

YIELD: 1 LOAF

1   teaspoon sugar
1   teaspoon active dry yeast
1/2 cup warm milk (105 to 115 degrees) plus 2 tablespoons
      milk, divided
1   cup plus 2 tablespoons flour
1   teaspoon baking powder
1/2 teaspoon salt
1   tablespoon melted butter or olive oil
3   tablespoons sesame seed

In small bowl combine sugar, yeast, and 1/2 cup warm milk. Mix well. Let stand until foamy. In food processor combine flour, baking powder, and salt. Process with several quick on and off turns. Add melted butter. With motor running pour yeast mixture slowly through tube. Process until ball forms. If dough is too wet add 1 teaspoon flour at a time, processing between each addition, to form soft dough.

On floured surface knead dough briefly. Cover with floured plastic wrap. Let stand 1 hour. Roll dough out to 12-inch diameter. Transfer to greased baking sheet. Brush with remaining 2 tablespoons milk and sprinkle with sesame seed, pressing into dough lightly. With long, thin implement such as chopstick, make indentations in dough crosswise at 2-inch intervals.

Bake on center rack in preheated 500-degree oven 3 to 5 minutes. Bread should puff up. Place under preheated broiler 30 to 45 seconds to brown top. Watch carefully. Serve hot, or cool and reheat in 300-degree oven immediately before serving.

CHEESE PEPPER PROSCIUTTO BREAD

YIELD: 2 LOAVES

2   **packages active dry yeast**
1   **tablespoon honey**
2   **cups warm water (105 to 115 degrees)**
1   **teaspoon salt**
1   **cup whole wheat flour**
4-5   **cups all-purpose white flour**
6-8   **slices thinly sliced prosciutto, divided**
1   **cup grated sharp Cheddar cheese, divided**
1   **cup grated Parmesan cheese, divided**
    freshly ground pepper
1/2   **cup cornmeal**
1   **egg white, lightly beaten**
1   **teaspoon water**
1/4   **cup sesame seed, optional**
1/4   **cup poppy seed, optional**

In large bowl stir yeast and honey into warm water. Let stand 5 to 10 minutes or until foamy. Add salt and whole wheat flour. Mix well. Add white flour gradually.

When dough becomes stiff transfer to floured surface and knead. Continue adding white flour until dough is smooth and not very sticky. Transfer dough to greased bowl, turning to coat all sides. Cover. Let stand at room temperature 1 to 1½ hours or until double in size.

Punch down dough. Divide in half. Flatten half of dough on floured surface. Spread half of prosciutto and half of both cheeses over dough. Sprinkle 1 grind of pepper over all. Roll dough into log, pinching ends and bottom seams to seal. Repeat with remaining dough, prosciutto, cheeses, and pepper.

Place loaves on cornmeal-sprinkled baking sheet or French bread loaf pan. Slash tops diagonally with knife. In small bowl mix egg white with water. Brush egg mixture over tops of loaves. Sprinkle with sesame and poppy seed, if desired.

Place loaves in cold oven. Set oven to 400 degrees. Bake 35 minutes or until tops are brown and loaves sound hollow when tapped on bottoms.

See photo page 79.

MARZIPAN BRIOCHE

8   **ounces canned almond paste, divided**
6   **jumbo eggs, divided**
3/4 **cup plus 3¼ teaspoons sugar, divided**
1   **package active dry yeast**
¼ **cup warm water (105 to 115 degrees)**
5   **cups flour, divided**
½ **teaspoon salt**
¼ **pound unsalted butter, in 10 pieces**
½ **cup warm milk (95 to 100 degrees) plus 3 tablespoons cold milk, divided**
   cooking spray
¼ **teaspoon almond extract**
3   **tablespoons sliced almonds**

In food processor or blender combine 4 ounces almond paste in small pieces, 1 egg white, and ½ cup sugar. Process until smooth. Line baking sheet with parchment or brown paper. Drop almond mixture onto paper in 12 small mounds. Flatten slightly. Bake in preheated 325-degree oven 30 minutes. Remove cookies from sheet. Cool on rack. Transfer 6 cookies to food processor or blender. Process into fine crumbs. Set aside. Store remaining cookies in airtight container for future use.

In small bowl sprinkle yeast over warm water. Add ¼ teaspoon sugar. Set aside. In large bowl combine 3 cups flour, ¼ cup sugar, salt, 3 eggs, and butter. Mix briefly.

Pour warm milk into another small bowl. Stir in yeast mixture. Yeast should be dissolved and starting to bubble. Add yeast-milk mixture to flour mixture. Mix well. Mixture will be very sticky. Stir in additional ½ cup flour.

Transfer dough to floured surface. Knead dough 15 minutes, gradually adding additional flour as needed, ½ to 1 cup. While dough is still very sticky, use spatula to lift from surface, sprinkle surface with flour, and replace dough. Continue kneading. When dough is smooth and no longer sticks to surface, form into ball. Place in large greased bowl, turning to coat all sides. Cover. Let rise in warm place 1½ to 2 hours until double in size. Coat 9-inch brioche pan with cooking spray. Let stand 2 minutes. Butter pan liberally.

continued

In food processor or blender combine remaining 4 ounces almond paste pieces, 2 egg whites, almond extract, and reserved cookie crumbs. Process until smooth. Cover tightly with plastic wrap.

Punch down risen dough and transfer to lightly floured surface. Knead 5 minutes. Remove fist-size piece of dough. Set aside. Roll dough into 14-inch square. Spread almond mixture over dough. Roll up. Bring ends together to form ring. Dampen ends slightly with several drops of water to make ends adhere.

Place ring of dough seam side down in brioche pan. Roll reserved piece of dough into teardrop shape. Using 1 hand to hold center of ring open, insert teardrop 1 inch into opening, leaving most of it out. Cover dough with towel. Let dough rise in warm place until above edge of pan.

In small bowl beat 1 egg yolk and 3 tablespoons cold milk. Brush risen bread with milk mixture. Sprinkle with almonds and 1 tablespoon sugar.

Bake in lower third of preheated 350-degree oven 15 minutes. Cover loosely with foil. Bake 35 minutes. Remove foil if browner bread is desired. Bake 10 to 15 minutes. Test for doneness by tapping top of bread with knuckle. Thoroughly baked bread will sound hollow. If bread sounds soft, bake additional 5 minutes. Cool bread in pan on rack 10 minutes. With narrow knife loosen bread around pan. Remove from pan.

Cool on rack loosely covered with towel. Wrap cooled bread in plastic bag to seal completely until served.

FENNEL AND BLACK PEPPER BREADSTICKS

YIELD: 60

1   **pound loaf frozen pizza dough, thawed**
1   **egg white, beaten**
4   **teaspoons grated Parmesan cheese, divided**
2   **teaspoons fennel seed, divided**
1   **teaspoon kosher salt, and as needed for sprinkling, divided**
1   **teaspoon medium grind black pepper, divided**

Divide dough into fourths. On lightly floured surface roll each fourth to about 12- by 6-inch rectangle. Brush with egg white. Sprinkle each rectangle with 1 teaspoon Parmesan cheese, 1/2 teaspoon fennel seed, and 1/4 teaspoon salt and pepper. Fold in half lengthwise to enclose toppings. Roll again to form 12- by 4-inch rectangles.

Slice dough into 1/4-inch strips with sharp knife or pizza roller. Transfer strips to parchment-lined baking sheets. If desired, brush strips with egg white and sprinkle lightly with kosher salt. Bake in preheated 350-degree oven 10 to 12 minutes or until lightly brown and crisp.

See photo page 78.

DESSERTS

CHOPPED APPLE PIE WITH BUTTER CRUMB TOPPING

SERVES 8 TO 10

FILLING:

6   **large McIntosh apples, unpeeled, coarsely chopped**
     juice of 1 lemon
⅔   **cup firmly packed light brown sugar**
¼   **cup flour**
¼   **teaspoon cinnamon**
     pinch nutmeg or mace
     pinch salt
2   **tablespoons butter, melted**

CRUST:

     pastry for 9-inch deep dish pie

TOPPING:

⅔   **cup firmly packed dark brown sugar**
⅔   **cup flour**
4   **tablespoons cold butter, in small pieces**
     pinch salt

In large bowl combine all filling ingredients. Mix well. Line 9-inch deep dish pie pan with pastry. Pour filling into pie shell.

In food processor combine all topping ingredients. Reduce to crumbs with 5 to 6 on and off turns. Completely cover filling with topping. Place pie pan on foil-lined jelly-roll pan to catch drippings.

Bake in preheated 400-degree oven 10 minutes. Reduce heat to 375 degrees. Bake 30 to 35 minutes. Cool on rack before slicing.

GINGER PEAR PIE

¼   **pound plus 4 tablespoons margarine, divided**
3   **ounces cream cheese**
1½   **cups flour, divided**
2   **eggs, beaten**
¼   **teaspoon salt**
¾   **teaspoon ginger**
    pinch nutmeg
½   **teaspoon grated lemon rind**
¼   **teaspoon vanilla**
¼   **teaspoon almond extract**
1   **cup sour cream**
4   **Anjou pears, peeled, in sections**
6   **tablespoons brown sugar**

In small bowl blend ¼ pound margarine, cream cheese, and 1 cup flour with pastry blender. Press mixture into bottom and up sides of 10-inch pie pan. Bake in preheated 350-degree oven 7 minutes.

In medium bowl combine eggs, salt, ginger, nutmeg, lemon rind, vanilla, almond extract, and sour cream. Mix well. Arrange pears in pie shell. Pour egg mixture over pears.

In another small bowl combine remaining ½ cup flour, brown sugar, and remaining 4 tablespoons margarine. Mix well. Sprinkle mixture over pie. Bake in preheated 325-degree oven 45 minutes or until top is golden brown.

FRESH PEACH GLAZED PIE

SERVES 6

4   **large ripe peaches, peeled, divided**
¾   **cup water**
1   **cup plus 1 tablespoon sugar, divided**
2   **tablespoons cornstarch**
1   **teaspoon fresh lemon juice**
1   **teaspoon butter**
    pinch salt
1   **9-inch baked pie shell**
1   **cup whipping cream**

Cut 1 peach into chunks. In medium saucepan combine peach and water. Cook 4 minutes. In small bowl mix 1 cup sugar and cornstarch. Add to mixture in saucepan. Cook until thick and clear. Blend in lemon juice, butter, and salt. Cool.

Slice remaining 3 peaches. Arrange slices in pie shell. Pour cooled glaze over peaches. Chill. When ready to serve, whip cream with remaining 1 tablespoon sugar in small bowl until stiff peaks form. Top pie with whipped cream.

Strawberries may be substituted for peaches.

FRESH RASPBERRY PIE

SERVES 8

1   **cup sugar**
¼   **cup flour**
1   **tablespoon tapioca**
4   **cups fresh raspberries or 2 cups fresh raspberries and**
    2 cups fresh black raspberries
2   **9-inch unbaked pie crusts (see page 360)**

In large bowl combine sugar, flour, and tapioca. Mix well. Add berries. Gently blend. Let stand 15 minutes. Carefully stir berries.

Line 9-inch pie pan with 1 crust. Spoon berry mixture into crust. Cover with lattice or well-pierced top crust. Bake in preheated 450-degree oven 10 minutes. Reduce heat to 350 degrees. Bake 35 to 40 minutes or until golden brown.

BLUEBERRY RHUBARB PIE

SERVES 8

1   **cup lard or shortening**
3   **cups plus 4 tablespoons sifted flour, divided**
1   **egg**
5   **tablespoons water**
1   **teaspoon cider vinegar**
1   **teaspoon salt**
2   **cups fresh blueberries**
1½   **cups diced fresh rhubarb, in ½-inch pieces**
1⅓   **cups sugar**
½   **teaspoon grated lemon rind**
    pinch cinnamon

In large bowl mix lard and 3 cups flour with pastry blender. In small bowl combine egg, water, vinegar, and salt. Mix well. Blend into flour mixture.

In medium bowl combine blueberries and rhubarb. In another small bowl mix sugar, remaining 4 tablespoons flour, lemon rind, and cinnamon. Pour mixture over fruit. Blend well.

Divide dough in half. Roll out half to 10-inch circle. Line 9-inch pie pan with pastry. Fill with fruit mixture. Roll out other half of dough to 9-inch circle. Cover pie. Crimp edges well. Cut steam vents in top crust. Bake pie in preheated 350-degree oven 45 to 55 minutes or until crust is golden brown.

MACADAMIA NUT TART

SERVES 10

CRUST:

¼ **pound unsalted butter, softened**

½ **cup sugar**

2 **egg yolks**

1 **teaspoon vanilla**

1½ **cups flour**

FILLING:

1 **cup firmly packed brown sugar**

5⅓ **tablespoons unsalted butter**

2 **tablespoons plus 1 teaspoon pure maple syrup**

2 **tablespoons plus 1 teaspoon light corn syrup**

3 **tablespoons whipping cream**

¾ **pound unsalted macadamia nuts, halved**

CRUST:

In large bowl cream butter and sugar until light and fluffy. Add egg yolks 1 at a time. Add vanilla. Stir in flour. Mix well. Between 2 sheets wax paper roll dough into circle 12 inches in diameter. Refrigerate in wax paper 30 minutes.

Remove 1 sheet wax paper. Place pastry paper side up in greased 9-inch tart pan with removable bottom. Remove wax paper. Cover pastry with aluminum foil. Top with dried beans or pastry weights. Bake in preheated 350-degree oven 15 minutes. Remove beans or weights and foil. Bake 3 to 5 minutes or until lightly golden. Cool on rack.

FILLING:

In medium saucepan combine brown sugar, butter, maple syrup, corn syrup, and cream. Bring to boil, stirring constantly. Boil 1 minute or until sugar is dissolved and mixture is caramel color.

Fill cooled crust with nuts. Pour hot filling over nuts. Bake in 350-degree oven 5 to 6 minutes or until filling bubbles. Cool on rack 2 hours. Remove sides of pan.

May serve with Semi-Sweet Hot Fudge Sauce, page 415.

See photo page 373.

MACADAMIA NUT CHIFFON PIE

SERVES 8 TO 10

4	large eggs, separated
1	cup plus 1 tablespoon sugar, divided
¼	teaspoon plus pinch salt, divided
1	cup milk
1	envelope unflavored gelatin
¼	cup cold water
3½	ounces macadamia nuts
¼-½	teaspoon almond extract
1	9- or 10-inch baked pie shell
1	cup whipping cream

In double boiler combine slightly beaten egg yolks, ½ cup sugar, ¼ teaspoon salt, and milk. Cook over simmering water until mixture is thickened and coats spoon, stirring constantly. Do not boil. Remove from heat. Stir in gelatin softened in cold water until dissolved. Cool.

In medium bowl beat egg whites and pinch salt until foamy. Gradually add ½ cup sugar, beating until very stiff and sugar is dissolved. Gently fold into cooled custard. Reserving some whole nuts for decorating, chop remaining nuts. Stir chopped nuts and almond extract into custard. Pour into pie shell. Chill.

In small bowl whip cream and remaining 1 tablespoon sugar until stiff peaks form. Top pie with whipped cream. Decorate with reserved whole nuts.

PEANUT BUTTER ICE CREAM PIE

SERVES 8

CRUST:

¼	pound butter
2	tablespoons brown sugar
1	cup flour
1	tablespoon peanut butter

FILLING:

½	gallon vanilla ice cream or nonfat frozen vanilla yogurt, divided
⅓	cup peanut butter
½	cup light corn syrup
1	cup unsalted peanuts, divided

continued

In medium bowl combine all crust ingredients. Mix well. Press into 10-inch pie pan. Bake in preheated 325-degree oven 15 minutes. Cool.

Press ¼ gallon ice cream or yogurt into pie shell. In small bowl combine peanut butter and corn syrup. Mix well. Pour half of peanut butter mixture over ice cream or yogurt. Sprinkle ½ cup peanuts over mixture. Press remaining ¼ gallon ice cream or yogurt over top, molding toward center. Top with remaining peanut butter mixture. Sprinkle with remaining ½ cup peanuts. Freeze 3 to 5 hours. Remove from freezer 15 minutes before serving. Slice with hot knife.

CHOCOLATE PECAN PIE

SERVES 8 TO 10

CRUST:
3   **ounces cream cheese, softened**
1   **cup flour**
¼   **pound butter or margarine**

FILLING:
4   **eggs**
1   **cup dark corn syrup**
2   **tablespoons butter, melted**
1   **cup brown sugar**
1   **teaspoon vanilla**
1   **cup pecan halves**
½   **cup semi-sweet chocolate chips**

In medium bowl combine all crust ingredients. Blend well. Press into 10-inch pie pan.

For filling, beat eggs in large bowl. Add corn syrup, butter, brown sugar, and vanilla. Mix well. Stir in nuts and chocolate chips. Pour into pie shell. Bake in preheated
350-degree oven 35 to 45 minutes.

FROZEN MARGARITA PIE

SERVES 8

CRUST:

¼ **pound plus 2 tablespoons butter or margarine, melted**

1¼ **cups finely crushed thin pretzel sticks**

½ **cup sugar**

FILLING:

14 **ounces sweetened condensed milk**

*½ **tablespoon lime juice**

1½ **tablespoons tequila**

1 **tablespoon plus 1 teaspoon orange liqueur**

2 **cups whipping cream**

fresh lime, thinly sliced

In medium bowl combine butter, pretzel crumbs, and sugar. Mix well. Press into bottom and up sides of greased 9-inch pie pan. Place in freezer while preparing filling.

For filling, combine condensed milk, lime juice, tequila, and liqueur in small bowl. Mix well. In another small bowl beat cream until soft peaks form. Fold into milk mixture. Pour into pie shell. Freeze at least 2 hours or until served. Garnish with lime slices.

*Lime juice may be increased to ⅔ cup if non-alcoholic pie is preferred.

PERFECT PIE CRUST

YIELD:

TWO 9-INCH

PIE CRUSTS

1 **cup shortening**

2⅓ **cups flour, divided**

1 **tablespoon white vinegar**

5 **tablespoons cold water**

In medium bowl combine shortening and 2 cups flour. Mix with pastry blender until texture resembles small peas.

In small bowl combine remaining ⅓ cup flour, vinegar, and cold water. Mix well. Add to flour-shortening mixture. Mix quickly, lightly, and minimally. Form into large disk. Divide in half. Form each half into disk. Wrap each disk in plastic wrap. Chill.

On floured surface roll each disk from center out, turning an eighth and repeating. Fit 1 crust into 9-inch pie pan. Add filling of choice. Fit second crust over top. Seal edges and flute, if desired. Bake according to filling directions.

APRICOT STRAWBERRY TART

SERVES 10 TO 12

CRUST:

¼	**pound plus 2 tablespoons unsalted butter, chilled**
1	**large egg plus 1 large egg yolk**
½	**cup confectioners sugar**
1	**tablespoon whipping cream or milk**
1⅔	**cups flour**

FILLING:

8	**dried apricot halves**
5	**tablespoons sugar**
2	**large egg yolks**
3	**tablespoons flour**
1½	**teaspoons orange liqueur or vanilla**
⅔	**cup whole milk, scalded**
½	**cup whipping cream, whipped**

TOPPING:

6-8	**fresh apricots, halved, pitted**
8	**small fresh strawberries, in thin slices**
⅓	**cup apricot preserves**

CRUST:

In food processor cut butter into bits. Add egg, egg yolk, confectioners sugar, and cream. Blend well. Add flour. Process just until dough comes together. Transfer to large plastic bag. Press into ball. Then flatten into disk. Refrigerate 30 minutes.

On floured surface roll dough to circle ⅛ inch thick. Press into bottom and up sides of 10-inch tart pan with removable bottom. Trim excess. Pierce several times with fork. Refrigerate 15 minutes. Bake in preheated 400-degree oven 18 to 20 minutes or until golden. Remove sides of pan. Cool on rack.

FILLING:

In food processor or blender combine dried apricots and sugar. Process until apricots are very fine. Add egg yolks. Mix well. Stir in flour and liqueur. Blend in scalded milk. Transfer to small saucepan. Cook over medium heat 4 to 5 minutes until very thick, stirring constantly. Transfer to medium bowl. Whisk until smooth. Refrigerate 1 hour. Fold in whipped cream. Spread filling over crust.

TOPPING:

Arrange circle of fresh apricots around outer edge of tart. Arrange circle of strawberries inside apricots and circle of apricots in center. In small saucepan melt preserves and put through fine strainer. Brush over fruit and top rim of crust. Refrigerate tart until served.

See photo page 374.

NECTARINE OR PEACH AND BERRY TART

SERVES 6

CRUST:
½ cup flour
6 tablespoons unsalted butter, in ¼-inch cubes
¼ teaspoon salt
4 tablespoons ice water, divided

STREUSEL TOPPING:
3 tablespoons butter
½ cup sugar
¼ cup flour
¼ teaspoon cinnamon

FILLING:
4 firm nectarines or peaches, peeled, sliced
1 cup fresh raspberries
½ cup fresh blueberries

1 tablespoon butter, melted
1 tablespoon sugar
⅛ teaspoon cinnamon

In large bowl combine flour, butter, and salt. Mix well. Add 2 tablespoons ice water. Mix well. Add remaining 2 tablespoons water. Blend well. Gather dough by hand. Knead briefly. Press into circular shape. Wrap dough in plastic and refrigerate 1 hour. Roll dough to circle 12 inches in diameter. Transfer to baking sheet lined with parchment paper.

In small bowl combine all streusel ingredients. Mix with pastry blender until texture resembles coarse crumbs.

Sprinkle 3 tablespoons streusel mixture in center of pastry, leaving 1½-inch border. Continuing to leave 1½-inch border arrange nectarine or peach slices evenly in overlapping circles. Top fruit with raspberries and blueberries. Sprinkle remaining streusel mixture over fruit only. Fold 1½-inch border up over edge of tart. Brush border with melted butter. Sprinkle with combined sugar and cinnamon.

Bake in preheated 400-degree oven 35 minutes. Cool on rack 20 minutes. Serve warm or at room temperature. May be served with vanilla ice cream, if desired.

See photo page 374.

CARAMELIZED APPLE TART

SERVES 8 TO 10

CRUST:

1¾ cups flour
2 tablespoons sugar
½ teaspoon salt
¼ pound butter, chilled, in small chunks
1 egg yolk
4-5 tablespoons ice water

FILLING:

4 large Granny Smith apples, peeled, finely sliced
1 cup sugar
¼ pound butter
1 tablespoon Calvados (apple brandy)

1 cup whipping cream, whipped, or vanilla ice cream

CRUST:

In medium bowl combine flour, sugar, and salt. Mix well. Transfer to food processor. Add butter and egg yolk. Process with 20 quick on and off turns or until mixture resembles coarse crumbs. (May be done in bowl cutting with pastry blender.)

Transfer mixture back to bowl. Slowly add ice water, mixing until dough can be formed into ball. Place ball on 12-inch sheet of aluminum foil or plastic wrap. Press ball into disk 5 inches in diameter and 1 inch thick. Bring excess foil or plastic wrap over top of disk. Refrigerate.

FILLING:

In large bowl mix apple slices with sugar. In heavy 12-inch ovenproof skillet melt butter. Add apple mixture. Cook over low heat about 40 minutes until juice evaporates and apples start to caramelize. Remove from heat. Sprinkle apples with Calvados.

Remove crust from refrigerator. On floured surface, using half of dough, roll crust into 13-inch disk. Remaining dough can be refrigerated or frozen. Arrange pastry over apples in skillet, tucking excess pastry under. Cut slits in pastry to allow steam to escape.

Bake in preheated 375-degree oven 25 to 30 minutes or until crust is lightly browned. Serve warm, pastry side down.* Skillet may be inverted onto serving platter or invert individual portions as they are sliced from skillet. Place dollop of whipped cream or scoop of ice cream on side of each portion.

*Invert just before serving to ensure crisp crust.

SERVES 6

CRUST:

1¼ cups flour
2 tablespoons superfine sugar
4 tablespoons unsalted butter, chilled
4 tablespoons margarine, chilled
1 egg yolk
2 tablespoons ice water

FILLING:

5 tablespoons orange juice, warmed
2½ tablespoons instant tapioca
1 teaspoon vanilla
4 large red plums, quartered, sliced crosswise
½ cup sugar
1 tablespoon water
2½ cups fresh raspberries, divided
1 teaspoon lemon juice
5 tablespoons raspberry jelly
1 teaspoon brandy, liqueur of choice, or fruit juice
4 kiwis, peeled, sliced

CRUST:

In food processor or in medium bowl with pastry blender combine flour, sugar, butter, and margarine until mixture resembles coarse cornmeal. In small bowl lightly beat egg yolk. Add ice water. Blend well. Add to flour mixture. Process or blend until combined. Do not overmix.

Place ball of dough in center of 20-inch sheet of foil. Fold ends over, leaving ample room at center. With heels of hands gently press dough into 8- to 9-inch disk shape. Chill 1 hour. With floured rolling pin roll out dough on floured surface. Transfer to 9-inch fluted tart pan with removable bottom. If pastry separates, push pieces together. Pierce bottom of crust at 1-inch intervals. Chill 1 hour before baking.

To bake line crust with circle of aluminum foil. Fill with dried beans or pastry weights. Bake in preheated 375-degree oven 12 minutes or until edges start to turn color. Remove beans or weights and foil. Bake 8 to 10 minutes until crust is light brown. Cool on rack.

continued

FILLING:

In small bowl combine orange juice, tapioca, and vanilla. Mix well. Let stand 10 to 15 minutes.

In medium saucepan combine plums, sugar, and water. Cook over medium heat 3 to 4 minutes until sugar is syrupy and plums soften, stirring frequently. Add tapioca mixture. Mix well. Cook 3 minutes, stirring occasionally. Add 1½ cups raspberries and lemon juice. Stir gently so as not to break berries. Cook 4 to 5 minutes, stirring carefully every minute. Remove from heat. Cool 30 minutes.

In small saucepan melt jelly. Stir in brandy. Brush some of mixture over bottom of crust. Pour cooked fruit into crust. One inch from edge of tart arrange overlapping kiwi slices in circle. Fill center and outer edges of tart with remaining 1 cup raspberries, placing individually with stem ends down. Brush top with remaining jelly glaze. Cool 4 hours before slicing.

DOUBLE-CRUSTED ALMOND CAKE

SERVES 10 TO 12

CRUST:
- 2⅔ **cups flour**
- 1⅓ **cups sugar**
- ½ **teaspoon salt**
- 1 **egg, beaten**
- 1⅓ **cups unsalted butter**

FILLING:
- 1 **cup finely chopped almonds**
- ½ **cup sugar**
- 1 **teaspoon grated lemon rind**
- 1 **egg, beaten**

  sliced almonds

In large bowl combine all crust ingredients. Mix well. Divide dough in half. Press half of dough into bottom of greased 9- to 10-inch springform pan.

In small bowl blend all filling ingredients. Spread over crust to ½ inch of edge. Roll out remaining dough between 2 sheets of wax paper to size of springform pan. Gently transfer to cover filling. Sprinkle with sliced almonds.

Bake in preheated 325-degree oven 45 to 55 minutes or until golden brown. Cool on rack 15 minutes. Remove sides of pan and cool completely.

BÊTE NOIRE WITH POACHED PEARS AND RASPBERRY SAUCE

SERVES 16 TO 24

1⅓ **cups sugar, divided**
½ **cup water**
8 **ounces unsweetened chocolate, in ½-inch pieces**
4 **ounces semi-sweet chocolate, in ½-inch pieces**
½ **pound butter, in small pieces**
5 **jumbo eggs**
confectioners sugar

In medium saucepan combine 1 cup sugar and water. Boil 4 minutes. Remove from heat. Add chocolate. Stir until melted. Add butter a few pieces at a time, beating well after each addition.

In large bowl beat eggs and remaining ⅓ cup sugar about 15 minutes until tripled in volume and lemon colored. Fold in chocolate mixture. Pour into greased 9-inch round cake pan lined with wax or parchment paper. Set cake pan in larger pan. Pour boiling water halfway up sides of cake pan.

Bake in preheated 350-degree oven 25 minutes or until inserted tester comes out clean. Cool 10 minutes. Turn onto wax paper dusted with confectioners sugar. Remove papers while cake is warm. When cool, refrigerate or freeze.

Serve sliced with Poached Pears and Raspberry Sauce.

POACHED PEARS AND RASPBERRY SAUCE

2 **quarts water**
4 **cups sugar**
8-12 **ripe Bosc pears, peeled**
2 **lemons, halved**

20 **ounces frozen red raspberries, thawed**
sugar to taste
1 **tablespoon Kirsch**
2 **tablespoons chopped, skinned raw pistachios or toasted, skinned almonds**

In large stainless steel (not aluminum) pot bring water to boil. Stir in sugar. Reduce heat to simmer. Rub pears with lemons. Add pears and lemons to water. If necessary, add additional water to barely cover pears. Gently poach pears uncovered 10 to 20 minutes or until they are slightly resistant to prick by fork. With slotted spoon remove pears from pot to large bowl. Discard lemons. Pour poaching liquid over pears. Refrigerate.

For sauce, puree berries with juice in food processor or blender. Strain to remove seeds. Sweeten puree with sugar to taste. Blend well. Stir in Kirsch. To serve, pour 2 tablespoons of sauce on individual dessert plates. Top with pear half or slices. Sprinkle with nuts.

See photo page 375.

OLD-FASHIONED CHOCOLATE CAKE

SERVES 12

¼ **pound butter or margarine**
1½ **cups sugar**
3 **eggs**
3 **tablespoons cocoa**
3 **tablespoons hot water**
2 **cups cake flour**
1 **teaspoon baking soda**
1 **cup sour cream**
1 **teaspoon vanilla**

FROSTING:
4 **ounces unsweetened chocolate**
6 **tablespoons butter or margarine**
5 **ounces evaporated milk**
3 **cups confectioners sugar**
1 **teaspoon vanilla**

In large bowl cream butter and sugar well. Add eggs 1 at a time, beating well after each addition. Dissolve cocoa in hot water. Add to butter mixture. In small bowl sift together flour and baking soda. Add flour and sour cream alternately to butter mixture. Add vanilla. Pour batter into 2 greased 9-inch round cake pans. Bake in preheated 350-degree oven 30 minutes or until inserted tester comes out clean. Cool.

For frosting, melt chocolate and butter in double boiler. In medium bowl combine chocolate mixture with evaporated milk, confectioners sugar, and vanilla. Beat at high speed 10 minutes. Spread frosting over 1 cake layer. Top with second layer. Frost entire cake.

CHOCOLATE MOUSSE TORTE

SERVES 8 TO 10

8 **ounces premium semi-sweet chocolate**
1 **tablespoon instant coffee**
¼ **cup boiling water**
8 **eggs, separated**
⅔ **cup sugar**
1 **teaspoon vanilla**
   pinch salt

TOPPING:

1 **cup whipping cream**
1½ **teaspoons vanilla**
⅓ **cup confectioners sugar**

In double boiler melt chocolate. Dissolve coffee in boiling water. Add to chocolate. Cover and let stand over low heat 5 minutes. Remove from heat. Stir until smooth. Cool slightly.

In large bowl beat egg yolks at high speed 5 minutes. Gradually add sugar. Continue to beat 5 minutes. Fold in vanilla and chocolate mixture. In medium bowl beat egg whites with salt until stiff but not dry. Fold into chocolate mixture. Remove 4 cups mixture and refrigerate. Pour remainder into greased 10-inch pie pan.

Bake in preheated 350-degree oven 25 minutes. Turn off heat. Leave pan in oven 5 minutes. Remove from oven. Cool on rack. When completely cool pour refrigerated mixture into baked shell. Refrigerate 2 to 3 hours.

In small bowl combine all topping ingredients. Beat until mixture stands in peaks. Spread over top of mousse. Refrigerate until served.

SERVES 12

MOUSSE:

2	**cups whipping cream**
1	**cup confectioners sugar**
1/2	**cup cocoa**
1 1/2	**teaspoons unflavored gelatin**
1/4	**cup cold water**
1	**teaspoon vanilla**
	pinch salt

CAKE:

2	**cups buttermilk**
2	**teaspoons baking soda**
2	**eggs**
2	**cups sugar**
2	**teaspoons vanilla**
4	**ounces unsweetened chocolate, melted**
1/4	**pound butter, melted**
2	**cups sifted cake flour**

FROSTING:

18	**ounces semi-sweet chocolate chips**
2	**cups sour cream, room temperature**
	pinch salt

For mousse, combine whipping cream, confectioners sugar, and cocoa in medium bowl. Mix well. Refrigerate 1 hour. In small bowl sprinkle gelatin over cold water. Let stand 5 minutes. Add vanilla and salt to chilled cream mixture. Beat until stiff. Refrigerate. In double boiler heat gelatin over hot water until dissolved. Cool briefly. Stir cooled gelatin into cream mixture, reserving 1/2 cup mixture. Pour remainder into 9-inch round cake pan lined with plastic wrap. Refrigerate 2 to 3 hours until firm.

For cake, combine buttermilk and baking soda in medium bowl. Mix well. In large bowl beat eggs. Add sugar. Mix well. Stir in vanilla. Blend in buttermilk mixture. Add chocolate and butter. Mix well. Add cake flour. Mix well. Pour into 2 greased, floured 9-inch round cake pans. Bake in preheated 350-degree oven 30 minutes. Cool.

For frosting, melt chocolate chips in double boiler. Remove from heat. Add sour cream and salt. Mix well.

Place 1 cake layer on serving plate. Cover top with mousse. Top with second layer. Spread frosting over top and sides of cake. Use reserved 1/2 cup cream mixture for decorating, if desired.

See photo page 379.

CHOCOLATE SHEET CAKE

SERVES 16

½   **pound margarine**
6   **tablespoons cocoa**
1   **cup water**
2   **cups sugar**
2   **cups flour**
1   **teaspoon baking soda**
½   **teaspoon salt**
2   **eggs, beaten**
½   **cup sour cream or plain yogurt**

FROSTING:
½   **cup margarine**
¼   **cup cocoa**
6   **tablespoons milk**
1   **pound confectioners sugar**
1   **teaspoon vanilla**

For cake, combine margarine, cocoa, and water in large saucepan. Bring to boil, stirring constantly. Remove from heat. Blend in sugar. In small bowl sift together flour, baking soda, and salt. Add to margarine mixture. Mix well. Add eggs and sour cream alternately to mixture. Pour into greased jelly-roll pan. Bake in preheated 375-degree oven 20 minutes.

For frosting, combine margarine, cocoa, and milk in large saucepan. Bring to boil. Remove from heat. Beat in confectioners sugar and vanilla. Spread frosting on warm cake.

FALLEN CHOCOLATE SOUFFLÉ CAKE

SERVES 8 TO 10

16   **ounces semi-sweet or bittersweet chocolate**
½   **pound unsalted butter**
2   **tablespoons Kahlúa**
9   **eggs, separated**
1   **cup sugar**

In double boiler melt chocolate and butter. Stir until smooth. Cool to room temperature. Stir in Kahlúa.

In large bowl beat egg yolks and sugar. In medium bowl beat egg whites until soft peaks form. Fold a third of chocolate mixture into yolks. Fold a third of egg whites into mixture. Fold in remaining chocolate and then remaining egg whites. Pour into greased, floured 9-inch springform pan. Bake in preheated 350-degree oven 25 to 30 minutes.

GINGER CAKE

SERVES 8 TO 10

2	tablespoons unsalted butter or margarine, softened
2	tablespoons sugar
1	egg
¼	cup plus 2 tablespoons honey
2	tablespoons grated fresh ginger root
1	teaspoon grated lemon zest
1	teaspoon vanilla
1½	cups sifted flour
1	teaspoon baking soda
¼	teaspoon baking powder
½	teaspoon coriander
⅛	teaspoon cardamom
½	teaspoon cinnamon
	pinch salt
2	tablespoons finely chopped crystallized ginger
½	cup buttermilk
2	teaspoons confectioners sugar

In large bowl combine butter and sugar. Beat until light and fluffy. Whisk in egg, honey, ginger root, lemon zest, and vanilla. Mixture will curdle slightly. In small bowl sift together flour, baking soda, baking powder, coriander, cardamom, cinnamon, and salt.

In another small bowl toss crystallized ginger with ½ teaspoon dry ingredients to coat completely. Set aside. Add dry ingredients and buttermilk alternately to butter mixture, beating well after each addition. Stir in crystallized ginger. Pour batter into greased 8-inch round cake pan. Bake in preheated 350-degree oven 25 minutes or until inserted tester comes out clean. Cool in pan on rack 10 minutes. Run knife around edge of cake and turn out of pan. Return cake right side up to rack. Cool completely. Sift confectioners sugar over top.

ORANGE LIQUEUR CAKE

SERVES 8 TO 10

CAKE:

18½   **ounces yellow cake mix**

3   **eggs**

⅓   **cup sour cream**

1   **cup orange juice**

1   **tablespoon lemon juice**

⅓   **cup vegetable oil**

1   **tablespoon grated orange rind plus ½ tablespoon
extra slivers for top of cake, divided**

1   **tablespoon orange liqueur**

SOAKING SYRUP:

⅓   **cup orange juice**

⅓   **cup brown sugar**

2   **tablespoons butter**

⅓   **cup orange liqueur**

GLAZE:

½   **cup apricot preserves**

2   **tablespoons orange marmalade**

In large bowl combine all cake ingredients except orange rind slivers. Mix well. Pour into greased 12-cup bundt pan. Bake in preheated 350-degree oven according to cake mix directions.

While cake bakes combine orange juice, brown sugar, and butter for soaking syrup. Melt on high in microwave 1 minute or in small saucepan over medium heat. Stir in orange liqueur.

When cake is removed from oven transfer in pan to rack. With long toothpick or fine skewer poke holes in cake. Immediately pour soaking syrup evenly over cake. Leave in pan 24 hours.

Invert cake onto serving plate. For glaze, heat apricot preserves and orange marmalade in small saucepan. Strain into bowl. Brush glaze evenly over cake. Just before serving add slivers of orange rind to top.

CLOCKWISE FROM LEFT: APPLE WALNUT CAKE, LEMON CHEESECAKE, PEACH SEMIFREDDO WITH RASPBERRY SAUCE, AND MACADAMIA NUT TART

TOP TO BOTTOM:
TRIPLE CHOCOLATE
CAKE, BLACK AND
WHITE BROWNIES, AND
CHOCOLATE MOUSSE
IN CREPE CUPS

FRESH
COCONUT CAKE

378

AMARETTO CAKE

SERVES 10 TO 12

CAKE:
- ½ **cup sliced almonds**
- 2 **tablespoons butter**
- 18½ **ounces butter cake mix**
- 4 **eggs**
- ½ **cup Amaretto**
- ½ **cup water**
- ½ **cup vegetable oil**

GLAZE:
- 1 **cup sugar**
- ¼ **pound margarine**
- ½ **cup water**
- ¼ **cup Amaretto**

In small skillet brown almonds in butter. Drain. Sprinkle over bottom of greased, floured bundt pan. In large bowl combine cake mix, eggs, Amaretto, water, and oil. Beat 2 minutes. Pour over nuts. Bake in preheated 325-degree oven 45 minutes or until inserted tester comes out clean.

While cake bakes combine all glaze ingredients in small saucepan. Boil 3 minutes.

When cake has cooled in pan 5 minutes drizzle glaze over top. Let stand 2 hours. Remove cake from pan.

USE DIAGRAM TO IDENTIFY COOKIES ON OPPOSITE PAGE

1. PINWHEELS
2. APPLE SPICE COOKIES
3. ONE-MINUTE CHOCOLATE DROPS
4. COCONUT CRANBERRY BARS
5. CHOCOLATE MARSCAPONE SANDWICHES
6. WHITE CHIP TOFFEE COOKIES
7. CARAMEL SHORTBREAD COOKIES
8. POPPY SEED SUNBURSTS
9. MARZIPAN THIMBLES
10. SPRINGERLE
11. ITALIAN ANISE COOKIES
12. SURPRISE ROLL-UPS
13. CHOCOLATE MADELEINES
14. JITTERBUGS

SPANISH ORANGE ALMOND CAKE

SERVES 8

⅓   **cup shortening**
1   **cup plus 2 tablespoons sugar, divided**
1   **large egg**
4   **teaspoons grated orange rind**
1¼   **cups flour**
1½   **teaspoons baking powder**
½   **teaspoon salt**
¾   **cup milk**
½   **cup sliced almonds**
¼   **cup orange liqueur**

In large bowl cream shortening and 1 cup sugar until light and fluffy. Add egg and orange rind. Mix well. In small bowl sift together flour, baking powder, and salt. Add dry ingredients and milk alternately to shortening mixture. Beat at high speed 3 minutes. Pour batter into greased, floured 9-inch round or 8-inch square baking pan. Sprinkle with almonds.

Bake in preheated 350-degree oven 40 minutes or until golden. Remove from oven. With toothpick poke 20 holes halfway through cake. Sprinkle with remaining 2 tablespoons sugar. Drizzle with liqueur. Cool on rack before slicing.

See photo page 376.

ORANGE CAKE

SERVES 8 TO 10

2   **large oranges, unpeeled, preferably seedless**
6   **eggs**
1   **cup sugar**
1½   **cups ground almonds**
1   **teaspoon baking powder**
¾   **teaspoon salt**

In large saucepan combine unpeeled oranges with water to cover. Boil 30 minutes or until oranges are very soft. Drain, cool, and cut in quarters. Remove seeds. Place quarters in food processor. Process to medium puree. Small bits of orange rind should remain.

In large bowl beat eggs and sugar until thick. Stir in almonds, baking powder, salt, and pureed oranges. Mix well. Pour into greased, floured 9-inch round cake pan.

continued

Bake in preheated 400-degree oven 1 hour or until lightly browned and firm to touch. Cool on rack. Using sharp knife remove cake from pan.

May be served with whipped cream or ice cream, or garnished with fresh fruit.

LEMON YOGURT CAKE

YIELD: ONE
10-INCH CAKE

½ **pound butter, softened**
2¾ **cups sugar, divided**
3 **eggs, separated**
16 **ounces lemon yogurt**
4 **tablespoons grated lemon rind, divided**
2 **tablespoons fresh lemon juice**
2 **teaspoons vanilla**
3 **cups flour**
1 **tablespoon baking powder**
1 **teaspoon baking soda**
½ **teaspoon salt**
¼ **teaspoon cream of tartar**
¾ **cup water**
3 **tablespoons Grand Marnier**
confectioners sugar, optional

In large bowl cream butter and 2 cups sugar well. Add egg yolks 1 at a time, beating well after each addition. Stop mixer. Add yogurt, 3 tablespoons lemon rind, lemon juice, and vanilla. Stir gently until just combined.

In medium bowl sift together flour, baking powder, baking soda, and salt. Fold into batter. In small bowl beat egg whites until foamy. Add cream of tartar. Beat until soft peaks form. Fold egg whites by thirds into batter. Do not stir. Pour into greased, floured 12-cup bundt pan. Bake in preheated 350-degree oven 60 to 70 minutes or until inserted tester comes out clean.

While cake bakes combine remaining ¾ cup sugar and water in small saucepan. Bring to boil. Cook 1 minute. Reduce heat. Simmer uncovered 20 minutes. Syrup will thicken slightly. Stir in liqueur. Remove from heat.

Cool cake in pan on rack 15 minutes. Insert fork at 2-inch intervals. Brush warm cake with syrup, allowing it to soak into cake. Repeat brushing until cake is well covered.

Cool cake completely in pan. Invert onto serving plate. Sprinkle with confectioners sugar, if desired, and remaining 1 tablespoon lemon rind.

FRESH COCONUT CAKE

SERVES 8 TO 10

CAKE:

*1	large coconut
2	tablespoons milk
¼	pound plus 4 tablespoons butter
1¾	cups sugar
2¾	cups flour
2½	teaspoons baking powder
½	teaspoon salt
2	tablespoons orange juice
½	teaspoon coconut extract
2	teaspoons finely grated orange rind
¾	teaspoon vanilla
4	egg whites, stiffly beaten

ORANGE FILLING:

½	cup plus 1 tablespoon confectioners sugar
1	egg yolk
6	tablespoons unsalted butter, softened
½-1	teaspoon Grand Marnier
1	teaspoon finely grated orange rind

GRAND MARNIER FROSTING:

2⅔	cups confectioners sugar
¼	pound unsalted butter, softened
3	tablespoons milk
1½	teaspoons Grand Marnier

Split coconut, reserving clear inner liquid. Using vegetable peeler, peel "curls" from white interior of coconut. Set aside. Break coconut halves in smaller pieces with hammer. Trim off brown rind. In food processor or with hand grater coarsely grate 1 cup coconut.

In small bowl combine grated coconut and milk. Set aside.

In large bowl combine butter and sugar. Beat until light and fluffy. In medium bowl sift together flour, baking powder, and salt. Strain reserved liquid from coconut. Add enough water to measure 1 cup. In another small bowl combine coconut, water mixture, orange juice, coconut extract, orange rind, and vanilla. Mix well. Add a third of flour mixture to butter mixture. Blend well. Stir in a third of coconut mixtures. Repeat with remaining flour and coconut mixtures. Mix well. Carefully fold in egg whites. Divide batter between 2 greased, floured 9-inch round cake pans.

*May substitute 2 cups packaged shredded coconut.

continued

Bake in preheated 375-degree oven 25 to 30 minutes or until inserted tester comes out clean. Cool in pans on rack 10 minutes. Remove from pans. Cool completely.

In small bowl combine all filling ingredients. Beat well. In another small bowl combine all frosting ingredients. Beat well.

To assemble, place 1 cake layer on serving plate. Cover with filling. Top with second layer. Spread frosting over top and sides of cake with decorative swirls. Decorate top with reserved coconut "curls."

VARIATION:
Orange filling may be tripled and used as both filling and frosting.

CRYSTALLIZED ROSE PETALS: (optional)
    rose petals
1   egg white, slightly beaten
    sugar

Dip rose petals in egg white. Sprinkle petals with sugar. Place on rack to dry. Use to decorate cake.

See photo page 378.

BLUEBERRY CAKE WITH LEMON GLAZE

SERVES 8 TO 10

CAKE:

¼ **pound unsalted butter**
1½ **cups sugar**
2 **eggs**
2 **cups fresh blueberries**
¼ **cup plain yogurt**
1 **teaspoon vanilla**
2¼ **cups sifted cake flour**
¾ **teaspoon baking soda**
½ **teaspoon baking powder**
¼ **teaspoon salt**

FILLING:

2 **cups fresh blueberries**
2 **tablespoons superfine sugar**
1 **tablespoon lemon juice**
1 **tablespoon water**
4 **teaspoons finely grated lemon rind**

GLAZE:

3 **tablespoons lemon juice**
1 **cup confectioners sugar**

For cake, beat butter until fluffy in large bowl. Gradually add sugar. Add eggs 1 at a time. In food processor or blender process berries until coarsely chopped. Transfer to small bowl. Stir in yogurt and vanilla.

In medium bowl sift together flour, baking soda, baking powder, and salt. Add dry ingredients to butter mixture in thirds, alternately with berry mixture. Do not overbeat. Pour into 2 greased 9-inch round cake pans.

Bake in preheated 350-degree oven 30 minutes or until golden brown and inserted tester comes out clean. Invert onto rack. Cool.

For filling, combine all filling ingredients in medium saucepan. Simmer 25 minutes, stirring occasionally for first 15 minutes and nearly constantly for last 10 minutes. Mixture should be jamlike.

For glaze, combine glaze ingredients in small bowl. Stir until smooth.

Place 1 layer of cooled cake on serving plate. Cover with berry filling. Top with second layer. Brush with glaze, allowing some to run down sides.

SAUCY CHERRY TORTE

SERVES 12

TORTE:
2	eggs
1-1½	cups sugar
1½	cups flour
1	teaspoon baking soda
1	teaspoon cinnamon
¼	teaspoon salt
20	ounces canned sour pitted cherries, drained, juice reserved
1	cup chopped pecans or walnuts
2	tablespoons butter, melted

SAUCE:
8	ounces reserved cherry juice
1½	tablespoons cornstarch
¼-½	cup sugar
	vanilla ice cream

In large bowl beat eggs. Add sugar. Mix well. In small bowl sift together flour, baking soda, cinnamon, and salt. Add to egg mixture. Add drained cherries, nuts, and butter to batter. Mix well. Pour into greased 11- by 7- by 1½-inch baking pan. Bake in preheated 350-degree oven 40 minutes.

In small saucepan combine all sauce ingredients. Cook over medium heat until thickened, stirring constantly.

Serve square of torte cold or warm, with vanilla ice cream and warm sauce.

APPLE WALNUT CAKE

1²/₃ cups sugar

2 eggs

½ cup vegetable oil

2 teaspoons vanilla

2 cups flour

2 teaspoons baking soda

1½ teaspoons cinnamon

1 teaspoon salt

¼ teaspoon nutmeg

4 cups chopped unpeeled apples

1 cup chopped walnuts

FROSTING:

6 ounces cream cheese, softened

3 tablespoons butter, softened

1 teaspoon vanilla

1½ cups confectioners sugar

In large bowl beat sugar and eggs. Add oil and vanilla. Mix well. In medium bowl sift together flour, baking soda, cinnamon, salt, and nutmeg. Add to sugar mixture. Blend well. Stir in apples and nuts. Pour into greased 9- by 13-inch baking dish. Bake in preheated 350-degree oven 50 to 55 minutes.

For frosting, combine cream cheese, butter, and vanilla in small bowl. Beat until well blended. Gradually add confectioners sugar until mixture reaches spreading consistency.

May be served without frosting topped with warm caramel sauce and vanilla ice cream.

See photo page 373.

APPLE CAKE

SERVES 12

2 **cups sugar**

3 **eggs**

1¼ **cups vegetable oil**

¼ **teaspoon salt**

¼ **cup orange juice**

3 **cups flour**

1 **teaspoon baking soda**

1 **teaspoon cinnamon**

1 **teaspoon vanilla**

1 **cup peeled chopped apple**

1 **cup shredded coconut**

1 **cup chopped nuts**

SAUCE:

6 **tablespoons butter**

1 **cup sugar**

½ **cup buttermilk**

½ **teaspoon baking soda**

In large bowl combine sugar, eggs, oil, salt, orange juice, flour, baking soda, cinnamon, and vanilla. Mix well. Blend in apple, coconut, and nuts with spoon. Pour into greased tube pan. Bake in preheated 325-degree oven 1½ hours.

Shortly before cake is finished baking combine all sauce ingredients in small saucepan. Bring to boil over medium heat, stirring constantly. Pour over baked cake. Let stand at least 1 hour before removing from pan.

BUTTERMILK POPPY SEED CAKE

SERVES 12 TO 16

½   **pound butter, room temperature**
1½   **cups sugar**
3   **eggs**
½   **teaspoon vanilla**
2½   **cups flour**
3   **teaspoons baking powder**
1   **teaspoon cinnamon**
½   **teaspoon salt**
1   **cup buttermilk**
⅓   **cup poppy seed**
1½   **teaspoons grated lemon rind**
2   **teaspoons confectioners sugar**

In large bowl cream butter and sugar. Add eggs and vanilla. Mix well.

In medium bowl sift together flour, baking powder, cinnamon, and salt. Add dry ingredients and buttermilk alternately to butter mixture. Stir in poppy seed and lemon rind. Pour into greased, floured 9-cup tube or bundt pan.

Bake in preheated 350-degree oven 50 minutes or until inserted tester comes out clean. Cool in pan 10 minutes. Remove from pan to rack. Cool completely. Sprinkle with confectioners sugar.

POPPY SEED CAKE

SERVES 12 TO 14

18½   **ounces butter cake mix**
4   **eggs**
⅓   **cup poppy seed**
3½   **ounces instant French vanilla pudding mix**
1   **cup sour cream**
½   **cup cream sherry**
½   **cup vegetable oil**
1-2   **tablespoons confectioners sugar**

In large bowl combine all ingredients except confectioners sugar. Beat at medium speed 5 minutes. Pour into greased 10-inch bundt pan.

Bake in preheated 350-degree oven 1 hour. Cool in pan on rack 15 minutes. Remove from pan. Cool on rack. Sprinkle with confectioners sugar.

CINNAMON SHORTCAKE WITH STRAWBERRIES IN BALSAMIC VINEGAR

SERVES 8

2   **cups flour**
8   **tablespoons sugar, divided**
1   **tablespoon baking powder**
2   **teaspoons cinnamon**
¼   **teaspoon salt**
2   **cups whipping cream, divided**
2   **eggs**
6   **tablespoons unsalted butter, room temperature, divided**
4   **cups fresh strawberries, hulled**
2   **teaspoons balsamic vinegar**
2   **teaspoons vanilla**
    mint leaves, optional

In large bowl sift together flour, 3 tablespoons sugar, baking powder, cinnamon, and salt. Add ½ cup cream and eggs. Beat well. With wooden spoon blend in 4 tablespoons butter. Dough will be sticky. Roll into ball. Wrap in wax paper. Refrigerate 1 hour.

Divide dough into 8 balls. With rolling pin roll each ball into circle ½ inch thick. Transfer to ungreased baking sheet. Bake in preheated 425-degree oven 12 to 15 minutes.

One hour before serving combine berries (cut large berries in half), 2 tablespoons sugar, and vinegar in medium bowl. Cover and refrigerate. Just before serving whip remaining 1½ cups cream, remaining 3 tablespoons sugar, and vanilla in small bowl until stiff peaks form. Cut each shortcake in half horizontally. Spread remaining 2 tablespoons butter on bottom halves. Spoon berries over butter. Top with whipped cream. Cover with top halves of shortcakes. Add more berries and whipped cream over top. Garnish with mint leaves, if desired.

WALNUT MERINGUE TORTE

SERVES 8 TO 10

8   **egg whites, room temperature**
2¼   **cups plus 2 tablespoons sugar, divided**
2   **teaspoons vanilla**
1   **teaspoon white vinegar**
2   **cups finely chopped walnuts**
1   **cup whipping cream, whipped**
2   **cups fresh strawberries**

In large bowl beat egg whites at high speed until frothy. Add 2¼ cups sugar 1 tablespoon at a time, continuing to beat until stiff, glossy peaks form. Add vanilla and vinegar. Mix well at low speed. Beat at high speed 30 seconds. Fold in walnuts by hand. Pour batter into 2 greased, floured 9-inch round cake pans with circle of wax paper fitted in bottoms.

Bake in preheated 350-degree oven 45 minutes or until lightly browned. Cool in pans on rack. Run knife around edges of torte layers. Invert onto plates. Remove wax paper.

Transfer 1 layer onto serving platter. Spread top of layer with whipped cream. Fit second layer over whipped cream. Torte may fall. Refrigerate until served. Serve each slice on bed of strawberries pureed with remaining 2 tablespoons sugar.

See photo page 377.

ALMOND CREAM PUFF RING

SERVES 10

RING:
1   cup water
¼   pound plus 1 teaspoon butter, divided
¼   teaspoon salt
1   cup flour
4   eggs

FILLING:
3   ounces instant vanilla pudding mix
1¼   cups milk
1   teaspoon almond extract
1   cup whipping cream, whipped to stiff peaks

GLAZE:
½   cup chocolate chips
1   tablespoon butter
1½   teaspoons milk
1½   teaspoons light corn syrup

In medium saucepan combine water, ¼ pound butter, and salt. Heat until butter melts. Remove from heat. Add flour all at once. With wooden spoon stir until smooth. Add eggs 1 at a time, beating well after each addition.

With remaining 1 teaspoon butter draw circle 7 inches in diameter on baking sheet. Drop batter in 10 equal mounds inside of circle or drop batter into 10 individual unconnected mounds. Bake in preheated 400-degree oven 40 minutes or until golden. Turn off oven. Leave in oven 15 minutes. Remove from oven. Cool. Carefully slice top off baked ring or individual puffs.

For filling, combine pudding mix and milk in small bowl. Mix well. Blend in almond extract. Fold in whipped cream. Spread mixture over lower half of ring or individual puffs. Place top over filling.

For glaze, melt chocolate chips and butter in double boiler or microwave. Blend in milk and corn syrup. Drizzle over top of ring or individual puffs. Refrigerate well before serving.

See photo page 376.

GINGER ROLL

4	eggs
1	cup sugar
1	tablespoon grated orange rind
2	tablespoons orange juice
1	cup flour
1	teaspoon baking powder
1	teaspoon ginger
½	teaspoon cinnamon
¼	teaspoon salt
	confectioners sugar
1	cup whipping cream, whipped
¾	cup ginger marmalade

In large bowl beat eggs 10 minutes. Gradually add sugar, mixing well. Stir in orange rind and orange juice. In small bowl sift together flour, baking powder, ginger, cinnamon, and salt. Sift dry ingredients over top of egg mixture. Blend in carefully. Pour mixture into 10- by 15-inch jelly-roll pan lined with greased wax paper. Bake in preheated 375-degree oven 15 to 17 minutes.

Turn cake out onto towel sprinkled with confectioners sugar and roll up. Unroll cake when cool. In small bowl combine whipped cream and ginger marmalade. Spread mixture over cake. Reroll. Dust with confectioners sugar.

See photo page 377.

TIRAMISU

*24   **ladyfingers, separated**
6   **egg yolks**
½   **cup sugar**
1   **pound mascarpone cheese**
1   **teaspoon vanilla**
1   **cup espresso coffee
2   **tablespoons coffee liqueur**
1   **tablespoon brandy**
½   **cup finely grated bittersweet chocolate**

Arrange ladyfingers in single layer on baking sheet. Bake in preheated 350-degree oven 15 minutes or until crisp, turning once. Set aside. Reassemble when cool.

In top of double boiler combine egg yolks and sugar. Beat until thick and lemon colored. Place top of double boiler over bottom of double boiler half-filled with simmering water. (Top pan should not touch water.) Beat egg yolk mixture over low heat 8 to 10 minutes or until mixture thickens slightly. Remove top of double boiler from heat. Cool slightly.

In small bowl blend cheese and vanilla until smooth. Combine with egg mixture. Mix well. Set aside. In another small bowl combine espresso, liqueur, and brandy. Mix well.

Line bottom of ungreased 9½- by 11-inch pan with reassembled ladyfingers that have been dipped quickly in espresso mixture. Spread egg-cheese mixture evenly over ladyfingers. Sprinkle chocolate over top. Refrigerate covered 6 hours or overnight. Serve in 3- to 4-inch squares.

*If Italian-style ladyfingers are used they need not be toasted.

**Instant espresso may be used.

LEMON IGLOO

3.4   ounces lemon pudding and pie filling mix
¼   cup fresh lemon juice
⅓   cup sugar
2   large egg yolks
6   ounces half and half
2   cups whipping cream, divided, plus 1 cup whipping cream, optional
2   packets stabilizer for whipping cream, divided, plus 1 packet, optional
1   angel food cake, very thinly sliced
2-4   tablespoons confectioners sugar, divided

SAUCE:
16   ounces frozen raspberries in sugar syrup, thawed
1-4   tablespoons Kirsch or Grand Marnier

Prepare pudding according to package directions, substituting lemon juice for ¼ cup water and including ⅓ cup sugar and 2 egg yolks. As cooked pudding cools add half and half gradually to prevent mixture from firming. In small bowl whip 1 cup cream and 1 packet stabilizer until stiff. Fold into cooled pudding.

Line large bowl with angel food cake slices, overlapping edges. Slices do not have to come up to rim. Add a third of filling to bowl. Cover filling with layer of overlapping angel food cake slices. Repeat layers, ending with cake. Refrigerate covered overnight.

To serve, place serving platter over uncovered bowl and invert. In small bowl beat 1 cup cream, 1 packet stabilizer, and 2 tablespoons confectioners sugar until stiff. Frost cake with whipped cream. If desired, whip 1 cup cream, 1 packet stabilizer, and 2 tablespoons confectioners sugar until stiff. This may be used to simulate "ice blocks" on "igloo."

For sauce, puree raspberries and syrup in food processor or blender. Add liqueur to taste. Serve sauce with slices of cake.

ORANGE CHOCOLATE CHEESECAKE

SERVES 10

1¼   **cups vanilla cookie crumbs**
¼   **cup butter, melted**
12   **ounces semi-sweet chocolate**
½   **cup orange juice**
16   **ounces cream cheese**
1   **cup sugar**
4   **eggs**
2   **teaspoons vanilla**
    zest of 1 orange
1   **cup whipping cream**
1   **tablespoon Grand Marnier**

In medium bowl combine cookie crumbs and butter. Press into bottom of 10-inch springform pan.

Melt chocolate in double boiler or microwave. Add orange juice. Mix well.

In large bowl beat cream cheese until light. Gradually add sugar, beating continually. Add eggs 1 at a time, continuing to beat. Stir in vanilla. Add chocolate-orange juice mixture. Mix well. Fold in orange zest. Pour batter into prepared springform pan.

Bake in preheated 325-degree oven 55 minutes. Turn off oven. Open oven door. Let cake cool in oven 2 to 3 hours. Top may crack. Before serving whip cream in small bowl until frothy. Add Grand Marnier. Whip until stiff. Remove sides of springform pan and frost top of cheesecake with whipped cream.

APPLE CHEESECAKE

SERVES 8

1   **cup graham cracker crumbs**
1   **cup sugar, divided**
3   **tablespoons margarine, melted**
1   **teaspoon cinnamon, divided**
16 **ounces cream cheese, softened**
2   **eggs**
½ **teaspoon vanilla**
4   **cups peeled, thinly sliced apples, preferably Rome Beauty**
½ **cup chopped pecans**

In small bowl combine graham cracker crumbs, 3 tablespoons sugar, margarine, and ½ teaspoon cinnamon. Mix well. Press into bottom and several inches up sides of greased 9-inch springform pan. Bake in preheated 350-degree oven 10 minutes.

In medium bowl combine cream cheese and ½ cup sugar. Add eggs 1 at a time, beating well after each addition. Mix well. Blend in vanilla. Pour into crust.

Place layer of apples over filling. In small bowl mix remaining ⅓ cup sugar and ½ teaspoon cinnamon. Sprinkle small amount over apples. Repeat layer of apples, followed by cinnamon-sugar mixture until all ingredients are used. Arrange pecans over top.

Bake in preheated 350-degree oven 1 hour 10 minutes. Cool before removing sides of springform pan.

CARAMEL PECAN CHEESECAKE

SERVES 8 TO 10

CRUST:

1   **cup graham cracker crumbs**
2   **tablespoons sugar**
4   **tablespoons margarine, melted**

FILLING:

24   **ounces cream cheese, room temperature**
¾   **cup sugar**
2   **tablespoons flour**
1   **teaspoon vanilla**
3   **eggs**
*½   **cup caramel topping**
½   **cup chopped pecans**

TOPPING:

1¼   **teaspoons margarine**
1   **tablespoon packed brown sugar**
1½   **teaspoons water**
½   **cup pecan halves**
*2   **tablespoons caramel topping**

In medium bowl combine all crust ingredients. Mix well. Press mixture into bottom of 9-inch springform pan. Bake in preheated 325-degree oven 10 minutes.

For filling, combine cream cheese, sugar, flour, and vanilla in large bowl. Beat at medium speed until well blended. Add eggs 1 at a time, beating well after each addition. Remove 1 cup cream cheese batter to small bowl. Stir in caramel topping. Mix well. Pour half of plain cream cheese batter into cooled crust. Cover with caramel mixture. Sprinkle with nuts. Top with remaining plain batter.

Bake in preheated 450-degree oven 7 minutes. Reduce heat to 250 degrees. Bake 30 minutes. Loosen cake from sides of pan and cool before removing sides. Chill.

For topping, melt margarine and brown sugar in small saucepan, mixing well. Add water. Bring to boil. Add nuts. Cook 2 minutes, stirring constantly. Spread nuts on wax paper to cool. Brush top of cheesecake with caramel topping and garnish with nuts.

*Available in jars.

LEMON CHEESECAKE

CRUST:

2   **cups crushed cinnamon graham crackers (about 26)**
6   **tablespoons unsalted butter, melted**

FILLING:

24   **ounces cream cheese, softened**
1½   **cups sugar**
3   **eggs**
¼   **cup fresh lemon juice**
1   **tablespoon grated lemon rind**
2   **teaspoons vanilla**

TOPPING:

2   **cups sour cream**
3   **tablespoons sugar**
1   **teaspoon vanilla**

GLAZE:

¾   **cup water**
⅓   **cup fresh lemon juice**
1   **egg yolk**
½   **cup sugar**
1½   **tablespoons cornstarch**
¼   **teaspoon salt**
1   **tablespoon butter**
2   **teaspoons lemon rind**

  lemon slices

In medium bowl blend crumbs and melted butter. Press mixture into bottom and up sides of greased 9-inch springform pan. Bake in preheated 350-degree oven 5 minutes.

For filling, beat cream cheese in large bowl until soft and fluffy. Gradually add sugar. Mix well. Add eggs 1 at a time, beating well after each addition. Stir in lemon juice, lemon rind, and vanilla. Pour into crust. Bake in preheated 350-degree oven 40 minutes or until lightly puffed.

In small bowl combine all topping ingredients. Mix well. Spread over baked filling. Bake in 350-degree oven 15 minutes. Cool 30 minutes.

For glaze, combine water, lemon juice, and egg yolk in small heavy saucepan. Mix well. Stir in sugar, cornstarch, and salt. Bring to boil over low heat about 10 minutes, stirring constantly. Add butter and lemon rind. Stir until butter melts. Cool glaze 20 minutes. Spread on cooled cheesecake. Refrigerate until thoroughly chilled. Garnish with lemon slices. Serve cold.

See photo page 373.

MELON BAKED ALASKA

SERVES 4

2 **small cantaloupes, halved**
¾ **cup fresh strawberries, hulled, halved**
¾ **cup fresh blueberries**
5 **egg whites**
¼ **teaspoon salt**
¾ **cup sugar, divided**

Remove seeds from melons. Scoop out flesh, leaving thin rim of flesh in each half. Slice thin piece from outside bottom of each half so melon will stand evenly.

Place melon halves open side down on baking sheet lined with 3 layers of paper towels. Refrigerate 2 hours. Dice scooped-out melon flesh to make 1½ cups. In medium bowl mix diced melon and berries. Refrigerate 2 hours.

Fifteen minutes before serving beat egg whites and salt in another medium bowl until foamy. Reserving 3 tablespoons sugar, gradually beat in remaining sugar until stiff and glossy. Fill each melon half with fruit mixture. Spread meringue over open side of melon, covering rim of flesh and fruit filling. Sprinkle tops with reserved sugar. Bake on ungreased baking sheet in preheated 500-degree oven 2 to 3 minutes or until lightly browned. Serve immediately.

VARIATION:
Melon halves may be filled with combination of fruit and ¼ cup each of raspberry, orange, and lemon sherbet.

FROSTED MELON

1   large ripe honeydew melon
4   cups combined fresh blueberries and raspberries or
      fruit of choice
10 ounces cream cheese, softened
2   tablespoons blue cheese spread
¼   cup whipping cream
1   teaspoon almond extract
4   ounces coconut, toasted
3   ounces sliced almonds, toasted

Peel melon, removing tough rind. Cut lid from top of melon. Remove thin slice from bottom so melon will stand. Scoop interior, removing all seeds. Fill center with berries. Replace top.

In medium bowl combine cheeses, cream, and almond extract. Mix well. Frost melon with cheese mixture. Sprinkle with coconut. Insert almonds porcupine style. Surround melon with extra fruit. Refrigerate at least 2 hours.

GRAPES BRÛLÉE

2½-3   pounds green grapes
6   ounces sour cream or sour half and half
*6   ounces lite Cool Whip
2   tablespoons vanilla
1   teaspoon Grand Marnier, or to taste
½-¾ pound dark brown sugar

In 9- by 13-inch baking dish spread grapes. In medium bowl combine sour cream, Cool Whip, vanilla, and Grand Marnier. Mix well. Pour mixture over grapes. Sprinkle brown sugar over top.

Place baking dish in large pan filled with ice. In preheated broiler broil about 2 minutes until sugar crystallizes. Refrigerate 8 hours.

Will keep several days.

*May omit Cool Whip and replace with more sour cream or sour half and half.

RING-AROUND-THE-FRUIT

SERVES 10 TO 12

2   **cups whipping cream**
3/4   **cup superfine sugar**
1½   **envelopes unflavored gelatin**
3/4   **cup cold water**
2   **cups sour cream**
1   **teaspoon vanilla**
4   **cups fresh berries or sliced fresh fruit**
½   **cup Grand Marnier or Chambord**
     brown sugar

In small saucepan warm cream over low heat. Add sugar gradually and stir until dissolved. Remove from heat. In another small saucepan soften gelatin in cold water. Bring to boil, stirring constantly to dissolve gelatin. Remove from heat. Blend into cream mixture.

In large bowl slowly add cream-gelatin mixture to sour cream, mixing until smooth. Add vanilla. Blend well. Pour into ungreased 6-cup ring mold. Cover and refrigerate overnight.

Just before serving combine berries and Grand Marnier in medium bowl. Let stand 15 to 20 minutes. Unmold ring onto serving plate. Fill center and surround sides of ring with fruit. Sprinkle top with brown sugar and serve.

BLUEBERRY BETTY

SERVES 8 TO 10

4   **cups fresh blueberries or 20 ounces frozen blueberries**
1   **tablespoon lemon juice**
¼   **teaspoon cinnamon**
1½   **cups flour**
1½   **cups sugar**
¼   **pound plus 4 tablespoons margarine**
     vanilla ice cream

Place berries in greased 1½-quart casserole. Drizzle with lemon juice. Sprinkle cinnamon over top.

In medium bowl blend flour, sugar, and margarine. Spread over berries. Bake in preheated 375-degree oven 1 hour. Serve warm with vanilla ice cream.

RASPBERRY PEACH COBBLER

SERVES 8 TO 10

2½   **pounds peaches, peeled, sliced**
2   **cups fresh raspberries**
1¼   **cups sugar, divided**
2   **tablespoons water**
¼   **teaspoon almond extract**
1   **cup flour**
¼   **pound unsalted butter**
1   **cup whipping cream, whipped, or vanilla ice cream**

In bottom of 9- by 13-inch baking dish arrange peach slices. Top with berries. In small bowl combine ¾ cup sugar, water, and almond extract. Pour over fruit.

In medium bowl combine flour and remaining ½ cup sugar. Cut in butter with pastry blender until well blended. Sprinkle evenly over fruit. Bake in preheated 350-degree oven 50 minutes. Cool to room temperature before serving. Serve with dollop of whipped cream or ice cream.

VARIATION:
For Raspberry Pear Cobbler, substitute peeled, sliced pears for peaches.

WINE COUNTRY PEARS

SERVES 4 TO 5

4   **Bosc pears, slightly underripe, peeled, halved, cored**
4   **tablespoons butter**
1-2   **teaspoons lemon juice**
1½   **sticks cinnamon**
2½-3   **cups zinfandel or other young, dry red wine**
1   **bay leaf**
¾-1   **cup sugar**
1   **teaspoon fresh mint**
1   **teaspoon cassis**
1   **cup whipping cream, stiffly whipped, crème anglaise, or vanilla ice cream**

continued

In large skillet sauté pears in butter until lightly browned. Sprinkle with lemon juice to prevent discoloration. Add cinnamon, wine, bay leaf, and sugar. Stir mixture until sugar is dissolved. Cook over low heat until liquid is reduced to syrup, spooning wine over pears occasionally.

Spoon syrup onto serving plates. Place 1 to 2 pear halves on top. Serve with fresh mint and a few drops of cassis blended with stiffly whipped cream or crème anglaise, or vanilla ice cream.

PEACHES WITH CHAMPAGNE SAUCE

SERVES 6

3	**cups water**
1½	**cups sugar, divided**
2	**tablespoons lemon zest**
3	**large peaches, peeled, halved, pitted**
1	**tablespoon vanilla**
6	**egg yolks**
½-1	**cup champagne**
½	**cup crème fraîche**
1	**quart pistachio or praline ice cream or flavor of choice**

In large pot boil water, 1 cup sugar, and lemon zest 5 minutes. Reduce heat. Add peaches. Simmer 10 minutes until tender and glazed. Remove pot from heat. Add vanilla. Cool. Drain.

In double boiler beat egg yolks and remaining ½ cup sugar over hot water until mixture ribbons. Add champagne gradually, beating until thick. Fold in crème fraîche.

On individual dessert plates arrange peach half and scoop of ice cream side by side. Top peach with champagne sauce, adding more to plate.

CHOCOLATE MOUSSE IN CREPE CUPS

CHOCOLATE MOUSSE:

12　ounces semi-sweet chocolate

9　eggs, separated

2　generous tablespoons brandy

CREPES:

3　large egg yolks

2/3　cup milk

2/3　cup water

3　tablespoons vegetable oil

1/4　teaspoon salt

1　cup flour

SABAYON SAUCE:

4　egg yolks

3/4　cup sugar

3/4　cup sherry

1/4　cup whipping cream, lightly whipped

2　cups fresh raspberries or strawberries, optional

CHOCOLATE MOUSSE:

The day before serving melt chocolate over hot, not boiling, water in double boiler. Remove from heat. In medium bowl add small amount of chocolate to lightly beaten egg yolks. Add yolk mixture to chocolate and heat thoroughly. Cool, stirring occasionally. Blend in brandy. Fold in stiffly beaten egg whites. Cover and refrigerate overnight.

CREPES:

The day before serving blend egg yolks in medium bowl. Add milk, water, oil, and salt. Blend well. Gradually stir in flour. Cover and refrigerate overnight. Next day cook 5-inch-diameter crepes in non-stick skillet or hot greased crepe pan. Separate cooked crepes with wax paper or aluminum foil.

SABAYON SAUCE:

In double boiler filled with hot, not boiling, water combine egg yolks, sugar, and sherry. Beat until thick. Transfer top of double boiler to pan filled with ice. Beat sauce until cold. Fold in cream. May be frozen.

TO ASSEMBLE:

Arrange each crepe in greased muffin tin. Fill each crepe with chocolate mousse. Refrigerate several hours. Remove crepe from muffin tin. Serve in pool of sabayon sauce. Garnish with berries, if desired.

continued

VARIATION:

With spoon or small spatula fill each crepe with 2 to 3 tablespoons mousse and roll up. Arrange seam side down on foil-lined baking sheet. (May be wrapped and frozen.) Refrigerate until served. To serve, place several tablespoons sauce on individual dessert plate. Place 2 filled crepes in center of plate. Cover with more sauce. Surround with 3 or 4 berries.

See photo page 379.

LIGHT RASPBERRY CREAM

SERVES 6

1	pint nonfat frozen vanilla yogurt, softened
1	pint raspberry sorbet, softened
¼	cup softened frozen orange juice concentrate
¼	cup fresh raspberries, optional

In medium bowl mix yogurt, sorbet, and concentrate until blended but not melted. Pour into goblets. Top with raspberries, if desired.

AMARETTO PUDDING

SERVES 8

1¼	pounds cream cheese, softened
1	cup sugar
4	eggs, separated
¼	cup whipping cream
3	ounces semi-sweet chocolate, grated, divided
8	ounces amaretti cookies (Italian macaroons), in fine crumbs
¾	cup liquid instant espresso coffee
2	teaspoons Amaretto, optional

In large bowl combine cream cheese, sugar, egg yolks, and cream. Beat until smooth. Fold in 2 ounces chocolate. Mix well. In medium bowl beat egg whites until stiff peaks form. Gently fold into cream cheese mixture.

In small bowl combine cookie crumbs and coffee. Mix well. Stir into cream cheese mixture. Add liqueur, if desired. Divide among 8 stemmed glasses. Refrigerate at least 2 hours. Serve garnished with remaining grated chocolate.

BURNT SUGAR PUDDING

SERVES 8

1   **cup plus 3 tablespoons sugar, divided**
1   **tablespoon plus ¼ cup water, divided**
¼-⅓   **cup chopped almonds**
2   **cups half and half**
3   **egg yolks**
1   **tablespoon unflavored gelatin**
1   **teaspoon vanilla**
1   **cup whipping cream, whipped**

In small heavy saucepan combine 1 cup sugar and 1 tablespoon water. Cook until sugar is brown. Stir in almonds. Pour into well-greased 8- or 9-inch square metal pan. Cool. Break into small pieces with back of spoon.

In double boiler heat half and half. When hot, add egg yolks beaten with remaining 3 tablespoons sugar. Cook until slightly thickened. Remove from heat. Add gelatin softened in ¼ cup cold water. Stir in vanilla. Cool. Blend in burnt sugar pieces. Fold in whipped cream. Pour into 1½-quart glass bowl or mold. Refrigerate until firm. Serve with Caramel Sauce, page 413.

RHUBARB BREAD PUDDING

SERVES 4 TO 6

4   **tablespoons margarine, melted**
3   **cups rhubarb, in ½-inch pieces**
2   **cups buttered, cubed white or cinnamon raisin bread**
½   **cup sugar**

In medium bowl combine all ingredients. Mix well. Spoon mixture into shallow 8-inch baking pan. Bake in preheated 350-degree oven 40 minutes. Serve warm.

CHEESE ROMANOFF

SERVES 6

¼ **pound unsalted butter or margarine, softened**
¾ **cup sugar**
1 **pound farmer cheese**
1¼ **cups sour cream**
2 **teaspoons vanilla**
  fresh strawberries

In large bowl cream butter and sugar. Add cheese. Beat at medium speed. Add sour cream and vanilla. Beat until smooth. Spoon into individual glass bowls to form a mound. Refrigerate until very cold. Serve garnished with strawberries. Spoon raspberry sauce over.

RASPBERRY SAUCE:

10 **ounces frozen raspberries, thawed**
6-8 **tablespoons sugar**
2 **tablespoons lemon juice**

In medium saucepan combine all ingredients. Cook over low heat 25 minutes, stirring occasionally. Sieve through fine strainer. Refrigerate.

FRESH PEACH ICE CREAM

YIELD:
2½ QUARTS

6 **cups finely chopped, peeled fresh peaches**
2 **cups sugar**
  juice of 1 lemon
5 **cups whipping cream**

In large skillet simmer peaches in sugar 5 to 10 minutes until softened. Cool. Blend in lemon juice and cream. Freeze in ice cream maker according to directions.

FIG ICE CREAM

YIELD: 2 QUARTS

2 **eggs, beaten**
2 **cups sugar (1 cup if sweetened fruit is used)**
½ **cup honey**
3½ **cups drained canned figs, pureed**
2 **cups whipping cream**
½ **teaspoon vanilla**
¼ **teaspoon salt**
   juice of 1 lemon
   rind of 1 lemon, grated

In double boiler combine eggs, sugar, and honey. Heat over boiling water until mixture foams, stirring constantly. Remove from heat.

In large bowl combine egg mixture and remaining ingredients. Mix well. Freeze in ice cream maker according to directions.

May substitute pureed strawberries or peaches for figs.

RHUBARB ICE CREAM

YIELD: 2 QUARTS

4½ **cups thinly sliced rhubarb**
1½ **cups sugar**
1½ **tablespoons lemon juice**
4 **cups whipping cream, whipped**

In large casserole combine rhubarb and sugar. Cover and bake in preheated 375-degree oven 30 minutes. Cool. Stir in lemon juice. Fold in whipped cream. Cover and freeze.

GINGER SORBET

2   **cups sugar**
2   **tablespoons peeled minced fresh ginger root**
2   **teaspoons finely grated lemon rind**
4   **cups water**
⅓   **cup fresh lemon juice**

In heavy non-aluminum saucepan combine sugar, ginger root, lemon rind, and water. Mix well. Heat to boiling, stirring frequently. Boil uncovered over medium heat 10 minutes. Cool. Stir in lemon juice. Freeze mixture in ice cream maker according to directions or transfer to shallow metal cake pan or metal ice cube tray. Freeze about 6 hours until almost solid.

Break into chunks. Process in food processor until smooth. Transfer to airtight container. Return to freezer 30 to 60 minutes or until firm.

May be made ahead and stored in freezer up to 4 days. Thirty minutes before serving transfer to refrigerator to soften slightly.

GRAPEFRUIT CAMPARI SORBET

**YIELD:
2 TO 3 QUARTS**

3   **cups sugar**
2   **cups water**
½   **gallon grapefruit juice**
6   **ounces Campari**

In medium saucepan combine sugar and water. Boil 1 minute. Refrigerate until chilled.

In large bowl blend sugar-water, grapefruit juice, and Campari. Transfer to ice cream maker and freeze according to directions or place in covered bowl in freezer for about 8 hours, stirring every 2 hours until frozen.

PEACH SEMIFREDDO WITH RASPBERRY SAUCE

SERVES 8 TO 10

4   medium ripe peaches, divided
     juice of 1 lemon
⅔   cup sugar, divided
⅔   cup part-skim ricotta cheese
1½   cups whipping cream
2   cups fresh raspberries

Quarter and pit 3 unpeeled peaches. Combine in food processor with lemon juice, ½ cup sugar, and ricotta cheese. Puree. Strain mixture into medium bowl to remove bits of peach skin. Refrigerate.

In small bowl whip cream until stiff. Fold into peach mixture. Line 9- by 5-inch loaf pan with aluminum foil that covers bottom and long sides and extends 3 inches beyond edges. Ends of pan need not be covered. Pour mixture into prepared pan. Fold foil ends over top. Freeze 8 hours or overnight.

Reserving 6 raspberries, puree remaining berries with remaining sugar. Strain to remove seeds. Refrigerate.

One to three hours before serving remove pan from freezer. Unmold and refrigerate until served. Garnish with reserved berries and slices of remaining peach. Cut loaf into thick slices. Spoon raspberry sauce on each serving.

See photo page 373.

BUTTERSCOTCH SAUCE

YIELD: 1½ CUPS

⅔   cup firmly packed light brown sugar
¼   cup light corn syrup
3   tablespoons butter
     pinch salt
⅓   cup whipping cream
1½   teaspoons vanilla

In medium saucepan combine brown sugar, corn syrup, butter, and salt. Bring to boil over medium-high heat. Boil until sugar is dissolved. Simmer 3 minutes, swirling mixture in pan. Remove from heat. Add cream and vanilla. Mix well.

CARAMEL SAUCE

YIELD: 4 CUPS

14 **ounces caramels**
¼ **pound butter**
14 **ounces sweetened condensed milk**
1 **pound brown sugar**
1 **cup dark corn syrup**

In large saucepan combine all ingredients. Bring to boil. Reduce heat. Simmer 20 to 25 minutes until candy thermometer registers 238 degrees, stirring constantly.

Will keep refrigerated in airtight jar for long period. Reheat in double boiler or in microwave until soft.

LEMON SAUCE

YIELD:
2 TO 3 CUPS

LEMON CURD:
1 **egg, beaten**
¾ **cup sugar**
1½ **tablespoons butter**
3 **tablespoons lemon juice**
 rind of 1 lemon, grated

1 **cup whipping cream, whipped to soft peaks**
½ **cup crème fraîche**
1 **tablespoon grated lemon rind**
3 **tablespoons lemon juice**

In medium saucepan combine all lemon curd ingredients. Cook until thick, stirring constantly. Cool.

In medium bowl combine ⅔ cup lemon curd, cream, crème fraîche, lemon rind, and lemon juice. Mix well. Serve over fresh fruit or use to top fruit soup.

Refrigerate remaining lemon curd and use as spread.

RASPBERRY SAUCE

YIELD: 2 CUPS

20 ounces frozen raspberries with syrup, thawed
¼ cup sugar
1½ tablespoons cornstarch
 pinch salt
¼ teaspoon almond extract

Drain berries, reserving syrup. Add enough water to syrup to make 1½ cups liquid.

In medium saucepan combine sugar, cornstarch, and salt. Mix well. Gradually add syrup-water mixture, blending until very smooth. Cook over medium heat until sauce thickens and becomes translucent, stirring gently. Do not boil. Simmer 1 to 2 minutes. Remove from heat. Stir in raspberries and almond extract. Refrigerate.

CHOCOLATE RASPBERRY SAUCE

YIELD:
3 TO 4 CUPS

¾ cup cocoa
¾ cup half and half or milk
4 tablespoons butter, melted
1½ cups sugar
⅓ cup light corn syrup
12 ounces frozen raspberries, thawed, pureed, strained

In medium saucepan combine cocoa and half and half. Mix well. Stir in butter, sugar, corn syrup, and raspberries. Bring to boil. Simmer 8 minutes without stirring. Remove from heat. Refrigerate in covered container.

May be made several days ahead.

Delicious over poached pears, ice cream, or angel food cake.

SEMI-SWEET HOT FUDGE SAUCE

YIELD: 1³/4 CUPS

Sauce hardens on ice cream.

1½ **cups semi-sweet chocolate chips**
¼ **cup sugar**
6 **ounces evaporated milk**
½ **teaspoon vanilla**

In double boiler combine chocolate chips, sugar, and evaporated milk. Heat until chocolate is melted, stirring constantly. Remove from heat. Stir in vanilla. Serve warm.

BITTERSWEET CHOCOLATE SAUCE

YIELD: 2 CUPS

3 **ounces unsweetened chocolate**
¼ **pound butter**
1¼ **cups confectioners sugar**
½ **cup sugar**
½ **cup cocoa**
1 **tablespoon instant espresso powder**
1 **cup whipping cream**
1 **teaspoon vanilla**

In double boiler melt chocolate and butter. Add confectioners sugar, sugar, cocoa, and espresso powder. Beat until chocolate begins to stick to beaters. Slowly beat in cream. Beat until smooth and creamy. Blend in vanilla.

HOT FUDGE SAUCE

YIELD: 4 CUPS

A mild version.

¼ **pound butter**
4 **ounces unsweetened chocolate**
3 **cups sugar**
12 **ounces evaporated milk**
½ **teaspoon salt**

In double boiler melt butter over low heat. Add chocolate. Blend well. Stir in sugar, evaporated milk, and salt. Cook 20 minutes, stirring frequently. May be made ahead and refrigerated.

BLACK AND WHITE BROWNIES

YIELD: 24

5 **ounces bittersweet or semi-sweet chocolate**
2 **ounces unsweetened chocolate**
¼ **pound plus 4 tablespoons butter**
2 **cups sugar, divided**
5 **eggs, divided**
¾ **cup plus 1 tablespoon flour**
  pinch salt
16 **ounces cream cheese, softened**
1 **teaspoon vanilla**

In double boiler melt chocolates and butter. Stir in 1¼ cups sugar. Cool to luke-warm. In small bowl lightly beat 3 eggs. Add flour and salt. Mix well. Add to chocolate mixture, blending well. Spread in 9- by 13-inch baking pan.

In medium bowl combine cream cheese, vanilla, remaining ¾ cup sugar, and remaining 2 eggs. Beat until smooth. Pour over chocolate mixture. With knife, draw through both layers until desired amount of chocolate layer appears at top, creating marbleized effect. Bake in preheated 325-degree oven 50 minutes. Refrigerate. Cut into squares.

See photo page 379.

RICHEST PECAN BROWNIES

YIELD:

SIXTEEN 2-INCH BROWNIES

¼   **pound plus 2 tablespoons butter, in large chunks**

12   **ounces semi-sweet chocolate, in small chunks or large chips, divided**

2   **ounces unsweetened chocolate**

2   **eggs, beaten**

1   **tablespoon instant espresso powder or other instant coffee**

1   **tablespoon vanilla**

¾   **cup sugar**

½   **cup flour**

1   **teaspoon baking powder**

½   **teaspoon cinnamon**

1   **cup pecan halves or large pieces**

In double boiler combine butter, 6 ounces semi-sweet chocolate, and unsweetened chocolate. Stir over simmering water until melted and smooth. Cool 15 minutes.

In large bowl combine eggs, espresso or instant coffee, vanilla, and sugar. Mix well. Add chocolate mixture. Stir until smooth. Do not beat. In small bowl sift together flour, baking powder, and cinnamon. Stir into chocolate mixture until smooth. Blend in remaining 6 ounces semi-sweet chocolate and pecans. Pour into greased 8-inch square baking pan.

Bake in preheated 350-degree oven 30 to 40 minutes or until inserted tester comes out clean. Cool completely before cutting and removing from pan.

CAPPUCCINO BROWNIES WITH ESPRESSO GLAZE

YIELD: FIFTY-FOUR
1- BY 2-INCH
PIECES

BROWNIE LAYER:

½ pound plus 2 tablespoons unsalted butter
12 ounces bittersweet chocolate
3 tablespoons instant espresso powder
1 tablespoon boiling water
2¼ cups sugar
3 teaspoons vanilla
6 large eggs
1½ cups flour
¾ teaspoon salt
1½ cups chopped walnuts

CHEESECAKE LAYER:

12 ounces cream cheese, room temperature
¼ pound butter, room temperature
2¼ cups sifted confectioners sugar
1½ teaspoons vanilla
1½ teaspoons cinnamon

GLAZE:

4½ ounces bittersweet chocolate
1½ tablespoons butter
¼ cup whipping cream
1⅛ tablespoons instant espresso powder
¾ tablespoon boiling water

In microwave or double boiler melt butter and chocolate. Dissolve espresso powder in boiling water. Stir into butter and chocolate until smooth. Cool to lukewarm. Transfer to large bowl. Add sugar and vanilla. Mix well. Add eggs 1 at a time, beating well after each addition. Blend in flour and salt. Mix well. Stir in nuts. Pour into greased, floured 9- by 13-inch glass baking dish. Bake in preheated 350-degree oven 22 to 25 minutes or until inserted tester comes out clean. Cool completely in dish on rack.

For cheesecake layer, beat cream cheese and butter in medium bowl until fluffy. Add confectioners sugar, vanilla, and cinnamon. Mix well. Spread evenly over brownie layer. Refrigerate 1 hour.

For glaze, melt chocolate and butter in microwave or double boiler. Remove from heat. Add cream and espresso powder dissolved in boiling water. Stir until smooth. Cool to room temperature. Carefully spread over cheesecake layer. Refrigerate 3 hours or overnight. Slice into 1- by 2-inch pieces. Serve cold or at room temperature.

BUTTERSCOTCH NUT BARS

YIELD: 60

1½ cups flour
¾ cup brown sugar
¼ pound plus 2 tablespoons butter, divided
15 ounces chopped pecans or chopped salted mixed nuts
½ cup light corn syrup
6 ounces butterscotch chips

In food processor combine flour, brown sugar, and ¼ pound butter. Blend well. Press mixture into 9- by 13-inch baking pan. Bake in preheated 350-degree oven 10 minutes. Cool.

Spread nuts over crust. In small saucepan combine remaining 2 tablespoons butter, corn syrup, and chips. Heat over low heat until chips melt. Mix well. Pour over nut covered crust. Bake in preheated 350-degree oven 10 minutes. Cool before cutting into 1-inch squares.

MAPLE NUT BARS

YIELD: 30

¾ cup brown sugar
¾ cup flour
¼ pound plus 2 tablespoons butter, divided
1 egg
½ teaspoon baking powder
pinch salt
½ cup chopped walnuts
1 teaspoon vanilla
1½ cups confectioners sugar
⅛ teaspoon maple flavoring
milk

In medium saucepan combine brown sugar, flour, ¼ pound butter, egg, baking powder, and salt. Stir over low heat until blended. Add nuts and vanilla. Mix well. Spread in greased, floured 9-inch square baking pan. Bake in preheated 350-degree oven 20 minutes. Cool.

In small saucepan melt remaining 2 tablespoons butter. Add confectioners sugar alternately with maple flavoring and enough teaspoons of milk to bring mixture to spreading consistency. Spread on baked layer. Cut into squares.

COCONUT CRANBERRY BARS

YIELD: 36

CRUST:

¼ **pound butter**
½ **cup brown sugar**
½ **teaspoon salt**
1 **cup flour**
½ **cup finely chopped pecans**

FILLING:

1¼ **cups sugar**
2 **tablespoons flour**
½ **teaspoon baking powder**
2 **eggs, beaten**
1 **tablespoon milk**
1 **teaspoon vanilla**
1 **tablespoon finely grated orange rind**
1 **cup fresh cranberries, coarsely chopped**
½ **cup flaked coconut**
½ **cup pecans, chopped**

CRUST:

In medium bowl combine butter, brown sugar, and salt. Mix well. Add flour. Blend well. Stir in nuts. Press mixture into bottom of 9- by 13-inch baking pan. Bake in preheated 350-degree oven 15 to 20 minutes.

FILLING:

While crust bakes combine sugar, flour, and baking powder in medium bowl. Mix well. Add eggs, milk, vanilla, and orange rind. Blend well. Fold in cranberries, coconut, and pecans. Spread mixture over hot baked crust. Return to 350-degree oven. Bake 25 to 30 minutes. Cool in pan on rack. Cut into bars.

See photo page 380.

ORANGE-ALMOND SHORTBREAD SQUARES

YIELD: 16

1¼ **cups flour**
½ **cup confectioners sugar**
zest of 1 large orange, finely cut
1 **teaspoon almond extract**
¼ **pound plus 2 tablespoons butter, softened**
½ **cup sliced, unskinned almonds**

continued

In food processor combine all ingredients except almonds. Process until dough forms ball. Press dough evenly into ungreased 9-inch square baking pan. Score into 16 squares. Pierce each square twice with fork. Sprinkle almonds over top, pressing gently into dough.

Bake in preheated 325-degree oven 20 to 25 minutes or until lightly browned. Cool in pan 5 minutes. Cut squares completely through. Cool thoroughly in pan. Store in airtight container.

PUMPKIN BARS

YIELD:
TWENTY 3- BY
2¹/₂-INCH BARS

BARS:

4	eggs
1	cup vegetable oil
1	cup canned pumpkin
2	cups sugar
2	cups flour
2	teaspoons cinnamon
1	teaspoon baking powder
1	teaspoon baking soda
¹/₂	teaspoon salt
1	cup chopped walnuts

FROSTING:

3	ounces cream cheese, softened
6	tablespoons butter or margarine, softened
³/₄	pound sifted confectioners sugar
1	teaspoon vanilla
3	teaspoons milk

BARS:

In large bowl combine all ingredients. Mix well. Pour into greased, floured jelly-roll pan. Bake in preheated 350-degree oven 20 to 25 minutes.

FROSTING:

In medium bowl combine cream cheese, butter, confectioners sugar, and vanilla. Stir in 1 teaspoon milk at a time until mixture has spreading consistency. Spread on warm bars. Cool completely. Slice into 3- by 2¹/₂-inch bars.

CARAMEL SHORTBREAD COOKIES

YIELD: 36

½ **pound plus 2 tablespoons unsalted butter, divided**
½ **cup plus 2 tablespoons sugar, divided**
½ **teaspoon plus pinch salt, divided**
1 **teaspoon vanilla**
½ **teaspoon almond extract**
2 **cups less 2 tablespoons flour**
¼ **cup rice flour**
⅔ **cup brown sugar**
⅓ **cup corn syrup**
½ **cup whipping cream**
36 **pecan halves**

In large bowl cream ½ pound butter, ½ cup sugar, and ½ teaspoon salt. Add vanilla and almond extract. Beat until mixture is light and fluffy. Add flour and rice flour. Mix well. Refrigerate dough 1 hour.

Roll dough to ⅛- to ¼-inch thickness. Cut out cookies with heart-shaped or other cookie cutter. Arrange on ungreased baking sheet. Bake in preheated 350-degree oven 12 to 15 minutes. Cool on rack.

In small saucepan combine brown sugar, corn syrup, cream, remaining 2 tablespoons sugar, and pinch salt. Mix well. Boil gently until mixture thickens to form soft balls, stirring frequently. Remove from heat. Immediately stir in remaining 2 tablespoons butter. Top each cookie with dollop of caramel mixture. Place pecan half on top of caramel.

See photo page 380.

SOUTHERN GINGER COOKIES

YIELD: 72

2 **cups flour**
⅔ **cup sugar**
1 **teaspoon ground ginger**
1 **teaspoon salt**
½ **pound unsalted butter, in pieces**
6 **tablespoons crystallized ginger, finely diced**

In small bowl sift together flour, sugar, ground ginger, and salt 3 times. In food processor or with pastry blender combine dry ingredients with butter. Mix well. Dough should have pie crust texture. Blend in crystallized ginger.

Divide dough into 3 portions. Roll each portion into 10-inch length. Wrap each roll in plastic wrap. Freeze 30 to 60 minutes or until firm. Unwrap and cut into ⅛- to ¼-inch slices. Bake on ungreased baking sheet in preheated 350-degree oven 10 minutes or until lightly browned.

POPPY SEED SUNBURSTS

YIELD: 36

½ **pound butter**
½ **cup sugar**
2 **egg yolks**
1 **teaspoon vanilla**
2 **cups flour**
¼ **teaspoon salt**
3 **tablespoons poppy seed**
¾ **cup semi-sweet chocolate chips, melted**

In large bowl cream butter and sugar. Add egg yolks and vanilla. Mix well. Blend in flour, salt, and poppy seed. Shape into 1-inch balls. Arrange 1 inch apart on greased baking sheet. Make depression in center of each ball.

Bake in preheated 375-degree oven 10 minutes. Do not allow cookies to brown. Remove from oven. Fill depressed area of cookies with melted chocolate. To create sunburst effect, draw chocolate to sides of cookies with toothpick. Transfer to freezer for 5 minutes or until chocolate hardens.

See photo page 380.

WHITE CHIP TOFFEE COOKIES

YIELD: 36 to 40

- ¼ **pound butter or margarine**
- 6 **tablespoons sugar**
- 6 **tablespoons brown sugar**
- 1 **teaspoon vanilla**
- 1 **egg**
- 1⅛ **cups flour**
- ½ **teaspoon baking soda**
- ¾ **cup vanilla milk chips**
- ¾ **cup toffee bits**
- ½ **cup halved macadamia nuts**

In large bowl cream butter until fluffy. Add sugars and vanilla. Mix well. Add egg. Mix well. In small bowl sift together flour and baking soda. Slowly add dry ingredients to butter mixture, beating constantly. Stir in remaining ingredients.

Drop dough by level tablespoonfuls onto ungreased baking sheet. Bake in preheated 375-degree oven 10 to 12 minutes until light golden. Transfer to rack. Cool.

Dough may be made 1 week ahead, chilled for 1 hour, rolled into 16-inch log, wrapped in wax paper, and refrigerated. To bake, slice in ⅓-inch slices and bake in preheated 375-degree oven 8 to 10 minutes.

See photo page 380.

GINGER LEMON COOKIES

YIELD: 70 TO 80

- ¼ **pound plus 4 tablespoons unsalted butter, softened**
- 1 **cup sugar**
- 1 **egg**
- 4 **tablespoons molasses**
- 1 **teaspoon finely grated fresh ginger root**
  rind of 3 large lemons, finely grated, divided
- 2 **cups flour**
- 2 **teaspoons baking soda**
- 1 **teaspoon cinnamon**
- ½ **teaspoon ground cloves**
- ½ **teaspoon ground ginger**
- ½ **cup superfine sugar**

continued

In large bowl beat butter at high speed 2 minutes until light and fluffy. Add sugar, egg, molasses, ginger root, and grated rind of 1 lemon. Mix well. In small bowl sift together flour, baking soda, cinnamon, cloves, and ground ginger. Add to butter mixture. Combine but do not overbeat. Wrap dough in wax paper. Refrigerate 3 to 4 hours.

In another small bowl combine superfine sugar with remaining grated rind of 2 lemons. Form dough into ½-inch-diameter balls. Roll in sugar-rind mixture. Arrange on baking sheets lined with wax or parchment paper. Flatten each ball slightly with back of fork.

Bake in preheated 350-degree oven 10 minutes or until lightly browned. Cool on rack. Store in airtight container to prevent hardening.

BREAKFAST COOKIES

YIELD: 36 TO 48

- ¾ **cup flour**
- ⅓ **cup margarine**
- ⅓ **cup butter**
- ⅓ **cup brown sugar**
- 1 **large egg**
- 1½ **teaspoons vanilla**
- ¾ **teaspoon cinnamon**
- ½ **teaspoon baking powder**
- 1½ **cups oats**
- 1 **cup grated Cheddar cheese**
- 1 **cup coarsely chopped apple**
- ¾ **cup raisins**

In large bowl combine flour, margarine, butter, brown sugar, egg, and vanilla. Mix well. In small bowl toss cinnamon and baking powder with oats. Blend well with flour mixture. Stir in remaining ingredients.

Bake on very lightly greased baking sheet in preheated 350-degree oven 12 minutes for heaping teaspoon size or 15 to 16 minutes for heaping tablespoon size. Cool on rack. To store, cover tightly and refrigerate.

VARIATION:
Substitute chopped cranberries for apple and add 2 tablespoons granulated sugar.

ALMOND OATMEAL CRUNCH COOKIES

YIELD: 48

¼ **pound plus 4 tablespoons butter, softened**
¾ **cup brown sugar**
½ **cup sugar**
1 **egg**
1½ **teaspoons vanilla**
1½ **cups oats**
1 **cup flour**
½ **teaspoon baking soda**
6 **ounces toffee bits or chopped chocolate-covered toffee**
1 **cup sliced almonds**

ICING: (optional)
½ **cup confectioners sugar**
4 **teaspoons fresh lemon juice**

In large bowl cream butter and sugars. Beat until light. Add egg and vanilla. Mix well. Stir in oats. In small bowl sift together flour and baking soda. Add to butter mixture. Mix well. Fold in toffee and almonds.

Place dough in 1-tablespoonful mounds on lightly greased baking sheet. Flatten slightly. Bake in preheated 350-degree oven 9 to 10 minutes. Cool on baking sheet 1 to 2 minutes. Remove to rack. Cool completely.

May be stored in airtight container. If icing cookies, do so just before serving. In small bowl combine confectioners sugar and lemon juice. Mix well. Place ¼ teaspoon of icing in center of each cookie.

CURRANT CRISPS

YIELD: 120

½ **pound unsalted butter, softened**
1 **cup sugar**
1 **large egg, slightly beaten**
2 **teaspoons vanilla**
1½ **cups flour**
1 **cup cornstarch**
1 **teaspoon baking powder**
½ **teaspoon salt**
1 **cup currants**

continued

In large bowl cream butter. Gradually add sugar. Mix well. Add egg and vanilla. Beat 1 minute. In medium bowl sift together flour, cornstarch, baking powder, and salt. Add dry ingredients to butter mixture in 2 batches, until just combined. Stir in currants. Refrigerate dough covered at least 3 hours or overnight.

Roll level teaspoonfuls of dough into balls. Arrange 2 inches apart on ungreased baking sheet. Flatten each ball with back of fork. Bake in preheated 375-degree oven 8 to 9 minutes or until golden around edges. Cool on racks. Store in airtight container.

SCHOOLHOUSE CARROT COOKIES

YIELD: 36 TO 40

¼	**pound butter or margarine, softened**
¾	**cup brown sugar**
1	**egg**
1	**teaspoon vanilla**
1½	**cups flour**
1	**teaspoon baking powder**
¼	**teaspoon baking soda**
¼	**teaspoon salt**
¾	**teaspoon cardamom**
½	**teaspoon cinnamon**
1	**cup grated carrots**
1	**cup chopped walnuts or pecans**
½	**cup golden raisins**

In large bowl cream butter and brown sugar until light. Add egg and vanilla. Mix well. In small bowl sift together flour, baking powder, baking soda, salt, cardamom, and cinnamon. Stir dry ingredients into butter mixture. Add carrots, nuts, and raisins. Mix well. Drop by tablespoonfuls 2 inches apart onto lightly greased baking sheet.

Bake in preheated 325-degree oven 20 to 25 minutes or until lightly browned. Cool on rack.

YIELD: 36 TO 48

*1 cup shortening (may use any combination of lard, butter, margarine, or vegetable shortening)
1/2 cup brown sugar
1/2 cup sugar
2 eggs, beaten
2 teaspoons vanilla
1 1/2 cups flour
1 teaspoon baking powder
1 teaspoon baking soda
1/2 teaspoon salt
1/2 teaspoon cinnamon
1/4 teaspoon freshly grated nutmeg
2 cups oats
2 cups cornflakes
1 cup grated coconut
1 cup chopped dry roasted unsalted peanuts

In large bowl cream shortening. Beat in sugars, eggs, and vanilla. In medium bowl sift together flour, baking powder, baking soda, salt, cinnamon, and nutmeg. Stir into shortening mixture. Add remaining ingredients. Mix well.

Roll dough into 1-inch balls. Place 2 inches apart on greased baking sheet. Bake in preheated 350-degree oven 8 to 10 minutes.

*1/2 cup lard and 1/2 cup butter make crisp cookies.
1/2 cup margarine and 1/2 cup vegetable shortening make soft cookies.

ONE-MINUTE CHOCOLATE DROPS

YIELD: 36 TO 48

2   cups sugar
¼   pound butter or margarine
½   cup milk
¼   teaspoon salt
3   cups quick-cooking oats
½   cup cocoa
1   teaspoon vanilla

In large saucepan combine sugar, butter, milk, and salt. Boil 1 minute. Remove from heat.

In small bowl combine oats, cocoa, and vanilla. Mix well. Combine with sugar mixture. Mix well. Drop by teaspoonfuls onto wax paper. Cookies will harden as they cool.

See photo page 380.

CRINKLES

YIELD: 96

½   pound butter
1   cup plus 4 tablespoons sugar, divided
1   cup firmly packed brown sugar
1   egg
1   cup vegetable oil
1   cup oats
1   cup crushed cornflakes
½   cup grated coconut
½   cup chopped pecans
3½   cups flour
1   teaspoon baking soda
1   teaspoon salt
1   teaspoon vanilla

In large bowl cream butter, 1 cup sugar, and brown sugar until light and fluffy. Add egg. Mix well. Add oil. Mix well. Add oats, cornflakes, coconut, and nuts. Blend well. Add flour, baking soda, salt, and vanilla. Mix well. Form mixture into small balls. Place on ungreased baking sheet. Flatten with fork dipped in water.

Bake in preheated 325-degree oven 12 minutes. Remove from oven. If desired, sprinkle warm cookies with 4 tablespoons sugar. Cool 2 minutes before removing from baking sheet.

PINWHEELS

YIELD:
24 TO 30

11-13	tablespoons butter, divided
4	ounces cream cheese
1	cup flour
1/2-3/4	cup brown sugar
1/2	cup chopped pecans
1	teaspoon cinnamon
1/2	cup confectioners sugar
2	tablespoons hot water
1/2	teaspoon vanilla

In food processor or by hand blend 8 tablespoons butter and cream cheese. Add flour. Mix well. Flatten mixture on sheet of plastic wrap or wax paper. Cover with second sheet. Refrigerate at least 1 hour.

On large sheet of wax paper roll out dough thinly into rectangle approximately 12 by 18 inches. Spread 2 tablespoons or more melted butter over top, followed by brown sugar, nuts, and cinnamon. Pat in gently. From long side of rectangle roll up tightly. Wrap roll tightly in plastic wrap or wax paper. Refrigerate at least 3 hours. Slice rolled dough diagonally in 1/4-inch pieces.

Arrange slices on greased baking sheet. Brush tops of cookies with 2 tablespoons melted butter as needed. Bake in preheated 350-degree oven 12 to 15 minutes or until done. Cool on rack.

In small bowl combine confectioners sugar, 1 tablespoon butter, hot water, and vanilla. Brush cooled cookies with glaze.

See photo page 380.

SURPRISE ROLL-UPS

YIELD: 48

½   **pound butter, room temperature**
2¾ **cups flour, divided**
8   **ounces sour cream**
12 **ounces canned apricot, cherry, prune, or poppy seed filling**
1   **cup sugar**
    confectioners sugar

In large bowl blend butter and 2½ cups flour with pastry blender. Add sour cream. Mix with fingers. Divide dough into 6 balls. Cover with wax paper. Refrigerate overnight. Use remaining ¼ cup flour to sprinkle rolling pin and rolling surface. Roll each ball into large, thin circle about 9 inches in diameter. Cut into 8 pie-shaped wedges. Place ½ teaspoon filling on center of wide end of each wedge. Roll up tightly. Sprinkle generously with sugar. Arrange on baking sheet.

Bake in preheated 350-degree oven 10 to 15 minutes or until golden. When cool sprinkle with confectioners sugar.

See photo page 380.

JITTERBUGS

YIELD: 24 TO 28

¼ **pound plus 6 tablespoons butter, softened**
1⅓ **cups flour**
2   **egg whites**
    pinch cream of tartar
1½ **cups sugar**

In medium bowl combine butter and flour. Mix well. Refrigerate 1 hour. On floured surface roll half of dough into 8- by 11-inch rectangle. In small bowl beat egg whites and cream of tartar until soft peaks form. Add sugar gradually, beating until stiff and glossy.

Spread half of meringue over rectangle, leaving 1-inch margin on all sides. Gently roll dough from long side. Press seams together. Slice into 12 to 14 pieces. Transfer to parchment-lined or non-stick baking sheet. Bake in preheated 375-degree oven 13 to 15 minutes or until golden brown. Repeat procedure with remaining dough and meringue.

See photo page 380.

APPLE SPICE COOKIES

YIELD: 30 TO 36

DOUGH:

¼ **pound butter**
1 **cup brown sugar**
1 **large egg**
2 **cups flour**
½ **teaspoon cinnamon**
¼ **teaspoon baking soda**
¼ **teaspoon nutmeg**
¼ **teaspoon allspice**
1 **teaspoon hot water**

FILLING:

1 **cup unpeeled, ¼-inch diced apple**
½ **cup raisins**
½ **cup ground walnuts**
½ **cup brown sugar**
1 **cup cornflakes**
1 **tablespoon butter, melted**
½ **teaspoon cinnamon**
⅛ **teaspoon salt**

DOUGH:

In large bowl cream butter and brown sugar. Beat egg into mixture. In medium bowl sift together flour, cinnamon, baking soda, nutmeg, and allspice. Gradually add dry ingredients to butter mixture with hot water. Form dough into ball. Cover and chill thoroughly. Roll into rectangle ¼ inch thick.

FILLING:

In medium bowl combine all filling ingredients. Mix well. Spread over rectangle. Roll up jelly-roll fashion. Chill well. Cut into ¼-inch slices. Arrange on greased baking sheet. Bake in preheated 350-degree oven 30 minutes.

See photo page 380.

MARZIPAN THIMBLES

YIELD: 20 TO 22

DOUGH:

⅓ **cup unsalted butter**
¼ **cup confectioners sugar**
1 **egg yolk**
¼ **teaspoon almond extract**
1 **cup flour**

FILLING:

⅓ **cup unsalted butter**
4 **ounces almond paste**
½ **cup sugar**
2 **eggs**
½ **teaspoon almond extract**

FROSTING:

¾ **cup confectioners sugar**
¼ **teaspoon almond extract**
4 **teaspoons lemon juice**

DOUGH:

In medium bowl cream butter and confectioners sugar. Add egg yolk and almond extract. Mix well. Blend in flour. Refrigerate 30 to 60 minutes. Pinch off walnut-size pieces of dough. Roll pieces into balls. Flatten each ball into circle with palm of hand. Fit each circle into bottom and up sides of ungreased mini-muffin tin. Bake in preheated 375-degree oven 7 to 8 minutes. Cool on rack.

FILLING:

In medium bowl cream butter and almond paste until well blended. Beat in sugar. Mix well. Add eggs and almond extract. Blend well. Spoon 1 tablespoon filling into each shell. Bake in preheated 350-degree oven 15 to 18 minutes or until golden brown. Center will fall slightly. Cool 10 minutes on rack. Remove from tins to rack.

FROSTING:

In small bowl combine confectioners sugar, almond extract, and lemon juice. Mix well. Spoon ¼ teaspoon of mixture into center of each warm "thimble."

See photo page 380.

CHOCOLATE MASCARPONE SANDWICHES

YIELD: 27

¼ **pound plus 4 tablespoons cold unsalted butter**
½ **cup plus 1 tablespoon sugar, divided**
1½ **cups flour**
    pinch salt
½ **cup sifted cocoa**
1 **cup mascarpone cheese**
¼ **teaspoon vanilla**

In large bowl combine butter and ½ cup sugar. Beat at low speed 15 seconds. Add flour, salt, and cocoa. Beat at low speed 3 to 5 minutes or until dough comes together.

Divide dough into thirds. On very lightly floured aluminum foil roll each third to ¼-inch thickness. Cover with second piece of foil and refrigerate 30 minutes.

Transfer chilled dough to lightly floured surface. Roll each third of dough to ⅛-inch thickness. Using 2-inch fluted round cookie cutter, cut out 54 cookies, reassembling scraps and rerolling as needed. Arrange cookies on parchment-lined baking sheets. Transfer baking sheets to freezer for 1 hour. Remove from freezer. Bake in preheated 250-degree oven 1 hour. Cool on paper towel.

In small bowl combine mascarpone cheese, remaining 1 tablespoon sugar, and vanilla. Mix well. Spread about 2 teaspoons mixture on half of cookies. Top with remaining cookies to make "sandwiches."

See photo page 380.

DYNAMITE MOCHA DROPS

YIELD: 36

4   **ounces unsweetened chocolate**
3   **cups semi-sweet chocolate chips, divided**
1/4 **pound unsalted butter, in bits**
1/2 **cup flour**
1/2 **teaspoon baking powder**
1/2 **teaspoon salt**
4   **large eggs, room temperature**
11/2 **cups sugar**
11/2 **tablespoons instant espresso powder**
2   **teaspoons vanilla**

In double boiler melt unsweetened chocolate, 1½ cups chocolate chips, and butter over simmering water. Stir until smooth. Remove from heat.

In small bowl sift together flour, baking powder, and salt. In large bowl beat eggs and sugar until thick and pale. Add espresso powder and vanilla. Fold in chocolate mixture. Add flour mixture. Mix well. Stir in remaining 1½ cups chocolate chips. Let batter stand 10 minutes.

Drop batter by heaping tablespoonfuls onto baking sheets lined with parchment paper. Bake in center of preheated 350-degree oven 8 to 10 minutes or until shiny and cracked on top. Cool on baking sheets.

TUXEDO COOKIES

YIELD: 48

1 **cup confectioners sugar**
1 **cup sugar**
1 **cup vegetable oil**
½ **pound margarine**
2 **eggs**
1 **teaspoon vanilla**
4¼ **cups sifted flour**
1 **teaspoon salt**
1 **teaspoon baking soda**
1 **teaspoon cream of tartar**
4 **ounces bittersweet chocolate or Frango mints, melted**

In large bowl cream sugars, oil, and margarine. Add eggs and vanilla. Mix well. In medium bowl sift together flour, salt, baking soda, and cream of tartar. Add to sugar mixture. Mix well. Divide dough into 4 equal portions. Wrap each portion in plastic wrap. Refrigerate 1 hour or until firm. Unwrap. Roll into cylinders 1 inch in diameter. Rewrap and freeze. Unwrap and cut dough into ¼-inch slices.

Arrange slices 2 inches apart on ungreased baking sheets. Bake in preheated 375-degree oven 7 to 9 minutes, watching closely so cookies do not brown. Cool. Spread ½ teaspoon melted chocolate or Frango mints on half of cookies. Top with another cookie, underside toward chocolate.

After filling, cookies are best served within 2 days. Unfilled cookies keep well in airtight container.

SPRINGERLE COOKIES

4   **large eggs**
1   **pound confectioners sugar**
1   **tablespoon lemon rind**
4   **cups flour**
1   **teaspoon baking powder**
1   **teaspoon butter, room temperature**
1   **teaspoon honey**
2   **tablespoons anise seed**
    apple or orange

In large bowl beat eggs 5 minutes until light. Add confectioners sugar. Mix well. Add lemon rind and flour sifted with baking powder. Blend well. Add butter and honey. Combine well with hands. Cover and refrigerate 1 hour.

On floured surface roll dough to ½-inch thickness. Using springerle rolling pin* or cookie stamps emboss dough with designs. Slice dough into cookies following designs. Sprinkle anise seed evenly over 2 greased baking sheets. Place cookies on top of anise seed. Let unbaked cookies stand uncovered at room temperature 12 hours.

Bake in preheated 325-degree oven 10 to 12 minutes. When cooled, store cookies in covered jar 2 to 3 weeks before serving. Add apple or orange to cookie jar to mellow cookies.

*A wooden rolling pin with carved designs. Available at specialty stores.

See photo page 380.

ITALIAN ANISE COOKIES

YIELD: 48

¼ **pound plus 4 tablespoons butter**
¾ **cup sugar**
3 **eggs**
2 **tablespoons anise seed**
2½ **cups flour**
½ **tablespoon baking powder**
1 **teaspoon baking soda**
1 **tablespoon vegetable oil**

In large bowl cream butter. Gradually add sugar. Add eggs 1 at a time. Add anise seed. Mix well. In medium bowl sift together flour, baking powder, and baking soda. Gradually mix into butter mixture. Blend in oil.

Divide dough into 3 equal portions. Shape each portion into 7½- by 2-inch loaf. Place loaves 3 inches apart on lightly greased, floured baking sheet.

Bake in preheated 350-degree oven 30 minutes. Cool slightly. Slice loaves diagonally to make ½-inch slices. Turn slices on sides to insure that both sides bake evenly. Return to oven. Bake 8 to 10 minutes.

See photo page 380.

MANDELBROT

YIELD: 40 TO 50

½ **pound butter or margarine**
1 **tablespoon shortening**
1 **cup plus 2 tablespoons sugar, divided**
3 **eggs, beaten**
3 **cups sifted flour**
1 **teaspoon baking powder**
¼ **teaspoon baking soda**
pinch salt
1 **teaspoon vanilla, lemon juice, or orange rind**
1 **cup chopped almonds or walnuts**
½ **teaspoon cinnamon**

continued

In large bowl cream butter, shortening, and 1 cup sugar. Add eggs. Mix well. In medium bowl sift together flour, baking powder, baking soda, and salt. Add to butter mixture. Stir in vanilla, lemon juice, or orange rind. Add nuts. Refrigerate dough 2 hours. Divide into 4 portions. Form each portion into roll 6 to 8 inches long and 2 inches wide. Place on greased baking sheet.

Bake in preheated 350-degree oven 25 to 30 minutes. Rolls will spread. While warm slice each roll lengthwise down the center. Then slice at slight angle crosswise. Turn each piece on its side. Sprinkle generously with combined cinnamon and remaining 2 tablespoons sugar. Bake 15 to 20 minutes or until lightly browned. Keeps well in airtight container.

CHOCOLATE MADELEINES

YIELD: 24

1	**tablespoon plus ¼ pound butter, divided**
4	**ounces premium semi-sweet chocolate**
2	**eggs**
½	**cup sugar**
1	**teaspoon dark rum**
½	**teaspoon vanilla**
½	**cup sifted flour**
½	**teaspoon baking powder**
3	**tablespoons confectioners sugar**

Brush 2 madeleine tins (12 forms per tin) with 1 tablespoon softened butter. In double boiler or microwave melt remaining ¼ pound butter and chocolate.

In medium bowl beat eggs well. Add sugar, continuing to beat. Blend in cooled butter-chocolate mixture, mixing well. Add rum and vanilla. Gently stir in flour and baking powder just until mixed. Spoon batter into prepared tins, filling each two-thirds full.

Bake in preheated 350-degree oven 10 to 12 minutes or until madeleines spring back when lightly touched. Invert onto rack. When cool sprinkle with confectioners sugar.

See photo page 380.

PECAN LACE CUPS

YIELD: 8

1/4 **cup brown sugar**
2 **tablespoons light corn syrup**
3 **tablespoons margarine or butter**
1/4 **cup flour**
1/4 **cup finely chopped pecans**
1/4 **teaspoon salt**

In small saucepan combine brown sugar, corn syrup, and margarine. Cook over medium heat until mixture bubbles, stirring constantly. Remove from heat. Stir in flour, pecans, and salt. Drop 4 separate tablespoonfuls onto greased or parchment-lined baking sheet. Bake in preheated 375-degree oven 9 minutes or until lightly browned. Cool 1 minute.

With pancake turner transfer each soft round to inverted custard cup or muffin tin. Cool. Carefully remove to dessert plates or storage tin. Repeat procedure with remaining batter.

Cups may be filled with ice cream, fruit, or mousse.

PEANUT BUTTER CLUSTERS

YIELD: 48

16 **ounces salted peanuts, divided**
1/4 **pound butter**
12 **ounces peanut butter chips**
14 **ounces sweetened condensed milk**
2 **cups marshmallows or 2 cups marshmallow creme**

In 9- by 9-inch or 7- by 11-inch baking pan spread 8 ounces peanuts. In double boiler combine and melt butter, peanut butter chips, condensed milk, and marshmallows. Pour melted mixture over peanuts. Sprinkle remaining 8 ounces peanuts over melted mixture. Refrigerate covered at least 2 hours before cutting into squares.

MELTING MOMENTS

YIELD:
2 POUNDS OR
80 TO 100 PIECES

A microwave fudge.

3 **cups semi-sweet chocolate chips**
14 **ounces sweetened condensed milk**
4 **tablespoons butter or margarine**
1-2 **cups chopped walnuts**

In flat 8-inch square microwavable dish combine chocolate chips, condensed milk, and butter. Microwave on medium 4 minutes, stirring once if microwave does not have turntable. Remove from microwave. Add walnuts. Blend well. Refrigerate until set.

ENGLISH TOFFEE

YIELD:
48 TO 60 PIECES

2½ **cups sugar**
½ **cup water**
¼ **cup light corn syrup**
1 **pound butter**
1 **pound chopped pecans, divided**
1 **pound semi-sweet chocolate chips**
1 **pound milk chocolate chips**

In heavy medium saucepan combine sugar, water, corn syrup, and butter. Heat to 285 degrees measured on candy thermometer, stirring frequently.

Spread pecans on 2 baking sheets, reserving some for topping. Pour cooked mixture over nuts. Top with chocolate chips. Spread with knife. Sprinkle reserved pecans over top. Cool. Break in pieces when hardened.

CRAZY CORN

YIELD:
8 TO 10 CUPS

8-10	**cups air-popped popcorn**
1½	**cups pecan halves**
⅔	**cup almonds**
½	**cup corn syrup**
1⅓	**cups sugar**
½	**pound margarine**
1	**teaspoon vanilla**

Combine popcorn and nuts on baking sheet, preferably with low sides. In medium saucepan combine corn syrup, sugar, and margarine. Boil gently over medium heat, stirring occasionally. Cook 15 minutes or until mixture changes from yellow to yellow-beige color. Remove from heat. Blend in vanilla.

Drizzle over popcorn-nut mixture. Mix gently with wooden spoons to coat popcorn and nuts. Spread on baking sheet to cool. When cool break in pieces and store in airtight container.

ALSO NOTEWORTHY

BULGUR FOR BREAKFAST

SERVES 4 TO 6

¾   **cup bulgur wheat**
¾   **teaspoon cinnamon**
    pinch nutmeg
1   **cup orange juice**
¼   **teaspoon grated orange rind**
2   **cups fresh blueberries**
2   **small peaches or nectarines, sliced**
⅓   **cup chopped walnuts**
1   **cup plain yogurt**
2   **tablespoons honey**
1   **teaspoon vanilla**

In large bowl stir together bulgur, cinnamon, and nutmeg. In small saucepan combine orange juice and rind. Bring to boil. Pour over bulgur. Mix well. Cover. Let stand 30 minutes or until liquid is absorbed. Cool completely. Fold in fruit and nuts.

In small bowl combine yogurt, honey, and vanilla. Serve yogurt topping over bulgur. See photo page 282.

PISTACHIO AND APRICOT GRANOLA

YIELD: 5½ CUPS

2½   **cups oats**
1   **cup wheat flakes (available in health food stores)**
½   **cup wheat germ**
1   **cup chopped unsalted pistachios**
2   **teaspoons cinnamon**
1   **teaspoon nutmeg**
½   **cup vegetable oil**
⅓   **cup honey**
¼   **cup orange juice**
½   **cup chopped dried apricots**

In large bowl combine oats, wheat flakes, wheat germ, and nuts. Mix well. In small saucepan combine cinnamon, nutmeg, oil, honey, and orange juice. Heat just to boiling. Pour over dry ingredients. Mix well. Spread over large baking pan with low sides.

Bake in preheated 325-degree oven 30 minutes, stirring every 5 minutes. Remove from oven. Stir in apricots. Cool. Store in airtight container.

Delicious served with milk or yogurt or sprinkled over fruit or ice cream.

PEACHY BLUEBERRY CONSERVE

YIELD: 8 CUPS

4   **cups fresh blueberries**
4   **cups peeled, chopped ripe peaches**
    rind of 1 lemon
2   **tablespoons lemon juice**
5½ **cups sugar**
½   **teaspoon ground cloves**
½   **teaspoon cinnamon**

In large pot combine blueberries, peaches, lemon rind, and lemon juice. Bring to boil. Reduce heat to low. Simmer 10 minutes, stirring occasionally. Add sugar. Mix well. Add cloves and cinnamon.

Increase heat and boil until mixture thickens and coats spoon. If using jelly thermometer, temperature should register 213 degrees or above. Remove from heat. Skim foam. Pour into sterilized jelly jars. Seal.

RASPBERRY CURRANT JELLY

YIELD:
11 TO 12 CUPS

3   **quarts fresh currants**
2   **quarts fresh raspberries**
8   **cups sugar (approximate)**
½   **cup orange juice**

In large pot cook and mash currants over medium heat until boiling. Add raspberries. Cook about 5 minutes until mixture turns gray. Remove from heat.

Arrange 6 layers of cheesecloth with large overhang over colander. Place over non-metallic bowl. Pour cooked currants and berries into cheesecloth and let slowly drip through into bowl. Do not force fruit through cheesecloth.

When mixture has stopped dripping measure strained liquid and return to clean pot. Cook over medium heat until warm. Add enough sugar to equal amount of strained liquid. Add orange juice. Heat until sugar dissolves, stirring frequently. Bring to boil. Reduce heat and simmer 5 to 8 minutes or until mixture coats wooden spoon and 2 drops of mixture on spoon run together into 1 drop. Remove from heat. Skim until only clear liquid remains. Ladle into sterilized jelly jars and seal with paraffin.

FIG JAM

YIELD: 2 CUPS

1   **large orange**
1¾ **cups chopped, peeled figs**
1   **cup sugar**
2   **tablespoons water**
2   **tablespoons lemon juice**

Using zester or grater, remove zest from orange. In medium saucepan combine figs, sugar, zest of orange, and water. Cook until tender. Peel white pith from orange. Chop orange segments and add to fig mixture. Cook 30 minutes. Add lemon juice. Mix well. Store in covered jars.

Use as condiment with lamb or as filling for kuchen.

LEMON BUTTER

YIELD: 3 CUPS

¼ **pound butter**
1   **cup sugar**
   juice and grated rind of 4 lemons
4   **eggs, well beaten**

In double boiler combine butter, sugar, lemon juice, and lemon rind. Heat until butter melts. Add eggs. Cook 5 to 6 minutes until thick, stirring constantly. Remove from heat. Mixture will continue to thicken as it cools. Refrigerate. Serve with muffins or scones.

CRANBERRY BUTTER

YIELD: 2¹/₂ CUPS

1   **cup fresh cranberries**
¾ **pound butter or margarine**
4   **teaspoons grated orange rind**
4   **teaspoons sugar**

In food processor chop cranberries finely. Add remaining ingredients and process with quick on and off turns until well blended and smooth. Refrigerate.

May be stored in refrigerator several weeks. Serve on scones, muffins, biscuits, and turkey sandwiches.

See photo page 186.

QUICK APRICOT CHUTNEY

YIELD: 2 CUPS

1 **cup apricot jam**
⅔ **cup minced red onion**
¼ **cup minced green pepper**
¼ **cup minced red pepper**
3 **tablespoons white vinegar**
1 **teaspoon sugar**
½ **teaspoon ground allspice**
½ **teaspoon ground ginger**
1 **teaspoon chopped crystallized ginger**
  salt to taste
  pepper to taste

In medium bowl combine all ingredients. Mix well. Store in covered jar in refrigerator.

Serve with fish or poultry. May also be served over cream cheese on crackers as an appetizer.

GARLIC JAM

YIELD: 1⅓ CUPS

4 **whole bulbs garlic**
1 **medium onion, unpeeled, halved**
3 **teaspoons olive oil, divided**
¼ **teaspoon salt**
  pinch white pepper

Slice ½ inch from top of each bulb of garlic. In shallow baking dish arrange garlic and onion halves cut side down. Add 1 teaspoon olive oil. Cover tightly with foil.

Bake in preheated 350-degree oven 15 minutes or until very soft. Uncover and cool 20 minutes.

Peel skin from onion and chop onion finely. Transfer to medium bowl. Squeeze garlic pulps from skins into bowl. Stir in remaining 2 teaspoons olive oil. With fork mash garlic and onion in oil until well blended. Add salt and white pepper. May be stored in airtight jar in refrigerator 2 weeks.

Delicious with roasted meats, croustades, and cold meat sandwiches. May mix a spoonful into salad dressings or sauces.

PRUNE PLUM CHUTNEY

YIELD: 4 QUARTS

2   **cups firmly packed light brown sugar**
2   **cups sugar**
1½   **cups cider vinegar**
2   **cups golden raisins**
½   **cup slivered crystallized ginger**
½   **cup thinly sliced white onion**
3   **teaspoons mustard seed**
2½   **teaspoons dried crushed red pepper**
4   **teaspoons salt**
40   **prune plums, pitted, quartered**

In large pot combine sugars and vinegar. Mix well. Bring to boil. Add remaining ingredients except plums. Mix well. Add plums. Reduce heat and simmer 50 minutes, stirring frequently. Pour into sterilized jelly jars. Seal tightly.

Excellent with cold or hot meats.

ZUCCHINI CHUTNEY

YIELD: 3 QUARTS

1   **quart cider vinegar**
½   **pound dark brown sugar**
1-1½   **pounds sugar**
*3-4   **quarts peeled, halved lengthwise, seeded zucchini**
10-12   **ounces currants**
1   **cup chopped walnuts**
1   **large onion, finely chopped**
3-4   **cloves garlic, finely chopped**
4   **dried chili peppers, seeded, finely chopped**
4   **jalapeño peppers, seeded, finely chopped**
1   **4-inch piece fresh ginger root, peeled, chopped**
1-2   **teaspoons cumin**
1-2   **teaspoons curry powder**
1-2   **teaspoons turmeric**
1   **teaspoon cardamom**
1   **teaspoon ginger**

In 6- to 8-quart stainless steel pot combine vinegar and sugars. Bring to boil. Add remaining ingredients. Simmer 30 minutes, stirring occasionally. Pour into sterilized jars with self-sealing lids.

*May substitute pears or quinces, if desired.

GARLIC CHUTNEY

YIELD: 4 CUPS

2 cups cider vinegar
1 cup apple juice
1 cup water
½ cup pineapple juice
5 Granny Smith apples, peeled, cored, chopped
1 large yellow onion, thinly sliced
1 tablespoon butter
4 whole bulbs garlic
1 tablespoon olive oil
½ cup chopped dried apricots
¼ cup dried cranberries
½ teaspoon ginger
½ teaspoon curry powder
½ teaspoon cumin
1 teaspoon cayenne pepper, or to taste
1½ teaspoons Worcestershire sauce
½ teaspoon salt
¼ teaspoon freshly ground pepper
½ cup raisins

In large saucepan combine vinegar, apple juice, water, pineapple juice, and apples. Mix well. In medium skillet sauté onion in butter until translucent. Add onion to saucepan. Bring to boil. Reduce heat and simmer 1 hour.

While apple mixture simmers arrange garlic bulbs on baking sheet. Sprinkle with olive oil. Bake in preheated 350-degree oven 40 minutes. Set aside.

Add apricots, cranberries, ginger, curry powder, cumin, cayenne, Worcestershire sauce, salt, and pepper to saucepan. Simmer until thickened.

Separate baked garlic cloves, remove from skins, and add to saucepan with raisins. Simmer to thick consistency, stirring frequently. Refrigerate in jar with tight fitting lid.

PLUM RELISH

YIELD: 2 CUPS

16   Italian plums, pitted
1   medium Granny Smith apple, unpeeled, quartered, seeds removed
1   orange, including rind, quartered, seeds removed
1   cup sugar or sugar substitute
½   teaspoon red food coloring

In food processor combine plums, apple, and orange. Process until finely chopped. Remove to medium bowl. Mix with sugar. Stir in food coloring. Refrigerate until served.

UNCOOKED CRANBERRY-ORANGE RELISH

YIELD: 6 CUPS

2   pounds fresh cranberries
2   oranges, including rind and pulp, seeds removed
½   lemon, including rind and pulp, seeds removed
1-1½   cups sugar
¼   cup Amaretto

In food processor combine cranberries, oranges, and lemon. Grind coarsely. Stir in sugar and Amaretto. Refrigerate in covered container at least 2 days, stirring occasionally.

May be made 1 week in advance. Improves with age.

HONEY, I SHRUNK THE PICKLES

YIELD: 1 QUART

*1   quart whole kosher dill pickles, in 1-inch slices
1   large clove garlic, minced, or to taste
½   cup sugar
4   sticks cinnamon

In large glass jar or crock combine all ingredients. Mix well. Cover and let stand at room temperature 2 to 3 days, stirring several times each day. Refrigerate until served.

*Available in refrigerated case in food markets.

JACK'S HORSERADISH

YIELD: 2½ CUPS

2   **large, firm pieces fresh horseradish, peeled, in pieces**
8   **ounces pickled beets, drained**
⅓   **cup white vinegar**
2   **packets artificial sweetener**
1   **cup water**

In food processor or blender puree horseradish. Add beets, vinegar, sweetener, and water. Blend well. Spoon into jars. Seal and refrigerate.

CRANBERRY KETCHUP

YIELD: 2 CUPS

⅔   **cup water**
12   **ounces fresh cranberries**
1   **cup white wine vinegar**
2½   **cups finely chopped onions**
2   **large cloves garlic, minced**
⅔   **cup sugar**
1   **tablespoon ground allspice**
1   **teaspoon salt**

In large saucepan combine all ingredients. Simmer 20 minutes or until thickened, stirring occasionally. Increase heat to medium and cook 15 to 20 minutes, stirring frequently. Remove from heat. Cool 30 minutes.

Transfer mixture to food processor and puree. Strain into large bowl, discarding pulp remaining in strainer. Pour mixture into jars. Seal and refrigerate. Will keep 2 months.

A different, delicious spread for turkey or ham sandwich.

DOUBLE MUSTARD MAYONNAISE

YIELD: 2 CUPS

2	**large egg whites**
2	**tablespoons fresh lemon juice**
2	**tablespoons coarse-grained Dijon mustard**
3/4	**cup vegetable oil**
2/3	**cup olive oil**
1/4	**cup honey mustard**
	salt to taste
	pepper to taste
2	**tablespoons plus 2 teaspoons sherry**

In food processor or blender combine egg whites, lemon juice, and Dijon mustard. Process 10 seconds. With motor running add oils in slow steady stream until mixture thickens. Add honey mustard, salt, and pepper. Process briefly. Remove from processor. Slowly stir in sherry.

Excellent with ham, turkey, or beef.

GRAVLAX SAUCE

YIELD: 3/4 CUP

4	**tablespoons dark, highly seasoned prepared mustard**
1	**teaspoon dry mustard**
3	**tablespoons brown sugar**
2	**tablespoons white vinegar**
1/3	**cup vegetable oil**
2	**teaspoons dill weed or 3 tablespoons chopped fresh dill**

In small bowl combine mustards, brown sugar, and vinegar. Mix well. With wire whisk or wooden spoon slowly beat oil into mixture until thickened. Stir in dill weed. Refrigerate in tightly covered jar. Will keep several weeks.

Excellent accompaniment to salmon.

PESTO MOUSSE

2   tablespoons unflavored gelatin
¼   cup cold water
1   cup Basil Pesto Sauce (see below)
1½   cups mayonnaise
¾   cup whipping cream, whipped
     watercress, basil leaves, or parsley, optional

In small saucepan soften gelatin in cold water. Stir over low heat until dissolved. Cool until thick.

In medium bowl combine Basil Pesto Sauce and mayonnaise. Mix well. Stir in gelatin. Fold in whipped cream. Pour into lightly oiled 6-cup mold. Refrigerate covered 2 hours or until firm.

Loosen edges with sharp knife. Invert onto serving platter. Garnish with watercress, basil leaves, or parsley, if desired. Serve in thin slices.

Good with cold meats, ham, and poached or cold fish.

BASIL PESTO SAUCE

2   cups fresh basil leaves, coarsely chopped
2   tablespoons chopped, toasted pine nuts
¼   cup olive oil
2   cloves garlic, crushed
1   teaspoon salt
½   cup freshly grated Parmesan cheese

In food processor combine basil, pine nuts, olive oil, garlic, and salt. Blend well. Stir in cheese.

BRANDIED MARDI GRAS COFFEE

SERVES 6

1 **cup premium brandy**
5 **tablespoons superfine sugar**
  rind of 1 small orange, in fine
      julienne strips
  rind of ½ large lemon, in fine
      julienne strips
½ **teaspoon whole cloves**
1 **1-inch stick cinnamon**
4 **cups freshly brewed New Orleans style coffee**
      (with chicory), or French roast coffee

In large saucepan combine all ingredients except coffee. Simmer, stirring frequently to dissolve sugar. With long matchstick light mixture. Burn 25 to 30 seconds. Cover saucepan to extinguish flame. Combine mixture with coffee. Serve hot.

HOT BUTTERED RUM

YIELD: 10 CUPS
OF PREPARED MIX

1 **pound butter**
2 **cups brown sugar**
2 **cups confectioners sugar**
1½ **teaspoons nutmeg**
1½ **teaspoons cinnamon**
1 **quart vanilla ice cream**
1½ **tablespoons rum per serving as needed**

In food processor or blender combine all ingredients except rum. Blend well. Store in freezer until needed.

To serve, for each cup combine 1½ tablespoons rum, 2½ tablespoons prepared mix, and boiling water to fill mug. Sprinkle with pinch of nutmeg.

FROZEN BANANA SHAKE

SERVES 1

1   **frozen banana (peeled, cut into 8-10 pieces, and
frozen in plastic bag)**
½   **cup milk, divided**
1   **teaspoon vanilla**
1   **tablespoon toasted wheat germ**

In food processor or blender combine banana and ¼ cup milk. Puree with quick
on and off turns. Add vanilla and wheat germ. Blend well. Add enough additional milk for desired consistency. Pour into glass.

SMOOTHIE

SERVES 2

1   **cup orange or apple juice**
1   **cup fresh strawberries**
1   **cup ice cubes**
2   **tablespoons plain or vanilla yogurt**

In food processor or blender combine all ingredients. Blend until smooth and
frothy. Pour into glasses.

See photo page 282.

SCARLETT O'HARA

SERVES 1

1-1½   **ounces Southern Comfort
(no substitutes)**
1   **ounce cranberry juice**
4   **teaspoons Real-lime juice**
1-2   **teaspoons grenadine
crushed ice**

Combine all ingredients. Mix well. Shake with crushed ice. Strain into glass filled
with crushed ice.

The Women's Board of the Ravinia Festival would like to thank those who submitted, tested, and proofread recipes. We also gratefully acknowledge the expertise, guidance, and generosity of all who helped in making this book a reality.

Aaron, Patricia
Adams, Rebecca
Adams, Mary Lou
Alger, Judith
Allen, Anne
Alt, Jane
Alves, Dorothy
Anderson, Gayle
Anderson, Ruth
Anderson, Mary
Andrews, Amy
Angelo, Constance
Anson, Margery
Antoniou, Irene
Appleby, Preston
Appleby, Julie
Armstrong, Jane
Asencio & Associates
    Inc.
Atkin, Eva
Ault, Valerie
Auschatz, Peggy
Austin, Jodelle
Bacon, Marguerite
Bailey, Sharon
Baker, Karen
Baldauf, Pat
Bales, Anne
Ball, Virginia
Banaszek, Nancy
Barber, Nancy
Barlow, Barbara
Barnard, Sally
Barrett, Elizabeth
Barron, Zoe
Bartlett, Janice
Bassett, Susan
Bauer, Sue
Bauer, Marilyn
Bay, George
Bay, Mrs. James
Bealey, Karen
Beard, Susan
Beatty, Fran
Beatty, Ann
Beautyman, Daphne

Beckett, Ann
Begley, Harry
Begley, Karen
Behner, Kathleen
Beider, Marlys
Beliley, Karen
Bell, Sharon
Below, Nancy
Bendy, Celine
Benson, Chris
Bentz, Jon
Bentz, Chuckie
Berghoff, Jean
Berghorst, Debbie
Bergman, Birgitta
Berry, Carol
Bertolli, Louise
Bertolli, Tom
Bruce, Vivienne
Bryan, Neville
Buckley, Amy
Buckley, David
Buckley, Ann
Buehler, Mignon
Buhl, Kay
Bullard, Beverly
Burnell, Devin
Burnstine, Ann
Burt, Lynn
Burton, Deborah
Caccamo, Jane
Caldarelli, Janna
Calhoun, Shirley
Calhoun, Deborah
Campbell, Heather
Campbell, Jane
Canovi, Claudia
Caplin, Arthur
Carey, Claire
Carmichael, Kay
Carr, Cynthia
Carter, Catherine
Cartland-Bode, Susan
Carton, Ann
Casper, Ann Marie
Castle, Peggy
Caylor, Jo
Cedervall, Helen
Chaffetz, Sara
Chainski, Mary Jane
Chalmers, Georganne
Chamberlin, Annette
Chapman, Jane

Chomsky, June
Cleeland, Betty
Clements, Kathy
Clements, Cynthia
Cleveland, Candy
Clouser, Jean
Cobbs, Sue
Colburn, Carolyn
Coleman, Mrs. A.B.
Coleman, Diane
Coleman, Jean
Colson, Kirby
Condon, Marilyn
Condon, Kit
Connery, Mimi
Connor, Ruth
Coon-Ryan, Ann
Cooper, Cheryl
Cooperman, Jane
Cordesman, Shirley
Cork, Jean
Cormier, Dorothy
Coulter, Debbie
Cowen, Saralee
Coyle, Darla
Crabbe, Mrs. Gerald
Cramer, Corli
Crane, Margaret
Crown, Sandy
Cruikshank, Alice
Cunningham, Marsha
Currie, Jean
D'Ancona, Terri
D'Angelo, Becky
Daniel, Madlyn
Darrow, Anita
Dart, Susan
Dart, Joan
David, Joan
David, Pam
Davis, Marjorie
Davis, Gloria
Davis, Dee
De Costa, Alyce

Deaton, Florence
Dell, Sharon
DeMar, Edith
Dennelly, Daphne
DeWitt, Eleanor
Dolin, Jenny
Domash, Rivia
Donaldson, John
Donnelley, Mary Beth
Dooley, Willie
Dorn, Michael
Douglass, Louise
Dreyfuss, Sandra
Drummond, Lorie
Dufour, Vicki
Duncan, Deuel
Dunn, Lori
Dunphy, Kelly
Earnest, Gayle
Eberhardt, Margy
Eberle, Suzanne
Ecker, Babette
Edwards, Nancy
Eklund, Kristin
Elkins, Nancy
Ellis, Debbie
Engel, Barbara
Epkins, Carol
Erwin, Rick
Fabbri, Clara
Falk, Janet
Falls, Alice
Feccheimer, Elaine
Feinberg, Carolyn
Feitler, Joan
Feld, Betsy
Felsenthal, Geoff
Felsenthal, Marla
Felton, Kimberley
Fenninger, Anne
Fields, Marcia
Fish, Anne
Fishbein, Ann
Florian III, Paul
Foley, Michael
Foran, Jean
Foreman, Hinda
Forman, Laberta
Forman-Geimetz,
    Diane

continued on next page

Forsythe, Sandra
Forward, Phyllis
Fowler, Peggy
Fowler, Janeen
Freehling, Joan
Freeto, Betty
Freivogel, Caroline
Frellsen, Betty
Frenkel, Anne
Frew, Jo
Frey, Mary
Fritsch, Mrs. Jack
Fulton, Muriel
Futterman, Pam
Gaertner, Dorothy
Gandelman, Mary
Gapers
Gatzert, Tudy
Gemini, Cisco
Gianni, Christian
Gignilliat, Ellen
Gillis, Pat
Gilmore, Edna
Gilson, Elva
Gingiss, Helene
Gisemer, Jan
Gladstone, Vicki
Glasser, Louise
Glazer, Marilyn
Gleason, Kathy
Glenn, Sandy
Glickman, Sarita
Goldman, Ann
Goldstick, Myla
Goldsticker, Marcia
Golin, June
Goltra, Carolyn
Good, Alison
Goodman, Diane
Goodman, Joan
Goodman, Judith
Goodman, Mary
Gordon, Ed
Goss, Lisa
Gotoff, Myra
Gottlieb, Gloria
Govert, Mary
Gramm, Annemie
Gray, Mary
Greco, Marion
Greene, Peggy
Greenebaum, Helen

Gregory, Lee
Grube, Ann
Gruenhans, Gay
Guercio, Diane
Gunn, Ann
Guthman, Pat
Guthrie, Lou
Haarlow, Lynne
Haarlow, Bill
Haber, Robin
Haber, Dorothy
Hadland, Judy
Hadley, Char
Halpern, Madeline
Handley, Denise
Hanson, Eleanor
Harley, Elizabeth
Harmet, Joan
Harris, Margaret
Harris, Ilo
Harroun, Barb
Hart, Gail
Hart, Richard
Hartley, Peggy
Hartman, Betsy
Harvey, Mary Neal
Haufler, Joan
Haugh, Jane
Hayford, Marylou
Heald, Mo
Heath, Marilyn
Heath, Tom
Hegwood, Janet
Heilig, Steve
Heller, Liz
Heller Catering
Henderson, Cindy
Henricks, Bonnie
Hersch, Judy
Hetzel, Susan
Heuser, Katherine
Hewett, Mrs. Robert
Heymann, Pat
Hill, Ann
Hirsch, Connie
Hodgkins, Bandy
Holbeck, Linda
Holceker, Nancy
Holden, Janet
Hoover, Stan
Hoover, Margaret
Horner, Nancy
Horwich, Layne
Hughes, Mim
Huizenga, Heide
Hunter, Maxine

Hutchinson, Linda
Idone, Christopher
Ihrke, Wendie
Irwin, Dorothy
Isaacs, Eilene
Isaacson, Susan
Isserman, Barbara
Jackson, Anne
Jackson, Ginny
James, Sunny
James, Jeannie
James, Connie
James, Ginger
Jarke, Aline
Jensen, Carol
Jensen, Jim
Jensen, Arlene
Jensen, Dona
Jessup, Mary
Jochem, Judy
Johnson, Gail
Johnson, Paul
Johnson, Nancy
Johnson, Julie
Johnston, Jr., Richard
Jones, Darlene
Jorndt, Pat
Jorndt, Mary
Lane, Crete
Kadet, Kathy
Kalso, Mrs. Donald
Kane, Jean
Kaplan, Kathy
Kaplan, Janice
Kaplan, Morris
Kaplan, Dorothy
Kaplan, Judie
Karger, Nancy
Karris, Mary Ann
Kates, Linda
Kauffman, Mike
Keen, Frank
Kehoe, Susan
Keim, Buffy
Kelley, Rowena
Kelly, Barbara
Kerth, Dawn
Kijac, Maria
Kindsvater, Connie

King, Diane
King, Catherine
Kirkland, Mary Glenn
Klesi, Tweedie
Klimczak, Jane
Kline, Robin
Knight, Emily
Knight, Becky
Knops, Kathryn
Koelling, Catherine
Kohler, Dawn
Kolar, Brooke
Korr, Jay
Korshak, Mrs. Sidney
Kovach, Marilyn
Kozartis, Patricia
Kraff, Sandra
Krask, Mary Ann
Kravitt, Beverly
Krebs, Anne
Krenzer, Joan
Krol, Joe
Kuhn, Josephine
Kunkler, Diane
Lachner, Ruth
Laking, Elizabeth
Landow, Mrs. Wallace
Lane, Claudia
Lawton, Mary
Leckman, Sandi
LeClercq, Susie
Legg, Marianne
Leider, Peggy
Lepman, Bill
Lepman, Gina
Leslie, Joanne
Levì, Kate
Levin, Marliss
Levin, Gloria
Levine, Helen
Levine, Sheri
Levitt, Gary
Levy, Carolyn
Levy, Lois
Levy, Ellen
Levy, Sara
Lewis, Frumie
Lieberman, Susan
Lieberman, Jack
Lincoln, Gwen
Lind, Nancy
Lins, Louise
Lipsky, Nancy
Lirkland, Mary Glenn
Livingston, Anne
Lizzadro, Carol
Lizzadro, Reva
Lloyd, Marilyn

Lochner, Ruth
Locke, Nora
Lockwood, Carol
Lockwood, Rima
Lombardi, Robin
London, Andy
Long, John
Lott, Betsy
Lovelace, Judy
Lowenbaum, Barbara
Lowrimore, Larry
Lubeck, Jeanne
Lubin, Amy
Ludcke, Jeanette
Luke, Ceil
Lustenberger, Johann
Lynch, Dolores
Lyon, Mrs. A.B.
Lyon, Marilyn
Lyons, Marilyn
Mackler, Natalie
MacLeod, Martha
Maconachy, Margery
Maentz, Ashley
Maggiano's
Maggiacomo, Sande
  Rase
Magrone, Paul
Mahr, Anne
Maloney, Kay
Manley, Maxine
Mann, Sada
Mann, Sara
March, Patricia
Mariani, Paula Katz
Markovich, Susan
Marks, Celia
Marks, Virginia
Marlowe, Ina
Marshall, Annie
Marshall, Jack
Marshall, Barbara
Martay, Peggy
Marzano, Arlene
Mason, Parsla
Mason, Anabel
Mason, Julie
Mason, Christopher
Mass, Audrey
Massey, Heather
Mather, Melissa
Mathews, Elaine
Mathy, Dottie

Matteoni, Irma
Mattson, Sue
May, John
Mazius, Louise
McCain, Susan
McCann, Karen
McCarter, Judy
McCashland, Gail
McClory, Doris
McClung, Fawn
McClung, Jean
McClung, Lisa
McClung, Marcella
McDermott, Ann
McKittrick, Caroline
McLaren, Jan
McMahon, Carol
McNally, Carolynn
McQuown, Gretchen
Mecarg, Bill
Mehta, Zarin
Meltzer, Jean
Mendelson, Linda
Metz, Maryanne
Metzger, Jan
Meyer, Carol
Meyer, Barb
Mezzanotte
  Restaurant
Mickels, Heather
Miles, Pam
Miller, Helen
Miller, Joan
Miller, Jr., Mrs. J.
  Carter
Minnow, Jo
Missimer, Jane
Monroe, Barbara
Mooney, Mary
  Martha
Morelli, Janice
Morris, Fanny
Morrison, Adeline
Morrissey, Jane
Mosior, Dorothy
Mueller, Margaret
Mueller, Donna
Mulroy, Dorothy
Munro, Opie
Munson, Ginny
Murphy, Sheila
Murphy, Breege
Nadick, Kimberley
Narrod, Sharon
Nath, Ruth
Nathan, Boots

Nathan, Lionel
Nathan, Louise
Nathan, Peggy
Nathanson, Evelyn
National Pork
 Producers
Nebergall, Lynn
Needham, Kay
Neilsen, Cam
Nejdl, Liz
Nelson, Linda
Nelson, Marti
Nelson, Anne
Neuhauser, Eva
Neuman, Linda
Neumeier-Roche
Newton, Judy
Nicholson, Margaret
Nicolette, Judy
Nied, Priscilla
Nielson, Jane
Nitka, Hilary
Noll, Mary Lou
Novitsky, Mrs. Byron
O'Mara, Nancy
O'Neil-Mansfield, Beth
O'Neill, Jane
O'Rourke, Susan
Oelman, Sue
Ogden, Heidi
Oliver, Susan
Oliver-Hoffman,
 Camille
Orenstein, Beverly
Osterman, Joan
Otis, Jane
Otting, Mrs. Donald
Ozburn, Dorothy
Pace, Patsy
Pagano, Kim
Palmer, A.T.
Pappas, Bette
Parsons, Barbara
Parsons, Russell
Pasquesi, Mary
Patchen, Elaine
Patterson, B.
Patton, Linda
Pattou, Suzanne
Paullin, Marjorie
Pearsall, Jane
Pendery, Mrs. Ralph
Perry, Joy

Petersen, Diane
Peterson, Jane
Pettersen, Marianne
Pfaelzer, Alice
Phelps, Kelly
Philipsborn, Anita
Phillips, Maggie
Pickholtz, JoAnn
Pigott, Karen
Piskorski, Mary
Pither, Margaret
Platt, Pam
Plum, Betty
Pollokoff, Amy
Pollokoff, Lori
Ponerantz, Jan
Porino, Trilby
Potts, Joan
Powell, Ruth
Powell, Mary
Power, Ruthie
Pratt, Marilyn
Presman, Helen
Price, Gladys
Prindle, Kathleen
Pritzker, Cindy
Purcell, Cecile
Puth, Betsey
Rabert, Bonnie
Rademacher, Carolyn
Rahe, Maribeth
Randolph, John
Rappel, Lynn
Ratcliff, Patty
Reed, Joan
Reinhold, Jil
Reskin, Merle
Resseguie, Kathryn
Reynolds, Holly
Reynolds, Peggy
Richland, Lucy
Riedel, Karen
Rinella, Barbara
Ritter, Mary
Roberta, Betty
Robertson, Diane
Robson, Elizabeth
Roeber, Charlotte
Roeske, Gloria
Roffe, Roy
Rohr, Jimmy
Rosenheim, John
Rosenthal, Marie-
 Louise
Rosenthal, Harriet
Rosenzweig, Betsy
Ross, Frances
Rossi, Sandy

Rossi, Yolanda
Roth, Muriel
Roth, Don
Rupp, Nina
Russell, Ann Marie
Ryder, Jan
Sadow, Carol
Sanchez, Adrian
Sanchez, Linda
Santi, Carol
Sault & Pepper & Co.
Sayre, Ruth
Sazama, Susan
Schamberg, Katharine
Schnadig, Patricia
Schonberg, Rosemary
Schubel, Ella
Schuetz, Bea
Schultz, Barbara
Schuppan, Susan
Schwabe, Lisa
Schwarten, Helen
Schwartz, Alan
Scott, Connie
Scott, Merridy
Scott, Sallie
Scribner, John
Scribner, Patti
Segal, Diane
Semaya, Susan
Sethness, Bill
Sethness, Jeff
Seweloh, Kathleen
Seymour, Marlyne
Shapiro, Kate
Shapiro, Louis
Shelton, Bernice
Shenker, Judy
Sherman, Marge
Shevick, Shirley
Shilka, June
Shorney, Erika
Shoup, Lisa
Sick, Stephanie
Sickle, Sue
Sikorovsky, Pat
Simmons, Carol
Simon, Roslyn
Simon Pierce
 Restaurant
Simpson, Nancy
Skilling, Alice
Sklansky, Sharon
Slaughter, Florence
Small, Shirley
Smart, Sue

Smith, Margaret
Smith, Muriel
Smith, Joan
Smith, Sally
Sokolofski, Diane
Spears, Susan
Speltz, Birnie
Spencer, Marty
Spiel, Mrs. George
Spock, Tina
St. Germaine, Georgia
Stanley, Barbara
Staub, E. Norman
Steans, Lois
Steans-Gail, Robin
Steans, Jennifer
Stearns, Grace
Stearns, Bonnie
Steif, Susan
Stephan, Sue
Stern, Mona
Stocker, Marilyn
Stompanato, Claudia
Stone, Susan
Strane, Lillian
Straub, Jane
Straus, Linda
Sullivan, Jeanne
Sutter, Deanna
Svingos, Cookie
Swam, Carol
Swan, Sue
Swaney, Pat
Swanson, Shirley
Swanson, Ellie
Swartchild, Peggy
Swift, Mary Anne
Swingle, Mary
Swirsky, Carla
Taft, Edgar
Taich, Mrs. James
Taliaferro, Barbara
Tanton, Mary Lou
Tardy, Martha
Taus, Bea
Taylor, Betty
Taylor, Donna
Teichen, Mrs. E.
 Howard
Temple, Dana
Temple, Elizabeth
Tencate, Lana
Terny, Patricia
Terzakis, Renata
Testa, Martha
Tetzlaff, Marian
Thomas, Susan
Thomas, Lisa
Thomas, Dean
Thomas, Janet
Thomas, Helen

Thorne, Sue
Torgerson, Mary
Tower, Jackie
Trone, Beverly
Tufer, Pat
Turley, Kelen
Turner, Barbara
Tyler, Marian
Uhlmann, Karen
Uhrig, Cornelia
Ulmas, Evelyn
Un Grand Cafe
Vale, Virginia
Valentine, Beverly
VanWert, Shannon
Varick, Lois
Vignocchi, Mary
Vogel, Pam
Volhert, Mary
Volotzky, Sallie
vonSchlegall, Ann
vonSchlegall, Abbie
vonSchlegall, Fran
Wade, Miriam
Wahle, Molly
Walker, Sarah
Walton, Karen
Ward, Jean
Warren, Debra
Warrick, Jill
Wass, Karen
Watts, Mark
Weaver, Catherine
Webber, Myra
Webster, Heather
Webster, Joanane
Weeden, Jane
Weil, I.B.
Weil, Donna
Weil, Jane
Weil, Janis
Weingarten, Marla
Weinstein, Mary
Weis, Penny
Weiss, Flo
Weiss, Ginger
Wellman, Barbara
Wendrow, Eta
Wharton, Dorothy
Wheelan, Betsy
White, Mrs. Edwin
White, Patti

Whitman, Barbara
Whitten, Mary
Wiedlin, Regina
Wiley, Sally
Wilhelm, Carol
Wilkens, Ardeth
Williams, Bridgit
Wilson, Janie
Wing, Joan
Wolff, Ann
Woloson, Carol
Wood, Pat
Woodstock Inn and
 Resort
Wool, Lynn
Woulfe, James
Woulfe, Nancy
Woulfe, Virginia
Wright, Meg
Yao, Louise
Yastrow, Alison
Younger, Suzanne
Zabel, Joan
Zaunbrechery, Sue
Zeisler, Marlies
Ziebarth, Patience
Zimmer, Barbara
Zobel, Claudette
Zuker, Rooh

INDEX

G

NOTES

TO REORDER

Please send _____ copies
$20.00 each. . . . . _____

Add shipping and handling
$5.00 each . . . . _____

For books to be sent
to an Illinois address add
7% sales tax
$1.40 each . . . . _____

_____

GRAND TOTAL _____

METHOD OF PAYMENT

Please print carefully

☐ Check payable to NOTEWORTHY TWO
enclosed or

☐ Please charge to:
☐ MasterCard
☐ VISA

Card Number

_____
Expiration Date

_____
Signature

continued on other side 👉

ORDER FORM

....
cut on dotted line

TO REORDER

Please send _____ copies
$20.00 each. . . . . _____

Add shipping and handling
$5.00 each . . . . _____

For books to be sent
to an Illinois address add
7% sales tax
$1.40 each . . . . _____

_____

GRAND TOTAL _____

METHOD OF PAYMENT

Please print carefully

☐ Check payable to NOTEWORTHY TWO
enclosed or

☐ Please charge to:
☐ MasterCard
☐ VISA

Card Number

_____
Expiration Date

_____
Signature

continued on other side 👉

ORDER FORM

ORDERED BY:

Name

Address

City

State   Zip

Daytime Telephone

MAIL OR FAX TO:

NOTEWORTHY TWO
Ravinia Festival
P.O. Box 1603
Highland Park, Illinois 60035

Telephone 708/266-5043
Fax 708/433-7983

Please allow three weeks for delivery

All proceeds from the sale of NOTE-WORTHY TWO will be used to benefit the Steans Institute for Young Artists at the Ravinia Festival.

Thank you for your order

For information about ordering the original award-winning NOTEWORTHY, call 708/266-5043 or fax 708/433-7983.

cut on dotted line ✂

. . . .

ORDERED BY:

Name

Address

City

State   Zip

Daytime Telephone

MAIL OR FAX TO:

NOTEWORTHY TWO
Ravinia Festival
P.O. Box 1603
Highland Park, Illinois 60035

Telephone 708/266-5043
Fax 708/433-7983

Please allow three weeks for delivery

All proceeds from the sale of NOTE-WORTHY TWO will be used to benefit the Steans Institute for Young Artists at the Ravinia Festival.

Thank you for your order

For information about ordering the original award-winning NOTEWORTHY, call 708/266-5043 or fax 708/433-7983.